# Test-Driven Development:
## A Practical Guide

David Astels

PRENTICE
HALL
PTR

Prentice Hall PTR
Upper Saddle River, NJ 07458
www.phptr.com

**Library of Congress Cataloging-in-Publication Data**

A CIP catalog record for this book can be obtained from the Library of Congress

*Editorial/Production Supervision*: Kathleen M. Caren
*Cover Design Director*: Jerry Votta
*Cover Illustration*: M. C. Escher
*Art Director*: Gail Cocker-Bogusz
*Manufacturing Manager*: Alexis R. Heydt-Long
*Executive Editor*: Paul Petralia
*Editorial Assistant*: Michelle Vincenti
*Marketing Manager*: Christopher Guzikowski

© 2003 Pearson Education, Inc.
Publishing as Prentice Hall Professional Technical Reference
Upper Saddle River, New Jersey 07458

**Prentice Hall PTR offers excellent discounts on this book when ordered in quantity for bulk purchases or special sales. For more information, please contact: U.S. Corporate and Government Sales, 1-800-382-3419, corpsales@pearsontechgroup.com. For sales outside of the U.S., please contact: International Sales, 1-317-581-3793, international@pearsontechgroup.com.**

Printed in the United States of America

Eighth Printing

ISBN 0-13-101649-0

Pearson Education Ltd.
Pearson Education Australia Pty., Limited
Pearson Education Singapore, Pte. Ltd.
Pearson Education North Asia Ltd.
Pearson Education Canada, Ltd.
Pearson Educación de Mexico, S.A. de C.V.
Pearson Education—Japan
Pearson Education Malaysia, Pte. Ltd.

# The Coad Series
Peter Coad, *Series Editor*

———■———

## About the Series

The Coad Series is a growing collection of practical guides "from the trenches." The series focuses on key "must be addressed" IT pain points, felt by leaders around the globe. The series is especially suited for CIOs, IT department managers, technology leaders, and change agents. The Coad Series addresses the four dimensions of successful IT: technology, process, people, and vision. For the series, Peter Coad personally selects authors and topics and then mentors the authors at a strategic level along the way.

## About the Series Editor

Peter Coad (pronounced "code") is senior vice president and chief strategist of Borland (http://www.borland.com) Software Corporation. Coad collaborates with fellow Borland execs in formulating long-term business and product strategies. Peter also represents Borland worldwide as a thought leader, industry luminary, and evangelist among CXOs, technical department managers, and developers.

Peter is globally recognized as an accomplished business strategist, model builder, and thought leader. As business strategist, Peter formulates long-term competitive strategies for Borland. Previously, as Chairman, CEO, and President of TogetherSoft, he led in growing that company 11.6 times revenue in the span of two years, overall profitably. As model builder, Peter has built hundreds of models for nearly every business imaginable, fully focused on building-in strategic business advantage. As thought leader, Peter writes books (six to date) on building better software faster; he speaks at industry events worldwide; and he is the Editor-in-Chief of The Coad Series, published by Prentice Hall; in addition, Peter was an invited speaker on business strategy at the 2003 "Future in Review" conference.

Coad attended the Stanford Executive Program for Growing Companies and received a Master of Science in Computer Science (USC) and a Bachelor of Science with Honors in Electrical Engineering (OSU).

*To my parents who,*
*though they may not have always*
*approved or understood,*
*let me try.*

# Contents

# FOREWORD

My responsibility in writing this foreword is to help you decide whether to read this book. If you are interested in improving your programs and your programming skill, this book can help you.

Test-Driven Development is a practice that can make your programs better. If you're like me, using the techniques in Dave's book, you will find that your programs are more clear, that they come into being more easily, and that you'll have fewer defects than you used to.

I'm not saying that TDD is some kind of magic potion; quite the contrary. TDD isn't magic, it is something that you yourself do. By focusing attention on tests first, you'll be designing your program more from the viewpoint of the user. By doing the tests one at a time, you'll be creating a simple design that's focused exactly on the problem. As you work up all these little tests, you'll drive out most of the defects that otherwise slip into your code. Finally, by saving the tests, you make the program easier to maintain and improve as time goes on.

Dave's book is full of examples of Test-Driven Development. There's an extended example to show you how TDD works over a longer haul. There are small examples showing how to use most of the TDD-related tools that are available. There are even examples in most of the languages where TDD is used, though the book's main focus is on examples in Java. This is a book about practice, with real examples rather than dry theory.

But wait! There's more! Dave also gives a good introduction to refactoring, and to programming by intention. And he introduces Mock Objects, an advanced and powerful technique in testing and Test-Driven Development. Plus, he has a section on one of the tricky areas in TDD, creating GUIs in test-first fashion.

You'll also find a quick and valuable summary of eXtreme Programming, a look at Agile Modeling, and a comprehensive list of online resources relating to all the book's topics.

All these things are good and serve as reasons to buy this book. The core value of Dave's book, the real meat, is in the code. Test-Driven Development is a technique that we use as we program. No matter what design or modeling we have done before we begin programming, TDD helps us make the code better. I'm sure that it will help you, if you'll give this book, and what it teaches, a chance.

Test-Driven Development has made my programs better, and those of many other programmers as well. It's a technique that is worth adding to your bag of tricks. This book will help you improve as a programmer. That's why I'm recommending it.

*Ron Jeffries*
*www.XProgramming.com*
*Pinckney, Michigan*
*18 December 2002*

# PREFACE

This isn't a book about testing.

This is a book about a way of programming that leads to simple, clear, robust code. Code that is easy to design, write, read, understand, extend, and maintain.

This is a book about thinking, designing, communicating, and programming. It's just a really nice side effect that we end up with a comprehensive[1] suite of tests.

This book explores Test-Driven Development, Test-First Programming, call it what you will: programming by writing the tests first, then writing the code needed to make the tests pass. Specifically, working in the smallest steps possible: write just enough of a test to fail, write just enough code to make it pass, refactor to clean up the mess you made getting the test to pass.

This book focuses on the Java programming language and uses Java examples throughout. It is assumed that the reader has at least an intermediate understanding of Java (and a working Java system if you want to try out the examples for yourself). Example code and other support material is available at my website[URL 54].

Even though the focus is on Java, Part IV looks at other prominent members of the xUnit family for several popular languages. This is done by taking the first task from Chapter 10 and recasting it in the various languages. This provides a good comparison of the different frameworks.

## EXTREME PROGRAMMING

Test-Driven Development is a core part of the agile process formalized by Kent Beck called *eXtreme Programming* (XP). XP is probably the most agile of the agile processes, being extremely low overhead, and extremely low ceremony. However, it is extremely high discipline, very effective, and incredibly resilient to change.

That being said, you do not need to adopt XP in order to practice TDD and gain the benefit from it. TDD is worth doing on its own. The quality of your code will improve. Of course, if you are doing XP it's well worth it to get really good at TDD.

---

[1] How comprehensive depends on how good we become at it.

TDD is one of the main design tools that we have in XP.[2] As I mentioned earlier, the fact that we end up with a set of tests is a very pleasant by-product. Because we have those tests, we can have confidence we haven't inadvertently broken anything if the tests ran successfully before the change and after it. Conversely, if a test fails after we make a change we know exactly what broke and are in the best position to find the problem and fix it. The only thing that could have caused the failure was the change we made since the last time the tests ran clean.

All this means is that because the tests are there, we can safely use another of the XP practices: refactoring. As we will see in Chapter 2, refactoring is the process of making changes to the structure of code without changing its external behavior. The tests let you confirm that you haven't changed the behavior. This gives you the courage necessary to make (sometimes drastic) changes to working code. The result is that the code is cleaner, more extensible, more maintainable, and more understandable.

Appendix A talks a bit more about eXtreme Programming. For more exhaustive information, you can browse the bibliography and explore the online XP resources listed in Appendix C.

## WHO SHOULD READ THIS BOOK?

Should you read this book? Helping you answer that question is why I wrote this preface. There was once an informal survey on the XP Yahoo Group as to the purpose that a preface should serve. The general opinion was that by reading the preface you should get a good idea of whether you should buy and read the book. I hope I've done a good job of it!

Read this book if you want to adopt eXtreme Programming. As stated earlier, being able to do TDD well is worth the time and effort it takes to get good at it. TDD is at the heart of XP, so doing TDD well makes the entire process that much more effective.

Read this book if you want to write code that is clearer, more robust, easier to extend, and as slim (as opposed to bloated) as possible.

Read this book if you know there must be a better way than spending weeks or months drawing pictures before writing a line of code.

Finally, read this book if you want to know how to make programming fun again.

In terms of what you should know before reading this book, it would help if you had at least an intermediate understanding of Java. Having a good background in another OO language or two (such as Smalltalk, C++, Python, or Ruby) will, however, enable you to get even more out of this book.

As this book goes to print there is one other TDD book available[9] (although I'm sure many will follow). I was aware of that book being written as I wrote much of this one, and it was always a partial goal to be complementary to it. From it you will get the philosophy and metaphysics of TDD, mixed with enough

---

[2]The other is refactoring.

pragmatics to make it real. If you are so inclined, I encourage you to read it first. The book you hold in your hands is, as the title says, a *practical* guide to doing TDD. It's focused on one language (not the best language, but arguably one that is very popular and well supported for TDD), and presents not only concepts and principles, but tools and techniques.

## THE STRUCTURE OF THIS BOOK

This book is divided into four parts:

**I Background** In Part I we examine some topics that relate to the main body of material in the book (i.e., TDD in Java). We start with an introduction to TDD. This is followed by chapters on refactoring and programming by intention. These two techniques are also prominent in XP and are required and enabled by TDD.

**II Tools and Techniques** In Part II we take an in-depth look at various tools that are useful for practicing TDD with Java, and how to use them. We start with a tutorial introduction to JUnit, the defacto standard Java TDD framework. We continue by exploring some of the standard (i.e., included in the distribution) and nonstandard extensions to JUnit. Next, we explore some tools that support the use of JUnit and other tools that are completely independent of JUnit but work well with it. The final chapters in this part examine specific techniques or issues and the related tools.

**III A Java Project: Test-Driven End to End** This is a practical hands-on book. To that end, Part III (which makes up the bulk of the book) is built around the development of a real system, not a toy example. We work through this project test-first. Along the way we draw on material from the previous parts of the book.

**IV xUnit Family Members** JUnit is just one member of a large and growing family of programmer test frameworks. In Part IV we have a look at some of the other members of the family. We don't look at all of them, but we go over several for the more popular languages. So that we get a good comparison, we go through the same set of stories (i.e., requirements) for each. Specifically, these are the initial stories from the Java project. This lets us compare the various members with JUnit as well.

There are also four appendices:

**A eXtreme Programming** This appendix provides a very brief introduction to XP.

**B Agile Modeling** This appendix provides an introduction to and overview of Agile Modeling.

**C Online Resources** Throughout the book I refer to Web sites where you can find information as well as downloads. This appendix contains a categorized, annotated list of these sites.

**D Answers to Exercises** Many of the chapters in this book contain exercises for the reader. This appendix contains all exercises in the book, with answers.

## CONVENTIONS USED IN THIS BOOK

I've adopted a handful of visual conventions which I've used throughout this book to make it easier for you, the reader, to differentiate between different sorts of information.

**Source Code** This book contains a large amount of source code. When one of more complete lines of code is being presented, it is indented and set in a sans-serif font, like this:

```
public int getAverageRating() {
  return totalRating / numberOfRatings;
}
```

When only part of a line is being presented, it is set in the same font, but kept in the body of the text. This often includes class names (Movie), methods (equals()), and constants (true, "a string", 42).

In general, when a method is referred to parameters are not included, but empty parentheses are, so that it is obvious that it is a method as opposed to some other type of identifier, for example: aMethod().

In blocks of code, package and import statements are generally left out.

**Filesystem and console I/O** Terms relating to the filesystem are set in a serif, monospaced font. This includes items like filenames (`filter.properties`) and commands and their output:

```
$ java \
> -classpath bin:/usr/local/java/lib/MockMaker.jar \
> mockmaker.MockMaker \
> com.saorsa.tddbook.samples.mockobjects.IntCalculator \
> >src/com/saorsa/tddbook/samples/mockobjects/MockIntCalculator.java
```

**Tips and Sidebars** I've used a couple of different callout mechanisms to highlight information that is important to take note of, or is interesting but doesn't fit in the body of the text for some reason.

Throughout the book there are small bits of wisdom that you may find especially useful. These are set apart the way this paragraph is.

---

### A Sample Sidebar

This is an example of a very short sidebar; most are a half to full page in length.

---

I've used sidebars to separate short passages that are not directly related to the main body of text. Sidebars get placed as LaTeX sees fit, usually at the top of a page. There's one around here somewhere as an example.

**Terminology**   I learned OO in the context of Smalltalk and I've used Smalltalk terminology from the beginning. If you're not familiar with Smalltalk, I include a few terms that I use, and how they map to Java and C++:

**instance variable** A variable whose scope is an object. Each object has a separate copy of this variable. (Java: *field* or *member variable*, C++: *data member*.)

**class variable** A variable whose scope is a class. All instances of the class share a single copy of the variable. (Java: *static field*, C++: *static data member*.)

**method** A functional member of a class. (Java: *method*, C++: *member function*.)

**sending messages to an object** A more abstract way to refer to calling an object's methods.

**senders** Methods that send a specific message, that is, call a specific method (commonly called *references* to a method).

## ACKNOWLEDGEMENTS

A preface is not complete without acknowledging the other people that make a book possible. Being an author is like being at the peak of a pyramid... you are being supported (and your work made possible) in various ways by a multitude of other people. This is my chance to acknowledge and thank them... by name for the ones I'm aware of.

Kent Beck for making TDD and XP household words—at least in my household—and for his support of this book.

Miroslav Novak for first turning me on to this new way of programming that a bunch of smart people were talking about on something called a Wiki. Miroslav may be my junior in terms of time spent programming, but I've learned more from him than I sometimes care to admit.

Patrick Wilson-Welsh for several things: for always reminding me of the big picture when I got mired down in the details of the moment; for being the best sounding board and copy editor that an author could ask for; and for having the courage to leave an established life in Washington, D.C. to move to small-town Canada to become my co-founder and first apprentice.

Dave Thomas of "The Pragmatic Programmers"[URL 55] for letting me use the LaTeX macros he wrote for the book "The Pragmatic Programmer"[25]. That book was inspiring in its layout and typesetting as well as catalytic in bringing about a turning point in my thoughts about programming.

Hand in hand with "The Pragmatic Programmer" went "Software Craftsmanship"[34] by Pete McBreen. I mean that literally,... I read them back-to-back. Pete provides a wonderful introduction to and discussion of software as a craft. A fabulous book, it was another contributing factor to my career-shaking epiphany (the third being XP). Thanks, Pete.

Peter Coad, to whom I owe a great debt for taking me under his wing in many ways and helping me to get this project off the ground. I have to thank him also for letting me charge ahead with a TDD edition of The Coad Letter[URL 61].

Paul Petralia, my acquisitions editor at Prentice Hall, and the fine crew that works with him. Thanks for letting us convince you that this book isn't about "Testing," and for believing in it wholeheartedly once we had accomplished that.

Craig Larman must be mentioned here for his encouragement, support, and advice. I still have great memories of spending a day with Craig at his home outside Dallas, discussing UML and Together[URL 34] and drinking homemade Chai.

And a big thanks to Ron Jeffries for writing the foreword for me, as well as being generally supportive of my XP-related endeavors, specifically (well, what comes to mind as I write this) this book, and the TDD Coad Letter. Also, for doing so much to bring XP so far.

Special thanks and a hearty acknowledgement to members of the TDD Yahoo! group that sent me their JUnit tips: Darren Hobbs, J. B. Rainsberger, and Derek Weber.

Very special thanks to those that contributed to the book by writing and letting me use material on subjects that they are the experts in, specifically (in order of appearance):

**Mike Clark** for the section on JUnitPerf,

**Jens Uwe Pipka** for the section on the Daedalos extensions,

**Tim Bacon** for the section on xmlUnit,

**Mike Bowler** for the section on the Gargoyle extensions,

**Bryan Dollery** for the section on IDEA,

**James Newkirk** for the chapter on NUnit,

**Bob Payne** for stepping in at the last minute with the chapter on PyUnit,

**Kay Pentecost** for the chapter on vbUnit, and

**Scott Ambler** for the appendix on agile modeling.

Thanks to all the folks in the XP community who gave me feedback (in no particular order): Kay Pentecost, Edmund Schweppe, Aldo Bergamini, Mike Clark, Francesco Cirillo, and my friends, colleagues, and past co-authors: Randy Miller and Miroslav Novak. As with all authors, I'm sure I've missed someone. Sorry about that.

I need to acknowledge and thank my reviewers as well: Alan Francis and William Wake.

And yes, as Kent Beck says in the preface of his TDD book[9], it is cliché to thank our families, but they heartily deserve it. To my wife, Kate, for saying "I'll clean up the kitchen. You go write." To my kids, Tasha and Jason, for being understanding when I had to write, and for thinking that it's so cool to have a Dad who writes books. Finally, to my youngest child, Leah, who is too young to notice what I'm doing but simply smiles when she sees me and gives me a hug when I pick her up.

This book was produced using a variety of open source software. All my computers run Redhat Linux. The manuscript was prepared using GNU Emacs, and typeset using LaTeX. Image manipulation was done with Gimp. The xdvi previewer was used extensively. The PDF version was created using dvips, and ps2pdf. Several packages were used with LaTeX, some off the shelf (lgrind, draftcopy, and fixme), several courtesy of Dave Thomas (for exercises, extended cross reference support, and url references), and several of my own (chapter heading quotes, story/task/test management, sidebars, and tips).

Part I

# BACKGROUND

This part of the book provides an introduction to Test-Driven Development and associated techniques and issues: refactoring and programming by intention.

# Chapter 1

# TEST-DRIVEN DEVELOPMENT

*To vouch this, is no proof,*
*Without more wider and more overt test*

*- Othello, Act 1 Scene 3*
*William Shakespeare*

From programmers to users, everyone involved in software development agrees: testing is good. So why are so many systems so badly tested? There are several problems with the traditional approach to testing:

- If testing is not comprehensive enough, errors can make it into production and cause potentially devastating problems.

- Testing is often done after all the code is written, or at least after the programmer who wrote the code has moved on to other things. When you are no longer living and breathing a particular program, it takes some time and effort to back *into* the code enough to deal with the problems.

- Often tests are written by programmers other than those who wrote the code. Since they may not understand all of the details of the code, it is possible that they may miss important tests.

- If the test writers base their tests on documentation or other artifacts *other than the code*, any extent to which those artifacts are out of date will cause problems.

- If tests are not automated, they most likely will not be performed frequently, regularly, or in exactly the same way each time.

- Finally, it is quite possible with traditional approaches to fix a problem in a way that creates problems elsewhere. The existing test infrastructure may or may not find these new problems.

Test-Driven Development solves all of these problems, and others.

- The programmer does the testing, working with tests while the code is freshly in mind. In fact, the code is based on the tests, which guarantees testability, helps ensure exhaustive test coverage, and keeps the code and tests in sync. All tests are automated. They are run quite frequently and identically each time.

- Exhaustive test coverage means that if a bug is introduced during debugging, the test scaffolding finds it immediately and pinpoints its location. And the test-debug cycle is kept quite short: there are no lengthy delays between the discovery of a bug and its repair.

- Finally, when the system is delivered, the exhaustive test scaffolding is delivered with it, making future changes and extensions to it easier.

So from a pure testing standpoint, before we begin to discuss non-testing benefits, TDD is superior to traditional testing approaches. You get more thoroughly tested code, period.

But you do indeed get much more than that. You get simpler designs. You get systems that reveal intent (describe themselves) clearly. The tests themselves help describe the system. You get extremely low-defect systems that start out robust, are robust at the end, and stay robust all the time. At the end of every day, the latest build is robust.

These are benefits for all project stakeholders. But perhaps the most immediate and most tangible benefit is exclusively the programmer's: more fun. TDD gives you, the programmer, small, regular, frequent doses of positive feedback while you work. You have tangible evidence that you are making progress, and that your code works.

There is a potential problem with all this, of course. It is more addictive than caffeine. Once you're hooked, you'll want to program this way, and only this way, from then on. And I for one certainly hope you do.

This chapter will give you an overview of Test-Driven Development, including a short example of a programming session.

## WHAT IS TEST-DRIVEN DEVELOPMENT?

Test-Driven Development (TDD) is a style of development where:

- you maintain an exhaustive suite of Programmer Tests,

- no code goes into production unless it has associated tests,

- you write the tests first,

- the tests determine what code you need to write.

Let's look at each of these in turn.

## Maintain an exhaustive suite of Programmer Tests

You have Programmer Tests to test that your classes exhibit the proper behavior. Programmer Tests are written by the developer who writes the code being tested. They're called Programmer Tests because although they are similar to unit tests, they are written for a different reason. Unit tests are written to test that the code you've written works. Programmer Tests are written to define what it means for the code to work. Finally, they're called *Programmer* Tests to differentiate them from the tests that the *Customer* writes (called, logically enough, *Customer Tests*) to test that the system behaves as required form the point of view of a user.

Using Test-Driven Development implies, in theory, that you have an exhaustive test suite. This is because there is no code unless there is a test that requires it in order to pass. You write the test, then (and not until then) write the code that is tested by the test. There should be no code in the system which was not written in response to a test. Hence, the test suite is, by definition, exhaustive.

## No code goes into production unless it has associated tests

One of eXtreme Programming's tenets is that a feature does not exist until there is a suite of tests to go with it. The reason for this is that everything in the system has to be testable as part of the safety net that gives you confidence and courage. Confidence that all the code tests clean gives you the courage (not to mention the simple ability) to refactor and integrate. How can you possibly make changes to the code without some way to confidently tell whether you have broken the previous behavior? How can you integrate if you don't have a suite of tests that will immediately (or at least in a short time) tell you if you have inadvertently broken some other part of the code?

## Write the tests first

Now we're getting eXtreme. What do I mean by *write the tests first*? I mean that when you have a task to do (i.e., some bit of functionality to implement) you write code that will test that the functionality works as required before you implement the functionality itself.

Furthermore, you write a little bit of test, followed by just enough code to make that test pass, then a bit more test, and a bit more code, test, code, test, code, etc.

## Tests determine what code you need to write

By writing only the code required to pass the latest test, you are putting a limit on the code you will write. You write only enough to pass the test, *no more*. That means that you do *the simplest thing that could possibly work*. I think an example is in order. Let's say you are working on a list class. The logical place to start is with the behavior of an empty list (it makes sense to start with the basis, or simplest, case). So you write the test:

```
public void testEmptyList() {
    MovieList emptyList = new MovieList();
    assertEquals("Empty list should have size of 0", 0, emptyList.size());
}
```

To pass this test we need a MovieList class that has a size() method.

When you are working this way, you want to work in small increments...sometimes increments that seem ridiculously small. When you grasp the significance of this, you will be on your way to mastering TDD. Later we'll explore the important and sometimes unexpected benefits and side effects of testing and coding in tiny increments.

## LET THE COMPUTER TELL YOU

Write your tests (and your code for that matter) without worrying about what classes or methods you will need to add. Don't even bother keeping a To Do list. Well, at least in terms of what classes, methods, etc., you need to create. You will likely want a To Do list to keep track of tests you want to write and other higher level items. Just write your test and compile.

If you need to add a class or method the compiler will tell you. It provides a better To Do list than you could, and faster. In the previous example when I compile[1] after writing the test (with nothing else written) I get the error:

```
MovieList cannot be resolved or is not a type.
```

This immediately tells me that I need to create a new MovieList class, so I do:

```
public class MovieList {
}
```

I compile again and get another error:

```
The method size() is undefined for the type MovieList
```

In response to this I add a stub size() method:

```
public int size() {
  return 0;
}
```

Now it will compile. Run the test, and it works. Due to Java requiring a return statement when a return type is defined, we need to combine the steps of creating the method and adding the simplest return statement. I have made a

---

[1]Modern Java programming environments will alert me to these missing items even before I compile. Furthermore, they will offer solutions and do the work of creating the stubs for me.

habit of always stubbing methods to return the simplest value possible (i.e., 0, false, or null).

What!?! Just return 0? That can't be right. Ah... but it is right. It is the simplest thing that could possibly work to pass the test we just wrote. As we write more tests we will likely need to revisit the size() method, generalizing and refactoring, but for now return 0 is all that is required.

## A QUICK EXAMPLE

Let's take a peek into the development of the project from later in the book. We have a Movie class which now needs to accept multiple ratings (e.g., 3 as in "3 stars out of 5") and give access to the average.

As we go through the example, we will be alluding to a metaphor for the TDD flow originated by William Wake: The TDD Traffic Light[URL 9][URL 61].

We start by writing a test, and we start the test by making an assertion that we want to be true:

```
public void testRating() {
    assertEquals("Bad average rating.", 4, starWars.getAverageRating());
}
```

Now we need to set the stage for that assertion to be true. To do that we'll add some rating to the Movie:

```
public void testRating() {
    starWars.addRating(3);
    starWars.addRating(5);
    assertEquals("Bad average rating.", 4, starWars.getAverageRating());
}
```

Finally, we need to create the Movie instance we are working with:

```
public void testRating() {
    Movie starWars = new Movie("Star Wars");
    starWars.addRating(3);
    starWars.addRating(5);
    assertEquals("Bad average rating.", 4, starWars.getAverageRating());
}
```

When we compile this, the compiler complains that addRating(int) and getAverageRating() are undefined. This is our yellow light. Now we make it compile by adding the following code to Movie:

```
public void addRating(int newRating) {
}
```

```
public int getAverageRating() {
  return 0;
}
```

Note that since we are using Java, we must provide a return value for getAverageRating() since we've said it returns an int.

Now it compiles, but the test fails. This is the red light (aka red bar). This term is derived by the JUnit interfaces that present a progress bar that advances as tests are run. As long as all tests pass, the bar is green. As soon as a test fails, the bar turns red and remains red. The message we get is:

```
Bad average rating. expected:<4> but was:<0>
```

Now we have to make the test pass. We add code to getAverageRating() to make the test pass:

```
public int getAverageRating() {
  return 4;
}
```

Recompile and rerun the test. Green light! Now we refactor to remove the duplication and other smells that we introduced when we made the test pass.

You're probably thinking "Duplication...what duplication?" It's not always obvious at first. We'll start by looking for constants that we used in making the test work. Sure enough, look at getAverageRating(). It returns a constant. Remember that we set the test up to get the desired result. How did we do that? In this case we gave the movie two ratings: 3 and 5. The average result is the 4 that we are returning. So, that 4 is duplicated. We provide the information required to compute it, as well as returning it as a constant. Returning a constant when we can compute its value is a form of duplication. Let's get rid of it.

Our first step is to rewrite that constant into something related to the provided information:

```
public int getAverageRating() {
  return (3 + 5) / 2;
}
```

Compile and run the tests. We're OK. We have the courage to continue. The 3 and 5 are duplicate with the arguments to addRating() so let's capture them. Since we add the constants we can simply accumulate the arguments. First we add a variable to accumulate them:

```
private int totalRating = 0;
```

Then we add some code to addRating():

```
public void addRating(int newRating) {
   totalRating += newRating;
}
```

Now we use it in getAverageRating():

```
public int getAverageRating() {
   return totalRating / 2;
}
```

Compile, test, it works! We're not finished yet, though. While we were refactoring we introduced another constant: the 2 in getAverageRating(). The duplication here is a little subtler. The 2 is the number ratings we added, i.e., the number of times addRating() was called. We need to keep track of that in order to get rid of the 2.

Like before, start by defining a place for it:

```
private int numberOfRatings = 0;
```

Compile, run the tests, green. Now, increment it every time addRating() is called:

```
public void addRating(int newRating) {
   totalRating += newRating;
   numberOfRatings++;
}
```

Compile, run the tests, green. OK, finally we replace the constant 2 with numberOfRatings:

```
public int getAverageRating() {
   return totalRating / numberOfRatings;
}
```

Compile, run the tests, green. OK, we're done. If we want to reinforce our confidence in what we did, we can add more calls to addRating() and check against the appropriate expected average. For example:

```
public void testLotsOfRatings() {
   Movie godzilla = new Movie("Godzilla");
   godzilla.addRating(1);
   godzilla.addRating(5);
   godzilla.addRating(1);
   godzilla.addRating(2);
   assertEquals("Bad average rating.", 2, godzilla.getAverageRating());
}
```

I need to underline the fact that I recompiled and ran the tests after each little change above. This cannot be stressed enough. Running tests after each small change gives us confidence and reassurance. The result is that we have courage to continue, one little step at a time. If at any point a test failed we know exactly what change caused the failure: the last one. We back it out and rerun the tests. The tests should pass again. Now we can try again... with courage.

The above example shows one school of thought when it comes to cleaning up code. In it we worked to get rid of the duplication that was embodied in the constant. Another school of thought would leave the constant 4 in place and write another test that added different ratings, and a different number of them. This second test would be designed to require a different returned average. This would force us to refactor and generalize in order to get the test to pass.

Which approach should you take? It really depends on how comfortable you are with what you are attempting. Remember that you do have the test to safeguard you. As long as the test runs, you know that you haven't broken anything. In either case you will want to write that second test: either to drive the generalization, or to verify it.

## SUMMARY

We've explored what Test-Driven Development is:

- an exhaustive suite of Programmer Tests,

- no code without tests,

- tests first,

- tests determine the code.

We've seen how to leverage feedback from the computer to keep track of what we should do next: if we need to create a class, method, variable, etc., the system will let us know.

We've even seen a quick example of TDD in action, step by step, building some code to maintain the average rating of a movie.

However, before we can jump in and start practicing it in earnest, we need to make sure we have a few basic techniques and skills that TDD builds on. The next few chapters will explore these.

## Agile Modeling and TDD

A primary benefit of both modeling and TDD is that they promote a *think before you act* approach to development. Just because they offer the same type of benefit doesn't mean that they are incompatible with one another. Instead, experience shows that we can and should model on a project taking a TDD approach.

Consider XP projects that clearly take a TDD approach. Modeling is definitely an important part of XP. XP practitioners work with user stories, and user stories are clearly agile models. XP practitioners also create CRC cards whenever they need to, also agile models. In *eXtreme Programming Explained* [8], Kent Beck even includes sketches of class diagrams. Heresy? No. Just common sense. If creating a model can help our software development efforts then that's what we do. It's as simple as that.

Creating agile models can help our TDD efforts because they can reveal the need for some tests. As an agile modeler sketches a diagram they will always be thinking, "How can I test this?" in the back of their minds because they will be following the practice *consider testability*. This will lead to new test cases. Furthermore, we are likely to find that some of our project stakeholders or even other developers simply don't think in terms of tests; instead, they are visual thinkers. There's nothing wrong with this as long as we recognize it as an issue and act accordingly—use visual modeling techniques with visual thinkers and test-driven techniques with people that have a testing mindset.

TDD can also improve our agile modeling efforts. Following a test-first approach, agile developers quickly discover whether their ideas actually work or not—the tests will either validate their models or not—providing rapid feedback regarding the ideas captured within the models. This fits in perfectly with AM's practice of *Prove it With Code*.

Agile Modeling (AM) and Test-Driven Development (TDD) go hand in hand. The most effective developers have a wide range of techniques in their intellectual toolboxes, and AM and TDD should be among those techniques.

See Appendix B for more information on Agile Modeling.

# Chapter 2

# REFACTORING

*Urge the necessity and state of times,*
*And be not peevish-fond in great designs.*

*- Richard III, Act 4 Scene 4*
*William Shakespeare*

This chapter is here because refactoring is so important to TDD. We'll have a quick look at some of the ideas and techniques—just enough to get a firm enough grasp of it to tackle the project later in the book. For everything we ever wanted to know about refactoring check out [16], [29], [41], [URL 4], and [URL 10].

## WHAT IS REFACTORING?

Refactoring is the process of making changes to existing, working code without changing its external behavior. In other words, changing *how* it does it, but not *what* it does. The goal is to improve the internal structure.

Refactoring is closely related to TDD in two ways:

- After doing the simplest thing possible to make a test pass (breaking any/all rules in the process), we refactor to clean up, mostly removing duplication we introduced getting the test to pass.

- If we are practicing TDD, then we have the safety net of tests in place that allows us to refactor with confidence.

## WHEN TO REFACTOR

Generally speaking, we refactor whenever we need to. However, there are three situations when we must refactor:

1. when there is duplication

2. when we perceive that the code and/or its intent isn't clear

3. when we detect code smells, that is, subtle (or not so subtle) indications that there is a problem.

## Duplication

Duplicated code in its various forms is the death of good code. We absolutely must get rid of it. Duplication is such a problem that several people have warned against it at length, including Ron Jeffries *et al.* ("Say Everything Once and Only Once" [27]) and Dave Thomas & Andrew Hunt ("Don't Repeat Yourself" [25]).

If we see duplicated code, we need to look closely to see what it's doing. It's likely that there is something useful or important being done. We need to put it in one place. We can do this by extracting duplicate code into separate methods that can then be called from multiple locations. If the duplication is in an inheritance hierarchy, we may be able to push the duplicated code up the hierarchy. If the structure of some code is duplicated but not the details, we can extract the differing parts and make a template method of the common structure.

Some cases of duplication will be simple, others won't be. Some will be obvious, but some will be very subtle.

An example of a simple case of duplication is an expression (or sequence of expressions) that appears in multiple methods. In this case, it is simply a matter of moving the duplicated expression(s) into a separate method and replacing the original occurrences with calls to the new method.

Here's an example of simple duplication. The majority of these two methods are identical. The only difference is the first line of saveAs():

```java
public boolean save() throws IOException {
  if (outputFile == null) {
    return false;
  }

  FileWriter writer = new FileWriter(outputFile);
  movies.writeTo(writer);
  writer.close();
  return true;
}

public boolean saveAs() throws IOException {
  outputFile = view.getFile();
  if (outputFile == null) {
    return false;
  }

  FileWriter writer = new FileWriter(outputFile);
  movies.writeTo(writer);
  writer.close();
  return true;
}
```

We can remove the duplication by chaining to save() after getting the file in saveAs(), like so:

```
public boolean saveAs() throws IOException {
  outputFile = view.getFile();
  save();
}
```

A more subtle form of duplication was shown in the example on page 9. That case deals with duplication between a constant and the information supplied to calculate it. Notice how, in that example, refactoring to remove duplication drove the code toward a more general solution.

Another form of duplication occurs at runtime when the same information is maintained redundantly. In the following example, we've moved from keeping track of how many times add has been called (satisfying initial tests that verify the list size) to storing the added movies. To satisfy a test that verifies that the list contains the movies that were added and not ones that weren't added we needed to add storage for the added movies. We properly just added the required code to get the new test passing, without much regard for the code that is there already.

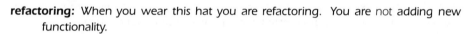

When you are practicing TDD, you have two hats[16]:

**coding:** When you wear this hat you are adding new functionality to the system. You are not refactoring.

**refactoring:** When you wear this hat you are refactoring. You are not adding new functionality.

When you are getting a test to pass, you wear your coding hat. Once the test is passing, you switch hats and refactor to clean up.

Now we need to refactor the old code out since it is now maintaining redundant information. Here's the code before refactoring:

```
public class MovieList {
  private int numberOfMovies = 0;
  private Collection movies = new ArrayList();


  public int size() {
    return movies.size();
  }
}
```

```
public void add(Movie movieToAdd) {
  movies.add(movieToAdd);
  numberOfMovies++;
}
}
```

After removing the maintenance of the redundant information, the code looks like this:

```
public class MovieList {
  private Collection movies = new ArrayList();

  public int size() {
    return movies.size();
  }

  public void add(Movie movieToAdd) {
    movies.add(movieToAdd);
  }
}
```

## Unclear Intent

The code is the most important deliverable. Because of that, it must be as clear and understandable as possible. It's not always possible to write it this way at the beginning, so we refactor the code to make it more understandable. One powerful and simple way to clarify intent is to choose better names for things. We can often pick a name *out of the air* that is close but not exactly what we want. One trick is to keep a thesaurus on hand and use it when we are having trouble coming up with a name that communicates our exact intent.

Using TDD helps make our intent clear when writing code by forcing us to think about the interface of a class rather than its implementation. We have a chance to decide what makes the most sense from the point of view of a user of the class, without getting mired in implementation details. Chapter 3 goes into detail on how to make intent clear when coding.

## Code Smells

The concept of *code smells*[1] is widely used by the eXtreme Programming community to refer to characteristics of code that indicate less than acceptable quality. In this section we will briefly overview a few of the more important smells.

When we find smells in our code, we refactor to get rid of them. In fact, one very useful feature of [16] is a cross reference of smells to indicated refactorings.

One thing to remember is that many of these smells don't always indicate a problem, but they do indicate something that we should have a closer look at to see if there is a problem.

---

[1]The term *code smells* was first used by Fowler and Beck in [16].

**Comments**   Most comments are written either because they are required by the process being used or to compensate for poorly written code. If we see a comment or feel compelled to write a comment, consider refactoring or rewriting the code first. See Chapter 3 for details on how to make code more understandable.

Here's some code that has comments that serve to break the method into separate functional units. Here, the comments indicate that those functional units should be extracted into separate methods. Look on page 29 to see this done.

```
public void init() {
  // set the layout
  getContentPane().setLayout(new FlowLayout());

  // create the list
  movieList = new JList(myEditor.getMovies());
  JScrollPane scroller = new JScrollPane(movieList);
  getContentPane().add(scroller);

  // create the field
  movieField = new JTextField(16);
  getContentPane().add(movieField);

  // create the add button
  addButton = new JButton("Add");
  addButton.addActionListener(new ActionListener() {
    public void actionPerformed(ActionEvent e) {
      myEditor.add(movieField.getText());
      movieList.setListData(myEditor.getMovies());
    }
  });
  getContentPane().add(addButton);
}
```

**Data Class**   This is a class that is essentially an evolved **record** or **struct**. It simply contains data and has little behavior. Don't be fooled by accessor methods that are only there to support the data. A real stink is the existence of public instance variables (fields/attributes).

If we look around the code, we may find other classes that operate on instances of the data class. We need to merge the two either by moving data into the other class or moving behavior into the data class.

Here's a simple example:

```
public class Point {
  private int x;
  private int y;

  public Point() {
    this(0, 0);
  }
}
```

```
public Point(int initialX, int initialY) {
  x = initialX;
  y = initialY;
}

public int getX() {
  return x;
}

public int getY() {
  return y;
}

public void setX(int newX) {
  x = newX;
}

public void setY(int newY) {
  y = newY;
}
}
```

Here's an even stinkier version of the same thing:

```
public class Point {
  public int x;
  public int y;

  public Point() {
    this(0, 0);
  }

  public Point(int initialX, int initialY) {
    x = initialX;
    y = initialY;
  }
}
```

This version should, initially, be refactored to encapsulate the instance variables. That would result in the first version of Point. Data classes are often manipulated by code that lives in other classes. The next step in this example would be to look at the code that uses Point to see if there is code that would be better placed in Point. For example:

```
public class Shape {
  private Point center;

  public Shape() {
    center = new Point();
  }
```

```
    public void translate(int dX, int dY) {
      center.setX(center.getX() + dX);
      center.setY(center.getY() + dY);
    }
  }
```

The code in translate() should be moved into Point:

```
  public class Point {
    //...

    public void translate(int dX, int dY) {
      x += dX;
      y += dY;
    }
  }

  public class Shape {
    //...

    public void translate(int dX, int dY) {
      center.translate(dX, dY);
    }
  }
```

**Duplicated Code**   This is one of the worst smells.  We discussed duplication earlier in this chapter.

**Inappropriate Intimacy**   This is the case where a class knows too much about another's internal details.  To deal with this, methods should be moved so that the pieces that need to know about each other are together.

For example, consider this method in a class MovieList which writes the list to a Writer:

```
  public void writeTo(Writer destination) throws IOException {
    Iterator movieIterator = movies.iterator();
    while (movieIterator.hasNext()) {
      Movie movieToWrite = (Movie)movieIterator.next();;
      destination.write(movieToWrite.getName());
      destination.write(' | ');
      destination.write(movieToWrite.getCategory().toString());
      destination.write(' | ');

      try {
        destination.write(Integer.toString(movieToWrite.getRating()));
      } catch (UnratedException ex) {
        destination.write("-1");
      }
      destination.write('\n');
    }
  }
```

This method has and uses full knowledge of the structure of the class Movie. If the structure of Movie changes (e.g., multiple ratings are supported), then this method, in a different class, must change to match. In short, this method uses too much knowledge about Movie. The solution is to extract the portion that deals with writing a single Movie and move it to the Movie class. The final result is:

```java
public class MovieList {
  //...
  public void writeTo(Writer destination) throws IOException {
    Iterator movieIterator = movies.iterator();
    while (movieIterator.hasNext()) {
      Movie movieToWrite = (Movie)movieIterator.next();;
      movieToWrite.writeTo(destination);
    }
  }
}

public class Movie {
  //...

  public void writeTo(Writer destination) {
    destination.write(getName());
    destination.write(' | ');
    destination.write(getCategory().toString());
    destination.write(' | ');

    try {
      destination.write(Integer.toString(getRating()));

    } catch (UnratedException ex) {
      destination.write("-1");
    }

    destination.write('\n');
  }
}
```

This can also be a common problem with inheritance, where subclasses know more than they should about the implementation details of their ancestors. To deal with this we can decouple the relationship by replacing the inheritance with delegation or by making the details of the ancestors private.

**Large Class**   If we find a class that is disproportionately larger than most of the other classes in the system, look carefully at it. Why is it so large? Does it try to do too much? Does it know too much? Is much of the behavior conditional? If so we might be able to extract subclasses and use polymorphism to see that the appropriate code is executed. If there are definite sets of subfunctionality they may be able to be extracted into classes of their own.

There are two ways to quickly find classes that might be too large:

1. Run a lines-of-code metric and look for inordinately large results. See Figure 2.1.

2. Visualize the code as UML and look for large classes. See Figure 2.2.

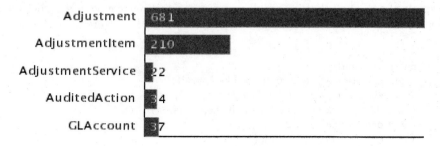

**Figure 2.1** Finding a large class with a LOC metric.

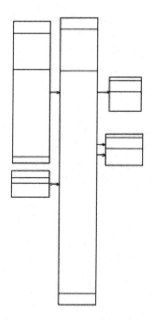

**Figure 2.2** Finding a large class by visualizing in UML.

**Lazy Class**   This is the opposite of Large Class. A Lazy Class doesn't pull its weight and should be merged with another class as appropriate. You can use the same techniques as you do when looking for large classes, but look for the other extreme, that is, unusually small classes.

**Long Method**   Just as an overly large class is a problem, so is an overly large method. Extracting functionally cohesive blocks of code into their own methods reduces the size of the method and makes the code more understandable. What's long? If you look at line count, then anything more than 10 lines, plus or minus. Another thing to consider is cognitive length—how many things is the method trying to do? In this case, long is anything more than one. Consider the following example of a method that isn't really long in terms of line count (it's borderline), but it's doing four different things. See page 29 to see how to refactor it.

```
public void init() {
  getContentPane().setLayout(new FlowLayout());
  movieList = new JList(myEditor.getMovies());
  JScrollPane scroller = new JScrollPane(movieList);
  getContentPane().add(scroller);
  movieField = new JTextField(16);
  getContentPane().add(movieField);
  addButton = new JButton("Add");

  addButton.addActionListener(new ActionListener() {
    public void actionPerformed(ActionEvent e) {
      myEditor.add(movieField.getText());
      movieList.setListData(myEditor.getMovies());
    }
  });
  getContentPane().add(addButton);
}
```

**Switch Statements**   The free use of switch statements (aka case statements) indicate a lack of deep understanding of object-oriented principles. Switch statements often result in *Shotgun Surgery*. We can often use polymorphism to accomplish the same goal in a much better, cleaner way.

Here's an example that we'll see refactored on page 32:

```java
public class Employee {
  // 0 - engineer, 1 - salesman, 2 - manager
  private int employeeType;

  public String departmentName() {
    switch (employeeType) {
      case 0:
        return "Engineering";
      case 1:
        return "Sales";
      case 2:
        return "Management";
      default:
        return "Unknown";
    }
  }
}
```

**Shotgun Surgery**   This isn't so much a smell from the code, but more from how we work with the code. The problem is evidenced when we need to make a single functional change and find that we need to make changes to code in several places. An example is having to add a clause in switch statements in several methods. This is a disaster waiting to happen. The solution is to move things that change together to the same place. This can often be done by using the *Replace Conditional with Polymorphism* refactoring (see page 32).

## HOW TO REFACTOR

First of all, we really need to have automated tests in place that will give us feedback as to whether we've broken anything as we are refactoring. The key to refactoring is that we don't want to change behavior, and having tests that verify that behavior will let us know as soon as it has changed.

Refactoring is done in small steps, running the tests after each one. That way we know as soon as we have broken something. By taking small steps, we will know exactly what caused the break: the last step we took. We must back it out and try again.

It really helps if we can use a good refactoring tool. The original refactoring tool was the refactoring browser for Smalltalk[URL 38]. There are several tools available for Java that provide refactoring support. Some are plugins for IDEs (such as jFactor[URL 39] and RefactorIt[URL 40]). Some IDEs are starting to include refactoring support as core features. These include Eclipse[URL 32] (which has included refactoring support from even early builds), IDEA[URL 33], Together[URL 34], and jBuilder[URL 35].

Refactoring has been done almost exclusively in source code, but it doesn't need to be limited to that. Working with code using a UML tool (specifically

class and sequence diagrams) has advantages in some cases. Some smells are
easy or easier to find when we can see the system graphically. Likewise, some
refactorings can be easily performed on a class diagram. See [5], [11] for more
information.

## SOME IMPORTANT REFACTORINGS

OK, time for Dave's ten favorite refactorings. Refactorings are like design patterns: the more we know, and the better we know them, the more benefit we will
get from them. The following are, in my experience, some of the most useful and
beneficial refactorings. Consider them a place to start, because, as with patterns,
more are being codified regularly.

**Extract Class**   When a class gets too big, or its behavior is unfocused, we need to
split it into pieces that have cohesive behavior, creating new classes as required.
**Extract Class** deals with extracting one of these sets of behavior into a new
class. Another reason why we might want to use this refactoring is if we will
need multiple implementations of some behavior. In this case, we can extract the
variable code into a separate class. Once there, we can extract an interface and
then go about writing the required implementations.

In the following example, the code to write a list of movies is in the MovieList
and Movie classes:

```java
public class MovieList {
  //...
  public void writeTo(Writer destination) throws IOException {
    Iterator movieIterator = movies.iterator();
    while (movieIterator.hasNext()) {
      Movie movieToWrite = (Movie)movieIterator.next();;
      movieToWrite.writeTo(destination);
    }
  }
}


public class Movie {
  //...
  public void writeTo(Writer destination) {
    destination.write(getName());
    destination.write(' | ');
    destination.write(getCategory().toString());
    destination.write(' | ');

    try {
      destination.write(Integer.toString(getRating()));
```

```
    } catch (UnratedException ex) {
      destination.write("-1");
    }
    destination.write('\n');
  }
}
```

We'd like to extract the writing functionality to a separate class so that it is easier to replace or enhance. Rather than have it spread over two classes, we'd like it in one place:

```
public class MovieListWriter {
  Writer destination = null;

  public MovieListWriter(Writer aWriter) {
    destination = aWriter;
  }

  public void writeMovieList(MovieList aList) throws IOException {
    Iterator movieIterator = aList.getMovies().iterator();
    while (movieIterator.hasNext()) {
      Movie movieToWrite = (Movie)movieIterator.next();;
      writeMovie(movieToWrite);
    }
  }

  private void writeMovie(Movie aMovie) {
    destination.write(aMovie.getName());
    destination.write(' | ');
    destination.write(aMovie.getCategory().toString());
    destination.write(' | ');

    try {
      destination.write(Integer.toString(aMovie.getRating()));

    } catch (UnratedException ex) {
      destination.write("-1");
    }
    destination.write('\n');
  }
}
```

Now, if we need to change the format of the output, it's all in one place. Also, notice that we've simplified the public interface in the process. Now only the top level call (i.e., writeMovieList()) is exposed. The details are now hidden.

**Extract Interface**   We might want to extract an interface for several reasons. We may want to abstract away from a concrete implementation so that we can use a technique like Mock Objects more easily. It is often advantageous to have interfaces defining the important behavior groups in a system.

Suppose we had a class that implements the management of a list of movies called MovieList. As we are going about our development we get to a point where we are developing a class that is responsible for being a bridge between a user interface and the movie list. To better isolate that new class we may want to mock (see Chapter 7) the movie list. Our existing class (MovieList) is concrete, but to make a mock we should have an interface (and sometimes we need one, e.g., if we want to use EasyMock). So, we need to extract an interface from MovieList. It's generally a good idea to keep interfaces small and focused, so only extract what you need and/or what makes sense.

Here's the class; it's still simple, but we'd like to be able to mock it:

```
public class MovieList {
  private Collection movies = new ArrayList();

  public int size() {
    return movies.size();
  }

  public void add(Movie movieToAdd) {
    movies.add(movieToAdd);
  }

  public boolean contains(Movie movieToCheckFor) {
    return movies.contains(movieToCheckFor);
  }
}
```

To extract an interface, we create an interface with abstract methods corresponding to those in the concrete class that are of interest. In this case, we're interested in all the methods in MovieList:

```
public interface IMovieList {
  int size();
  void add(Movie movieToAdd);
  boolean contains(Movie movieToCheckFor);
}
```

Now we change MovieList to implement our new interface:

```
public class MovieList implements IMovieList {
  //...
}
```

The final step is to change references to MovieList to be references to IMovieList. We can now easily create other implementations of the IMovieList interface, including a mock.

Choosing names for interfaces can be difficult and controversial. A well accepted best-practice is to use an adjective to name interfaces whenever possible and meaningful. So, we have interfaces like Serializable, Runnable, and Remote. Note that interfaces will often be named with adjectives ending in –able or –ible. Sometimes that doesn't make sense. A second best strategy is to prefix the interface name with I or Int. In our example, MovieListable doesn't make much sense, so I went with IMovieList. This is often typical when you are extracting an interface to make mocking easier and/or possible.

**Extract Method**   When a method gets too long or the logic is too complex to be easily understood, part of it can be pulled out into a method of its own. Here's another example from the code we will see in Chapter 8. Here's some code that builds a user interface:

```java
public void init() {
  getContentPane().setLayout(new FlowLayout());
  movieList = new JList(myEditor.getMovies());
  JScrollPane scroller = new JScrollPane(movieList);
  getContentPane().add(scroller);
  movieField = new JTextField(16);
  getContentPane().add(movieField);
  addButton = new JButton("Add");
  addButton.addActionListener(new ActionListener() {
    public void actionPerformed(ActionEvent e) {
      myEditor.add(movieField.getText());
      movieList.setListData(myEditor.getMovies());
    }
  });
  getContentPane().add(addButton);
}
```

This method does several different things. It sets a layout and it creates and adds three components: a list, a field, and a button. That's rather busy. To make the situation more extreme, I've made sure there are no blank lines to split up the different bits of functionality. One approach would be to add blank lines and explanatory comments, like this:

```java
public void init() {
  // set the layout
  getContentPane().setLayout(new FlowLayout());
```

```
  // create the list
  movieList = new JList(myEditor.getMovies());
  JScrollPane scroller = new JScrollPane(movieList);
  getContentPane().add(scroller);


  // create the field
  movieField = new JTextField(16);
  getContentPane().add(movieField);


  // create the add button
  addButton = new JButton("Add");
  addButton.addActionListener(new ActionListener() {
    public void actionPerformed(ActionEvent e) {
      myEditor.add(movieField.getText());
      movieList.setListData(myEditor.getMovies());
    }
  });
  getContentPane().add(addButton);
}
```

Is that any better? Maybe a little, but the method is even longer! All
we've really done is try to mask the smell with some deodorant comments. A
better solution is to use **Extract Method** to pull each of the different bits of
functionality out into its own method:

```
public void init() {
  setLayout();
  initMovieList();
  initMovieField();
  initAddButton();
}


private void setLayout() {
  getContentPane().setLayout(new FlowLayout());
}


private void initMovieList() {
  movieList = new JList(getMovies());
  JScrollPane scroller = new JScrollPane(movieList);
  getContentPane().add(scroller);
}


private void initMovieField() {
  movieField = new JTextField(16);
  getContentPane().add(movieField);
}
```

```
    private void initAddButton() {
      addButton = new JButton("Add");
      addButton.addActionListener(new ActionListener() {
        public void actionPerformed(ActionEvent e) {
          myEditor.add(movieField.getText());
          movieList.setListData(getMovies());
        }
      });
      getContentPane().add(addButton);
    }
```

Notice how much clearer this is. Each functional unit is in its own method. The init() method is not extremely clear, but from the decomposition and naming it is self-evident what is happening. For details on any one aspect, you can simply look at the appropriate method.

**Replace Type Code with Subclasses**   We can use this refactoring when we have a class that indicates subtypes using a type-code (e.g., an employee is either an Engineer or a Salesman). We make a subclass for each alternative. Doing this will often help break up complex conditionals and switch statements that decide based on the type code. Here's a simple example:

```
    public class Employee {
      // 0 - engineer, 1 - salesman, 2 - manager
      private int employeeType;

      //..
    }
```

This isn't very object-oriented. Replacing employeeType with subclasses we get the following code, which is also shown as UML in Figure 2.3:

```
    abstract public class Employee {
      //...
    }

    public class Engineer extends Employee {
      //...
    }

    public class Salesman extends Employee {
      //...
    }

    public class Manager extends Employee {
      //...
    }
```

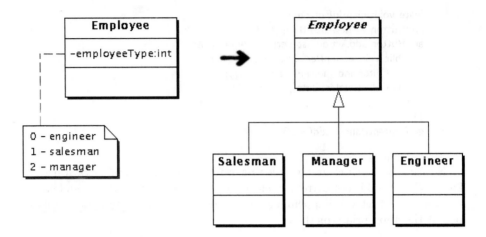

**Figure 2.3** Replacing a typecode with subclasses.

**Replace Conditional with Polymorphism**    When we find switch statements, consider creating subclasses to handle the different cases and get rid of the switch. If
there are subclasses already, maybe the conditional behavior can be pushed into
them?

We can revisit the previous example for an illustration. Here's more of the
original code:

```
public class Employee {
  // 0 - engineer, 1 - salesman, 2 - manager
  private int employeeType;

  public String departmentName() {
    switch (employeeType) {
      case 0:
        return "Engineering";
      case 1:
        return "Sales";
      case 2:
        return "Management";
      default:
        return "Unknown";
    }
  }
}
```

After extracting subclasses for each type of employee (as in the previous
example) we can use polymorphism to replace the switch statement in **depart-
mentName()**:

```
abstract public class Employee {
  public abstract String departmentName();
}


public class Engineer extends Employee {
  public String departmentName() {
    return "Engineering";
  }
}


public class Salesman extends Employee {
  public String departmentName() {
    return "Sales";
  }
}


public class Manager extends Employee {
  public String departmentName() {
    return "Management";
  }
}
```

**Form Template Method** We can use this when we have a similar method in multiple classes that have a common structure but different details. We want to end up with a method having the common structure in the superclass (which may have to be created) and the extracted detail methods in subclasses. Polymorphism takes care of calling the proper detail methods.

We'll reuse our employment example again, with a different twist. Here are methods that compute an XML representation of employees:

```
public class Engineer extends Employee {
  public String asXML() {
    StringBuffer buf = new StringBuffer();
    buf.append("<employee name=\"");
    buf.append(getName());
    buf.append("\" department=\"Engineering\">");
    //...
    return buf.toString();
  }
  //...
}
```

```
public class Salesman extends Employee {
  public String asXML() {
    StringBuffer buf = new StringBuffer();
    buf.append("<employee name=\"");
    buf.append(getName());
    buf.append("\" department=\"Sales\">");
    //...
    return buf.toString();
  }
  //...
}
```

```
public class Manager extends Employee {
  public String asXML() {
    StringBuffer buf = new StringBuffer();
    buf.append("<employee name=\"");
    buf.append(getName());
    buf.append("\" department=\"Management\">");
    //...
    return buf.toString();
  }
  //...
}
```

Notice how all three methods are almost identical. This is a sure indication that refactoring is required. To refactor to a template method, we first push one of the methods up to the superclass, in this case that is **Employee**:

```
public class Employee {
  public String asXML() {
    StringBuffer buf = new StringBuffer();
    buf.append("<employee name=\"");
    buf.append(getName());
    buf.append("\" department=\"Engineering\">");
    //...
    return buf.toString();
  }
  //...
}
```

Next, we extract the differences into separate methods. In this case that's the department name. See the description of *Replace Conditional with Polymorphism* on page 32 on how this is done. Now, given that we have departmentName() methods in place, the next step is to call that polymorphic method from the template method in **Employee**:

```
public class Employee {
  public String asXML() {
    StringBuffer buf = new StringBuffer();
    buf.append("<employee name=\"");
    buf.append(getName());
    buf.append("\" department=\"");
    buf.append(departmentName());
    buf.append("\">");
    //...
    return buf.toString();
  }
  //...
}
```

Finally, delete the **asXML()** methods in each of the **Employee** subclasses. All the tests should pass as before.

**Introduce Explaining Variable**   When we have a complex expression that is difficult to understand, we can extract parts of it and store the intermediate results in well-named temporary variables. This breaks the expression into easy-to-understand pieces, as well as making the overall expression clearer.

Consider the following:

```
public Money calculateTotal() {
  return getSubtotal().plus((getTaxableSubtotal().times(0.15)))
               .minus((getSubtotal().asDouble() > 100.0)
                        ? (getSubtotal().times(0.10))
                        : 0);
```

The above code is quite simple, but it could certainly be clearer. There's also a potential performance issue since **getSubtotal()** is called repeatedly. We can refactor this, breaking the complex expression up into simpler pieces and using well-named variables to better communicate the intent:

```
public Money calculateTotal() {
  Money subtotal = getSubtotal();
  Money tax = getTaxableSubtotal().times(0.15);
  Money total = subtotal.plus(tax);
  boolean qualifiesForDiscount = getSubtotal().asDouble() > 100.0;
  Money discount = qualifiesForDiscount
                        ? subtotal.times(0.10)
                        : new Money(0.0);
  return total.minus(discount);
```

**Replace Constructor with Factory Method**  If we have several constructors that
create different flavors of the class, it can be confusing since, in Java and C++
(as opposed to Smalltalk), all constructors have the same name. Instead of using
hard-coded constructors, we can use static factory methods. This lets us give
each one a meaningful name.

We'll use the following as an example:

```java
public class Rating {
  private int value = 0;
  private String source = null;
  private String review = null;

  public Rating(int aRating) {
    this(aRating, "Anonymous", "");
  }

  public Rating(int aRating, String aRatingSource) {
    this(aRating, aRatingSource, "");
  }

  public Rating(int aRating, String aRatingSource, String aReview) {
    value = aRating;
    source = aRatingSource;
    review = aReview;
  }

  //...
}
```

This isn't too bad. We're chaining constructors to provide default arguments
to the next more specific one. In this way the functionality of the constructor is
implemented only in the most specific one. However, we can communicate the
intent more clearly by refactoring to convert these to factory methods:

```java
public static Rating newAnonymousRating(int value) {
  return new Rating(value, "Anonymous", "");
}

public static Rating newRating(int value, String source) {
  return new Rating(value, source, "");
}

public static Rating newReview(int value, String source, String review) {
  return new Rating(value, source, review);
}

private Rating(int aRating, String aRatingSource, String aReview) {
  value = aRating;
  source = aRatingSource;
  review = aReview;
}
```

Part of refactoring this is changing all references to use the factory methods. When tests all pass again we can delete the unnecessary constructors and mark the ones that remain as private. For example, constructor calls such as:

```
starWars.addRating(new Rating(2));
starWars.addRating(new Rating(4, "NY Times"));
starWars.addRating(new Rating(5, "Jason", "A really fun movie!"));
```

get changed to calls to a factory method:

```
starWars.addRating(Rating.newAnonymousRating(2));
starWars.addRating(Rating.newRating(4, "NY Times"));
starWars.addRating(Rating.newReview(5, "Jason", "A really fun movie!"));
```

Making the constructors private also gives us more control over where and how instances are created.

**Replace Inheritance with Delegation**   Inheritance should only be used when the subclasses are *special kinds of* the superclass, or they extend the superclass and not just override parts of it[12]. If inheritance is being used just to reuse some of the capabilities of the superclass (e.g., subclassing Vector to be able to store objects sequentially), it should be replaced with delegation by making the Vector an instance variable and using it to store the objects.

For example, consider this code for a class representing a company department that contains a collection of employees:

```
public class Department extends Vector {
}
```

The idea here is to get *for free* the collection maintenance support from Vector. Big mistake. There is no type-safety at all. Anything can be added to the department, and anything coming out of it has to be cast to Employee. Consider the following code:

```
public class Company {
  private HashMap departments = new HashMap();

  public Company() {
    departments.put("Engineering", new Department());
    departments.put("Sales", new Department());
  }

  public Department getDepartmentNamed(String departmentName) {
    return (Department)departments.get(departmentName);
  }
}
```

```
public int rollCall() {
  int absentees = 0;
  Collection allDepartments = departments.values();
  Iterator deptIterator = allDepartments.iterator();
  while (deptIterator.hasNext()) {
    Department aDepartment = (Department)deptIterator.next();
    Department.DepartmentIterator employees =
    aDepartment.iterator();

    while (employees.hasNext()) {
      Employee somebody = employees.next();
      if (!somebody.atWork()) {
        absentees++;
      }
    }
  }
  return absentees;
}
}
```

Not a very good design. Any code can get a department object and add any-thing it wants to it. By extending Vector to reuse the collection implementation we've totally discarded any control over what goes into Department. Talk about equal-opportunity hiring!

What can we do? Well, the first step would be to refactor out the collection management and provide a type-safe iterator:

```
public class Department {
  private Vector employees = new Vector();

  public void hire(Employee newHire) {
    employees.add(newHire);
  }

  public DepartmentIterator iterator() {
    return new DepartmentIterator();
  }

  public class DepartmentIterator {
    Iterator underlying = employees.iterator();

    public boolean hasNext() {
      return underlying.hasNext();
    }

    public Employee next() {
      return (Employee)underlying.next();
    }
  }
}
```

Now the only way to add to the collection is to use the hire() method. This provides type-safety. Since we now have that, we can create the customer iterator to encapsulate the cast.

**Replace Magic Number with Symbolic Constant** Having hard-coded literal values embedded in code is a very bad thing. They are harder to see, changing them is shotgun surgery, and it's blatant duplication. We can use a well-named symbolic constant instead. Then when it has to change, it's only in one place. This is really more general, and applies to any literal values, such as strings.

Consider this code:

```
public void testAdd() {
    Vector movieNamesWithAddition = new Vector(movieNames);
    movieNamesWithAddition.add("Lost In Space");
    MockControl control = EasyMock.controlFor(MovieListEditor.class);
    MovieListEditor mockEditor = (MovieListEditor) control.getMock();

    mockEditor.getMovies();
    control.setReturnValue(movieNames, 1);

    mockEditor.add("Lost In Space");
    control.setVoidCallable(1);

    mockEditor.getMovies();
    control.setReturnValue(movieNamesWithAddition, 1);

    control.activate();

    MovieListWindow window = new MovieListWindow(mockEditor);
    window.init();
    window.show();

    JTextField movieField = window.getMovieField();
    movieField.setText("Lost In Space");

    JButton addButton = window.getAddButton();
    addButton.doClick();

    JList movieList = window.getMovieList();
    ListModel movieListModel = movieList.getModel();
    assertEquals("Movie list is the wrong size after add",
                 movieNamesWithAddition.size(),
                 movieListModel.getSize());

    assertEquals("Movie list doesn't contain new name",
                 "Lost In Space",
                 movieListModel.getElementAt(movieNames.size()));

    control.verify();
}
```

The smell here is the duplication of the literal string "Lost In Space". We start by introducing a constant to hold the value:

```
private static final String LOST_IN_SPACE = "Lost In Space";
```

Then we replace every occurrence of the literal string with LOST_IN_SPACE. The resulting code is:

```
public void testAdd() {
    Vector movieNamesWithAddition = new Vector(movieNames);
    movieNamesWithAddition.add(LOST_IN_SPACE);
    MockControl control = EasyMock.controlFor(MovieListEditor.class);
    MovieListEditor mockEditor = (MovieListEditor) control.getMock();

    mockEditor.getMovies();
    control.setReturnValue(movieNames, 1);

    mockEditor.add(LOST_IN_SPACE);
    control.setVoidCallable(1);

    mockEditor.getMovies();
    control.setReturnValue(movieNamesWithAddition, 1);

    control.activate();

    MovieListWindow window = new MovieListWindow(mockEditor);
    window.init();
    window.show();

    JTextField movieField = window.getMovieField();
    movieField.setText(LOST_IN_SPACE);

    JButton addButton = window.getAddButton();
    addButton.doClick();

    JList movieList = window.getMovieList();
    ListModel movieListModel = movieList.getModel();
    assertEquals("Movie list is the wrong size after add",
            movieNamesWithAddition.size(),
            movieListModel.getSize());

    assertEquals("Movie list doesn't contain new name",
            LOST_IN_SPACE,
            movieListModel.getElementAt(movieNames.size()));

    control.verify();
}
```

This provides several benefits, including:

- the literal value appears only once, so only one change is needed if the value needs to change.

- all uses of the string are synchronized, so we no longer need to worry about references being the same.

**Replace Nested Conditional with Guard Clauses**  I know I said this was my ten favorite refactorings, but I thought I'd throw in a bonus.

Many people have been taught that a method should have only a single exit point (i.e., **return** statement). There is no valid reason for this, certainly not at the expense of clarity. In a method that should exit under multiple conditions, this leads to complex, nested conditional statements. A better, and much clearer, alternative is to use guard clauses to return under those conditions.

Here's a simple example:

```
public int fib(int i) {
  int result;
  if (i == 0) {
    result = 0;
  } else if (i <= 2){
    result = 1;
  } else {
    result = fib(i - 1) + fib(i - 2);
  }
  return result;
}
```

It's correct, but very ugly and crowded. And the conditional isn't even deeply nested. Now let's refactor it to use guard clauses instead of the conditional:

```
public int fib(int i) {
  if (i == 0) return 0;
  if (i <= 2) return 1;
  return fib(i - 1) + fib(i - 2);
}
```

---

This is one case where I will drop the braces surrounding the body of an if: guard clauses that perform one very simple action, typically a return. The intent is revealed much more by using this format rather than the more canonical:

```
public int fib(int i) {
  if (i == 0) {
    return 0;
  }
  if (i <= 2) {
    return 1;
  }
  return fib(i - 1) + fib(i - 2);
}
```

---

Using guard clauses results in code that is much cleaner, shorter, and clearer.

## REFACTORING TO PATTERNS

Design patterns are distillations of proven design ideas. To be good programmers we should know as many patterns as possible, and be constantly learning new ones. More than that, we need to know when to use them and, just as important, when not to.

If we don't know design patterns and/or don't use them, we are at risk of under-engineering. We won't see similarities as easily, and will find ourselves solving the same problems again and again. Knowing patterns helps us recognize recurring problems and gives us approaches to solving them.

The danger of design patterns is getting caught up in them. Many programmers overdo it when they discover design patterns. They begin seeing *Composites* around every requirement. Worse yet, they design by using patterns at the outset.

So, how should we be using patterns? The answer (if you haven't guessed yet, then you should reread this chapter before continuing) is as targets for refactoring. The thing to remember is that we shouldn't drop patterns into the design in final form, rather we should gradually evolve into using them via refactoring... but *only when we need to.*

## SUMMARY

Now we know a bit about refactoring: what it is, some of the specific techniques, and some of the indicators that tell us that refactoring may be required.

It is very important to engrain the habit of refactoring and to become proficient at refactoring. Both are accomplished through practice. We can start by pulling out some recent code and sniffing through it for code smells with a newly critical nose. Then we can apply specific refactorings as appropriate.

The problem with refactoring working code is that our changes might break it. That's where TDD comes in. If we are practicing TDD, all of the code is checked by our tests to ensure its proper behavior. We must always refactor as we do any TDD coding: in tiny increments. After making each component change in a refactoring, we run the tests again to catch any small bugs that might have been introduced. The level of confidence this gives us must be experienced to be understood.

Pretty soon we will have the courage to continually whittle down our code to the leanest, sparest possible implementation. As we become proficient at refactoring through TDD, we'll find that we develop a more discriminating eye (and nose!) for coding excellence, and a deeper level of software craft.

## Refactoring Test Code

Just as we need to continually refactor application code to make it cleaner and clearer, we also need to refactor test code for the same reasons. Here are some things we should keep in mind:

- Always use the appropriate assertion. For example:
  - If you are asserting the equality of values, use assertEquals(expected, actual) rather than assertTrue(actual == expected) or assertTrue(actual.equals(expected)).
  - If you are asserting that a value is false, use assertFalse(value) rather than assertTrue(!value).

- Stay alert for opportunities to consolidate duplicate fixture code within test methods into a single setup() method.

- Stay alert for fixtures that are not used uniformly by all the test methods in the TestCase. Look for opportunities to split TestCases to keep them focused on specific fixtures.

- Stay alert for ways to collect TestCases into TestSuites. Make sure that TestCases are not themselves serving as TestSuites (organized around structure or functionality instead of common fixture requirements).

- Don't duplicate information in test method and TestCase names. Name the TestCase to reflect the fixture (e.g., TestEmptyList) and the test methods to reflect the behavior tested (e.g., testSize()).

- Look for ways to keep test methods independent of each other. Look for opportunities to mock state-sensitive resources that bind your test methods together.

- Always look for better ways to organize your hierarchy of TestSuites and TestCases.

For more on test code smells and test code refactoring, see [39], [40].

# Chapter 3

# PROGRAMMING BY INTENTION

> *'Tis but thy name that is my enemy;*
> *. . .*
> *O, be some other name!*
>
> *- Romeo and Juliet, Act 2 Scene 2*
> *William Shakespeare*

This chapter discusses *programming by intention*, a central idea in XP. It means making your intent clear when you write code.

Have you ever had to work on a piece of code and found that it was hard to understand? Maybe the logic was convoluted, the identifiers meaningless, or worse, misleading. You say there was documentation? Was it readable? Did it make sense? Was it up to date with the code? Are you sure? How do you know?

The main idea of programming by intention is communication, specifically, the communication of our *intent* to whomever may be reading the code. The goal is to enable them to understand what we had in mind when we wrote the code.

Let's look at what we need to do in order to have our code be as understandable and intent-revealing as possible.

## NAMES

By *names* I mean the identifiers we choose to name the various classes, variables, methods, etc., that we create as we work. We need to choose names that are *semantically transparent*, that is, they say what they mean and mean what they say.

When I'm talking about choosing names, I like to pull out the quote from *Romeo and Juliet* that appears at the beginning of this chapter. We can use whatever word/name we like to refer to a thing, but if it does not convey the meaning that we intend then it is an enemy of clarity and may serve to confuse people who read or work on this code in the future. The lesson here is to use names that make sense. . . call it what it is.

My oldest daughter used to have a cute, although somewhat annoying, habit of coming up with her own names for songs and stories that she liked. She would focus on one line from the whole song/story and derive a name from that. Many nights at bedtime she would ask frantically for a new favorite, while we went through a game of *Twenty Questions* to try and deduce what she was talking about. This is a danger of using non-obvious names for things. Sure, it may make sense to us, but what about everyone else?

There are several patterns that we can use when choosing names; we discuss them in detail next.

**Use nouns or noun phrases for class names.** Name classes for what they represent or what they do:

```
public class Movie {
  //...
}

public class MovieRatingComparator implements Comparator {
  //...
}

public class XMLMovieListReader implements MovieListReader {
  //...
}
```

**Use either adjectives or generic nouns and noun phrases for interfaces.** Interfaces are a bit different. If an adjective is used for an interface name it usually ends with *-able*, for example, Runnable, Serializable. My advice is to avoid conventions that prepend or append "I" to the name when possible. Sometimes there isn't a good name for an interface other than "interface to *something*." In that case, ISomething is acceptable.

```
public interface Serializable {
}

public interface MovieListWriter {
  void write(MovieList movieList) throws IOException;
}
```

**Use verbs and verb phrases for method names.** Methods do something, so using verbs to name them makes sense. Examples include add and fetchReview.

```
private int calculateAverageRating() {
  int totalRating = calculateTotalRating();
  return totalRating / ratings.size();
}
```

**Use accepted conventions for accessors and mutators.** Many languages have generally accepted conventions for how to retrieve and modify instance variables. For instance, if you are working in Java, you are advised to use the Java Beans conventions of **getX** and **setX** to retrieve/modify a variable named x.

```java
public Category getCategory() {
  return category;
}

public void setCategory(Category aCategory) {
  category = aCategory;
}

public boolean isOfCategory(Category aCategory) {
  return category.equals(aCategory);
}
```

To access a boolean variable, use isX in both Java and Smalltalk. An alternative in some cases is to use the form isX() where X refers to an optional part of the object; for example, either of the following could be used:

```java
public boolean isRated() {
  return !ratings.isEmpty();
}

public boolean hasRating() {
  return !ratings.isEmpty();
}
```

Note that this applies to computed properties as well as actual instance variables, for example, when a circular queue class needs a method to query whether it is full, we suggest isFull.

Sometimes it is clearer to drop the **get** prefix. For example, I tend to use size rather than **getSize** to fetch the size of a composite object. This is often the case when the value you are asking for is a property of the object as opposed to one of its attributes.

```java
public int size() {
  return movies.size();
}
```

In this case, we are also conforming to the convention used in the Java class libraries. It is a good idea to conform to the naming idioms of the environment you are working in because that is what others who will be reading your code will be accustomed to.

**Don't put redundant information in method names.** If I needed a method to add an instance of X, I would tend to call the method add rather than addX since the parameter will be an X. This has the benefit that if later refactoring changes the type of the argument (even simple renaming of the class), then the method name is out of sync with its argument. The innocent redundancy has now become misleading and confusing. Another benefit is that you gain clarity if you need to support adding of different types by the ability to overload the method name.

```
public void add(Movie movieToAdd) throws DuplicateMovieException {
  if (this.contains(movieToAdd)) {
    throw new DuplicateMovieException(movieToAdd.getName());
  }
  movies.add(movieToAdd);
}
```

There are always exceptions. Sometimes it is just clearer, and reads better, if you have type information in the method name.

```
public void addRating(Rating ratingToAdd) {
  ratings.add(ratingToAdd);
}
```

**Use nouns and noun phrases for variable names.** Variables hold *things*, so nouns make sense, for example, rating, movies, connectionToReviewServer.

```
public class Movie {
  private String name = "";
  private Category category = Category.UNCATEGORIZED;
  private List ratings = null;

  //...
}
```

Choose names carefully, but don't spend too much time at it. Remember, they are easy to change. If later we decide that a different name would communicate the intent better, it can be changed. That's one of the most basic refactorings. Using a tool that has automated refactoring support helps.

## SIMPLICITY

When we are explaining something unfamiliar to someone we speak as simply as we can. Likewise, when we write code we should write it as simply as we can. Keep in mind that someone will be reading that code later, trying to understand what it does and how it does it. We should strive to keep our code as clear and intent-revealing as possible.

## Do the Simplest Thing

So how do we keep our code clear? One way is to use simple algorithms as much as possible. Always assume that the simplest way of doing something is the best. If it proves not to be, we can always change it. One of the phrases heard a lot in the eXtreme Programing world is *"What is The Simplest Thing That Could Possibly Work?"*

"What," you may ask, "does that mean?" Well, consider this simple test:

```
public void testEmptyList() {
  MovieList emptyList = new MovieList();
  assertEquals(0, emptyList.size());
}
```

In order to get this test to pass once it is compiling, we do the simplest thing that could possibly work. Specifically:

```
public int size() {
  return 0;
}
```

When we do this we know that the size() method is too simple, but at this point we don't know what it should be, and returning zero is the simplest thing that makes the test pass. We will have to generalize this method later, but not until we write tests for non-empty list behavior.

## Keep It Simple by Refactoring

Another way to keep code simple and intent-revealing is to change unclear code so that it is clear. This is one way that refactoring is used. Chapter 2 has a more in-depth discussion of this incredibly important topic.

There are many refactorings that deal with increasing the intent-revealing quality of a piece of code. While it could be argued that most of Fowler's refactorings make code clearer, we only consider a handful here. See [15] and [16] for more information on these and the remainder. The simplest of these include renaming classes, methods, variables, etc. Some of the more complex intent-revealing refactorings are explained next.

**Introduce Explaining Variable** If we have a complex expression, we take parts of it and put those intermediate values in temporary variables with names that explain the purpose of the subexpression.

**Extract Method** If we have a method that is getting overly complex, we make part of it into a separate method. This is also useful if we see common code in multiple methods: we extract the common part (possibly parameterized) into a separate method that can be called by multiple clients.

**Extract Class** If we have a class that is doing too much or that has multiple responsibilities, we extract related responsibilities into separate classes.

**Replace Temp with Query** Rather than computing a value and storing it in a temporary variable, we extract the computation into a method that returns the result, and call that instead.

**Split Temporary Variable** If we find a case where a temporary variable is reused, we create a new temporary variable for each use.

**Remove Assignments to Parameters** If we find code that assigns to a parameter, we use a temporary variable instead.

## WARRANTED ASSUMPTIONS

The test in the section titled *Programming by Intention* was the first test written in the project it came from. It was written as shown and no other code had been written yet. Why is this significant? Well, if we look at the test code we will see that it makes some assumptions:

1. there is a class called MovieList,

2. MovieList has a zero-argument constructor, and

3. MovieList has a method named size which takes no parameters and returns an int.

Making these assumptions as we write tests (and later when we write the *real* code) gives us the ability to design interfaces from the point of view of code that will use them. This allows us to choose names that make sense and that read well, that is, are understandable and clear. It also allows us to decide what behavior is required from a much better point of view: again, that of the client. This limits the behavior to exactly what is required, which lets us write less code, which lets us work faster, which lets us deliver sooner and more often.

How does this let us write less code? Primarily by deferring the addition of any code until it is proven to be required. This not only includes implementation detail, but also the existence of classes and methods. You do not create a class until you have a test that creates an instance of it. Likewise, you do not add a method until you have a test that calls it.

When you are writing code (especially tests), write what you want, without worrying about how to do it. Make up the support classes, methods, and variables you want and worry about their implementation later. This keeps you focused on what you have in mind at the time. The compiler will remind you about the assumptions you made.

# HOW TO PROGRAM BY INTENTION

There are several techniques that can be used to enhance the communication of intent by your code. We explore them and how to use them. Some of these include: use of metaphor, test first, refactor, make assumptions, and let the compiler tell you what your next step is.

## Common Vocabulary

Everyone involved with the project should use a common vocabulary to talk about the domain and the system. This can be based on the reality of the situation or it can be metaphorical if that eases understanding.

Having a common vocabulary helps us with two things:

**Understanding the domain** Because the activity of developing a complex software system involves people with different backgrounds and areas of knowledge it can be difficult to have everyone understand everyone else. However, to be an effective team we need to achieve a common understanding of the problem domain and the specific problem that the system is to solve. The difficulty here is that the technical members of the team will very likely not have a deep knowledge of the business. The opposite problem is making sure that the business people involved are able to have a clear understanding of what the system does, and to a large extent, how it works. Using a metaphor helps us bridge these two gaps by providing a description of the domain and the system that all parties can understand. It does this by providing a description in terms that everyone understands.

The original XP project at Chrysler is a prime example. The people at Chrysler understood factory and assembly line terminology. The programmers used that as a metaphor for the payroll system they were developing. An employee's paycheck was the product, constructed from *dollar parts*. It passed through various workstations, each of which performed some operation such as converting *hour parts* to *dollar parts*, taking a deduction, adding a bonus, etc.

**Choosing names** If we choose names from the common vocabulary, everyone knows what we mean. Having a common vocabulary means that everyone is using the same terms to mean the same thing. A great deal of confusion and miscommunication can be avoided, and a great deal of time and money can be saved. Not only should the terminology be used by everyone involved, it should also make sense in a fairly obvious way.

## Test First

One of the biggest effects of working a test first is that we have a large suite of programmer tests that make it possible for us to refactor mercilessly. Also, by writing the tests first, we have time to think about *what* we need to do before we have to think about *how* to do it.

Another benefit to writing the test first is that when the test passes, we're done. This has at least two advantages:

1. it helps you work faster, because when the test passes we're done and can move on to something else, and

2. because we stop when we have the test passing, it's easier to avoid overengineering a more complex solution than is required. This improves the overall quality of our code, as well as making it smaller and more understandable.

## Make Assumptions

This is closely related to writing tests first, but isn't limited to writing tests. You can make assumptions during implementations as well. By making assumptions as we work, we first decide what we need and what it should be called, and then create it. This lets us think about what we want to accomplish before worrying about the technical details of how to accomplish it. It also allows us to focus on the task at hand. If we made some assumptions that turn out to be invalid (i.o., what we assumed existed isn't there yet), we will find out when we try to compile. At that point we can deal with it; we have finished what we were doing when we had to make the assumption. The alternative is to deal with our assumptions as we make them. If we do that we risk losing track of what we were originally doing. Keep a notepad or stack of blank cards next to the workstation for jotting down notes and To Do items.

## Refactor

By refactoring as we see the need for it, we can change what we have already done to make our intention clearer. Refactoring was discussed earlier in this chapter as well as in Chapter 2.

## Let the Compiler Tell You

This technique helps us to defer work until it is required, by allowing us not to worry about keeping track of the assumptions we make. When we make an assumption which turns out to be false (i.e., the class, method, etc., that we are using in our code does not yet exist) the computer will inform us. In some cases (e.g., Java and C++) the compiler will report that something is missing and we will have to correct the issue (by stubbing the missing classes or methods). In other cases (such as Smalltalk) will we receive notification at runtime that a class, method, etc., is missing.

For example, consider the following test which was the first written for a project:

```
public void testEmptyListSize() {
  MovieList emptyList = new MovieList();
  assertEquals("Size of empty movie list should be 0.", 0, emptyList.size());
}
```

If this is the first code written in a project, compiling will produce the following message:

```
MovieList cannot be resolved or is not a type.
```

So we create the required class:

```
public class MovieList {
}
```

Compiling again results in:

```
The method size() is undefined for the type MovieList
```

Next, we add a stub for the method:

```
public int size() {
  return 0;
}
```

By leveraging the compiler like this, you can stop worrying about the assumptions you made that have to be dealt with... *let the compiler tell you*. This is also a way to avoid doing more than you absolutely need to.

## Do the Simplest Thing

I've said it before, but it's worth repeating: *Strive for simplicity*. If code starts out simple it's easier to keep it simple than to make complex code into simple code. You may not always do the simplest thing, but your code will be simpler and clearer if you take the time to figure out what the simplest thing would be. An earlier section discussed simplicity in more detail.

There is a difference of opinion on this point. Some advise always *doing* the simplest thing that could possibly work. I agree that forcing yourself to do the simplest thing is preferred when you are just starting out. Get into the habit of being simple. Once you have that, actually doing the simplest thing is not as important as long as you are aware of what it is.

## "NO COMMENT"

There are valid reasons to write comments. We'll talk about these later. However, as we discussed in Chapter 2, most comments are not written for valid reasons. Fowler's *Refactoring*[16] calls comments "deodorant"... they are there to try to hide the bad smell of the code. The code is unclear, the code is poorly written, names are badly chosen, the logic is obtuse, etc. Comments were added to try to explain what the code does. The code should have been, and should be, refactored to make the comments unnecessary.

Don't get me wrong. I'm not saying "Don't write documentation." Nobody really doing XP will say that. Sometimes it is important to the customer to have specific documentation written. Also, I'm not saying "Never write comments." What I am saying is "Never write unnecessary comments." Most comments are unnecessary if the code is written so that the intent is clear. If and when we do write comments, we need to make sure they communicate *why* and not *how*.

## Valid Comments

As I mentioned above, there are several valid reasons for us to write comments.

**Incomplete code** This type of comment serves as a note to what we were in the midst of working on, or how we see the code evolving. There generally is not much need for this type of comment, since tasks should be no larger than what can be accomplished in a single day. If you find that you do need to make such a note, choose a standard tag for it so you can quickly search for loose ends. And stay away from generic not done yet comments. I'd suggest something like:

```
// TODO: The tree should be balanced after doing the insertion.
```

A valid use for this type of comment might be to note code that could benefit from being refactored. Maybe we saw the need to refactor but didn't have time to do it. Make a note so that someone will spot it and do the refactoring when there is time. It might be prudent to use standard wording for these "refactoring To Do" comments so that a global search can be performed as a rough code-debt metric. I suggest something similar to the following:

```
// CODE DEBT: the looping structure is a bit convoluted, could use
// some method extraction.
```

**Refactoring doesn't make it clear enough** This isn't really a valid comment, rather it is more like the previous type...it's an IOU. If refactoring doesn't clean up the code, either someone else should try their hand at it, or (more likely) the code in question should be scrapped and rewritten.

```
// NEEDS WORK: I tried extract method, but it's still awkward.
// Maybe refactoring to a Strategy would clean it up?
```

**Use of an unusual algorithm** If we use an uncommon algorithm for some reason, we should make a note of it with a comment. Point the reader to where they can learn more. Don't try to document the algorithm in a huge comment. Just note what algorithm it is, why it was used, and where to find more information.

```
// I used an AVL Tree algorithm here to keep the tree balanced.
```

**Use of a published algorithm** If we use an algorithm that is published somewhere, we should add a comment saying where and giving credit to the author. This type of comment is often used with the previous type.

```
// This AVL alorithm was based on Brad Appleton's implementation at
// http://www.enteract.com/~bradapp/ftp/src/libs/C++/AvlTrees.html
```

**Performance tuning** This is important. If we tune for performance, we should add a comment explaining it. At the very least we need to add a note saying that the method in question has been tuned. If we tune without adding such a note we may find that someone later refactors to make the code clearer, undoing the optimization in the process. Keep in mind that we generally shouldn't be performance tuning until late in the project, once performance has been measured and actual bottlenecks have been found.

```
// A circular queue is used here for performance reasons: to avoid
// having to move elements around.
```

**Class comment** This is the one case that is often useful, in spite of the general disapproval of comments. Not much is required. A simple note at the beginning of the class briefly explaining why the class exists and what it is used for will suffice. Avoid writing a *how to use this class* tutorial. That's one of the things the tests are for.

```
/**
 * This class represents a single movie title. It is responsible for
 * maintaining its own ratings, reviews, etc.
 */
```

A final note related to comments. Programmers often sign their work by including a comment in the file header noting who wrote it. That's fine; credit where credit is due and all that, except:

1. If we are practicing XP, specifically collective code ownership, everyone will likely work on that code. It is owned by the team.

2. A record of who worked on each file will be maintained by the source code control system (SCCS). It is redundant to include the information in the file itself as well. Another comment on this: Please don't include an expandable change log in the file (e.g., $Log$ in CVS). This clutters the code, makes the files larger, and duplicates information that is easy to extract from the SCCS.

## SUMMARY

In this chapter we've seen how even seemingly minor details, like picking a name for something, can have a great impact on the code quality. We've discussed several techniques for choosing names, achieving simplicity, staying focused, and making your code intent-revealing. The benefit to practicing these techiques is code that is simple, understandable, and maintainable.

Sooner or later, someone *will* read our code. We will ourselves reread our code, sometimes after a long absence. Any readers, including us, will be hindered or thwarted by code that is awkward, complex, obscure, or in the worst case, misleading.

Well-crafted, simple, clear, intent-revealing code will speed us in our work instead. Such code also helps teach readers how to program well. It teaches good solutions to problems, and teaches how to express those solutions succinctly.

Learning to code with this clear intent is well worth any programmer's effort.

Part II
_____

# TOOLS AND TECHNIQUES

In this part of the book we will explore and discuss tools that can be used for TDD. The most important of these is JUnit (and by extension, the whole xUnit family) and its extensions. We also look at some other tools that are of use when practicing TDD and work in conjunction with JUnit. Finally, we look at tools that are not specific to TDD, but make practicing TDD easier, or have features that do so.

# Chapter 4

# JUNIT

*I do owe them still*

*- Coriolanus, Act 2 Scene 2*
*William Shakespeare*

In this chapter we'll be looking at and learning a bit about the de facto tool for Test-Driven Development using Java: the JUnit programmer test framework. Specifically, we'll be looking at the latest released version as of this writing: JUnit 3.8.

The esteem in which developers hold JUnit is evidenced by the fact that it has repeatedly won honors at the Java-World Editors Choice Awards in the *Best Java Performance Monitoring/Testing Tool* category.

## ARCHITECTURAL OVERVIEW

First let's look at how JUnit is structured. Figure 4.1 shows a high-level UML class diagram of the core of JUnit: the junit.framework package.

The class junit.textui.TestRunner and its superclass are included to show how the test runners are hooked up to the framework. Let's look at each class in turn and see what it does and how it fits in.

**Test** This is the interface that all types of test classes must implement. Currently in the framework there are only two such classes: TestCase and TestSuite.

**TestCase** This class is the main class you will be extending when you write your tests. It is the simplest type of Test. A concrete TestCase (i.e., a class that extends TestCase) has methods that implement individual tests as well as optional setUp and tearDown methods (see the section later on "Writing a TestCase" for details).

**TestSuite** This is another subclass of Test. Its purpose is to collect together Tests: TestCases, other TestSuites, or any combination of the two. Later we'll explore techniques and conventions for collecting tests together into suites.

**Assert** This is the superclass of TestCase that provides all of the assert methods that are available to you when you write your tests.

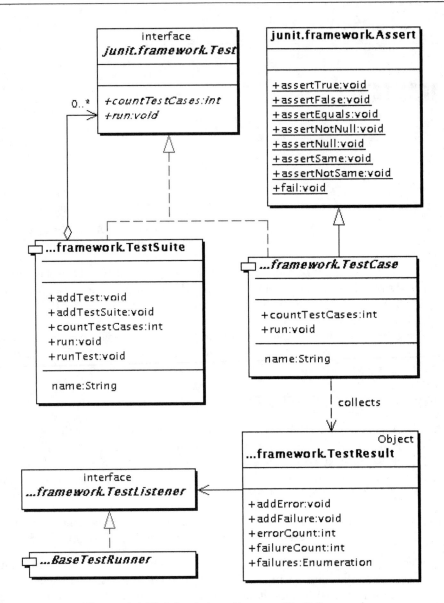

**Figure 4.1** High-level class diagram of junit.framework.

**TestFailure** This class simply encapsulates an error or failure that occurs during a test run. It keeps track of the Test that failed and the exception that was responsible for the error or failure (in the case of a failure this will be an AssertionFailedError).

**TestResult** This class accumulates the results of running the tests. It is also responsible for informing any interested parties of the start and end of a test, as well as failures and errors. It is this facility that enables the Graphical User Interface's (GUI) progress bar to move for each test, and the results to be displayed.

**TestListener** This is an interface that is implemented by any class that wishes to track the progress of a test run. Methods are declared for notification of the start and end of each test, as well as the occurrence of errors and failures.

**TestRunner** JUnit comes with a selection of TestRunner classes. Each extend junit.runner.BaseTestRunner and provide various interfaces to the JUnit framework.

For more discussion of the framework and how it is composed of design patterns, see [20].

## THE ASSERTIONS

When you are writing test methods you make heavy use of the capabilities you inherit (by way of TestCase) from Assert. For all Assert methods there are two versions: with an initial String parameter that contains a message to be displayed in the case of failure, and without.

### fail

The simplest method (really we'll be talking about pairs of methods, but from here on I'll just consider them single methods) is fail().

```
void fail()
void fail(String message)
```

Calling fail() causes an immediate test failure. This is useful in cases where the test can get to a point that indicates something went wrong. An example is when you expect a method call to throw a specific exception. You would place a call to fail() immediately after the method call inside the try block. The following example demonstrates this:

```
public void testDivisionByZero() {
  try {
    int x = 3 / 0;
    fail("Division by zero didn't throw an exception");
  } catch (ArithmeticException ex) {
  }
}
```

## assertTrue and assertFalse

The next methods of interest are assertTrue() and assertFalse(). assertTrue() used to be named assert() but has been changed due to the addition of the assert keyword in J2SE 1.4..

```
void assertTrue(boolean condition)
void assertTrue(String message, boolean condition)
void assertFalse(boolean condition)
void assertFalse(String message, boolean condition)
```

If condition is false, the test fails. The assertFalse() method does the opposite, failing if the value of the condition is true. This is provided as a cleaner alternative to using assertTrue() with a negated condition.

Here's an example:

```
public void testEmptyList() {
    assertTrue("An empty list should report empty", emptyList.isEmpty());
    Enumeration emptyEnumerator = emptyList.movies();
    assertFalse("Empty list should have empty Enumeration",
            emptyEnumerator.hasMoreElements());
}
```

## assertNull and assertNotNull

Next are two method pairs for checking for null or not null:

```
void assertNull(Object object)
void assertNull(String message, Object object)
void assertNotNull(Object object)
void assertNotNull(String message, Object object)
```

Each of these takes an Object and checks whether it is or isn't null, then fails if it isn't as expected.

```
public void testEmptyListEnumeration() {
    Enumeration emptyEnumerator = emptyList.movies();
    assertNotNull("Empty list should have non-null Enumeration",
            emptyEnumerator);
}
```

## assertSame and assertNotSame

```
void assertSame(Object expected, Object actual)
void assertSame(String message, Object expected, Object actual)
void assertNotSame(Object expected, Object actual)
void assertNotSame(String message, Object expected, Object actual)
```

These methods succeed if the two supplied arguments are the same object (for assertSame()) or different objects (for assertNotSame()).

```java
public void testIteration() {
    Enumeration threeMovieEnumerator = scifiList.movies();
    assertSame("First movie from threeMovieEnumerator is bad",
            starWars,
            (Movie) threeMovieEnumerator.nextElement());
    assertSame("Second movie from threeMovieEnumerator is bad",
            stargate,
            (Movie) threeMovieEnumerator.nextElement());
    assertSame("Third movie from threeMovieEnumerator is bad",
            starTrek,
            (Movie) threeMovieEnumerator.nextElement());
}
```

## assertEquals

This is really a family of methods, one for each Java type. Each method tests for equality using the appropriate mechanism (i.e., = for primitives and the equals() method for objects). For this reason I've omitted types for expected and actual.

```java
void assertEquals(expected, actual)
void assertEquals(String message, expected, actual)
```

It is important to understand the difference between assertSame and assertEquals. The former passes only when the two objects being compared are the same object. Make sure you understand that.. the same object. . . not objects that are equals.

There is a set of methods (with and without an initial message parameter) for the following types: boolean, byte, char, double, float, int, long, Object, and short.

The version for Object makes use of the equals method of the expected argument.

```java
public void testRemoving() {
    assertEquals("Bad initial size", 3, scifiList.size());
    scifiList.remove(starWars);
    assertEquals("Bad size after removing the first movie",
            2,
            scifiList.size());
```

```
scifiList.remove(stargate);
assertEquals("Bad size after removing the second movie",
             1,
             scifiList.size());

scifiList.remove(starTrek);
assertEquals("Should be empty after removing third movie",
             0,
             scifiList.size());
}
```

The version for **double** and **float** have an additional parameter (of type **double** or **float**, respectively) that specifies the maximum difference allowed between the expected and actual values.

## WRITING A TESTCASE

**TestCase** is the class most often used in JUnit. You begin by creating a subclass of **TestCase** to which you will add related test methods. The examples here will be taken from the project that forms the core of the book: keeping track of a list of movies you would like to see, with ratings, recommendations, and so forth. We start with the idea of supporting a list of movies. Here is what the skeletal test class looks like:[1]

```
import junit.framework.TestCase;

public class TestMovieList extends TestCase {
}
```

The name of the class is important. It should either be of the form **TestMyClass** or **MyClassTest**. Using one of these forms of naming allows the collectors to automatically find your test classes. The same applies to **TestSuites**.

Now that we have a skeleton set up we can start writing tests. We do this by writing methods that follow the basic pattern:

- set up preconditions

- exercise functionality being tested

- check postconditions

Interestingly, it is best to write the tests in the opposite order:

1. write the assertions that test what you want as a result (one small assertion at a time)

---

[1]Note that prior to JUnit 3.8 a constructor was required which took a **String** parameter, which was then passed to the superclass' constructor. As of version 3.8 this is no longer required.

2. do what needs to be done to achieve those results

3. set up any preconditions (this may be done implicitly by setUp(); more on this later).

Doing it this way leads to smaller, more focused tests.

Test methods should be short and to the point. Each method should test a specific bit of functionality. In keeping with the TDD mantra of *test a little, code a little*, don't write all the tests then go about writing code. Write one test method... now make it run... write another test... make it run... and so on. And try to focus on keeping those tests as small as you can. Time for another example: time to write the first test. This is often an awkward point: *How do you start testing? What test should you start with?* My advice is to find the simplest thing to test. If there is a basis case, test that first, then move incrementally to the larger cases.

In this example our basis case is an empty list of movies. Here's a test method for empty list behavior, from which we can learn several things:

```
public void testEmptyList() {
  MovieList emptyList = new MovieList();
  assertEquals("Size of an empty list should be zero.", 0, emptyList.size());
  assertTrue("An empty list should report empty.", emptyList.isEmpty());
}
```

The first thing to notice is that we use a fairly specific method signature. All test methods should have a signature of the form public void testWhatever(). This allows them to be found and collected automatically by the JUnit framework.

Next, notice the pattern:

- set up preconditions... create a new MovieList, get its Enumeration of Movies.

- exercise functionality... call emptyList.size(), emptyList.isEmpty(), etc.

- check postconditions... check that size() returned 0, check that isEmpty() returned true, etc.

Next, notice the assert... method calls. The final thing to notice is that the test refers to classes (MovieList and Movie) as well as methods (size(), isEmpty(), and movies()) none of which have been written yet. This is Test-Driven Development in action.

As we'll explore later on, you also want to be on the lookout for opportunities to refactor your test code just as you do with the production code. Test code has characteristic smells of its own. At XP2001 there was a great paper on refactoring test code[40].

## RUNNING YOUR TESTS

Now that we've discussed how to write tests we should look at what you do with your tests once you've written them. This section will look at the TestRunner implementations that are part of JUnit, as well as plugins for some IDEs. As an example for comparison, we'll use the samples test suite from the JUnit 3.8 build.

### Errors and Failures

When you run tests there are two types of feedback you get for each test:

- whether the test passed or failed

- if the test failed, whether it was an error or a failure, and what caused it

Additionally, you get feedback on the test run as a whole: pass (the diligently-sought-after green bar) or fail (the not-so-pleasant, but still invaluable, red bar). The overall pass/fail feedback is commonly referred to as a greenbar/redbar due to the implementation of the graphical test runners: the progress bar is green as long as tests are passing but turns red if one test fails (and stays red). This provides immediate and undeniable feedback.

As mentioned above, when a test fails it can be due to an error or a failure. An *error* indicates that the test terminated unsuccessfully due to an unexpected exception being thrown. A *failure* indicates an unsuccessful termination due to an assertion failure.

### JUnit's Text UI

We'll start with the simplest thing that could possibly work: a command line, textual TestRunner.

You simply run junit.textui.TestRunner, passing it the name of the Test to run, as shown in Figure 4.2. As each test is run, a character is printed to the console (actually System.out): . for a pass, E for an error, or F for a failure.

Following the individual test status output, a failure trace is output for each unsuccessful test.

### JUnit's Swing GUI

The junit.swingui.TestRunner, shown in Figure 4.3, provides a much more elaborate interface for running tests. A notable addition in respect to the AWT GUI is the test hierarchy tab that allows you to open test suites to recursively see the component tests. Each test case is annotated by a green check or red X, indicating the pass/fail status of that particular test. Selecting a test and clicking on the *Run* button will rerun that particular test.

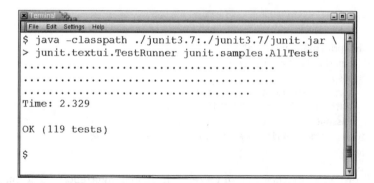

**Figure 4.2** The text TestRunner.

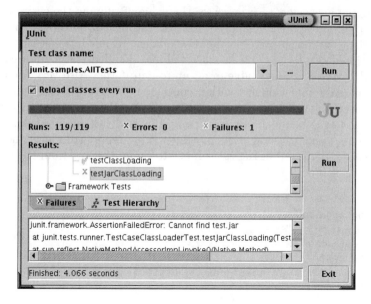

**Figure 4.3** The swing TestRunner.

## Running Tests as an ANT TASK

There are two tasks in the *optional* task jar for using JUnit from within an ANT build file. Both support a variety of attributes that we won't cover here. The ANT documentation does a more than adequate job.

The first task is junit, which runs a set of JUnit tests. The screen output from a junit task is minimal, and not overly useful. Here's a build.xml snippet that shows basic use of the junit task which specifies an XML formatter that is needed in support of the task we'll discuss in a moment:

```
<junit printsummary="on">
  <formatter type="xml" />
  <classpath>
    <pathelement location="${dist}" />
    <pathelement location="${dist}/junit.jar" />
  </classpath>
  <test name="junit.samples.AllTests" />
</junit>
```

ANT provides another task for use with JUnit: junitreport. The purpose of this task is to take status reports (in XML) that are generated by one or more junit tasks, consolidate them, and generate a nested set of HTML pages that present the test results.

Using the junitreport task increases the value of running the entire test suite as part of an automated build. The HTML output can be copied (by another ANT task) to a known place on the development team's intranet site. By running the build regularly, you can make full and detailed status information (as described by the tests) available in an up-to-date form. Also very useful is the high-level test count. Coupled with a continuous integration and build process (e.g., CruiseControl [URL 37]) you can literally see the test count increase over the course of even hours. In an XP setting, this feedback is quite valuable.

Figures 4.4 and 4.5 show parts of the resulting report (top level and details, respectively). Here's a `build.xml` snippet to build a report from the output of the previous snippet:

```
<junitreport todir=".">
  <fileset dir=".">
    <include name="TEST-*.xml"/>
  </fileset>
  <report format="frames" todir="./html"/>
</junitreport>
```

## The JUnit plugin for Eclipse

Erich Gamma was one of the original developers of JUnit, and his team at OTI has done a splendid job of integrating JUnit into Eclipse. They don't just spawn the Swing JUnit TestRunner like many IDE integrations do. They have written a TestRunner that is fully integrated into the Eclipse workbench, taking full advantage of the Eclipse plugin architecture.

Figure 4.6 shows an Eclipse session with a JUnit view open (center right). The Eclipse TestRunner is a view within workbench. It can be made into a *fast view* (i.e., docked in the perspective bar and popped back on demand), run in debug mode, and invoked by running a class as a *JUnit Test*. This tight integration also provides the ability to double-click a line of the failure trace and have an

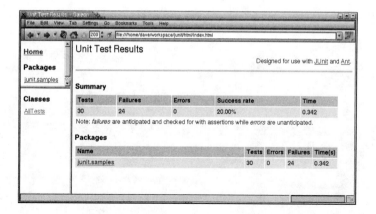

**Figure 4.4** Top-level output report from the ANT junitreport task.

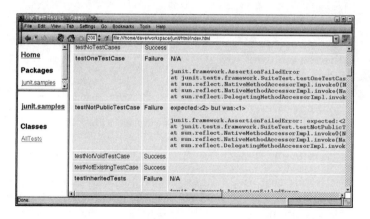

**Figure 4.5** Detailed output from the ANT junitreport task.

editor open on the corresponding file, positioned at the line causing the failure. Nifty. Clicking on the name of a test in the *Failures* or *Hierarchy* tabs opens an editor on the source of that test. Having JUnit this integrated speeds up the programming experience greatly: make a change, a quick keystroke to save and compile, and another quick keystroke to rerun the last set of tests. These features coupled with Eclipse's other TDD supporting features (and the fact that it is open source) make it a great choice of IDE for TDD.

## USING SETUP() AND TEARDOWN()

As you write test methods you may find that you are creating the same test object(s) in multiple test methods. Hey, that smells! What you do in this situation is create a **public void setUp()** method and move the shared test setup code there,

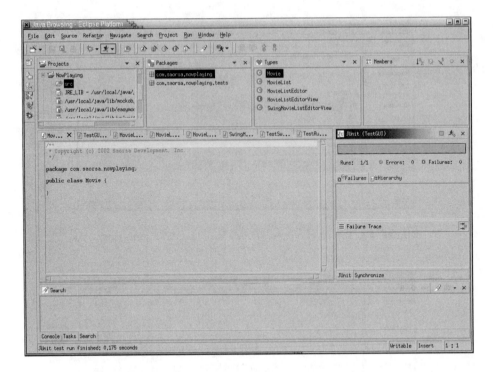

**Figure 4.6** The JUnit view in Eclipse.

creating a test fixture that establishes a context in which your test methods will run. When you move fixture creation into a setUp() method, don't forget to make the local variables into instance variables. If we found that we needed emptyList in other tests we could add the following bit of code and just use emptyList as required in the test methods.

```
private MovieList emptyList;

public void setUp() {
  emptyList = new MovieList();
}
```

The counterpart of setUp() is tearDown() in which you perform any required clean up of the test fixture. This is most useful if, as part of the fixture, you need to allocate limited resources that will not be reclaimed automatically, such as databases and communication connections.

The setUp() method is called before each test method, and tearDown() is called after each one. This keeps tests isolated and reduces the chance of side effects from test to test.If you want setUp() and tearDown() to be common for all tests in a **TestCase**, there is a decorator that does just that. Chapter 5 discusses this and other extensions.

## USING TESTSUITE

As mentioned earlier, **TestSuites** are used to collect a selection of **Tests** so that they can be run as a unit. Note that a **TestSuite** may recursively contain other **TestSuites**.

When you start out with JUnit you will likely be using **TestSuites** without even knowing it. The framework uses reflection to find and collect all of the test methods in a given **TestCase** whose signatures match:

```
public void testWhatever()
```

When you use this facility, you have no control over or any guarantee of the order in which the test methods will be run. Tests should be written in such a way that they are order independent, so this should not be a problem. If, however, you have a situation where you want or need tests to run in a specific order you can supply a **public static Test suite()** method which builds the **TestSuite** as required. Here is an example:

```
public static Test suite() {
  suite.addTest(new TestMovieList("testEmptyList"));
  suite.addTest(new TestMovieList("testAdding"));
  return suite;
}
```

I can't stress enough that test methods within a **TestCase** should be completely independent. You should seldom have to resort to writing your own **suite()** method. In xUnit for languages that lack a reflection mechanism, you will have to build suites by hand, as it were.

If you find that you want or need to have test methods run in a specific order you should see if there is a way to remove that requirement. It may be that you are relying on an external resource whose state is modified by each subsequent test. Try to find a way to tease apart those dependencies, setting up the appropriate fixture individually for each test. You might be able to do this by mocking such an external resource. For more on mock objects, see Chapter 7.

Another more valid use of **TestSuite**, in my opinion, is to create smaller **TestSuites** which include a specific subset of the tests. There are two main reasons to do this:

1. You can create custom suites of tests that relate directly to the task you are working on. By doing this you can save time running tests by focusing the tests that are run on the area of the code you are working on. But always keep that suite and the code it tests in sync. As you find yourself needing

to involve code that your suite doesn't test, be sure to add the tests for
that code to your suite so that you can proceed, protected and confident.

2. You will most likely want to have a **TestSuite** that tests a complete package
   or module. My practice is to have a suite in each package called **TestAll**
   that includes all tests in that package and all subpackages. By doing this,
   I can easily test any subtree of a project. Here's an example:

```
package com.saorsa.nowplaying.pd.tests;

import junit.framework.Test;
import junit.framework.TestSuite;

public class TestAll extends TestSuite {

    public TestAll() {
        super();
    }

    public static Test suite() {
        TestSuite suite = new TestSuite();
        suite.addTestSuite(TestMovie.class);
        suite.addTestSuite(TestMovieList.class);
        return suite;
    }
}
```

## HOW DOES IT ALL FIT TOGETHER?

Tests, cases, suites, fixtures. How do they all fit together? What really happens
when the tests run? This section will answer these questions. By the end of it,
you should have a much deeper understanding of what happens when we run
our tests. This will help us write and organize groups of tests that are simpler,
cleaner, more understandable, and more maintainable.

Let's begin by considering **TestCase**. It is used to group related tests together.
But what does *related* mean? It is often misunderstood to mean all tests for
a specific class or specific group of related classes. This misunderstanding is
reinforced by some of the IDE plugins that will generate a **TestCase** for a specified
class, creating a test method for each method in the target class. These test
creation facilities are overly simplistic at best, and misleading at worst. They
reinforce the view that you should have a **TestCase** for each class being tested,
and a test for each method in those classes. But that approach has nothing to
do with TDD, so we won't discuss it further.

This structural correspondence of tests misses the point. You should write
tests for behaviors, not methods. A test method should test a single behavior.
Examples include:

- The size of an empty list should be zero.

- An empty list should answer true when it is asked if it isEmpty().

- The iterator returned by an empty list should have no elements.

Here's a TestCase corresponding to the above behaviors:

```
public class TestEmptyList extends TestCase {
  private List emptyList;

  protected void setUp() throws Exception {
    emptyList = new ArrayList();
  }
  public void testSize() {
    assertEquals("Size of an empty list should be zero.",
                 0,
                 emptyList.size());
  }
  public void testIsEmpty() {
    assertTrue("Empty list should report empty.",
               emptyList.isEmpty());
  }
  public void testIterator() {
    Iterator emptyListIterator = emptyList.iterator();
    assertFalse("Iterator from empty list should be empty.",
                emptyListIterator.hasNext());
  }
}
```

TestCase is a mechanism to allow *fixture* reuse. Each TestCase subclass represents a fixture, and contains a group of tests that run in the context of that fixture. A fixture is the set of preconditions and assumptions with which a test is run. It is the runtime context for the test, embodied in the instance variables of the TestCase, the code in the setUp() method, and any variables and setup code local to the test method. In the above example, the fixture consisted of emptyList, an ArrayList with no elements.

An instance of a TestCase is created for each individual test method. When the TestCase object is run, it builds the fixture (using setUp()), runs its single test, and tears down the fixture (using tearDown()). Figure 4.7 shows this. Note that the two test case objects are the same object, but with methods from the super and subclass. By allowing TestCase to contain multiple tests (i.e., public void testXXX() methods) you are sharing a fixture definition.

This hardwired fixture-orientation makes TestCase a bad choice for grouping tests structurally or conceptually—TestSuite is better for that, as we'll see later. So instead of using TestCase to group tests for a given class, try thinking about it as a way to group tests that need to be set up in exactly the same way.

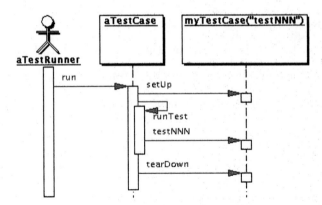

**Figure 4.7** Sequence of running a single TestCase.

A measure of how well your **TestCase** is mapping to the requirements of a single fixture is how uniformly that fixture (as described by the **setUp()** method) is used by all of the test methods. Whenever you discover that your **setUp()** method contains code for some of your test methods, and different code for other test methods, consider it a smell that indicates that you should refactor the **TestCase** into two or more **TestCases**.

Running a cohesion metric on your test code can help bring this to light.

Once you get the hang of defining **TestCases** this narrowly, you will find that they are easier to understand and maintain. And again, as we will see shortly, there are still lots of ways to organize the tests for a specific class (or for any other natural grouping) so that they are easy to identify.

For example, here is a **TestCase** similar to the one above, but with multiple fixtures:

```
public class TestList extends TestCase {
  private List emptyList;

  protected void setUp() throws Exception {
    emptyList = new ArrayList();
  }

  public void testEmptyListSize() {
    assertEquals("Size of an empty list should be zero.",
                 0,
                 emptyList.size());
  }
```

```
    public void testEmptyListIsEmpty() {
      assertTrue("Empty list should report empty.",
                emptyList.isEmpty());
    }

    public void testEmptyListIterator() {
      Iterator emptyListIterator = emptyList.iterator();
      assertFalse("Iterator from empty list should be empty.",
                emptyListIterator.hasNext());
    }

    public void testOneItemListSize() {
      List oneItemList = new ArrayList();
      oneItemList.add("One");
      assertEquals("Size of a one item list should be one.",
                1,
                oneItemList.size());
    }

    public void testOneItemListIsEmpty() {
      List oneItemList = new ArrayList();
      oneItemList.add("One");
      assertFalse("One item list should not report empty.",
                oneItemList.isEmpty());
    }
  }
```

Here, we want to extract the common fixture code in testOneItemListSize() and testOneItemListIsEmpty() into a common fixture using the setUp() method. The problem is that the other three tests don't need it. This class should be split into two fixtures, the earlier TestEmptyList and the following:

```
    public class TestOneItemList extends TestCase {
      private List oneItemList;

      protected void setUp() throws Exception {
        oneItemList = new ArrayList();
        oneItemList.add("One");
      }

      public void testOneItemListSize() {
        assertEquals("Size of a one item list should be one.",
                  1,
                  oneItemList.size());
      }

      public void testOneItemListIsEmpty() {
        assertFalse("One item list should not report empty.",
                  oneItemList.isEmpty());
      }
    }
```

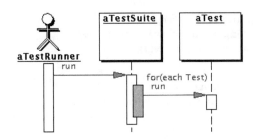

**Figure 4.8** Sequence of running a TestSuite.

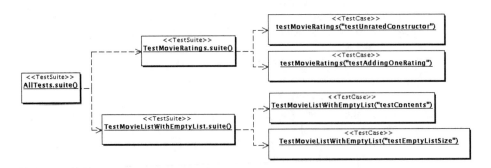

**Figure 4.9** A sample of the runtime structure of tests.

This is better, but notice that it leaves a little smell behind: overly long test method names that echo the fact that we are testing a list with one item. Because the class name makes it clear what size list we are testing, we can shorten these method names to describe just the behaviors being tested: testSize() and testIsEmpty().

TestSuite is a mechanism for grouping a collection of Test instances and running them sequentially. These can be either TestCases or, recursively, other Test-Suites. Figure 4.8 shows this.

TestCase has the ability to create a TestSuite containing all possible instances of itself. This is done by using reflection to create an instance for each constituent test. You also have the ability to create explicit TestSuites by subclassing Test-Suite and writing a custom public static Test suite() method. This is useful for collecting together groups of smaller TestSuites, which can be other custom Test-Suites, or TestSuites generated by TestCases.

Both TestSuite and TestCase implement the Test interface. The TestRunners work with objects that are Tests, hence, we can point a runner at any Test (i.e., TestSuite or TestCase) and recursively run all the contained tests. At runtime, after the Tests have been recursively collected, the structure looks something like that shown in Figure 4.9. The internal nodes are TestSuites and the leaves are TestCases (remember, each TestCase instance represents a single test method).

## WHERE DO TESTS BELONG?

Now that you are writing tests using JUnit, there is the issue of where you should put them. There are two main alternatives; we'll look at them in turn.

**With the code being tested.** This allows you to reference package-scoped members from your test code. A disadvantage is that it clutters your packages with test classes, making it less clear what is production code.

**In a subpackage.** Typically, this would be a subpackage named **tests**. For example, if you are testing code in the package **com.saorsa.nowplaying** the test code would be in the package **com.saorsa.nowplaying.tests**. This has the advantage of limiting access to only public members of the classes being tested.

A second issue is whether you put test code in the same source tree as the code being tested. My personal preference is to answer this with a resounding "yes." There is no real technical advantage either way, but I just like to keep the tests tightly bound to the tested code. Everything is in one place, and it reinforces the philosophy that code without tests doesn't exist. Also, not all tools handle multiple source trees very well.

Keep in mind that some organizations will have policies about where test code must reside, keeping test code separate from production code, or about what code is where in general. If that's the case, you'll generally have to go along with it.

Personally, I make a habit of placing my test code in a subpackage. I find that this clean separation between production and test code is beneficial. If all you have are TestCase and TestSuite subclasses, then that separation can be maintained by naming conventions. This becomes more problematic as you add other types of classes to the test scaffolding. Some, like mock objects (see Chapter 7), can use naming (e.g., Mock-CommPort), but often you will require other helper classes and the name space gets crowded. Another reason I use a subpackage is to reduce visibility to the public methods of the production code. After all, you are working with the behavior of the code, and this is made up of its public interface.

As for the question of using the same or parallel source tree, I use a single source tree. This keeps things simple, binds the test code closely to the corresponding production code, and works with all tools.

## TIPS

As with any technology or technique, there are certain idioms or rules of thumb that are helpful to know when you are practicing TDD. I've polled the TDD community and collected a list of what the leading practitioners consider good ideas.

## Test the simple stuff first

Some things are easier to test, or it's obvious how to write the tests. The types of things that this could include are:

- proper handling of null (but only in cases where null would be a potential value)

- empty collection or null object behavior

- generally, the basis case for recursive or iterative structures and computations.

By tackling these easy tests first you quickly get into the test-first rhythm.

## Use assertEquals

You should use the assertEquals() method as much as possible[31]. This is a matter of clarity.

## Use the message argument

All of the methods that are inherited from Assert have a form that takes a message as the initial argument. *Use it!*[31] If you feel that the test is clear and failure would be unambiguous, please disregard this advice. However, if you find that the failure isn't clear, including a message does help.

For example, if the test is as simple as possible, having only a single assertion, and is descriptively named then there is little reason to have a message in the assertion. It is simply redundant. However, if you have multiple assertions in a single test, use the message to aid in identifying them in the TestRunner output. If an assertion fails, the message will indicate which one.

Failure to use the message argument is one of the smells reported by Arie van Deursen et.al. at XP2001[40].

This message argument provides an explanation of the failure to the user. It makes it easier to understand why the test is failing. This can be especially useful when you are not running JUnit in an integrated environment where you can double-click on the error trace and jump to the assert line that failed. It also serves as documentation for the tests, stating explicitly what the failure condition is for that test.

In any case, the message shouldn't just echo what the test code, or the built-in error message, says.

## Keep test methods small

Most importantly, keep the number of assertions to a minimum in each test method. Doing this will keep your tests small and focused. This leads to easy-to-understand tests. The "extreme" of this is one assertion per test.

Here's an initial version of a test from Chapter 8 which has one monolithic test method:

```
public class TestWidgets extends TestCase {

  protected void testWidgets() {
    MockControl control = EasyMock.niceControlFor(MovieListEditor.class);
    MovieListEditor mockEditor = (MovieListEditor) control.getMock();
    control.activate();
    MovieListWindow window = new MovieListWindow(mockEditor);
    window.init();
    window.show();

    JList movieList = window.getMovieList();
    assertNotNull("Movie list should be non null", movieList);
    assertTrue("Movie list should be showing", movieList.isShowing());

    JTextField movieField = window.getMovieField();
    assertNotNull("Movie field should be non null", movieField);
    assertTrue("Movie field should be showing", movieField.isShowing());

    JButton addButton = window.getAddButton();
    assertNotNull("Add button should be non null", addButton);
    assertEquals("Add button should be labeled \"Add\"",
                 "Add",
                 addButton.getText());
  }
}
```

Notice that this one method, testWidgets(), sets up a fixture and tests three
different things: the list, the field, and the button. Oops! Time to refactor,
making a fixture and separating those tests. The result is shown below. Notice
how much cleaner and more understandable it is.

```
public class TestWidgets extends TestCase {
  private MockControl control;
  private MovieListEditor mockEditor;
  private MovieListWindow window;

  protected void setUp() {
    control = EasyMock.niceControlFor(MovieListEditor.class);
    mockEditor = (MovieListEditor) control.getMock();
    control.activate();
    window = new MovieListWindow(mockEditor);
    window.init();
    window.show();
  }

  public void testList() {
    JList movieList = window.getMovieList();
    assertNotNull("Movie list should be non null", movieList);
    assertTrue("Movie list should be showing", movieList.isShowing());
  }
```

```
public void testField() {
  JTextField movieField = window.getMovieField();
  assertNotNull("Movie field should be non null", movieField);
  assertTrue("Movie field should be showing", movieField.isShowing());
}

public void testButton() {
  JButton addButton = window.getAddButton();
  assertNotNull("Add button should be non null", addButton);
  assertTrue("Add button should be showing", addButton.isShowing());
  assertEquals("Add button should be labeled \"Add\"",
               "Add",
               addButton.getText());
}
}
```

## Test boundary conditions early

This is similar to testing null handling, but includes items such as empty strings, 0, and MAX_INT. Don't forget about domain-specific boundary conditions. These are often more restrictive than the natural ones. This is also a bootstrap or *tester's block* technique. These tests tend to be easy to write so if you're casting about for what to write, try these if there are any untested.

## Keep your tests independent of each other

Try writing tests in such a way as to make them as independent as possible. Conditions that cause one test to fail shouldn't (ideally) cause other tests to fail as well.

## Use fine-grained Interfaces liberally

When you are extracting interfaces keep them small. Interfaces are meant to be focused, so keep them that way. An interface that declares too much is a smell. Interfaces with less than three declarations are great.

An advantage of small, focused interfaces is that they make it easier to create and maintain mock implementations.

## Avoid System.out and System.err in your tests

A few lines of output per test look fine when running a small number of tests, but when you're running a suite of 1,000-plus tests, it just becomes so much screen garbage. Worse than that it can actually slow down the tests. One approach that you can take if there are log messages being generated is to reassign the log's output stream in the setUp() and tearDown() methods.

If you can check something visually, try to do the same with an assertion instead. After all, these tests are supposed to be automated, with programmatic assertions to do the work.

## Avoid testing against databases and network resources

When you are testing code that talks to a database or communications system (serial, wireless, network, etc.) use interfaces to decouple the code from the actual resources. Then you can use mocks (see Chapter 7 for more on mocks).

This decoupling is a good idea in any event, regardless of whether you are using TDD.

## Add a main() to your test cases

In each of your test cases, or suites for that matter, put in a main() method that runs that test in the textui TestRunner. The following would suffice:

```
public class TestSomething extends TestCase {
  //...
  public static void main(String[] args) {
    junit.textui.TestRunner.run(TestSomething.class);
  }
}
```

Doing this lets you easily run any test from the command line or other tool.

## Start with the assert

When you are writing a test, start by writing what you are testing: the assert. Then work backward and fill in whatever is needed to set things up for the assert.

## Always write a toString() method

The text of various JUnit failure reports use the toString() method of the expected and/or actual objects involved in the assertion. If meaningful implementations of toString() are provided, these failure reports will be more informative, saving time and effort.

## SUMMARY

There are a variety of frameworks available for writing unit/programmer tests in a variety of languages. The most effective are those that allow you to develop tests in the same language and same environment as the code being tested. In this book we use the xUnit family of test frameworks—JUnit, in particular, since we are working in Java.

We looked at the architecture of JUnit, its assertion statement syntax, and the structure and style of good JUnit TestCases and test methods. We looked at how to run JUnit tests and interpret the results. We looked at the JUnit plugin for the Eclipse IDE, and their TDD-friendly tight integration with each other. We discussed automatically running tests with an automated build system. We then discussed the differences and best uses of TestCase and TestSuite. We then discussed the topic of organizing test code in relation to production code, and finally closed with a number of JUnit-related TDD tips.

Part IV provides a look at the xUnit implementation for some other languages.

The xUnit family of frameworks are useful in any development context, but in eXtreme Programming projects their use is nearly universal. In a sense, XP and xUnit grew up together. The articulator of XP, Kent Beck, was also the author of SUnit (the original member of the xUnit family) and an author of JUnit. In the spirit of the Agile development process movement, JUnit is barely sufficient for the task. It provides just enough overhead to accomplish the task, and no more.

Another reason for JUnit's success is the fact that it is open source. This has allowed its users to create extensions and tools that work with JUnit to provide more complete or wide-reaching solutions to the challenge of testing. We cover a number of those extensions in the next chapter.

# Chapter 5

# JUNIT EXTENSIONS

*extended more than can be thought to begin from such a cottage*

*- Winter's Tale, Act 4 Scene 2*
*William Shakespeare*

This chapter discusses some of the useful extensions that have been made to JUnit. Some come with JUnit while others are independent efforts. I have the good fortune to have become friends with the creators of several of the extensions we will be looking at in this chapter. They have agreed to write about the extensions they've created.

## STANDARD EXTENSIONS

This section looks at the set of extensions that come as part of JUnit, in the package junit.extensions.

### ActiveTestSuite

This is a simple extension that allows you to write/run tests that must interoperate in realtime. When the suite is run, it runs each test in its own thread and waits until all terminate before completing. This is a subclass of **TestSuite**, so to use this capability we simply need to instantiate **ActiveTestSuite** and add tests to it rather than to a **TestSuite**.

### ExceptionTestCase

There are two ways to test that an **Exception** is being thrown when it should be. One is to do it explicitly, failing immediately following the statement that should throw it:

```
public void testForThrow() {
  try {
    shouldThrow();
    fail("Expected SpecialException");
  }
  catch (SpecialException e) {
  }
}
```

There is another way, which I do not recommend: ExceptionTestCase. To do that, write the test ignoring the exception that should be thrown and create a TestCase using ExceptionTestCase:

```
public class ThrowingTest extends ExceptionTestCase {
  public void testForThrow() {
    shouldThrow();
  }
}
```

Then you create the tests, passing the Exception to be thrown as well as the name of the test to run:

```
new ThrowingTest("testForThrow", SpecialException.class);
```

To use this effectively you will need to maintain your own suite() method in any test cases that are subclasses of ExceptionTestCase, in order to supply the Exception that should be thrown. For the above example you would need the following:

```
public static Test suite() {
  TestSuite suite = new TestSuite();
  suite.addTest(new ThrowingTest("testForThrow", SpecialException.class));
  return suite;
}
```

This approach is more limited than doing the Exception check explicitly (as in the first code snippet). Firstly, having the exception explicit in the test communicates intent better. Secondly, you can no longer rerun a single test method.

## TestDecorator

This extension is used to wrap some additional behavior around a test run. To do this, you subclass TestDecorator and overload the run() method to do whatever is required around a call to basicRun(). The following two extensions are built using TestDecorator. Note that any Test can be decorated.

I think a simple example is in order. Let's assume that we would like a test to be a bit more instrumented when run on the command line. We can use TestDecorator to achieve this.

```java
public class InstrumentedTest extends TestDecorator {

  public InstrumentedTest(Test arg0) {
    super(arg0);
  }

  public void run(TestResult result) {
    System.out.println("Starting " + fTest.toString());
    basicRun(result);
  }
}
```

And here's an example of how we could use this:

```java
public class InstrumentedTestTester extends TestCase {

  public void testMethod() {
    //...
  }

  public static Test suite() {
    TestSuite suite = new TestSuite();
    Test test = new InstrumentedTestTester("testMethod");
    suite.addTest(new InstrumentedTest(test));
    return suite;
  }

  public static void main(String args[]) {
    junit.textui.TestRunner.run(suite());
  }
}
```

The output from running this code is:

```
Starting testMethod(InstrumentedTestTester)
.
Time: 0.036

OK (1 tests)
```

## RepeatedTest

This class lets us run a test a specified number of times. To use it, we simply create an instance, passing it the test to be repeated and the number of times to repeat it. RepeatedTest is a subclass of TestDecorator so we can wrap it around any instance of Test.

Here's an example of a use of RepeatedTest which will run testMethod() ten times:

```
public class RepeatedTestTester extends TestCase {

  public void testMethod() {
  }

  public static void main(String args[]) {
    Test test = new RepeatedTestTester("testMethod");
    junit.textui.TestRunner.run(new RepeatedTest(test, 10));
  }
}
```

And here's the output from the textual TestRunner:

```
. . . . . . . . . .
Time: 0.096

OK (10 tests)
```

## TestSetup

This class is a Decorator that allows us to set up and tear down a fixture that stays in place for the duration of running the decorated test. Recall that the overriding goal is to have tests totally independent and not sharing a fixture. There are resources that are expensive enough that we don't want them to be allocated and freed for each test. That would cause the tests to run too slowly. For these cases, we can use TestSetup to do one-time setup and teardown for an entire set of tests (that are in a TestSuite). Resources that this could be done for include such things as database or network connections. Another approach is the use of TestResource that is described later.

Use this decorator by subclassing it and overriding setUp() and tearDown(). Here's a trivial example. It uses a RepeatedTest to run a trivial test five times (to show the local fixture), and decorates that with an instance of a TestSetup subclass, SetupExample (to show the global fixture).

```
public class SetupExample extends TestSetup {

  public SetupExample(Test arg0) {
    super(arg0);
  }

  public void setUp() {
    System.out.println("Setting up global fixture...");
  }
```

```
      public void tearDown() {
        System.out.println("Tearing down global fixture...");
      }

    }

    public class TestForSetupExample extends TestCase {

      public void testMethod() {
        System.out.println("testMethod");
      }

      public void setUp() {
        System.out.println("\nlocal setUp");
      }

      public void tearDown() {
        System.out.println("local tearDown");
      }

      public static void main(String args[]) {
        Test test = new TestForSetupExample("testMethod");
        Test repeatedTest = new RepeatedTest(test, 5);
        junit.textui.TestRunner.run(new SetupExample(repeatedTest));
      }
    }
```

Here's the output that shows the global and local fixtures being set up and torn down:

```
Setting up global fixture...
.
local setUp
testMethod
local tearDown
.
local setUp
testMethod
local tearDown
.
local setUp
testMethod
local tearDown
.
local setUp
testMethod
local tearDown
.
local setUp
testMethod
```

```
local tearDown
Tearing down global fixture...

Time: 0.037

OK (5 tests)
```

## ADDING MISSING ASSERTS WITH MockObjects

MockObjects is a framework to make it easier to create mocks of classes. We'll explore this important subject later in Chapter 7. Here we are restricting ourselves to looking at two classes in the MockObjects framework—AssertMo and TestCaseMo—that are useful for writing programmer tests in general.

AssertMo extends Assert from the JUnit framework and adds several assertion methods that are lacking in the standard JUnit distribution:[1]

### assertEquals for Object[]

assertEquals(String message, Object[] expected, Object[] actual)

This is another version of assertEquals that asserts that the length of two arrays is the same, and that each pair of objects at a given index are equal.

### assertExcludes

assertExcludes(String message, String substring, String target)

This asserts that substring does not appear in target.

### assertIncludes

assertExcludes(String message, String substring, String target)

As assertExcludes(), but asserts that substring does appear in target.

### assertStartsWith

assertStartsWith(String message, String prefix, String target)

This asserts that prefix appears at the beginning of target.

## PERFORMANCE AND SCALABILITY WITH JUnitPerf
with Mike Clark

*This section was contributed by Mike Clark of Clarkware Consulting [URL 56], the developer and maintainer of JUnitPerf [URL 15].*

---

[1]In keeping with the philosophy of the folks who wrote MockObjects, these assert methods are available only in a version with the initial message parameter.

## Introduction

Good mountain bikers first learn to meticulously pick their way through every obstacle on every trail. Great mountain bikers must then learn to disregard smaller obstacles, crudely plowing over them to conserve energy for the toughest terrain. Similarly, good programmers optimize every line of code using a variety of techniques, but great programmers learn to write simple code first. They save optimizations for hot spots and performance-critical sections of code. The trick is identifying the most important code sections and continually measuring them over time as the software undergoes change.

JUnitPerf is an open source JUnit extension that uses the decorator pattern to adorn standard JUnit tests as performance or scalability tests. A **TimedTest** measures the elapsed time of an existing test. A **LoadTest** runs an existing test with a simulated number of concurrent users and iterations. Using JUnitPerf tests we can transparently leverage our existing tests to ensure that the functionality being tested continues to meet performance and scalability requirements over time.

Let's put JUnitPerf to the test with an example.

## Tackling New Customer Stories

Our team is building a Web-based application for the medical industry. Today's particular story involves querying the database for all prescriptions written by a given doctor, then displaying the prescription information to the user.

We started by writing clean and simple code that expressed intent, driven by tests that validate that the code is doing the right things. We've been wisely deferring any premature code optimizations because we don't want to speculate and overspend on performance until we identify a problem. But now that we've demonstrated working code, our customer decides there's value in improving the performance and scalability of this story.

We don't want to compromise the reliability of prescription queries by complicating the code for performance and scalability. JUnitPerf tests will fail if the tests they decorate fail, so we have confidence that tweaking performance won't adversely affect existing functionality.

## Tuning with Confidence

Our Web page is taking approximately 5.0 seconds to display 100 rows of prescription information. That's less than ideal for our users. So our customer writes a story stating that the response time of a Web page containing up to 100 prescriptions should not exceed 3.0 seconds. We've got our work cut out for us!

Many things happen behind that curtain of a Web page. We need to know which sections of the code contribute the most to the page's overall response time. We will then focus on tuning those performance-critical areas first. We fire up our favorite profiling tool, hit the Web page, and let the profiler hunt down the busiest code. Alas, it identifies the **Pharmacy.findPrescriptionsByPrescriber()** method, contributing approximately 3.5 seconds to the total response time.

Thankfully, we already have the following JUnit test for that method:

```
public void testFindPrescriptions() throws Exception {
    PrescriptionDatabase database = new PrescriptionDatabase();
    Pharmacy pharmacy = new Pharmacy(database);
    Collection prescriptions = pharmacy.findPrescriptionsByPrescriber("Dr. Jekyl");

    assertEquals(100, prescriptions.size());



    Iterator prescriptionIter = prescriptions.iterator();
    while (prescriptionIter.hasNext()) {
        Prescription p = (Prescription) prescriptionIter.next();
        assertEquals("Dr. Jekyl", p.getPrescriber());
    }
}
```

The test validates that indeed every prescription written by Dr. Jekyl is returned. The Pharmacy class employs a PrescriptionDatabase to perform the prescription query, without worrying about what kind of persistence strategy is being used under the hood. In this case a one-time test fixture was used to prepopulate the PrescriptionDatabase with exactly 100 prescriptions signed by the villainous Dr. Jekyl.

We're glad we wrote well-factored code from the start because in doing so we enabled the profiler to point us towards a single cohesive method that we can tune for maximum benefit. If we could only boost the performance of the Pharmacy.findPrescriptionsByPrescriber() method, our Web users would be much happier. But how do we know when to stop tuning? Write an automated test for the performance story, of course. When it passes, we're done!

## Using TimedTest for Performance Testing

With the performance story in hand, we write a PharmacyTimedTest that creates a TimedTest instance passing in the existing PharmacyTest.testFindPrescriptions() test case method and a maximum elapsed time of 1.5 seconds. By default, the TimedTest will wait for the completion of its decorated test and then fail if the maximum elapsed time was exceeded. The Web page contributes another 1.5 seconds in presentation overhead, so when this test passes we'll be on target for a 3.0 second total response time.

As a convenient way to run the PharmacyTimedTest, we define a suite() method called by a TestRunner in the main() method, as follows:

```
public class PharmacyTimedTest extends TestCase {

  public static Test suite() {
    long maxElapsedTimeInMillis = 1500;
    Test test = new PharmacyTest("testFindPrescriptions");
    Test timedTest = new TimedTest(test, maxElapsedTimeInMillis);
    return timedTest;
  }

  public static void main(String args[]) {
    junit.textui.TestRunner.run(suite());
  }
}
```

We run the PharmacyTimedTest and it fails with the following output:

```
.
TimedTest (WAITING): testFindPrescriptions(PharmacyTest): 3516 ms
F
Time: 3.516
There was 1 failure:
1) testFindPrescriptions(PharmacyTest)
junit.framework.AssertionFailedError:
Maximum elapsed time exceeded! Expected 1500ms, but was 3516ms.

FAILURES!!!
Tests run: 1, Failures: 1, Errors: 0
```

The expected elapsed time was exceeded—we expected 1.5 seconds but it actually took 3.5 seconds. We're not surprised, and now we have a goal to work towards, as well as a test that tells us if we're getting warmer or colder.

We then go after some low-hanging fruit: we tune the underlying SQL a bit and optimize some of the object-relational mapping logic necessary to create Prescription objects from database rows. Then we run the PharmacyTimedTest again and it passes with the following output:

```
.
TimedTest (WAITING):
testFindPrescriptions(PharmacyTest): 1452 ms

Time: 1.452

OK (1 tests)
```

Much better! We're making progress. Had the test failed we would have continued to optimize until it passed, but no further. Now that we have quantitative performance criteria in the form of an automated test, the test will continue to keep its performance in check as we refactor the code.

The elapsed time measured by a TimedTest decorating a single testXXX() test case
method includes the total time of the setUp(), testXXX(), and tearDown() methods.
For example, if the 100 test prescriptions were added to the database in the setUp()
method, then the TimedTest would include this setup overhead. Therefore, the maximum elapsed time should be adjusted accordingly to take into account the setup and
tear-down costs of the decorated test. One technique for establishing a baseline for this
overhead is to time an empty testXXX() method.

## Scaling Up

We've successfully demonstrated single-user response time with a repeatable test.
We haven't thought much about multiuser performance because up until now the
scalability requirements were unknown. Instead, we've been relying on simple,
modular code capable of responding when the customer writes a scalability story.
Now that it's a bit later in the project our customer has a better estimate of the
expected load on the production system.

   It is expected that multiple pharmacies will be hitting the same Web page
concurrently. So the customer writes a scalability story that states that the
response time of a Web page containing up to 100 prescriptions should not exceed
10.0 seconds under a load of 10 concurrent users.

## Using LoadTest for Scalability Testing

As with the performance story, we want to write an automated test that specifies
the expected response time of the existing code under load, then tune until it
passes. We write a PharmacyLoadTest that creates a LoadTest instance passing in
a TimedTest and a number of concurrent users (threads). The TimedTest in turn
decorates the existing PharmacyTest.testFindPrescriptions() test case method.

Similar to the TimedTest, the LoadTest decorates at the granularity of the setUp(),
testXXX(), and tearDown() method sequence. By default, the LoadTest uses the
same instance of the decorated test for all concurrent users. Therefore, each user will
run setUp(), testXXX(), and tearDown() concurrently with the same test instance. If
transient test data is being created in the setUp() method of the decorated test, use
the TestFactory class to ensure that each concurrent user operates on its own instance
of the decorated test. If persistent test data is being created in the setUp() method, as
in the case of the PrescriptionDatabase, consider using the junit.extensions.TestSetup
class to create a one-time test fixture.

The LoadTest will run the TimedTest with 10 concurrent users (threads), and each user will run the PharmacyTest.testFindPrescriptions() test case method once. We calculate 7.0 seconds to be a sufficient response time under load based on the Web page incurring 1.5 seconds of additional overhead. We write the following test that will fail if any user's response time exceeds 7.0 seconds:

```
public class PharmacyLoadTest extends TestCase {

  public static Test suite() {
    int users = 10;
    int iterations = 1;
    long maxElapsedTimeInMillis = 7000;
    Test test = new PharmacyTest("testFindPrescriptions");
    Test timedTest = new TimedTest(test, maxElapsedTimeInMillis);
    Test loadTest = new LoadTest(timedTest, users, iterations);
    return loadTest;
  }

  public static void main(String args[]) {
    junit.textui.TestRunner.run(suite());
  }
}
```

We chose this order of test decoration because the scalability story explicitly related to each user's individual response time under load. If instead the story were expressed in terms of throughput, we could switch the order of test decoration such that the TimedTest decorated the LoadTest which in turn decorated the PharmacyTest. This would fail if the cumulative response time of all concurrent users exceeded a threshold.

We run the PharmacyLoadTest and it fails with the following output:

```
. . . . . . . . . .
TimedTest (WAITING): testFindPrescriptions(PharmacyTest): 1522 ms
TimedTest (WAITING): testFindPrescriptions(PharmacyTest): 2353 ms
TimedTest (WAITING): testFindPrescriptions(PharmacyTest): 3175 ms
TimedTest (WAITING): testFindPrescriptions(PharmacyTest): 4016 ms
TimedTest (WAITING): testFindPrescriptions(PharmacyTest): 4837 ms
TimedTest (WAITING): testFindPrescriptions(PharmacyTest): 5678 ms
TimedTest (WAITING): testFindPrescriptions(PharmacyTest): 6519 ms
TimedTest (WAITING): testFindPrescriptions(PharmacyTest): 7371 ms
F
TimedTest (WAITING): testFindPrescriptions(PharmacyTest): 8212 ms
F
TimedTest (WAITING): testFindPrescriptions(PharmacyTest): 9063 ms
F

Time: 9.303
```

```
There were 3 failures:
1) testFindPrescriptions(PharmacyTest)
junit.framework.AssertionFailedError:
Maximum elapsed time exceeded! Expected 7000ms, but was 7371ms.
2) testFindPrescriptions(PharmacyTest)
junit.framework.AssertionFailedError:
Maximum elapsed time exceeded! Expected 7000ms, but was 8212ms.
3) testFindPrescriptions(PharmacyTest)
junit.framework.AssertionFailedError:
Maximum elapsed time exceeded! Expected 7000ms, but was 9063ms.

FAILURES!!!
Tests run: 10, Failures: 3, Errors: 0
```

Again, we're not surprised because we didn't concern ourselves with scalability when we wrote the original code. We notice that the response times increased for each successive user until the last three users failed the test. It appears to be a classic case of resource contention creating a bottleneck in our system. We quickly conclude that concurrent users must be contending for a single database connection. Ideally, we want to maximize our time by making a change with low cost and a high reward, so we decide to make a minor change to the PrescriptionDatabase class to use a database connection pool with 10 active connections. This should help the query scale.

We run the PharmacyLoadTest again and it passes with the following output:

```
..........
TimedTest (WAITING): testFindPrescriptions(PharmacyTest): 6830 ms
TimedTest (WAITING): testFindPrescriptions(PharmacyTest): 6790 ms
TimedTest (WAITING): testFindPrescriptions(PharmacyTest): 6780 ms
TimedTest (WAITING): testFindPrescriptions(PharmacyTest): 6850 ms
TimedTest (WAITING): testFindPrescriptions(PharmacyTest): 6910 ms
TimedTest (WAITING): testFindPrescriptions(PharmacyTest): 6850 ms
TimedTest (WAITING): testFindPrescriptions(PharmacyTest): 6840 ms
TimedTest (WAITING): testFindPrescriptions(PharmacyTest): 6870 ms
TimedTest (WAITING): testFindPrescriptions(PharmacyTest): 6910 ms
TimedTest (WAITING): testFindPrescriptions(PharmacyTest): 6950 ms

Time: 7

OK (10 tests)
```

Excellent! The scalability tests are passing and the decorated test continues to pass as well. We notice that the response times are nearly consistent for each user thereby confirming our theory about resource contention. If scalability starts to degrade in the future, the test will let us know by failing.

## Other Applications of JUnitPerf

Because JUnitPerf is based on decorating any class that implements JUnit's Test interface, we can use JUnitPerf tests to measure the performance and scalability of other areas, including:

- Web pages, by decorating HttpUnit tests

- servlets and Enterprise JavaBeans (EJB), by decorating Cactus tests

- algorithms and data structures

- changes to the database

- impacts of switching third-party software

As we write more performance and scalability tests, they may take a while to run, and we don't want these types of tests slowing down our development pace. We'll organize them in a special test suite to be run at least once a day. We won't run this test suite during our test-driven development cycle, unless of course we're fiddling with performance-critical code.

## Conclusion

It's all too easy to optimize early only to find out that the optimized code isn't executed frequently. Equally troubling and expensive are intended optimizations that instead degrade performance and scalability. It's always best to write simple code, identify performance-critical sections of code when the reward is high, and then create benchmarks in the form of repeatable JUnitPerf tests. The tests help reduce the stress of tuning and retain their value over time by failing whenever the response time and throughput of the software move in the wrong direction. They can be run automatically to continually measure performance in the face of change. Moreover, the tests tell us when to stop tuning and deliver the software.

# DAEDALOS JUNIT EXTENSIONS
with Jens Uwe Pipka

*This section was contributed by Jens Uwe Pipka of Daedalos Consulting GmbH [URL 57], the author and maintainer of The Daedalos JUnit Extensions[URL 17].*
  The Daedalos JUnit Extensions, or in short *djux*, provide additional tools to speed up programmer testing. The core components are *test resources*. Using test resources, it is possible to make static resources available for all tests during the whole development cycle. So, time-consuming initializations are done only once and remain active over a complete series of test runs. Furthermore, djux includes additional tools for database tests as well as for the integration of external test programs. You can download the latest version from the djux homepage.
  We will present an example of how you can implement and use your own test resources and show how tests are sped up. We will implement a test that checks entries inside a database. To do this, the test operates as follows:

- a database connection must be opened

- the test checks if certain data exists in the database (this unit test is implemented using the database checker that also comes with djux)

- the database connection has to be closed.

## A Programmer Test Implementation Using Test Resources

We start with a standard JUnit test. Our test case is named MyDatabaseTest and contains a class variable for the database name. We also need instance variables for the database connection as well as for our database checker. Furthermore, the constructor registers the appropriate driver to access our database. Here's the code:

```
public class MyDatabaseTest extends TestCase {
    private static final String DATABASE_NAME = "jdbc:odbc:MyDatabase";
    private DatabaseChecker dbChecker = null;
    private Connection connection = null;

    public MyDatabaseTest(String name) throws SQLException {
        super(name);
        DriverManager.registerDriver(new sun.jdbc.odbc.JdbcOdbcDriver()) ;
    }
}
```

Next, we implement the setUp() method to open the database connection and initialize the database checker. This is done by asking the DriverManager for the connection and passing it to the database checker's constructor.

```
public void setUp() throws SQLException {
    connection = DriverManager.getConnection(DATABASE_NAME);
    dbChecker = new DatabaseChecker(connection);
}
```

We also need to implement tearDown() to close the database connection properly:

```
public void tearDown() throws SQLException {
    if (connection != null)  {
        connection.close();
        connection = null;
        dbChecker = null;
    }
}
```

After implementing the necessary actions to open and close the database connection, we can start with the actual test. First, the existence of the table

BOOKS is checked. Using the djux database checker, this can be done fairly easily:

```
public void testTableBooksExists() throws SQLException {
  assertTrue(dbChecker.tableExists("BOOKS"));
}
```

Now we can run our first test. Assuming that the database is set up properly and the table BOOKS really exists, the test is successful. Now we can go on with defining additional tests; for example, one that checks that the table does not contain any records:

```
public void testTableBooksReallyEmpty() throws SQLException {
  assertEquals("There should be no records", 0, dbChecker.rowCount("BOOKS"));
}
```

Running the unit test again, it takes some time before the results are displayed. This is because for each test a new connection is opened and closed. This gets even worse if you are working with a remote database. This overhead can be reduced by implementing an appropriate TestSetup instead of using the setUp() and tearDown() inside the test case, but the connection is still opened and closed for each test run. Furthermore, it gets even more complex if several test cases refer to the same database connection. It then becomes necessary to implement specific TestSuites considering the different test runs.

Here is where the idea of test resources comes into play: using them, it is possible to open the database connection once and access it during the whole testing cycle. It is no longer necessary to reopen the database connection before a test run is executed.

But what does this mean for our implementation? Let's have a look at our test case. We only have to change the setUp() and tearDown() methods. Instead of handling the database connection there, we implement the functionality inside a test resource.

Generally, a test resource can be implemented like this:

1. Define the new resource as a subclass of com.daedalos.junit.TestResource

2. Override start() to initialize your resource

3. Override stop() to release your resource

4. Register your new test resource with TestResourceFactory

5. Afterwards, you can access your test resource directly within your test cases.

Now we are going to define the connection to our database as a TestResource. We start refactoring our existing testcase and implement a new class, DbConnectionTR, that inherits from com.daedalos.junit.TestResource. This new class holds the database connection. Therefore, the constructor is used to register the appropriate driver. Furthermore, we add an instance variable, connection, that holds the database connection. Finally, we define a constant for the database name.

```
public class DbConnectionTR extends TestResource {
  private static final String DATABASE_NAME = "jdbc:odbc:MyDatabase";
  private Connection connection = null;

  public DbConnectionTR() throws SQLException {
    super();
    DriverManager.registerDriver(new sun.jdbc.odbc.JdbcOdbcDriver()) ;
  }
}
```

Now we have to implement the inherited abstract methods start() and stop(). These methods are called when the test resource is started at the beginning and stopped at the end of the test cycle, respectively. We want to open the database connection when the TestResource is started and close it at the end of the development cycle. So, we move this functionality from the test case to the corresponding methods in the test resource.

The method start() tries to open the database connection. If it is successful, the return value is true, otherwise false is returned. The return value is essential to enable the TestResourceFactory to manage the state of the existing test resources.

```
public boolean start() {
  try {
    connection = DriverManager.getConnection(DATABASE_NAME);
  } catch (SQLException exc) {
    return false;
  }
  return true;
}
```

The method stop() closes the database connection. Again, the return value is true if the operation was successful and false otherwise:

```
public boolean stop() {
  try {
    if (connection != null) {
      connection.close();
      connection = null;
    }
  } catch (SQLException e) {
    return false;
  }
  return true;
}
```

Now we provide a getter method to access the database connection:

```
public Connection getConnection() {
  return connection;
}
```

It is also possible to provide a short description of the test resource. This is an optional but useful way to manage different test resources. To do this, we override the method getDescription() by returning the description:

```
public String getDescription() {
  return "A basic test resource example for holding a database connection";
}
```

As you can see, the implementation is exactly as in our test case before. All we have done is move the functionality to another class.

Finally, we have to adapt our test case itself. The test case has to inherit from the class com.daedalos.junit.TestResourceTestCase that is again a subclass from TestCase. In addition to moving the implementation for opening and closing the database to the test resource class, we must change the database access inside our test case. Instead of the database connection being accessed directly as in the original implementation, it is now accessed via the DbConnectionTR class.

This is done by using the TestResourceFactory that is the unique interface to handle test resources inside your tests. It uses the singleton pattern. To use a specific TestResource inside a test case, the method prepareTestResource() is expected. The argument is the name of the test resource, for example, Db-ConnectionTRString in our example. After registering the test resource, you can access it using the method getTestResource(), which also expects the test resource name as argument.

After these modifications, our test case looks like this:

```
public class MyDatabaseTest extends TestResourceTestCase {
  private DatabaseChecker dbChecker = null;

  public void setUp() {
    prepareTestResource("DbConnectionTR");
    TestResourceFactory  trFactory = TestResourceFactory.current();
    DbConnectionTR dbTestResource =
        (DbConnectionTR) trFactory.getTestResource("DbConnectionTR");
    dbChecker = new DatabaseChecker(dbTestResource);
  }

  public void testTableBooksExists() throws SQLException {
    assertTrue(dbChecker.tableExists("BOOKS"));
  }
```

```
public void testTableBooksReallyEmpty () throws SQLException {
  assertEquals("There should be no entries",
                 0,
                 dbChecker.rowCount("BOOKS"));
}
}
```

Now, the test methods themselves are not modified. The most important changes are made inside the setUp() method. Specifically, the database connection is not opened anymore. Instead, the DbConnectionTR is added to the active test resources. Afterwards, the connection is obtained from TestResourceFactory directly. It is necessary to cast the TestResource to its definition class if you want to access user defined methods. The other modifications are rather easy: The constructor now does nothing else but delegate the work to its parent constructor. And, finally, teardown is no longer necessary.

That's it! Now, you can run your TestCase inside your TestRunner, for example, junit.swingui.TestRunner. Running the test the first time, nothing seems to be changed: it still takes a fair amount of time for the test to go green. But try it again: Instantly, the test is green again. This is because, of course, the database connection must be opened by your first test run. But thereafter the connection stays open, until you finally close the whole test runner.

## Managing Your Test Resources

In the preceding example, the new test resource is accessed via its fully qualified class name, including the entire package name. Happily, it is possible to map your test resources to logical names instead, which keeps your test cases cleaner. For example, my.example.DBConnectionTestResource can be mapped to dbAccess.

For this purpose, the TestResourceFactory provides the method registerTestResource(). The first argument specifies the logical name you want to use for the test resource; the second the class it refers to. The registering of the TestResource inside the TestResourceFactory is only necessary one time. If it is not done directly using the TestResourceFactory, it can also be done by calling the mapper class RegisterTestResource. For the earlier example, you can register your test resource by executing the following command:

```
$ java -cp junitextensions.jar:junit.jar:$CLASSPATH \
> com.daedalos.junit.util.RegisterTestResource dbAccess DbConnectionTR
```

As a result of this command, a new test resource mapping is added to the file testresources.properties in your user directory. Now you can access the test resource inside your test case with its logical name:

```
public class MyDatabaseTest extends TestResourceTestCase {
  ...
  public void setUp() {
    prepareTestResource("dbAccess");
    TestResourceFactory  trFactory = TestResourceFactory.current();
    DbConnectionTR dbTes tResource =
        (DbConnectionTR) trFactory.getTestResource("dbAccess");
    dbChecker = new DatabaseChecker(dbTestResource);
  }
  ...
}
```

Furthermore, it is possible to reset your test resources. Simply call TestResourceFactory.reset() from within a test case.

## Using the TRTestRunner

Until now, a test case that uses a test resource is defined as a subclass from TestResourceTestCase. This class ensures that a specific test resource is accessible inside the test case, and that it is started automatically when, for example, it is accessed for the first time. Nevertheless, it is often better to manage the test resources manually in a more comprehensive test environment. For this purpose, djux provides a specialized test runner based on the original swing test runner. This test runner also includes a test resource browser that shows the current state of test resources and enables the user to manage test resources.

You can start the TRTestRunner by executing the following command:

```
$ java -cp junitextensions.jar:junit.jar:$CLASSPATH \
> com.daedalos.junit.gui.TRTestRunner
```

Then you can open the Test Resource Browser using the TestResourceBrowser entry in the JUnit menu. A new window pops up that shows the state of the currently registered TestResources (see Figure 5.1). You can start, stop, and reset test resources with this GUI. Furthermore, it is possible to register new test resources with their logical and class names, as well as remove them. This is much handier than the manual operation described earlier. You also have the option to "auto"-start your test resources, so that all registered test resources are started when you start the TRTestRunner.

Another advantage of the TRTestRunner is that test cases using test resources no longer have to be subclasses of TestResourceTestCase but can extend TestCase directly. It is also not necessary to add your test resource explicitly, because the handling is now done by the TRTestRunner and the TestResourceBrowser. You only have to access your test resources as known via the TestResourceFactory. Moreover, all other test cases will run as known without any limitation or change.

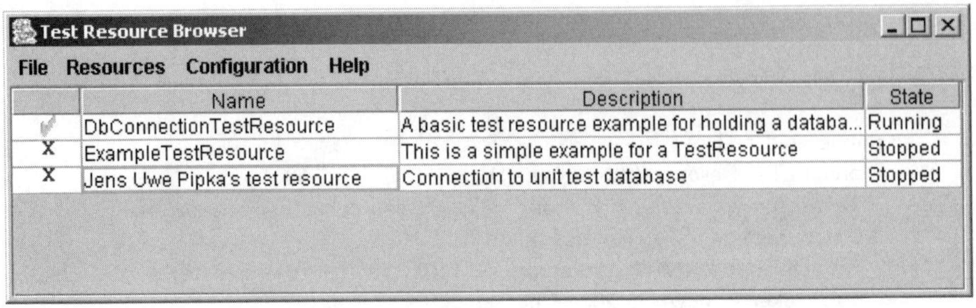

**Figure 5.1** The Test Resource Browser window.

Using the TRTestRunner, our test case will look as follows:

```java
public class MyDatabaseTest extends TestCase {
  private DatabaseChecker dbChecker = null;

  public void setUp() {
    TestResourceFactory  trFactory = TestResourceFactory.current();
    DbConnectionTR dbTestResource =
        (DbConnectionTR) trFactory.getTestResource("dbAccess");
    dbChecker = new DatabaseChecker(dbTestResource);
  }

  public void testTableBooksExists() throws SQLException {
    assertTrue(dbChecker.tableExists("BOOKS"));
  }

  public void testTableBooksExists() throws SQLException {
    assertEquals("There should be no entries",
                 0,
                 dbChecker.rowCount("BOOKS"));
  }
}
```

As you can see, this looks even more like a traditional JUnit test. After starting the dbAccess test resource via the Test Resource Browser, our test runs again showing the green bar. If the test resource is stopped, the unit test will fail with an Exception: "TestResource not available".

The decision about which approach to use to manage your test resources is dependent on your environment: If you work in a graphical environment, it is much more convenient to use the TRTestRunner that is fully compatible with the Swing TestRunner and offers additional tools to manage your test resources. But if your tests should also work with the AWT or the command-line-based test runner, you should implement your tests that access test resources as subclasses of TestResourceTestCase. In either case, the test resource implementation is identical, so you can use them in both environments.

## Additional JUnit Test Tools

### ExtensibleTestCase

Even though JUnit is a comprehensive testing tool, it is often necessary to also include external testing tools. To simplify the integration of external testing tools, djux provides an easy-to-use mechanism to plug in external testing tools as additional test cases: the ExtensibleTestCase.

This is based on the class com.Daedalos.junit.ExtensibleTestCase that is again a subclass of junit.framework.TestCase. First, the expected result can be passed as an argument to the method setExpectedResult(). All you have to do then is to implement the abstract method runTestSilently() which should implement the functionality to call the external tool and set the result value accordingly. Finally, the method postProcessTest() compares the expected result with the actual one. As an example of using ExtensibleTestCase, we have included code that shows how to integrate the execution of native programs with djux.

Despite setting the expected return value, ExtensibleTestCases are handled like any other standard test cases and need no additional setup. Therefore, ExtensibleTestCases can be executed using the standard JUnit TestRunner.

### DatabaseChecker

In the previous example, we used the DatabaseChecker. This is a djux test utility that allows executing simple database checks. In particular, the database checker provides checks concerning the database structure as well as its content. It provides a simple and easy way to verify if the application behavior has the expected effect on the persistent database content. If a middleware persistency framework is used, this cross check becomes particularly important.

To introduce the database checker in more detail, we continue with our previous example. Here we develop an application that provides a book list that allows adding and removing books. The requirements are that the book list be stored immediately in a database table BOOKS each time it is changed. The table contains the columns TITLE, AUTHOR, and ISBN.

In the example above, we have already checked that the table BOOKS exists. We continue defining the test case for the new user story. Therefore, a new test case BookListTest is created as a subclass of TestCase. It contains an instance dbChecker of class DatabaseChecker that is initialized in the setUp() method of our test by instantiating the class com.daedalos.dbcheck.DatabaseChecker. Note that the constructor expects a valid database connection that is used for all database access. Again, we use the database test resource that we developed in the previous example. We also use an instance variable booklist that manages the new class representing the book list.

```
public class BookListTestCase extends TestCase {
    private DatabaseChecker dbChecker = null;
    private BookList booklist;
```

```
public BookListTestCase(String name) {
  super(name);
}

public void setUp() {
  TestResourceFactory  trFactory = TestResourceFactory.current();
  DbConnectionTestResource dbTestResource =
      (DbConnectionTestResource) trFactory.getTestResource("dbAccess");
  dbChecker = new DatabaseChecker(dbTestResource.getConnection());
  booklist = new BookList();
  }
}
```

Now we are going to define the interface of the BookList class by defining
the test cases for our user story. Because all changes have a direct effect on the
database, DatabaseChecker is a valuable tool to verify the functionality of the
BookList class.

First, we have to initialize the book list. After this, it should contain no
entries. To check this, we use the database checker method rowCount(tableName)
that returns the number of rows for a specific table. In our example, we have to
check the table BOOKS:

```
public void testTableBooksExists() throws SQLException {
  booklist.initialize();
  assertEquals(0, dbChecker.rowCount("BOOKS"));
}
```

Next, a new book is added. If the book already exists, it should not be added to the
book list. To check if a book is added correctly, we use the method rowExists(tableName,
whereClause). It returns whether or not a row exists in the specified table for the given
where clause. The method returns true if there is exactly one row that fulfills the where
clause. If there exists more than one row or the entry is not found, the return value is
false.

```
public void testHandleABook() throws SQLException {
  booklist.initialize();
  this.assertEquals(0, dbChecker.rowCount("BOOKS"));

  Book newBook = new Book("Dinner for two", "Mike Gayle", "0340823429");
  booklist.add(newBook);

  String query = "title=\"Dinner for two\" " +
                 "and author=\"Mike Gayle\" " +
                 "and isbn=\"0340823429\"";
  this.assertTrue("Dinner for two should be there",
                  dbChecker.rowExists("BOOKS", query));

  booklist.add(newBook);
  assertTrue("Dinner for two should still be there",
             dbChecker.rowExists("BOOKS", query));
```

```
        assertEquals("Finally, only one entry expected",
                1,
                dbChecker.rowCount("BOOKS", "isbn=\"0340823429\""));
  }
```

Here, we add the same book two times. It is the task of the **BookList** class to meet the condition that there is only one entry for each book. If this doesn't work, the database checker method rowExists(tableName, whereClause) would cause the test to fail, because more than one entry is found in the database. To check the simple existence of a specific entry, where more than one entry is allowed, the database checker provides the method multipleRowsExists(tableName, whereClause) that returns true if any row matches.

With database checker method rowCount(tableName, whereClause) it is also possible to check how many entries for the specific entry exists. In the last test case in the example above, we use this method to verify that there is exactly one entry for the specific ISBN of the new entry.

Now we want to implement a test for removing a book. We add some books and then remove the second book. Again, we verify each step with the help of the database checker and the methods we used before:

```
public void testManageBooks() throws SQLException {
  Book book1 = new Book("Dinner for two", "Mike Gayle", "0340823429");
  Book book2 = new Book("High Fidelity", "Nick Hornby", "3426604361");
  Book book3 = new Book("Herr Lehmann", "Sven Regener", "3821807059");


  booklist.initialize();
  assertEquals("No entries expected", 0, dbChecker.rowCount("BOOKS"));


  booklist.add(book1);
  assertEquals("One entry expected", 1, dbChecker.rowCount("BOOKS"));
  booklist.add(book2);
  assertEquals("Two entries expected", 2, dbChecker.rowCount("BOOKS"));
  booklist.add(book3);
  assertEquals("Three entries expected", 3, dbChecker.rowCount("BOOKS"));


  booklist.remove(book2);
  assertEquals("Again, two entries expected", 2, dbChecker.rowCount("BOOKS"));


  assertEquals("Check the title for the first book",
               "Dinner for two",
               dbChecker.getStringColumn("BOOKS",
                                         "TITLE",
                                         "ISBN=\"0340823429\""));
  assertEquals("Check the author for the first book",
               "Mike Gayle",
               dbChecker.getStringColumn("BOOKS",
                                         "AUTHOR",
                                         "ISBN=\"0340823429\""));
```

```
assertEquals("Check the title for the third book",
             "Herr Lehmann",
             dbChecker.getStringColumn("BOOKS",
                                       "TITLE",
                                       "ISBN=\"3821807059\""));
assertEquals("Check the author for the secong book",
             "Sven Regener",
             dbChecker.getStringColumn("BOOKS",
                                       "AUTHOR",
                                       "ISBN=\"3821807059\""));

}
```

Here we check whether the number of books in the book list is growing constantly with the addition of each new book. Similarly, we verify that it is decreased when a book is removed. But the test is not complete until it checks whether the correct book is removed. We accomplish this by verifying that the book list still contains the entries for the other two books. We use the method getStringColumn(tableName, columnName, whereClause) that returns the value of the specified column of the first row that matches the given where clause in the specified table. Thus, we verify that for each ISBN the expected author and title are still available inside the book list.

With this test case it is now possible to implement the appropriate domain class BookList that contains the mapping between the Java code and the database content. This small example shows how the database checker can be used to verify if this mapping works as expected and the database content is consistent with the application behavior.

# WRITING XML-BASED TESTS WITH XMLUnit
with Tim Bacon

*This section was contributed by Tim Bacon of ThoughtWorks UK [URL 58], the author and maintainer of xmlUnit[URL 18].*

## What is XMLUnit?

XMLUnit enables JUnit-style assertions to be made about the content and structure of XML. It is an open source project hosted at sourceforge.net that grew out of a need to test a system that generated and received custom XML messages. The problem that we faced was how to verify that the system generated the correct message from a known set of inputs. Obviously, we could use a DTD or a schema to validate the message output, but this approach wouldn't allow us to distinguish between valid XML with correct content (e.g., element <foo>bar</foo>) and valid XML with incorrect content (e.g., element <foo>baz</foo>). What we really wanted was an assertXMLEquals() method so we could compare the message that we expected the system to generate and the message that the system actually generated. And that was the beginning of XMLUnit.

## Quick tour

XMLUnit provides a single JUnit extension class, XMLTestCase, and a set of supporting classes that allow assertions to be made about:

- the differences between two pieces of XML

- the validity of a piece of XML

- the outcome of transforming a piece of XML using XSLT

- the evaluation of an XPath expression on a piece of XML

- individual nodes in a piece of XML that are exposed by DOM Traversal

XMLUnit can also treat HTML content (even badly-formed HTML) as valid XML to allow these assertions to be made about Web pages.

## Glossary

As with many projects, some words in XMLUnit have particular meanings, so a quick review would probably be helpful. A piece of XML is either a DOM Document, a **String** containing marked-up content, or a **Reader** that allows access to marked-up content in some underlying source. XMLUnit compares the expected control XML to some actual test XML. The comparison can reveal that two pieces of XML are identical, similar, or different. The unit of measurement used by the comparison is a difference, and differences can be either recoverable or unrecoverable. Two pieces of XML are identical if there are no differences between them, similar if there are only recoverable differences between them, and different if there are any unrecoverable differences between them.

## Configuring XMLUnit

There are many Java XML parsers available, and XMLUnit should work with any JAXP-compliant parser library, such as Xerces from the Apache Jakarta project. To use the XSL and XPath features of XMLUnit a Trax-compliant transformation engine is required, such as Xalan, from the Apache Jakarta project. To configure XMLUnit to use your parser and transformation engine set three System properties before any tests are run:

```
System.setProperty("javax.xml.parsers.DocumentBuilderFactory",
                   "org.apache.xerces.jaxp.DocumentBuilderFactoryImpl");


System.setProperty("javax.xml.parsers.SAXParserFactory",
                   "org.apache.xerces.jaxp.SAXParserFactoryImpl");


System.setProperty("javax.xml.transform.TransformerFactory",
                   "org.apache.xalan.processor.TransformerFactoryImpl");
```

Alternatively, there are static methods on the **XMLUnit** class that can be called directly. The advantage of this approach is that you can specify a different parser class for control and test XML and change the current parser class at any time in your tests, should you need to make assertions about the compatibility of different parsers.

```
XMLUnit.setControlParser("org.apache.xerces.jaxp." +
                   "DocumentBuilderFactoryImpl");
XMLUnit.setTestParser("org.apache.xerces.jaxp.DocumentBuilderFactoryImpl");
XMLUnit.setSAXParserFactory("org.apache.xerces.jaxp.SAXParserFactoryImpl");
XMLUnit.setTransformerFactory("org.apache.xalan.processor." +
                   "TransformerFactoryImpl");
```

## Writing XML comparison tests

Let's say we have two pieces of XML that we wish to compare and assert that they are equal. We could write a simple test class like this:

```
public class MyXMLTestCase extends XMLTestCase {
  public MyXMLTestCase(String name) {
    super(name);
  }

  public void testForEquality() throws Exception {
    String myControlXML = "<msg><uuid>0x00435A8C</uuid></msg>";
    String myTestXML = "<msg><localId>2376</localId></msg>";

    assertXMLEqual("Comparing test xml to control xml",
               myControlXML,
               myTestXML);
  }
}
```

The assertXMLEqual test will pass if the control and test XML are either similar or identical. Obviously, in this case, the pieces of XML are different and the test will fail with the message:

```
Comparing test xml to control xml
[different] Expected element tag name 'uuid' but was 'localId' -
            comparing <uuid...> to <localId...>
```

When comparing pieces of XML, XMLUnit is creating an instance of the Diff class behind the scenes. The Diff class stores the result of an XML comparison and makes it available through the methods similar() and identical(). The XMLTestCase class tests the value of similar() in the assertXMLEquals() method and the value of identical() in assertXMLIdentical(). However, it is easy to create a Diff directly in test cases:

```
public void testXMLIdentical()throws Exception {
  String myControlXML = "<struct>" +
                   "<int>3</int>" +
                   "<boolean>false</boolean>" +
                 "</struct>";

  String myTestXML = "<struct>" +
                   "<boolean>false</boolean>" +
                   "<int>3</int>" +
                 "</struct>";

  Diff myDiff = new Diff(myControlXML, myTestXML);
  assertTrue("XML similar " + myDiff.toString(), myDiff.similar());
  assertTrue("XML identical " + myDiff.toString(), myDiff.identical());
}
```

This test fails as two pieces of XML are considered similar but not identical if their nodes occur in a different sequence. The failure message reported by JUnit from the call to myDiff.toString() looks like this:

```
[not identical] Expected sequence of child nodes '0' but was '1' -
                comparing <int...> to <int...>
```

For efficiency reasons, a Diff stops the comparison process as soon as the first difference is found. To get all the differences between two pieces of XML an instance of the DetailedDiff class, a subclass of Diff, is required. Consider this test:

```java
public void testAllDifferences() throws Exception {
    String myControlXML = "<news>" +
                            "<item id=\"1\">War</item>" +
                            "<item id=\"2\">Plague</item>" +
                            "<item id=\"3\">Famine</item>" +
                          "</news>";

    String myTestXML = "<news>" +
                            "<item id=\"1\">Peace</item>" +
                            "<item id=\"2\">Health</item>" +
                            "<item id=\"3\">Plenty</item>" +
                          "</news>";
    DetailedDiff myDiff = new DetailedDiff(new Diff(myControlXML, myTestXML));
    List allDifferences = myDiff.getAllDifferences();
    assertEquals(myDiff.toString(), 2, allDifferences.size());
}
```

This test fails with the following message as each of the three news items differs between the control and test XML:

```
[different] Expected text value 'War' but was 'Peace' -
            comparing <item...> to <item...>
[different] Expected text value 'Plague' but was 'Health' -
            comparing <item...> to <item...>
[different] Expected text value 'Famine' but was 'Plenty' -
            comparing <item...> to <item...>
expected <2> but was <3>
```

The List returned from the getAllDifferences() method contains instances of the Difference class. Difference objects are instantiated at runtime by XMLUnit using final static fields in the DifferenceConstants class, and these instances are passed in notification events to a registered DifferenceListener by the DifferenceEngine class as it compares two pieces of XML. The Diff class implements the DifferenceListener interface but it is possible to override the default behavior by implementing the interface in your own class.

The IgnoreTextAndAttributeValuesDifferenceListener class is an example of how to implement a custom DifferenceListener. It allows an XML comparison to be made that ignores differences in the values of text and attribute nodes, for example, when comparing a skeleton or outline piece of XML to some generated XML. The following test illustrates its use:

```java
public void testCompareToSkeletonXML() throws Exception {
    String myControlXML = "<location>" +
                            "<street-addr>22 any street</street-addr>" +
                            "<postcode>XY00 99Z</postcode>" +
                          "</location>";
```

```
    String myTestXML = "<location>" +
                       "<street-addr>20 east cheap</street-addr>" +
                       "<postcode>EC3M 1EB</postcode>" +
                       "</location>";

    DifferenceListener myDifferenceListener =
            new IgnoreTextAndAttributeValuesDifferenceListener();
    Diff myDiff = new Diff(myControlXML, myTestXML);
    myDiff.overrideDifferenceListener(myDifferenceListener);
    assertTrue("test XML matches control skeleton XML", myDiff.similar());
}
```

## Comparing XML Transformations

XMLUnit can test XSL transformations at a high level using the Transform class that
wraps a javax.xml.transform.Transformer instance. Knowing the input XML, input style-
sheet, and expected output XML, we can assert that the output of the transformation
matches the expected output as follows:

```
    public void testXSLTransformation() throws Exception {
      String myInputXML = ". . .";
      File myStylesheetFile = new File(". . .");

      Transform myTransform = new Transform(myInputXML, myStylesheetFile);
      String myExpectedOutputXML = ". . .";
      Diff myDiff = new Diff(myExpectedOutputXML, myTransform);
      assertTrue("XSL transformation worked as expected", myDiff.similar());
    }
```

The getResultString() and getResultDocument() methods of the Transform class can
be used to access the result of the XSL transformation programmatically if required,
for example, as seen here:

```
    public void testAnotherXSLTransformation() throws Exception {
      File myInputXMLFile = new File(". . .");
      File myStylesheetFile = new File(". . .");
      Transform myTransform = new Transform(new StreamSource(myInputXMLFile),
                                    new StreamSource(myStylesheetFile));

      Document myExpectedOutputXML =
      XMLUnit.buildDocument(XMLUnit.getControlParser(),
                      new FileReader(". . ."));

      Diff myDiff = new Diff(myExpectedOutputXML,
                          myTransform.getResultDocument());
      assertTrue("XSL transformation worked as expected", myDiff.similar());
    }
```

## Validation Tests

XML parsers that validate a piece of XML against a DTD are common; however, they rely on a DTD reference being present in the XML, and they can only validate against a single DTD. When writing a system that exchanges XML messages with third parties there are times when you would like to validate the XML against a DTD that is not available to the recipient of the message and so cannot be referenced in the message itself. XMLUnit provides a **Validator** class for this purpose.

```
public void testValidation() throws Exception {
    XMLUnit.getTestDocumentBuilderFactory().setValidating(true);
    // As the document is parsed it is validated against its referenced DTD
    Document myTestDocument = XMLUnit.buildTestDocument(". . .");

    String mySystemId = ". . .";
    String myDTDUrl = new File(". . .").toURL().toExternalForm();
    Validator myValidator = new Validator(myTestDocument, mySystemId, myDTDUrl);
    assertTrue("test document validates against unreferenced DTD",
               myValidator.isValid());
}
```

## Xpath Tests

One of the strengths of XML is the ability to programmatically extract specific parts of a document using XPath expressions. The **XMLTestCase** class offers a number of XPath related assertion methods, as demonstrated in this test:

```
public void testXPaths() throws Exception {
    String mySolarSystemXML = "<solar-system>" +
                        "<planet name='Earth'" +
                              "position='3'" +
                              "supportsLife='yes'/>" +
                        "<planet name='Venus' position='4'/>" +
                    "</solar-system>";

    assertXpathExists("//planet[@name='Earth']", mySolarSystemXML);
    assertNotXpathExists("//star[@name='alpha centauri']", mySolarSystemXML);
    assertXpathsEqual("//planet[@name='Earth']",
                      "//planet[@position='3']",
                      mySolarSystemXML);

    assertXpathsNotEqual("//planet[@name='Venus']",
                         "//planet[@supportsLife='yes']",
                         mySolarSystemXML);
}
```

When an XPath expression is evaluated against a piece of XML a **NodeList** is created that contains the matching **Nodes**. The methods in the previous test—assertXPath Exists(), assertNotXPathExists(), assertXPathsEqual(), and assertXPathsNotEqual()—use these **NodeLists**. However, the contents of a **NodeList** can be flattened (or String-ified) to a single value, and XMLUnit also allows assertions to be made about this single value, as in this test:

```
public void testXPathValues() throws Exception {
  String myJavaFlavours = "<java-flavours>" +
                          "<jvm current='some platforms'>1.1.x</jvm>" +
                          "<jvm current='no'>1.2.x</jvm>" +
                          "<jvm current='yes'>1.3.x</jvm>" +
                          "<jvm current='yes' latest='yes'>1.4.x</jvm>" +
                          "</java-flavours>";

  assertXpathEvaluatesTo("2", "count(//jvm[@current='yes'])", myJavaFlavours);
  assertXpathValuesEqual("//jvm[4]/@latest",
                         "//jvm[4]/@current",
                         myJavaFlavours);

  assertXpathValuesNotEqual("//jvm[2]/@current",
                            "//jvm[3]/@current",
                            myJavaFlavours);

}
```

Xpaths are especially useful where a document is made up largely of known, un-
changing content with only a small amount of changing content created by the system.
One of the main areas where constant *boilerplate* markup is combined with system-
generated markup is of course in Web applications. The power of XPath expressions
can make testing Web page output quite trivial, and XMLUnit supplies a means of
converting even very badly formed HTML into XML to aid this approach to testing.

The HTMLDocumentBuilder class uses the Swing HTML parser to convert marked-
up content to Sax events. The TolerantSaxDocumentBuilder class handles the Sax events
to build up a DOM document in a tolerant fashion, that is, without mandating that
opened elements are closed. (In a purely XML world this class would have no purpose as
there are plenty of Sax event handlers that can build DOM documents from well-formed
content.) The following test illustrates the use of these classes:

```
public void testXpathsInHTML() throws Exception {
  String someBadlyFormedHTML = "<html>" +
                               "<title>Ugh</title>" +
                               "<body>" +
                               "<h1>Heading" +
                               "<ul>" +
                               "<li id='1'>Item One" +
                               "<li id='2'>Item Two";

  TolerantSaxDocumentBuilder tolerantSaxDocumentBuilder =
        new TolerantSaxDocumentBuilder(XMLUnit.getTestParser());

  HTMLDocumentBuilder htmlDocumentBuilder =
        new HTMLDocumentBuilder(tolerantSaxDocumentBuilder);

  Document wellFormedDocument =
        htmlDocumentBuilder.parse(someBadlyFormedHTML);

  assertXpathEvaluatesTo("Item One",
                         "/html/body//li[@id='1']",
                         wellFormedDocument);

}
```

One of the key points about using Xpaths with HTML content is that extracting values in tests requires the values to be identifiable. (This is just another way of saying that testing HTML is easier when it is written to be testable.) In the previous example id attributes were used to identify the list item values that needed to be testable; however, class attributes or span and div tags can also be used to identify specific content for testing.

## Testing by Tree Walking

The DOM specification allows a Document to optionally implement the DocumentTraversal interface. This interface allows an application to iterate over the Nodes contained in a Document, or to *walk the DOM tree*. The XMLUnit NodeTest class and NodeTester interface make use of DocumentTraversal to expose individual Nodes in tests: the former handles the mechanics of iteration, and the latter allows custom test strategies to be implemented. A sample test strategy is supplied by the CountingNodeTester class that counts the nodes presented to it and compares the actual count to an expected count. The test here illustrates its use:

```
public void testCountingNodeTester() throws Exception {
    String testXML = "<fibonacci>" +
                        "<val>1</val>" +
                        "<val>2</val>" +
                        "<val>3</val>" +
                        "<val>5</val>" +
                        "<val>9</val>" +
                    "</fibonacci>";

    CountingNodeTester countingNodeTester = new CountingNodeTester(4);
    assertNodeTestPasses(testXML, countingNodeTester, Node.TEXT_NODE);
}
```

This test fails as there are five text nodes, and JUnit supplies the following message:

```
Expected node test to pass, but it failed!
Counted 5 node(s) but expected 4
```

Note that if your DOM implementation does not support the DocumentTraversal interface, then XMLUnit will throw an IllegalArgumentException informing you that you cannot use the NodeTest or NodeTester classes. Unfortunately, even if your DOM implementation does support DocumentTraversal, attributes are not exposed by iteration; however, they can be examined from the Element node that contains them.

While the previous test could have been performed easily using XPath, there are times when Node iteration is more powerful. In general, this is true when there are programmatic relationships between nodes that can be more easily tested iteratively. The following test uses a custom NodeTester class to illustrate the potential:

```java
public void testCustomNodeTester() throws Exception {
  String testXML = "<fibonacci>" +
                     "<val>1</val>" +
                     "<val>2</val>" +
                     "<val>3</val>" +
                     "<val>5</val>" +
                     "<val>9</val>" +
                  "</fibonacci>";

  NodeTest nodeTest = new NodeTest(testXML);
  assertNodeTestPasses(nodeTest, new FibonacciNodeTester(),
        new short[] {Node.TEXT_NODE, Node.ELEMENT_NODE}, true);
}
private class FibonacciNodeTester extends AbstractNodeTester {
  private int nextVal = 1, lastVal = 1, priorVal = 0;

  public void testText(Text text) throws NodeTestException {
    int val = Integer.parseInt(text.getData());
    if (nextVal != val) {
      throw new NodeTestException("Incorrect sequence value", text);
    }

    nextVal = val + lastVal;
    priorVal = lastVal;
    lastVal = val;
  }

  public void testElement(Element element) throws NodeTestException {
    String name = element.getLocalName();

    if ("fibonacci".equals(name) || "val".equals(name)) {
      return;
    }
    throw new NodeTestException("Unexpected element", element);
  }

  public void noMoreNodes(NodeTest nodeTest) throws NodeTestException {
  }
}
```

As expected, the test fails because the XML contains the wrong value for the last number in the sequence.

```
Expected node test to pass, but it failed!
Incorrect sequence value [#text: 9]
```

## GARGOYLE SOFTWARE JUNIT EXTENSIONS
with Mike Bowler

*This section was contributed by Mike Bowler of Gargoyle Software Inc. [URL 59], the author and maintainer of the Gargoyle JUnit Extensions[URL 19].*

As a consultant, I find myself being asked to write the same code over and over again. Many of my clients share the same needs and require the same base utility classes. Because each client owns the code that I wrote when working for them, I am unable to reuse that code for the next client and consequently end up rewriting the same classes repeatedly.

In 1998, I got sufficiently frustrated with this situation so I started writing these classes on my own time and releasing them as open source. This way I would only have to write each class once and I could reuse them for each one of my clients. This collection of classes has become the GSBase project.

The testing classes within GSBase originally started out as support for the testing of GSBase itself but have shown themselves to be generally useful for testing other projects.

## RecursiveTestSuite

The standard mechanism for running tests in JUnit is to build nested hierarchies of test suites. In addition to being very monotonous work, this way is extremely error prone as it is very easy to accidentally miss a test in a suite. I wanted JUnit to figure out where all my tests were and to just execute them. Because JUnit itself doesn't do this, I created RecursiveTestSuite, a special TestSuite that will recursively walk through the directory structure looking for subclasses of TestCase.

If you are using Ant for your builds then the Ant junit target provides the same kind of functionality as RecursiveTestSuite. If that target had been available when I first started using JUnit then writing this class would have been unnecessary.

The most common usage of RecursiveTestSuite is to create a subclass like this:

```
public class MainTestSuite extends RecursiveTestSuite {
  public MainTestSuite(final String name) throws IOException {
    super(new File("."), new AcceptAllTestFilter());
  }
}
```

The reason for creating a subclass is that you need a class that can be passed into the test runners that will initialize everything the way you want. When you have this class, you can invoke the gui test runner with this command:

```
java junit.swingui.TestRunner mypackage.MainTestSuite
```

...and the text test runner with this command...

```
java junit.textui.TestRunner mypackage.MainTestSuite
```

The RecursiveTestSuite has the following constructor

```
public RecursiveTestSuite(final File startingDirectory,
                          final TestFilter testFilter);
```

The first parameter that is passed into RecursiveTestSuite is the directory to start at. This is the root of your classpath.

The second parameter is a test filter. The main advantage to recursively walking the directories looking for tests is that you won't miss any by mistake. The main disadvantage is that you may include tests that you don't want to run. The test filter is intended to solve that problem. It allows you to exclude certain tests from the full run. The AcceptAllTestFilter specified in the example will accept all of the tests. If you want to selectively exclude tests then you need to implement the TestFilter interface yourself.

For example, if you have your infrastructure code separate from your business logic and you wanted to be able to run the tests for one or the other, only then you might write a test filter like this:

```
public class InfrastructureTestFilter implements TestFilter {
  public boolean accept(final Class clazz) {
    String name = clazz.getName();
    return name.startsWith("com.mycompany.myproduct.infrastructure");
  }
}

public class BusinessCodeTestFilter implements TestFilter {
  public boolean accept(final Class clazz) {
    String name = clazz.getName();
    return name.startsWith("com.mycompany.myproduct.business");
  }
}
```

In each case, the filter only accepts tests located within certain package structures. It checks the class name of the test class to see if it starts with a given prefix and accepts or rejects the class based on its package.

## OrderedTestSuite

Assuming that your tests are in a class that subclasses TestCase, there are two ways to identify which tests should be run. The easiest way is to use the TestSuite constructor that takes a class. This will automatically create a new test for every method that follows a specific naming convention

```
public void testNegativeValue() {
}
```

The other way is to use the default constructor for TestSuite and then manually add each test that you want run.

```
public static Test suite() {
  final TestSuite suite = new TestSuite();
  suite.addTest(new MoneyTest("testNegativeValue"));
  suite.addTest(new MoneyTest("testNullCurrency"));
  return suite;
}
```

The problem with the first approach is that there is no way to specify the order in which the tests will be run. The second approach solves that problem but introduces the potential for accidentally missing tests. What I wanted was something that automatically found the tests and yet allowed me to specify the order in which the tests would be run. OrderedTestSuite was created to solve this problem.

Whenever possible it is advisable to avoid order dependencies between your tests. If tests must be run in a specific order, then one failing test can often cause other subsequent tests to also fail. Ideally, every test is completely independent of all other tests so that one failing test will not cause any other tests to fail.

```
public static Test suite() {
  return new OrderedTestSuite(MoneyTest.class,
                new String[] {
                  "testNegativeValue",
                  "testNullCurrency"
                });
}
```

OrderedTestSuite will guarantee that testNegativeValue and testNullCurrency will be executed in order. It will then use reflection to find other methods starting with "test" and will execute them. This means that if you write testThree but forget to add it to suite() then it will still get executed, albeit not in a defined order.

## EventCatcher

When testing objects that fire events, it becomes neccessary to collect events to ensure that the right events were fired at the right time.

```
final List collectedEvents = new ArrayList();
final JFrame frame = new JFrame("test");
frame.addWindowListener(new WindowAdapter() {
  public void windowClosing(final WindowEvent event) {
      collectedEvents.add(event);
  }
});
```

The typical approach requires creating many inner classes for the various types of events that you want to listen for. This quickly becomes very tedious and introduces the potential for error as very similar code is written over and over again.

EventCatcher is the solution to this problem. This is a single object that can listen for any kind of event that might be fired.

```
final JFrame frame = new JFrame("test");
final EventCatcher eventCatcher = new EventCatcher();
eventCatcher.listenTo(frame);
```

In this example, the event catcher will register itself as a listener for every type of event that is thrown by frame. Note that this will work for any event so long as the object has a method for registering listeners that follows the form addXXXListener().

An EventCatcherRecord will be created for each event that is caught. This will contain the event itself, the method that was invoked on the listener, and the name of the thread on which this method was called. These records can be retrieved with EventCatcher.getEventRecordAt(int index).

The preceding example caught every event fired by the JFrame. Although convenient, sometimes that is too much information—sometimes you only want to catch one specific kind of event. EventCatcher provides support for this by generating listener objects which you can then manually add to the object you wish to listen to.

```
final JFrame frame = new JFrame("test");
final EventCatcher eventCatcher = new EventCatcher();
final WindowListener listener =
        (WindowListener)eventCatcher.getListener(WindowListener.class);

frame.addWindowListener(listener);
```

The getListener() method takes a class object that is a listener interface such as ActionListener or WindowListener. It returns an object that implements that interface and that will log all events that are passed into it.

A common testing idiom is to perform an assertEquals() on a collection of expected values and another collection of collected values. The problem in this case is that this idiom assumes that all objects in both collections implement the equals() method. None of the core events in Java implement equals() so this idiom doesn't work. Instead, we can take a best guess of whether they are equal

```
final List expectedEvents = new ArrayList();
final List collectedEvents = new ArrayList();
...
eventCatcher.assertEventsAppearEquals(expectedEvents, collectedEvents);
```

This will call every accessor on each object and compare the results. If the values of all the properties are the same, then we assume that the objects themselves are in fact equal. This isn't perfect—it is possible to get false positives—but it's accurate enough in most cases.

## EqualsTester

EqualsTester is used to test the equals contract on objects. The contract as specified by java.lang.Object states that if A.equals(B) is true then B.equals(A) is also true. It also specifies that if A.equals(B) is true then A.hashCode() will equal B.hashCode().

It is not a trivial exercise to fully test the equals contract, so many people don't bother. Instead, they assume that equals() and hashCode() are simple enough that they couldn't break and therefore don't need to be tested. Ironically enough, it is very common for this contract to be implemented incorrectly. Peter Haggar goes into depth on the common pitfalls when implementing the equals contract in his book *Practical Java*[23].

In my experience, the most common problems when implementing equals are as follows:

1. The null case isn't handled.

   According to the contract, the equals() method must return false but many implementations don't explicitly handle null and consequently throw a NullPointerException.

2. equals(Foo) is written instead of equals(Object)

   The problem with this is that the wrong method has been overridden and it will not be called in all situations.

   ```
   public boolean equals(final Movie movie) {
      . . .
   }
   ```

   Given this sample code:

   ```
   final Movie movie1 = new Movie("One");
   final Movie movie2 = new Movie("Two");
   final Object movieAsObject = movie2;
   ```

   movie1.equals(movie2) will call the method declared above and will correctly compare the two movies.

   movie1.equals(movieAsObject) will call the superclasses equals(Object) method which will not return the expected result.

3. An instanceof check was used for comparison rather than getClass()

   ```
   // Wrong comparison
   public boolean equals(final Object object) {
      if (object == null) return false;
      if (!(object instanceof Movie)) return false;
      final Movie otherMovie = (Movie)object;
      return getName().equals(otherMovie.getName());
   }
   ```

   This will return false positives in some situations when comparing against subclasses. If the class in question is final then using instanceof is safe to use, but if it can be overridden then getClass() should be used instead.

   The reason that false positives are possible is that instanceof checks to ensure that the object is an instance of this class or a subclass of this class. In the case of a subclass, then this object is not able to properly perform a comparison as it only knows about the fields that it has and is unable to perform a comparison against fields present in the subclass but not present in the superclass. As a result it is possible for a.equals(b) to not equal b.equals(a).

For example, if we have a Movie and its subclass RatedMovie:

```
public class Movie {
  private final String name;
  public Movie(final String newName) {
    name = newName;
  }

  public boolean equals(final Object object) {
    if (object == null) return false;
    if (!(object instanceof Movie)) return false;
    final Movie otherMovie = (Movie)object;
    return getName().equals(otherMovie.getName());
  }
}
public class RatedMovie extends Movie {
  private final String rating;

  public RatedMovie(final String newName, final String newRating) {
    super(newName);
    name = newName;
    rating = newRating;
  }

  public boolean equals(final Object object) {
    if (object == null) return false;
    if (!(object instanceof RatedMovie)) return false;
    final RatedMovie otherMovie = (RatedMovie)object;
    return getRating().equals(otherMovie.getRating() &&
            super.equals(object));
  }
}
```

then given the following instances, we can perform comparisons.

```
final Movie a = new Movie("The One");
final RatedMovie b = new Movie("The One", "Great");
```

This case, a.equals(b), will return true because b is an instance of Movie and the names are the same. The reverse is not true; however, b.equals(a) will return false as a is not an instance of RatedMovie. This has violated the portion of the equals contract that says a.equals(b) must be the same as b.equals(a).

Instead of using instanceof, the proper comparison should have been written as follows, using the getClass() method.

```
if(object != null && object.getClass() == getClass())
```

Had both **equals()** methods been written this way then both of them would have returned **false** which would have satisfied the contract.

4. **equals(Object)** was overridden but **hashCode()** was not

The contract states that if two objects return true for **equals()**, then they must return the same hash code. By default, the value returned by **hashCode()** is fairly random so if you override **equals()** to be safe, then you must also override **hashCode()**.

While it is possible for two objects to return different values from **equals()** at different times (as property values on the object change, for example), **hashCode** values must remain the same for the entire lifetime of the object. If the value of **hashCode** was to change after the object had been placed into a hash table then unpredictable behavior would result.

Note that it is perfectly acceptable to return a constant value (e.g., **return 2;**) from the **hashCode()** method. Be aware that if you do return a constant and this object is used as a key in a hash table then performance will be extremely bad. Many objects are not used as keys and therefore performance is not an issue.

```
public long hashCode() {
    return getName().hashCode();
}
```

A correct implementation of **equals()** resembles the following:

```
public boolean equals(final Object object) {
    if (object == null) return false;
    if (object.getClass() != this.getClass()) return false;
    final Movie otherMovie = (Movie)object;
    return getName().equals(otherMovie.getName());
}
```

---

*While it is perfectly legal to directly access instance variables within the equals() method, I prefer to use the accessors to ensure that the accessors themselves have been adequately tested.*

---

Many developers will also put in a check for **this** as a quick return. There is nothing wrong with this but it should be noted that this check is purely done for performance reasons—adding this check does not make the method any more "correct."

```
public boolean equals(final Object object) {
    if (object == this) return true;
    if (object == null) return false;
    if (object.getClass() != this.getClass()) return false;
    final Movie otherMovie = (Movie)object;
    return name.equals(otherMovie.name);
}
```

The EqualsTester is designed to test the contract and ensure that none of the common problems are present. A test using EqualsTester would look like this:

```
public void testEquals() {
  final Movie a = new Movie("A");
  final Movie b = new Movie("A");
  final Movie c = new Movie("B");
  final Movie d = new Movie("A") {};
  new EqualsTester(a, b, c, d);
}
```

The four values that you pass into the EqualsTester are as follows:

1. The original object that will be the reference for comparision.

2. Another object of the same class that has the same values as the first. We expect this object to return true when compared to the first.

3. Another object of the same class that has different values than the first. We expect this object to return false when compared to the first.

4. An instance of a subclass of the first class that has the same values as the first object. If the first object is final, then this must be null as it is not possible to subclass a final class.

If any part of the equals contract is broken then an AssertionFailedError will be thrown—this is the same as calling the fail() method in JUnit.

## Detailed exceptions

When testing parameter checking, we often write code like this:

```
public void testNullInMoneyConstructor() {
  final Currency currency = null
  try {
    new Money(55, currency);
    fail("Expected NullPointerException");
  }
  catch(final NullPointerException e) {
    // Expected path
  }
}
```

The problem with this code is that while we are checking to ensure that a NullPointerException was thrown, we aren't checking to ensure that the exception was thrown from the place we expected.

```
public Money(final int newValue, final Currency newCurrency) {
  getLog().trace("Entering Money constructor");
  value = newValue;
  currency = newCurrency;
```

```
    if(newCurrency == null) {
      throw new NullPointerException("newCurrency");
    }
  }
```

In this example, if **getLog()** returns null then a **NullPointerException** will be thrown out of this constructor. The test assumes that parameter validation was successful because the exception was thrown, although the cause of the exception had nothing to do with the value that we thought we were validating.

The next best solution would be to put the name of the null parameter in the exception and check that from the test code.

```
  public void testNullInMoneyConstructor() {
    try {
      new Money(55, null);
      fail("Expected NullPointerException");
    } catch(final NullPointerException e) {
      assertEquals("newCurrency", e.getMessage());
    }
  }
```

The problem with this is that expecting to get structured data out of a message field is always dangerous. Inevitably someone will change the message while they are debugging something else.

For this reason, I created **DetailedNullPointerException**, which is a subclass of **NullPointerException** and contains more detailed information about what was null.

```
  public Money(final int newValue, final Currency newCurrency) {
    getLog().trace("Entering Money constructor");
    value = newValue;
    currency = newCurrency;

    if(newCurrency == null) {
      throw new DetailedNullPointerException("newCurrency");
    }
  }
```

Then the test becomes:

```
  public void testNullInMoneyConstructor() {
    try {
      new Money(55, null);
      fail("Expected DetailedNullPointerException");
    } catch(final DetailedNullPointerException e) {
      assertEquals("newCurrency", e.getArgumentName());
    }
  }
```

In this case, if **getLog()** returns null then a regular **NullPointerException** will be thrown, which will not be caught by the test and will result in a failing test.

The same problem occurs with IllegalArgumentExceptions, so there is also a DetailedIllegalArgumentException.

There is also a DetailedIllegalArgumentException that subclasses IllegalArgumentException to provide additional information.

```
public Money(final int newValue, final Currency newCurrency) {
    getLog().trace("Entering Money constructor");
    value = newValue;
    currency = newCurrency;

    if(newCurrency == null) {
        throw new DetailedNullPointerException("newCurrency");
    }
    if(newValue < 0) {
        throw new DetailedIllegalArgumentException("newValue",
                                                   newValue,
                                     "Must be greater than zero");

    }
}
```

The test then looks like this:

```
public void testNullInMoneyConstructor() {
    try {
        new Money(-55, Currency.USD);
        fail("Expected DetailedIllegalArgumentException");
    } catch(final DetailedIllegalArgumentException e) {
        assertEquals("newCurrency", e.getArgumentName());
        assertEquals(new Integer(55), e.getArgumentValue());
    }
}
```

## BaseTestCase

BaseTestCase is the common superclass that all of the GSBase test cases inherit from. It includes common methods that we would like to see in JUnit such as assertInstanceOf() and assertCollectionsEqual(). It also overrides some existing methods in TestCase that don't normally provide enough information. For example, assertSame() doesn't tell you what the two objects are in the case that they are different. BaseTestCase overrides assertSame() to print out more information.

assertInstanceOf() asserts that the specified object is an instance of a given class.

```
final Page page = webClient.getPage(new URL("http://www.yahoo.com"));
assertInstanceOf("Should have returned an html document", page, HtmlPage.class);
```

assertCollectionsEquals() compares two collections for equality independent of order. Often, you don't care what order items have been added to a collection so long as all the items are present in the correct quantities. Calling equals() on the collection will in some cases compare against a specific ordering.

```
final Collection expectedErrorMessages = getExpectedErrorMessages();
final Collection collectedErrorMessages = getCollectedErrorMessages();
assertCollectionsEquals(expectedErrorMessages, collectedErrorMessages);
```

notImplemented() indicates that a given test has not yet been completed. This is a simple way to mark a class so that you get a simple reminder every time you run the tests. This method will print out a message indicating that the test is not complete and will provide the name of the test.

```
public void testNegativeMoneyValue() {
  notImplemented();
}
```

# Chapter 6

# JUNIT-RELATED TOOLS

*Sirs, take you to your tools.*

*- Titus Andronicus, Act 4 Scene 3*
*William Shakespeare*

In this chapter we'll discuss a few tools that help with practicing TDD and/or using JUnit. The first three assist in verifying that you can have confidence in your tests: one by giving us feedback on how precise our tests are, and the remaining two by letting us know how much of our code is being tested. We'll then look at two IDEs that provide support for TDD: Eclipse and Idea.

There's a great number of useful tools out there, with more written every day. I've selected a few that are handy and specifically related to TDD. Furthermore, I've mostly picked open source tools. Idea and Clover are the exceptions.

## JESTER

Jester is a tool written by Ivan Moore for finding code that is not tested. The way it works is by making systematic changes to your application's source code (as opposed to your tests' source code), recompiling, and running the test suite. If all the tests still pass after making the change, then there is potentially a problem and it is reported.

The Jester Web site[URL 21] has links to download as well as more information regarding installation and use. There was also a paper at XP2001 about Jester[35].

Jester makes changes textually, not syntactically. The changes it makes are selected to change the logic of the code, for example, replacing **true** with **false**, forcing a conditional to **true** or **false**, etc. The rationale is that if such a major logical change is made it should cause a test to fail. If all the tests still pass, then more than likely there is a problem.

As packaged, Jester makes a small number of simple changes to your code, shown in Figure 6.1. By editing the file, `mutations.cfg`, you can add more. Additionally, it changes numeric constants.

Let's see how we can use Jester to improve our tests. Here are a few tests that drove some initial development of the **Movie** class:

```
true   ↔    false
 if(   →    if(true ||
 if (  →    if (true ||
 if(   →    if(false &&
 if (  →    if (false &&
  ==   ↔    !=
  ++   ↔    --
```

**Figure 6.1** Standard Jester changes.

```java
public class TestMovie extends TestCase {

  private Movie starWars;

  public void setUp() {
    starWars = new Movie("Star Wars");
  }

  public void testTitle() {
    assertEquals("Bad title reported.", "Star Wars", starWars.getTitle());
  }

  public void testRating() throws RatingOutOfRangeException {
    assertEquals("Default rating should be 0", 0, starWars.getRating());
    for (int i = 1; i <= 5; i++) {
      starWars.setRating(i);
      assertEquals("Rating not what was set", i, starWars.getRating());
    }
  }

  public void testBadRating() {
    try {
      starWars.setRating(7);
      fail("Too big of rating was accepted");
    } catch (RatingOutOfRangeException ex) {
    }
  }

  public void testNegativeRating() {
    try {
      starWars.setRating(-1);
      fail("Negative rating was accepted");
    } catch (RatingOutOfRangeException ex) {
    }
  }

}
```

And here's the Movie class in `Movie.java`:

```java
/**
 * Copyright (c) 2002 Saorsa Development Inc.
 * author Saorsa Development Inc.
 */

public class Movie {
  private String title;
  private int rating;

  public Movie(String movieTitle) {
    title = movieTitle;
    rating = 0;
  }

  public int getRating() {
    return rating;
  }

  public void setRating(int newRating) throws RatingOutOfRangeException {
    if (newRating < 0 || newRating > 5) {
      throw new RatingOutOfRangeException("Rating set to " + newRating);
    }
    rating = newRating;
  }

  public String getTitle() {
    return title;
  }
}
```

Here's the supporting Exception class in RatingOutOfRangeException.java:

```java
/**
 * Copyright (c) 2002 Saorsa Development Inc.
 * author Saorsa Development Inc.
 */

/**
 * This Exception is thrown when a <code>Movie</code>'s rating is
 * set to a value outside of the allowed range.
 */

public class RatingOutOfRangeException extends Exception {
  public RatingOutOfRangeException() {
    super();
  }
```

```
  public RatingOutOfRangeException(String message) {
    super(message);
  }
}
```

To run Jester, you first have to set your CLASSPATH (*not* by using the -cp option of the java command) to include everything that your test needs to run. For this example the directory structure is:

```
TestMovie.class
src
  Movie.java
  RatingOutOfRangeException.java
```

The commands to run Jester on this code are:

```
$ CLASSPATH=/usr/local/java/lib/jester.jar:/usr/local/java/lib/junit.jar:./src:.
$ java jester.TestTester TestMovie ./src
```

**Be sure to run Jester only on a copy of your code. Jester makes changes to the source files. Don't let it loose on files you can't replace. But then again, you have everything under version control anyway, right? Right!**

Here's the Jester console output:[1]

```
For File ./src/Movie.java:
  2 mutations survived out of 4 changes.
  Score = 50
./src/Movie.java
  - changed source on line 2 (char index=21)
                  from "2"
                  to "3"
/**
 * Copyright (c) #2#002 Saorsa Development Inc.
 * @author Saors

./src/Movie.java
  - changed source on line 18 (char index=439)
                  from "5"
                  to "6"
(newRating < 0 || newRating > #5#) {
          throw new RatingOutOfRangeEx


For File ./src/RatingOutOfRangeException.java:
  1 mutations survived out of 1 changes.
  Score = 0
./src/RatingOutOfRangeException.java
```

---

[1]Edited slightly for formatting and clarity. The '#' characters show the bit of code that Jester changed.

```
  - changed source on line 2 (char index=21)
                  from "2"
                  to "3"
/**
 * Copyright (c) #2#002 Saorsa Development Inc.
 * @author Soars


3 mutations survived out of 5 changes. Score = 40
took 0 minutes
```

One shortcoming of the current implementation of Jester is immediately obvious: It makes (and counts) changes in comments.[2] This leads to false positives in the results since changes to comments will, of course, not cause tests to fail. Future versions of Jester will no doubt address this and other shortcomings, doing more syntactic analysis of the code when deciding what changes to make.

So, the comment changes account for two out of the three potential problems. What's the third one? Looking at the output we can see that this change was to the constant that sets the upper limit to valid ratings. The requirement was that valid ratings were in the range 0–5, inclusive. This code looks OK, so why did a change to the upper limit (changing it to 6) not break a test? You would think that a change to a limit should break a test—after all, boundary conditions should be tested! Hmm... let's look at the test that checks for rating above the acceptable range:

```java
public void testBadRating() {
  try {
    starWars.setRating(7);
    fail("Too big of rating was accepted");
  } catch (RatingOutOfRangeException ex) {
  }
}
```

OK, all together now: "Ah Ha!" Our test wasn't close enough to the boundary condition. It tests a rating too high. The upper limit could be changed to 6 and still let this test pass. The test is sloppy and needs to be tightened up. The value passed to setRating should be 6, which is one more than the allowable limit.

Making this change results in the following Jester output:

```
For File ./src/Movie.java:
  1 mutations survived out of 4 changes.
  Score = 75
./src/Movie.java
  - changed source on line 2 (char index=21)
                  from "2"
                  to "3"
/**
 * Copyright (c) #2#002 Saorsa Development Inc.
 * @author Saors

For File ./src/RatingOutOfRangeException.java:
  1 mutations survived out of 1 changes.
```

[2] As the writing of this book finished, Jester had some experimental code to skip comments.

```
   Score = 0
./src/RatingOutOfRangeException.java
  - changed source on line 2 (char index=21)
                       from "2"
                       to "3"
/**
 * Copyright (c) #2#002 Saorsa Development Inc.
 * @author Saors


2 mutations survived out of 5 changes. Score = 60
took 0 minutes
```

That's better. The spurious comment changes are still there, but everything else is as it should be. This example showed one way in which Jester can be used to improve a test.

Another way in which Jester can help us is if we found that a method contained several changes that did not cause a test to fail. In this case, it is likely that we need more tests. Let's give that a try. We'll add a **toString()** method to **Movie:**[3]

```java
public String toString() {
  StringBuffer result = new StringBuffer();
  result.append("(");
  result.append(title);
  result.append(" - ");
  if (rating == 0) {
    result.append("No Rating");
  } else {
    result.append(rating);
  }
  result.append(")");
  return result.toString();
}
```

Now when we run Jester we get this output:

```
For File ./src/Movie.java:
  5 mutations survived out of 8 changes.
  Score = 38
./src/Movie.java
  - changed source on line 2 (char index=21)
                       from "2"
                       to "3"
/**
 * Copyright (c) #2#002 Saorsa Development Inc.
 * @author Saors

./src/Movie.java
  - changed source on line 34 (char index=800)
                       from "if ("
```

---

[3]If we were doing this for real, we'd write a test first. Since we want to have an untested method, we'll just write the method. Don't try this at home!

```
                        to "if (true ||"
            tle);
            result.append(" - ");
            #if (#rating == 0) {
                    result.append("No Rating

   ./src/Movie.java
     - changed source on line 34 (char index=800)
                    from "if ("
                    to "if (false &&"
            tle);
            result.append(" - ");
            #if (#rating == 0) {
                    result.append("No Rating

   ./src/Movie.java
     - changed source on line 34 (char index=811)
                    from "=="
                    to "!="
            lt.append(" - ");
            if (rating #==# 0) {
                    result.append("No Rating");
            } else

   ./src/Movie.java
     - changed source on line 34 (char index=814)
                    from "0"
                    to "1"
            append(" - ");
            if (rating == #0#) {
                    result.append("No Rating");
            } else {

For File ./src/RatingOutOfRangeException.java:
  1 mutations survived out of 1 changes.
  Score = 0
./src/RatingOutOfRangeException.java
  - changed source on line 2 (char index=21)
                    from "2"
                    to "3"
/**
 * Copyright (c) #2#002 Saorsa Development Inc.
 * @author Saors


6 mutations survived out of 9 changes. Score = 34
took 0 minutes
```

What can we learn from this output? Well, Jester made four changes to line 34 of Movie.java (the if statement in the toString() method) that didn't cause any test to fail. That indicates that the toString() isn't being tested well enough. Well, that's no surprise since we added it explicitly to get this kind of result. But consider how useful it would be to run Jester occasionally (daily?) to catch this kind of hole in our tests. This example is somewhat overstated, since if we are practicing TDD, it's not likely that this much code would not be tested. But we can easily get ourselves into a situation where a branch of a conditional isn't being tested well enough. Jester can help you find cases like that. This is especially useful for teams that are in the process of transitioning to TDD and adding tests to their existing code.

In addition to the console output, Jester creates an XML file that contains comparable information. Here's an example:

```
<JesterReport>
  <JestedFile fileName="./src/Movie.java"
              numberOfChangesThatDidNotCauseTestsToFail="5"
              numberOfChanges="8"
              score="38">
    <ChangeThatDidNotCauseTestsToFail index="21" from="2" to="3"/>
    <ChangeThatDidNotCauseTestsToFail index="800" from="if (" to="if (true ||"/>
    <ChangeThatDidNotCauseTestsToFail index="800" from="if ("
                                      to="if (false &amp;&amp;"/>
    <ChangeThatDidNotCauseTestsToFail index="811" from="==" to="!="/>
    <ChangeThatDidNotCauseTestsToFail index="814" from="0" to="1"/>
  </JestedFile>
  <JestedFile fileName="./src/RatingOutOfRangeException.java"
              numberOfChangesThatDidNotCauseTestsToFail="1"
              numberOfChanges="1"
              score="0">
    <ChangeThatDidNotCauseTestsToFail index="21" from="2" to="3"/>
  </JestedFile>
</JesterReport>
```

Jester also has python scripts that take that XML file and use it to create a set of HTML pages that detail each change that it was able to make without breaking tests. Table 6.1 and Figure 6.2 show an example of this. This is the same information, but presented in a more meaningful way.

In Chapter 20 we will use Jester on our example project.

**Table 6.1** Jester Index for the Movie Example

| file name | score | number of changes where tests still passed | total number of changes |
|---|---|---|---|
| ./src/Movie.html | 38 | 5 | 8 |
| ./src/ RatingOutOfRangeException.html | 0 | 1 | 1 |

# NOUNIT

NoUnit allows you to see how good your JUnit tests are. It generates a report from your code to graphically show you how many of your project's methods are being tested, and how well.

The report (see Table 6.2 for a sample) includes a line for each method in your code indicating:

- Whether it's called directly, indirectly, or not at all from any test method. This is indicated by the color of the third and fourth columns and the icon in the third column:

```
public String toString() {
    StringBuffer result = new StringBuffer();
    result.append("(");
    result.append(title);
    result.append(" - ");
if (if (true ||if (false &&rating ==!= 01) {
            result.append("No Rating");
    } else {
            result.append(rating);
    }
    result.append(")");
    return result.toString();
}
```

**Figure 6.2** Sample Jester change report for the Movie example.

**Table 6.2** NoUnit Report for the Movie Example

| Depth | Volume | | Method Name | Class |
|-------|--------|---|-------------|-------|
| 0 | 1 | ✓ | init | Movie |
| 0 | 2 | ✓ | getRating | Movie |
| 0 | 1 | ✓ | getTitle | Movie |
|   |   | ✗ | toString | Movie |
| 0 | 3 | ✓ | setRating | Movie |
| 1 | 3 | ? | init | RatingOutOfRangeException |
| 2 | 3 | ? | init | RatingOutOfRangeException |

| green | ✓ | → | called directly |
|-------|---|---|-----------------|
| orange | ? | → | called indirectly |
| red | × | → | not called at all |

- how many times it's called for all test methods reported on (the second column)

- the minimum number of methods between it and a test method (the first column).

The fourth column also contains the method name being reported on in that line, and the fifth column indicates the class of that method.

NoUnit works by analyzing the class files from a project. It can answer several questions about your tests:

1. Are all methods called from a test?

2. Are all methods tested reasonably directly?

3. Where are the holes in our test *net*?

4. Are some areas better tested than others?

If you are practicing Test-Driven Development, NoUnit isn't as useful as it would be if you were writing tests after the code. Doing TDD implies there is no code in the system that wasn't written to get a test to pass. That means that everything should be covered by some test.

Even so, it is worth running NoUnit on your code occasionally to make sure something bad hasn't happened. If you are working with legacy code, NoUnit can be very useful as you are adding tests to existing code. Since NoUnit works with class files, and not the Java source code, you can even use it to analyze the test coverage of third-party libraries.

To see NoUnit in action, let's run it on the code we used in the final Jester example (i.e., including the untested toString() method):

```
$ pwd
  /home/dave/projects/books/tdd/samples/nounit
$ ls
  Movie.class
  Movie.java
  output
  RatingOutOfRangeException.class
  RatingOutOfRangeException.java
  TestMovie.class
  TestMovie.java
$ $NOUNIT_HOME/batch/nounit .
  Generating Report:
  XML in:./output/project.xml
  XSLT file:/home/dave/workspace/nounit/batch/../xslt/no-unit.xsl
  Output file:./output/index.html
  Transformation Successful
```

The results were shown in Table 6.2. It is much clearer in that report that the toString() method is not being tested. Also notice that it has identified that the constructors for the exception class are only called indirectly.

NoUnit excels at finding gaping holes in your test suite, that is, methods that are not tested, or only tested indirectly. Jester is better at finding smaller holes—conditional branches that aren't being tested.

The result of running NoUnit is an HTML page containing the report and legend, ready for posting on our project's intranet site. In the example, the table has been extracted from the entire page. The NoUnit Web site[URL 20] gives instructions on downloading, installing, and using NoUnit.

There are some problems with NoUnit that I found; it has some bugs and shortcomings. Fortunately, there is a fairly large online user community that has posted bug reports, solutions, and workarounds at the NoUnit SourceForge site. Since NoUnit is open source, you can easily fix the problems on your own, especially in the cases where someone else has figured it out and posted instructions.

In Chapter 20 we will use NoUnit on the project we develop, and in the process bring to light some of its shortcomings.

# CLOVER

Clover is a classic code coverage tool. During a run it measures what code is executed and how many times—down to the statement level. The results can be reported in a variety of formats, including a nice HTML format that lets you drill down to the source code level. At the package and class method it shows the percentage of the code which was executed. At the source level it shows how often each line was executed, and visually highlights lines that were not executed.

Clover works by instrumenting the source code. When the code is then compiled and run it writes execution information to a logfile which is later processed to generate the report. This instrumentation is transparent and automatic. All that you need to do is add some additional lines to your Ant build script. Clover is very nicely integrated with Ant, and hence with anything that can use Ant to perform builds. The instrumentation is done to a copy of your source; your source tree is untouched by the process.

Clover's Ant integration is done very nicely. Clover institutes its own compiler adapter in place of the standard `javac` adapter. The Clover adapter takes care of instrumenting the code in your source tree, placing the results in a temporary location (that it cleans up afterward), and then using the original compiler adapter to compile the instrumented code, placing the resulting class files in your project's build directory. Totally transparent. Nice job.

A benefit of Clover's approach (i.e., instrumenting the source) is that no modification or extensions are required to the runtime environment.

I won't go into detail here on how you hook Clover into your `build.xml`; the Clover site [URL 22] has a nicely done user guide and tutorial walking you through it. What I will show you is some examples of the HTML report. These were generated from the tutorial example that ships with Clover, the JUnit Money example. We'll start at the top level with the project report, shown in Figure 6.3. You can see the coverage results for the overall project, as well as for each top level package, of which there is a single one in this example.

By selecting the package, we can see the package level report, which shows us results for each class (and subpackages, if there were any). See Figure 6.4.

Selecting a class shows us the code with execution counts. Figure 6.5 shows us a piece of the Money class that Clover has found never to be executed: one branch in

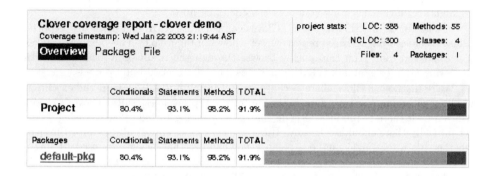

**Figure 6.3** Project level Clover report.

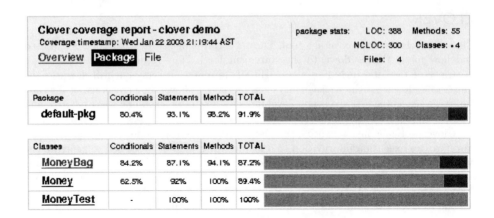

**Figure 6.4** Package level Clover report.

```
39  27    public boolean equals(Object anObject) {
40  27        if (isZero())
41   0            if (anObject instanceof IMoney)
42   0                return ((IMoney)anObject).isZero();
43  27        if (anObject instanceof Money) {
44  24            Money aMoney= (Money)anObject;
45  24            return aMoney.currency().equals(currency())
46                                && amount() == aMoney.amount();
47            }
48   3        return false;
49        }
```

**Figure 6.5** Class level Clover report.

the equals() method that handles comparing with a zero value Money. Notice the color highlighting on the execution counts of the offending lines.[4]

In addition to the HTML report, Clover can generate XML and plain text reports. It also includes a Swing-based report viewer, shown in Figure 6.6. This flexibility makes it a wonderful tool. You can quickly browse through the result on a local build with the Swing GUI, or generate HTML reports as part of a central build process.

We're discussing Clover here because it is especially useful for us if the execution used for gathering coverage data is the run of the top level test suite. Clover's report will tell us if there is production code that is not getting tested. If we're using TDD, theoretically there shouldn't be any. However, something almost always slips through, whether it's a toString() method, or an event handler that never gets used. Using a coverage analyzer like Clover in conjunction with Jester will provide you with a fairly complete picture of how comprehensive and effective your tests are.

---

[4]In reality the highlighting is pink, but that didn't have enough contrast when converted to grayscale... so I've taken artistic license.

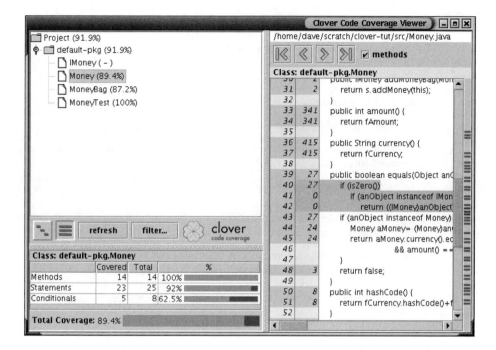

**Figure 6.6** Swing-based Clover report viewer.

One thing about Clover that sets it apart from most of the others we've looked at: it's a commercial product. Even so, the price is very reasonable. Given the data it provides it's worth what it costs.

## ECLIPSE

Eclipse[URL 32] is a fairly new development environment that is becoming very popular. It was written by Object Technology International (OTI), a subsidiary of IBM. OTI is the company behind IBM's Smalltalk and Java tools. IBM's Websphere Application Development Studio (WSAD) is built on top of Eclipse. Eclipse is an open source project that is freely available for download.

What makes Eclipse so interesting is how XP- and TDD-friendly it is. It should be no surprise that one of the people central to the Eclipse effort is Erich Gamma (coauthor of *Design Patterns* [19] and JUnit).

### JUnit integration

Eclipse is architected as a common core platform and a series of plugins. In fact, the Java development environment is itself a set of Eclipse plugins. The JUnit plugin is of special interest, in particular for the way it is integrated into the Java toolset. JUnit plugin's features include:

- a TestCase creation wizard

- a TestSuite creation and updating wizard

- a deeply integrated TestRunner that provides:

  - a *view* for test results

  - the ability to hide packages in the stack trace

  - clickable test lists and stack trace (clicking opens the corresponding file/line in an editor)

  - an easy way to rerun tests

- an integration with the *Run* menus, allowing a class to be run as a JUnit Test, including in the debugger

- the ability to keep JUnit running to increase the speed of running tests, and to allow the rerunning of individual tests.

Having JUnit integrated this tightly with the development environment greatly streamlines the TDD experience.

## Problem indication

Eclipse indicates problems that will prevent code from compiling. Offending code is underlined with a wavy red line, and the line is flagged in the left margin with a yellow lightbulb. You can have Eclipse offer corrections by clicking on the lightbulb, or positioning the caret on the offending code and typing CTRL-1. Select a correction from the list to have it applied. Figure 6.7 shows an example of this in action.

This capability gets us to the point where we have a compiling, failing test very quickly. It really streamlines the process of letting the compiler tell you what you need to do. You can skip the manual process of compiling, checking the error messages, adding the appropriate stubs, etc. You can have Eclipse add the stubs as appropriate (including classes, interfaces, methods, instance variables, and local variables) while you are still thinking about the problem at hand. Then you can get on with making the test pass.

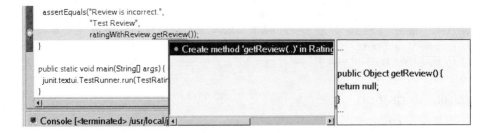

**Figure 6.7** Problem indication and correction in Eclipse.

## Refactoring support

Eclipse supports several automated refactorings that greatly speed development. Refactoring provided includes:

- Extracting a method
- Renaming a package
- Renaming a class or interface
- Renaming a method
- Renaming a field
- Renaming a local variable
- Renaming method parameters
- Reordering method parameters
- Extracting a local variable
- Inlining a local variable
- Self-encapsulating a field
- Replacing a local variable with a query
- Pulling members up to their superclass
- Moving static members between types

Being able to use automated refactorings increases both your confidence, since the refactorings are proven not to introduce errors, and your speed, since you don't have to perform each step of the refactoring manually.

Eclipse includes all of the standard features expected in an IDE, such as code assist, incremental compilation, documentation lookup, etc., all of which serve to streamline the programming process.

# IDEA
### with Bryan Dollery

*I've asked Bryan to talk about IDEA IDE from IntelliJ. Bryan is a well-known consultant in New Zealand and an outspoken IDEA user and advocate.*

IDEA[URL 33] has many features that will help with practicing TDD; in this section we will look at several of them.

If I use a class that hasn't yet been imported, IDEA will use a tool-tip to tell me, and offer to import it for me — very simple, very fast. Once the class is imported its methods and attributes are available to me for code completion.

If I use a class that doesn't exist, something that we all do at first with TDD, then IDEA puts a lightbulb in the gutter which, if I click on it, offers me a number of code generation options, including the option to create the class for me.

If I have an object and attempt to call a method that doesn't exist, IDEA will use the lightbulb again to tell me that it can help out. Clicking on it gives me the option to create the method. Here is where IDEA starts to show its real intelligence. When generating a method, IDEA has to make certain assumptions: the return type, the parameter types, and their names.

If I have started with:

```
fragment.doSomething("name");
```

within fragment's class, IDEA can generate:

```
void doSomething(String s) {
}
```

It will then put a red box (a live template query) around void, with my cursor in it. It's telling me that void was an assumption, and that I need to either accept it by pressing enter or tab, or change it. Once I'm happy with the return type, I can press enter to move to the next assumption, the type for the parameter. The final assumption here is the name for the parameter, which I don't like, so I can change it. Of course, if I provide it with more information, say, by assigning the return type to a variable, then IDEA will make better assumptions.

To run the tests I have a few choices available to me. I can compile, test, run, or debug, at a class level or a method level. If I right-click on a method then it assumes that I'm interested in that method and offers choices based on the method, but if I right-click on the class name (or a gap between methods) then I'll be offered these choices for the whole class (which is what I usually want). I can also choose to run all the tests within a given package.

To run or debug I don't need a main method, only the test methods. Being able to debug at a test-method level is very useful. I don't have to play around getting to the method I really want to test; it's all done for me.

The integration with JUnit is very tight. If the GUI runner shows a stack trace I can double-click on a line of the trace and be taken straight to that line in the editor. Fix the error, recompile, and alt-tab back to the GUI runner to rerun the tests. I can also choose to run the text-runner, the output of which appears in IDEA's messages window.

However, refactoring is the jewel in the crown for IDEA. Look at your current editor right now, and open the refactoring menu. If it's not at least half the size of your screen then you're really missing out.

There are 22 refactorings listed on its menu, but some of those are multirefactorings. Take, for example, the rename refactoring. It works on variables of any scope, methods, classes, and packages — that makes it four similar refactorings in one. When it renames a class, it also renames the file it's in, and when it renames a package it'll rename the directory and ensure that the change is recorded in CVS — this is a very bright tool, nothing is left unfinished.

One of my favorites is Change Signature — I can use it to add, remove, reorder, and rename parameters to a method — all at once. If I change a parameter's name it'll do a rename refactoring automatically for me, before it does the rest of the changes. If I add a parameter it asks for a default value. If I reorder the parameters it'll ensure that the method is called correctly throughout my project.

IDEA attempts to transparently automate repetitive and common tasks. It leaves nothing undone, and asks for clarification when it's guessing. It's highly polished, looks great, and will probably speed up your coding significantly.

# Chapter 7

# MOCK OBJECTS

> *You mock me, sir.*
> *- Hamlet, Act 5 Scene 2*
> *William Shakespeare*

What is the Holy Grail of TDD? What do you strive for when you write tests? Something like:

- focused tests: ideally one assert each
- independent tests: the fixture is built and cleaned up for each test, allowing tests to run in any order
- fast tests: you want to be able to run them frequently

There is a potential conflict here. Small, focused tests mean that you will have lots of tests, each very small and focused. To keep them independent you need to have a clean fixture for each. That means you need to rebuild (and re-cleanup) the fixture *for each test, every time it is run.* OK, so far so good. The last goal is the problem. We want the tests to be fast... as fast as possible... so that we can run them frequently. For trivial fixtures, that's OK. But what happens if your test fixtures get complex and time-consuming to build and cleanup?

You may simply have a lot of fixture to put in place, or you may be working in the context of a large, complex system. This could be a database, a workflow system, or some system for which you are developing an extension (e.g., an IDE). Your fixture may involve getting the system into a specific state so that it responds the way your tests require. This may be impossible to do quickly.

In light of such problematic test resources, how do we reconcile our three goals of focus, independence, and speed? Mock objects provide one approach that has proven successful. Mock objects are used when it is difficult or impossible to create the required state for a problematic resource, or when access to that resource is limited. There are other interesting uses for mock objects. In this chapter we'll talk about mock objects, what they are, how to use them, a framework for working with them, and some tools to make that easier.

## MOCK OBJECTS

Mock objects (we will follow convention and call them *mocks*) take the place of real objects for the purposes of testing some functionality that interacts with and is dependent on the *real* objects. An excellent paper on mocks was presented at XP2000[32], and there is a site dedicated to the idea[URL 23].

The basic idea behind mocks is to create lightweight, controllable replacements for objects you need in order to write your tests. Mocks also enable you to specify and test your code's interaction with the mocks themselves.

## AN ILLUSTRATIVE EXAMPLE

We're going to consider a simple, somewhat contrived example of a situation where mocks can help. First we will do it the hard way: creating our mocks entirely by hand. Later we will explore excellent tools for automating much of the business of mock creation and setup.

Our example involves writing an adventure game in which the player tries to rid the world of foul creatures such as Orcs. When a player attacks an Orc they roll a 20-sided die to see if they hit or not. A roll of 13 or higher is a hit, in which case they roll the 20-sided die again to determine the effect of the hit. If the initial roll was less than 13, they miss.

Our task at the moment is to test the code in **Player** that governs this process. Here's **Player** (I know, we aren't test driving this code... assume we inherited it):

```java
public class Player {
  Die myD20 = null;

  public Player(Die d20) {
    myD20 = d20;
  }
  public boolean attack(Orc anOrc) {
    if (myD20.roll() >= 13) {
      return hit(anOrc);
    } else {
      return miss();
    }
  }

  private boolean hit(Orc anOrc) {
    anOrc.injure(myD20.roll());
    return true;
  }

  private boolean miss() {
    return false;
  }
}
```

Here's the initial take at a test. We'll start simply with the case where the attack misses. We'll assume that a **Die** class already exists:

```java
public class Die {
  private int sides = 0;
  private Random generator = null;
```

```
public Die(int numberOfSides) {
  sides = numberOfSides;
  generator = new Random();
}

public int roll() {
  return generator.nextInt(sides) + 1;
}
}
```

Here's a first stab at the test for a missed attack:

```
public void testMiss() {
  Die d20 = new Die(20);
  Player badFighter = new Player(d20);
  Orc anOrc = new Orc();
  assertFalse("Attack should have missed.", badFighter.attack(anOrc));
}
```

The problem is that there is a random number generator involved. Sometimes the test passes, other times it fails. We need to be able to control the return value in order to control the preconditions for the test. This is a case where we cannot (or rather, should not) get the actual test resource into the state we need for the test. So instead, we use a simple mock object for that. Specifically, we can mock the Die class to return the value we want. But first we need to extract an interface from Die, and use it in place of Die:[1]

```
public interface Rollable {
  int roll();
}

public class Die implements Rollable {
  //...
}

public class Player {
  Rollable myD20 = null;
  public Player(Rollable d20) {
    myD20 = d20;
  }
  //...
}
```

Now we can create a mock for a 20-sided die that always returns a value that will cause an attack to miss, say, 10:

---

[1] There are other ways of approaching this, such as creating a subclass that returns the constant, but I like working with interfaces.

```
public class MockD20FailingAttack implements Rollable {
  public int roll() {
    return 10;
  }
}
```

Now we use the mock in our test:

```
public void testMiss() {
  Rollable d20 = new MockD20FailingAttack();
  Player badFighter = new Player(d20);
  Orc anOrc = new Orc();
  assertFalse("Attack should have missed.", badFighter.attack(anOrc));
}
```

There, the test always passes now. Next, we write a corresponding test with a successful attack:

```
public void testHit() {
  Rollable d20 = new MockD20SuccessfulAttack();
  Player goodFighter = new Player(d20);
  Orc anOrc = new Orc();
  assertTrue("Attack should have hit.", goodFighter.attack(anOrc));
}
```

This requires a new mock:

```
public class MockD20SuccessfulAttack implements Rollable {
  public int roll() {
    return 18;
  }
}
```

Now, these two mocks are almost identical, so we can refactor and merge them into a single parameterized class:

```
public class MockDie implements Rollable {
  private int returnValue;

  public MockDie(int constantReturnValue) {
    returnValue = constantReturnValue;
  }

  public int roll() {
    return returnValue;
  }
}
```

Our tests are now:

```
public void testMiss() {
  Rollable d20 = new MockDie(10);
  Player badFighter = new Player(d20);
  Orc anOrc = new Orc();
  assertFalse("Attack should have missed.", badFighter.attack(anOrc));
}

public void testHit() {
  Rollable d20 = new MockDie(18);
  Player goodFighter = new Player(d20);
  Orc anOrc = new Orc();
  assertTrue("Attack should have hit.", goodFighter.attack(anOrc));
}
```

Next, we want to write tests for the cases where an attack hurts the Orc, and where it kills it. For this we will need to extend MockDie so that we can specify a sequence of return values (successful attack followed by the amount of damage). In order to maintain the current behavior, MockDie repeatedly loops through the return value sequence as roll() is called.

```
public class MockDie implements Rollable {
  private Vector returnValues = new Vector();
  private int nextReturnedIndex = 0;

  public MockDie() {
  }
  public MockDie(int constantReturnValue) {
    addRoll(constantReturnValue);
  }
  public void addRoll(int returnValue) {
    returnValues.add(new Integer(returnValue));
  }
  public int roll() {
    int val = ((Integer)returnValues.get(nextReturnedIndex++)).intValue();
    if (nextReturnedIndex >= returnValues.size()) {
      nextReturnedIndex = 0;
    }
    return val;
  }
}
```

Using the Rollable interface allows us to easily and cleanly create mocks without impacting the Player class at all. We can see this in the class diagram shown in Figure 7.1.

So far we've written simple mocks, really just stubs that return some predefined values in response to a method call. Now we'll start writing and using a real mock, one that expects and can verify specific calls. Again, so far, we're doing it all by hand.

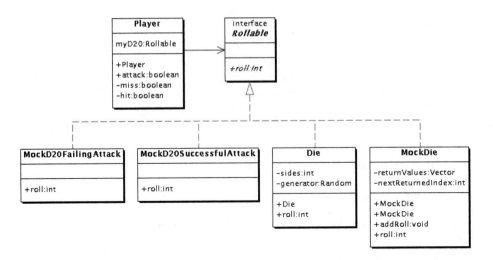

**Figure 7.1** Class diagram of the Player and Die aspects of the example.

First, consider this implementation of Orc and Game:

```
public class Orc {
  private Game game = null;
  private int health = 0;

  public Orc (Game theGame, int hitPoints) {
    game = theGame;
    health = hitPoints;
  }
  public void injure(int damage) {
    health -= damage;
    if (health <= 0) {
      die();
    }
  }
  private void die() {
    game.hasDied(this);
  }
  public boolean isDead() {
    return health <= 0;
  }
}
public interface Game {
  void hasDied(Orc orc);
}
```

Now we can write tests like this:

```
public void testNoKill() {
  MockGame mockGame = new MockGame();
  Orc strongOrc = new Orc(mockGame, 30);

  MockDie d20 = new MockDie();
  d20.addRoll(18);
  d20.addRoll(10);

  Player fighter = new Player(d20);
  fighter.attack(strongOrc);
  assertFalse("The orc should not have died.", strongOrc.isDead());
  mockGame.verify();
}
public void testKill() {
  MockGame mockGame = new MockGame();
  Orc weakOrc = new Orc(mockGame, 10);
  mockGame.expectHasDied(weakOrc);

  MockDie d20 = new MockDie();
  d20.addRoll(18);
  d20.addRoll(15);

  Player fighter = new Player(d20);
  fighter.attack(weakOrc);
  assertTrue("The orc should be dead.", weakOrc.isDead());
  mockGame.verify();
}
```

The one thing that is missing is MockGame. Here it is:

```
public class MockGame implements Game {
  private Orc deadOrc = null;
  private Orc orcExpectedToDie = null;

  public void hasDied(Orc orc) {
    if (orc != orcExpectedToDie) {
      Assert.fail("Unexpected orc died.");
    }
    if (deadOrc != null) {
      Assert.fail("Only expected one dead orc.");
    }
    deadOrc = orc;
  }

  public void expectHasDied(Orc doomedOrc) {
    orcExpectedToDie = doomedOrc;
  }
```

```
public void verify () {
   Assert.assertEquals("Doomed Orc didn't die.", orcExpectedToDie, deadOrc);
}
}
```

When an Orc dies it reports the fact to the game. In the case of the tests, this is a MockGame that checks that the dead orc is the one that was expected and that this is the only dead orc so far. If either of these checks fail, then the mock causes the test to fail immediately by calling Asert.fail(). When the mock is set up by the test it is told what orc it should expect to die. At the end of the test the MockGame can be asked to verify that the expected Orc died.

This is a trivial mock, but it should give you a taste of what is possible. Figure 7.2 shows this part of the class diagram, while Figure 7.3 shows the sequence diagram for testKill().

You can now easily see that as our mocks get more complex, they get harder to write and maintain, if we write them from scratch each time. The folks that evolved the mock objects concept found this out quickly, and as happens when you find yourself writing similar code a lot, they developed a framework for creating mocks and tools to make the job easier. Again, we'll have more on that later.

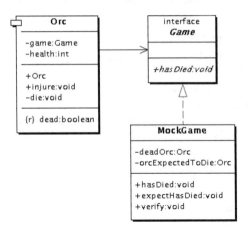

**Figure 7.2** Class diagram of the Orc and Game aspects of the example.

## USES FOR MOCK OBJECTS

Using mocks would seem to have several advantages beyond keeping test fixtures light-weight and fast to build and cleanup. There are several reasons to use mocks. We'll look at them in turn:

**To help keep the design decoupled.**   Using mocks helps to enforce interface-centric design. Programming against a mock removes the possibility of depending on the implementation of the objects being used.

**To check your code's usage of another object.**   By setting expectations in a mock, we can verify that the code we are working on properly uses the mocked interface.

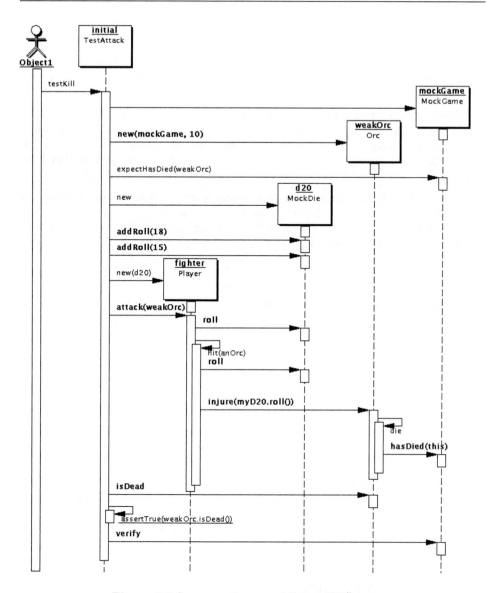

**Figure 7.3** Sequence diagram of the testKill() test.

**To test-drive your code from the inside out.**   By setting return values in the mocks, we can provide specific information to the code under development, then test that the resulting behavior is correct.

**To make your tests run faster.**   By mocking things like communications or database subsystems, we can avoid the overhead involved in setting up and tearing down connections, etc.

**To make it easier to develop code that interacts with hardware devices, remote systems, and other problematic resources.** If the code we are writing needs to interact with some tricky resource, we can create a proxy layer to isolate us from the real resource. Then we can use a mock of that layer. This allows us to develop code without needing access to the actual device or system.

**To defer having to implement a class.** We can use mocks for classes that we haven't written yet but that the code we are working on needs to interact with. This lets us defer implementing those classes, letting us focus on the interface between them and the code we are writing. This allows us to leave implementation decisions until we know more. If all you need for your test is to simulate the behavior, a mock will suffice.

**To let us test-drive components in isolation from the rest of the system.** By mocking the component(s) that the code being written has to interact with, we can focus on it in isolation. This lets us go faster, because complex interactions with other components are fully under our control.

**To promote interface-based design.** Mocks are easiest to use when you adopt an interface-heavy style of programming.[2]

**To encourage composition over inheritance.** This is related closely to the previous point. In general, inheritance is overused. As a result, monolithic functionality builds up in an inheritance hierarchy. A class is and always will be whatever it inherits. Mocking any aspect of a class in an inheritance hierarchy is difficult because of all of the baggage that the class inherits. The desire to mock certain aspects (e.g., persistence) tends to yield smaller classes that *get smart* by collaborating with other classes. Then different implementations of these classes, including mocks, can be easily interchanged.

**To refine interfaces.** Using a mock for a class you will eventually need to implement gives you an early chance to think about and refine the interface. This is especially true when using test-first design. You have to think about the interface from the view of a real class that will be using it — because you begin with a real test class that uses it.

**To test unusual, unlikely, and exceptional situations.** You can easily create a mock that will return values that don't usually occur, or that will throw exceptions on demand. This allows you to easily test exception handling. For example, you can mock a FileOutput Stream and have it throw an IOException upon writing the 10th byte. In general, you can write a mock to replicate any situation that might be hard (or even impossible) to arrange to happen for the purposes of a test.

## WOULDN'T IT BE NICE?

**Wouldn't it be nice** if the mock could be told what method calls to expect from the object(s) being tested? Then you could test the object behavior from the other side as

---

[2]This is simply a better way of programming. By using interfaces, you make it easier to decouple your classes. In their book on Java design techniques[12], Coad et al. dedicate more pages to interface-centric design than any of the other techniques they discuss. They boil down the reasons to use interfaces to three characteristics that an interface-rich system has: flexibility, extensibility, and plugability. Using mocks is made easier if you freely use interfaces, because if methods expect an interface, you can easily create a mock implementation and use that in place of a *real* implementation. It's no coincidence that **Extract Interface** is a very important refactoring.

well: not just the response to a call (i.e., the return value and state change), but also what methods in the mock were called from the class being developed.

**Wouldn't it be nice** if the mock could be told what value(s) to return from those calls? That would let you verify more complex interactions.

**Wouldn't it be nice** if it could be told to return different values each time a method is called? Again, this would let you test even more complex interactions.

**Wouldn't it be nice** if you could ask it to verify that everything that was expected to happen did, indeed, happen, and to throw an exception if any expectation was violated? Some conditions could be detected immediately (such as a method being called too many times, or with the wrong arguments), but some (such as a method not being called enough times) couldn't until the mock was asked to check what really happened against what was expected.

**Wouldn't it be nice** if the mock threw an Exception as soon as it knew it was being used in a way that wasn't desired? That would report the failure as close to the point of failure as possible, making it easier and faster to find and fix the problem.

**Wouldn't it be nice** if you had tools that made this easy and painless?

**Wouldn't it be nice** if you could do all that? Well, (as you might have guessed), you can indeed do all of that with the tools we'll be talking about in the remainder of this chapter.

## A COMMON EXAMPLE

In order to compare the different tools that we will explore in the remainder of this chapter we will adopt a common example that will be used in each section. The example we will use is derived from code in the MockObjects distribution. Specifically, we'll be using parts of the calculator example in the package com.mockobjects.examples.calcserver.

We will assume that the calculation engine has been developed and implements the following interface:

```
public interface IntCalculator {
    int calculate(int value1, int value2, String operation) throws CalculatorException;
}
```

The code we want to write takes an XML representation of a calculation and evaluates it using a concrete **Calculator**. The initial test case will pass the following XML string to an instance of **XmlCalculator** and verify the result (i.e., 2):

```
<calculate operation="/add">
  <argument>1</argument>
  <argument>1</argument>
</calculate>
```

There would, of course, need to be various other tests but this will suffice for the purpose of this chapter.

## THE MOCKOBJECTS FRAMEWORK

The MockObjects project[URL 23] is a generic framework whose goal is to facilitate developing programmer tests in the mock object style. Figure 7.4 shows a high-level view of the core of the framework. As we did with JUnit (see Chapter 4), we will look at each of these classes in turn, then show how to use them to create mocks.

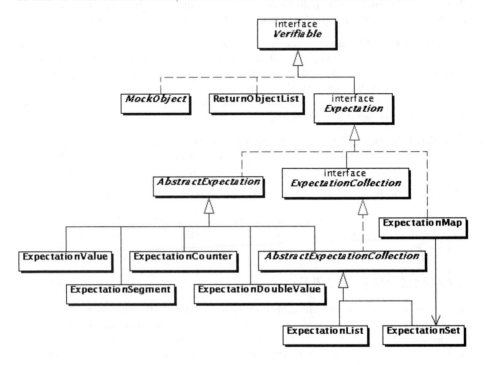

**Figure 7.4** High-level class diagram of com.mockobjects.

**Verifiable** provides an interface for classes that can be asked at the end of a test to confirm that the correct behavior occurred. As shown in the diagram, it is the root of the core of the framework.

**MockObject** is extended by mocks created with the framework. Its purpose is primarily to provide some convenience methods.

**ReturnObjectList** is used to contain an ordered sequence of objects that can be sequenced through. When the next object is requested, an assertion error will be thrown if there are no more objects. ReturnObjectList implements Verifiable and its verify() method throws an assertion error if there are any objects remaining.

This class can be used to manage a list of return values that are to be returned by successive calls to a given method in a mock.

**Expectation** is another interface that extends Verifiable. Its purpose is to provide an interface for classes that have the notion of expecting certain things to happen. The verify() method of an Expectation will check that the expectation was fulfilled.

The following classes are concrete implementations that embody specific types of expectations.

**AbstractExpectation** provides a superclass for specific kinds of expectations. Expectations can be named. There is also support for choosing when failure due to expectation violation occurs: either as soon as the actual situation is known (this is the default behavior) or when it is asked to verify.

**ExpectationValue** is used to set up a value expectation. When created, you set an expected value, and later (in response to calls by the class being tested) the actual value is set. Verification consists of checking for equality (using assertEquals()) of the expected and actual values.

This class is often used to capture expectations of argument values.

**ExpectationDoubleValue** is similar in purpose to ExpectationValue, except that it works with double values. The notable difference is that setExpected() takes an additional double argument that specifies the acceptable error when comparing the expected and actual double values.

**ExpectationSegment** is used for substring expectations. That is, you expect that the actual value contains a certain string.

Verification for this expectation checks that the expected string is a substring of the actual string.

**ExpectationCounter** lets you set up an expectation that something (e.g., a method call) should happen a specific number of times. You set it up with the expected count, increment it as required, and verify that the count was, in fact, as expected. If this expectation is set to fail immediately upon violation of the expectation, it will fail when incremented past the expected value.

**ExpectationCollection** provides an interface for classes that support multiple expected-actual value pairs.

Methods are defined to add expected and actual values, singly and in multiples as arrays, enumerations, and iterators.

**AbstractExpectationCollection** provides default implementations for the required methods (from the implemented interfaces). It also provides abstract accessors for the collections of expected and actual values.

**ExpectationList** is an implementation of AbstractExpectationCollection that uses two instances of ArrayList for storing expected and actual values. It is used when the order of the pairs is relevant.

**ExpectationSet** is another implementation of AbstractExpectationCollection that uses two instances of HashSet for storing expected and actual values. It is used when the order of the pairs is irrelevant.

**ExpectationMap** is used to manage expectations involving named or indexed values. It uses an ExpectationSet to manage the expected keys.

In addition to the mock framework, MockObject provides an extension to JUnit's Assert and TestCase classes. These were discussed in Chapter 5.

When you use mocks in your tests you will notice yourself working in a common pattern:

- create the mocks

- set state and expectations

- execute the code you are test-driving using the mocks

- have the mocks verify that expectations were met

If we look ahead at the example we can see this pattern. First, we create the mock:

```
MockCalculator mockCalculator = new MockCalculator();
```

Then we set expectations and state:

```
mockCalculator.setExpectedCalculation(1, 1, "/add");
mockCalculator.setupResult(2);
```

Then we execute our code using the mock (details omitted):

```
XmlCalculator xmlCalculator = new XmlCalculator(mockCalculator);
assertEquals("Bad simple add result", 2,
xmlCalculator.calculate(xmlString));
```

And finally have the mock verify its expectations:

```
mockCalculator.verify();
```

Let's return to our example. We need to use the MockObjects framework to write a mock for the calculator engine. Here it is, as it appears copied exactly from the examples package of the MockObjects distribution:

```
package com.saorsa.tddbook.samples.mockobjects;

import com.mockobjects.ExpectationValue;
import com.mockobjects.MockObject;

public class MockCalculator extends MockObject implements IntCalculator
{
  private int myResult;
  private ExpectationValue myValue1 = new ExpectationValue("value1");
  private ExpectationValue myValue2 = new ExpectationValue("value2");
  private ExpectationValue myOperation = new ExpectationValue("operation");

  public MockCalculator() {
    super();
  }
```

```
   public int calculate(int value1, int value2, String operation)
         throws CalculatorException {
     myValue1.setActual(value1);
     myValue2.setActual(value2);
     myOperation.setActual(operation);
     return myResult;
   }
   public void setExpectedCalculation(int value1, int value2, String operation) {
     myValue1.setExpected(value1);
     myValue2.setExpected(value2);
     myOperation.setExpected(operation);
   }
   public void setupResult(int result) {
     myResult = result;
   }

   public void verify() {
     myValue1.verify();
     myValue2.verify();
     myOperation.verify();
   }
 }
```

This mock used simple ExpectationValue instances to manage the pairs of expected and actual values. As such, it only supports a single call of the calculate() method.[3] Notice the general form:

- create an ExpectationValue for each parameter of the calculate() method

- have a variable to hold the return value

- have methods to set parameter expectations and return value

- have an implementation of the interface's method to set actual values and return the preset return value

- have a verify() method that has each Expectation verify itself

Now we can write our test case using this mock to drive the development of XmlCalculator:

```
package com.saorsa.tddbook.samples.mockobjects;

import junit.framework.TestCase;

public class TestXmlCalculator extends TestCase {

  public void testSimpleAdd() {
    MockCalculator mockCalculator = new MockCalculator();
    mockCalculator.setExpectedCalculation(1, 1, "/add");
    mockCalculator.setupResult(2);
```

---

[3]When we look at MockMaker in the next section we'll see a mock that can support multiple calls using the ExpectationCounter, ReturnValues, and ExpectationList classes.

```
XmlCalculator xmlCalculator = new XmlCalculator(mockCalculator);
String xmlString = "<calculate operation=\"/add\">" +
                   " <argument>1</argument>" +
                   " <argument>1</argument>" +
                   "</calculate>";

assertEquals("Bad simple add result", 2, xmlCalculator.calculate(xmlString));
mockCalculator.verify();
    }
}
```

## MOCKMAKER

MockMaker[URL 24] is a tool for creating mock classes from a given interface or class. MockMaker builds mock classes using the MockObjects framework.

Building mocks by hand using MockObjects is certainly better and easier than building them from scratch each time. It's still a fair bit of work. After you've built a few that way, you'll notice that they all look very much alike. They let a method be called some number of times, with specific parameters each time, returning specific values each time. The same folks who created the MockObjects framework have written a tool that automates this drudgery: MockMaker.

MockMaker takes an interface or class and creates a mock for it. We will take the example shown earlier and use MockMaker to create the mock. To keep things simple, we'll use MockMaker from the command line, as so:

```
$ java \
> -classpath bin:/usr/local/java/lib/MockMaker.jar \
> mockmaker.MockMaker \
> com.saorsa.tddbook.samples.mockobjects.IntCalculator \
> >src/com/saorsa/tddbook/samples/mockobjects/MockIntCalculator.java
```

This command results in the following in `MockIntCalculator.java`:[4]

```
package com.saorsa.tddbook.samples.mockobjects;

import mockmaker.ReturnValues;
import com.mockobjects.*;
import com.saorsa.tddbook.samples.mockobjects.IntCalculator;
import com.saorsa.tddbook.samples.mockobjects.CalculatorException;

public class MockIntCalculator implements IntCalculator {
```

---

[4] After adding a package statement, shortening the expectation names, and reformatting to make it fit on the page better.

```
    private ExpectationCounter myCalculateCalls =
            new ExpectationCounter("CalculateCalls");
    private ReturnValues myActualCalculateReturnValues =
            new ReturnValues(false);
    private ExpectationList myCalculateParameter0Values =
            new ExpectationList("CalculateParameter0Values");
    private ExpectationList myCalculateParameter1Values =
            new ExpectationList("CalculateParameter1Values");
    private ExpectationList myCalculateParameter2Values =
            new ExpectationList("CalculateParameter2Values");
    public void setExpectedCalculateCalls(int calls) {
      myCalculateCalls.setExpected(calls);
    }

    public void addExpectedCalculateValues(int arg0, int arg1, String arg2) {
      myCalculateParameter0Values.addExpected(new Integer(arg0));
      myCalculateParameter1Values.addExpected(new Integer(arg1));
      myCalculateParameter2Values.addExpected(arg2);
    }

    public int calculate(int arg0, int arg1, String arg2) throws CalculatorException {
      myCalculateCalls.inc();
      myCalculateParameter0Values.addActual(new Integer(arg0));
      myCalculateParameter1Values.addActual(new Integer(arg1));
      myCalculateParameter2Values.addActual(arg2);
      Object nextReturnValue = myActualCalculateReturnValues.getNext();
      return ((Integer) nextReturnValue).intValue();
    }

    public void setupCalculate(int arg) {
      myActualCalculateReturnValues.add(new Integer(arg));
    }

    public void verify() {
      myCalculateCalls.verify();
      myCalculateParameter0Values.verify();
      myCalculateParameter1Values.verify();
      myCalculateParameter2Values.verify();
    }
  }
```

Notice the differences between this and the mock in the previous section. This one supports an arbitrary number of method calls rather than a single call. This is more complex and uses a different approach to manage expectations about parameters and return values. Specifically:

- create an ExpectationCounter to count the number of method calls

- create an ExpectationList for each parameter

- create a ReturnValues to hold preset return values

- As before, we need methods to set expected parameter values and return values. An additional method is required to set the expected number of calls.

- We have a similar implementation of the interface's method to set the actuals and return an appropriate value.

- Also, we have a very similar verify() method.

Using this generated mock, our test would be written as so:

```
package com.saorsa.tddbook.samples.mockobjects;

import junit.framework.TestCase;

public class TestMockMakerXmlCalculator extends TestCase {


  public void testSimpleAdd() throws CalculatorException {
    MockIntCalculator mockCalculator = new MockIntCalculator();
    mockCalculator.addExpectedCalculateValues(1, 1, "/add");
    mockCalculator.setupCalculate(2);
    mockCalculator.setExpectedCalculateCalls(1);


    XmlCalculator xmlCalculator = new XmlCalculator(mockCalculator);
    String xmlString = "<calculate operation=\"/add\">"
              + " <argument>1</argument>"
              + " <argument>1</argument>"
              + "</calculate>";


    assertEquals("Bad simple add result", 2, xmlCalculator.calculate(xmlString));
    mockCalculator.verify();
  }
}
```

Since MockMaker generates a fairly general mock we can write more involved tests such as:

```
public void testComplexAdd() throws CalculatorException {
  MockIntCalculator mockCalculator = new MockIntCalculator();
  mockCalculator.addExpectedCalculateValues(1, 1, "/add");
  mockCalculator.setupCalculate(2);
  mockCalculator.addExpectedCalculateValues(2, 2, "/add");
  mockCalculator.setupCalculate(4);
  mockCalculator.setExpectedCalculateCalls(2);
```

```
    XmlCalculator xmlCalculator = new XmlCalculator(mockCalculator);
    String xmlString = "<calculate operation=\"/add\">"
                     + "  <argument>"
                     + "    <calculate operation=\"/add\">"
                     + "      <argument>1</argument>"
                     + "      <argument>1</argument>"
                     + "    </calculate>"
                     + "  </argument>"
                     + "  <argument>2</argument>"
                     + "</calculate>";
    assertEquals("Bad nested add result", 4, xmlCalculator.calculate(xmlString));
    mockCalculator.verify();
  }
```

One potential drawback of generating mocks by hand or with MockMaker is that you have another class that has to be managed. If the interface that is being mocked changes, the mock has to be changed or regenerated. The classes have to be stored, version controlled, packaged, etc. Next, we'll look at a MockObjects-based framework that gets around all of this in exchange for a few cycles at runtime.

## EASYMOCK

EasyMock[URL 25] is a framework for creating mock objects dynamically at runtime. It was written and is maintained by Tammo Freese, who presented it in a paper at XP2002[18].

Using EasyMock does, indeed, make things easier. We take the following test case from the MockMaker example in the previous section and rewrite it to use EasyMock. Then we'll look at how EasyMock is used in the example as well as some of its other capabilities.

```
public class TestEasyMockXmlCalculator extends TestCase {
  private MockControl control;
  private IntCalculator mockCalculator;

  protected void setUp() {
      control = EasyMock.controlFor(IntCalculator.class);
      mockCalculator = (IntCalculator)control.getMock();
  }
  public void testSimpleAdd() throws CalculatorException {
    mockCalculator.calculate(1, 1, "/add");
    control.setReturnValue(2);
    control.activate();

    XmlCalculator xmlCalculator = new XmlCalculator(mockCalculator);
    String xmlString = "<calculate operation=\"/add\">"
                     + "  <argument>1</argument>"
                     + "  <argument>1</argument>"
                     + "</calculate>";

    assertEquals("Bad simple add result", 2, xmlCalculator.calculate(xmlString));
    control.verify();
  }
```

```
public void testComplexAdd() throws CalculatorException {
  mockCalculator.calculate(1, 1, "/add");
  control.setReturnValue(2);
  mockCalculator.calculate(2, 2, "/add");
  control.setReturnValue(4);

  control.activate();

  XmlCalculator xmlCalculator = new XmlCalculator(mockCalculator);
  String xmlString = "<calculate operation=\"/add\">"
              + "  <argument>"
              + "    <calculate operation=\"/add\">"
              + "      <argument>1</argument>"
              + "      <argument>1</argument>"
              + "    </calculate>"
              + "  </argument>"
              + "  <argument>2</argument>"
              + "</calculate>";

  assertEquals("Bad nested add result", 4, xmlCalculator.calculate(xmlString));
  control.verify();
  }
}
```

## Basic Features

When creating a mock with EasyMock, you start by creating an instance of **MockControl** for the interface you want to mock. This is done with a call to a static factory method in the **EasyMock** class:

```
MockControl control = EasyMock.controlFor(IntCalculator.class);
```

The next step is to ask the control for a mock:

```
IntCalculator mockCalculator = (IntCalculator)control.getMock();
```

Now we can specify our expectations by using the newly created mock and the control. You set method call expectations by making the expected method call on the mock, with the expected arguments. For example:

```
mockCalculator.calculate(1, 1, "/add");
```

We can specify the result to be returned from this method call by using the control:

```
control.setReturnValue(2);
```

That's pretty much it. We continue this until our expectations have been specified. Then we make one more call to the control to switch the mock from specification mode to usage mode:

```
control.activate();
```

We then use the mock in our test as usual. At the end we ask the control to verify:

```
control.verify();
```

**Remember that we need to ask the control to verify the expectations, not the mock. This is a significant difference from working with hand-coded or MockMaker-generated mocks. Be sure to keep it in mind, especially if you're working with a mixture of the two.**

That's the basic idea. There are some additional capabilities we can take advantage of. If we set an expectation that a void method is to be called, then we can skip the step of setting the return value and it will be assumed to be void. If, however, we prefer to make that explicit, we can do so with the following instead of calling setReturnValue():

```
control.setVoidCallable();
```

## Advanced Features

So far, all of the expectations we've looked at simply specify the methods to be called, the expected arguments, and the value to return (or none if it's void). There are no expectations about how many times the method should be called. The only thing we set an expectation for is that it *will* be called. We can set an expectation about how many times a method is to be called by passing that number to the return-value-setting method of the control. For example, if we expected calculate(1, 1, "/add") to be called three times, returning 2 each time, we could use:

```
control.setReturnValue(2, 3);
```

The general form for a method that returns something is:

```
setReturnValue( <type> value, int count)
```

For a void method (i.e., no return value), we can use:

```
control.setVoidCallable(int count)
```

If more than the expected number of calls is made, an exception will be thrown on the first call that exceeds the expectation. If fewer than the expected number of calls are made, an exception will be thrown by the control when it is asked to verify the expectations. The following two examples show this.

First, an example of setting an expectation for two calls, and making three.

```
public void testTooManyCalls() throws CalculatorException {
    MockControl control = EasyMock.controlFor(IntCalculator.class);
    IntCalculator mockCalculator = (IntCalculator)control.getMock();
    mockCalculator.calculate(1, 1, "/add");
    control.setReturnValue(2, 2);
    control.activate();

    mockCalculator.calculate(1, 1, "/add");
    mockCalculator.calculate(1, 1, "/add");
    mockCalculator.calculate(1, 1, "/add");

    control.verify();
}
```

We get the following exception trace on the third call to **calculate()** (trimmed for clarity and space):

```
junit.framework.AssertionFailedError:
  EasyMock for interface
com.saorsa.tddbook.samples.mockobjects.IntCalculator:
method call calculate(1, 1, "/add"): calls expected: 2, received: 3
  at org.easymock.AbstractMockControl.invoke(AbstractMockControl.java:55)
  at $Proxy0.calculate(Unknown Source)
  at com.saorsa.tddbook.samples.mockobjects.TestEasyMockXmlCalculator
    .testTooManyCalls(TestEasyMockXmlCalculator.java:78)
```

The second example is of setting the same expectation (two calls) and only making one.

```
public void testTooManyCalls() throws CalculatorException {
    MockControl control = EasyMock.controlFor(IntCalculator.class);
    IntCalculator mockCalculator = (IntCalculator)control.getMock();
    mockCalculator.calculate(1, 1, "/add");
    control.setReturnValue(2, 2);
    control.activate();

    mockCalculator.calculate(1, 1, "/add");

    control.verify();
}
```

In this case we don't get the expectation until **verify()** is called:

```
junit.framework.AssertionFailedError:
    EasyMock for interface
    com.saorsa.tddbook.samples.mockobjects.IntCalculator:
    Expectation failure on verify:
method call calculate(1, 1, "/add"): calls expected: 2, received: 1
  at org.easymock.AbstractMockControl.verify(AbstractMockControl.java:45)
  at com.saorsa.tddbook.samples.mockobjects.TestEasyMockXmlCalculator
    .testNotEnoughCalls(TestEasyMockXmlCalculator.java:114)
```

Sometimes we will want a mock method to throw an exception when called rather than return a value. To do this, use setThrowable() rather than setVoidCallable() or setReturnValue(). Here's an example:

```
control.setThrowable(new RuntimeException());
```

Note that you can specify the number of expected calls as with setVoidCallable() and setReturnValue().

One nice feature of EasyMock is that after making the method call to set the expected arguments, you can make repeated calls to setVoidCallable(), setReturnValue(), and setThrowable() (with the count parameter) to specify behavior for each subsequent call. I don't have a good example from our Calculator code, but here's one from the EasyMock documentation:

```
mockRepository.getText("Text");
control.setReturnValue("The text you wanted", 2);
control.setThrowable(new RuntimeException(), 3);
control.setReturnValue("The text you really wanted");
```

Throwing an AssertionFailedError is the default behavior for methods in the mocked interface for which you haven't set an expectation, or methods called with arguments other than those set in an expectation. You can change the default for methods called with arguments other than those specified by using one of the following, after the expectation-setting call to the mock:

```
control.setDefaultReturnValue(<type> toBeReturned);
control.setDefaultThrowable(Throwable toBeThrown);
control.setDefaultVoidCallable()
```

To change the default behavior for methods for which you set no expectation, you can use a *nice control* for which the default behavior is to return the appropriate null value (i.e., 0, null, or false). We get a nice control by using the following factory method in EasyMock:

```
MockControl control = EasyMock.niceControlFor(AnInterface);
```

## EasyMock Summary

One very important advantage of EasyMock is that the mock is specified in the test. This means that the mock is tightly bound to the test it serves.

There are some downsides to using EasyMock, though:

1. There's a performance hit that you take at runtime. It takes some time to build the mock on the fly. As you specify the mock, you not only specify what methods are mocked, but also the expectations. This rolls two steps into one. This makes the mocks easier to build and more localized, but means that unique mocks need to be built for each test, since each test will have different expectations to verify.

2. You are limited to the mocks as EasyMock creates them. When you handcraft mocks or use MockMaker you can tweak the mock as required.

3. Not being able to tune expectations may lead to over-specification in tests. There may be cases where you only really want to test one parameter. If you are hand-coding you just write an expectation-setting method that does just that. If you are using MockMaker you can tweak the generated methods, or add what you need. With EasyMock you are stuck with expectations fully specifying exactly the methods in the interface being mocked.

4. EasyMock-generated mocks are passive: you specify expected calls and provide return values. There is no way to have the mock make calls into your objects. This generally isn't a problem. When it is, use MockMaker or build it by hand.

5. You can only mock interfaces with EasyMock whereas MockMaker will generate mocks for classes as well. This can be an issue if you are creating mocks for legacy code that wasn't designed in an interface-centric way.

6. EasyMock only works with Java 1.3.1 or later due to its reliance on new classes in the java.lang.reflect package, specifically InvocationHandler and Proxy.

## SUMMARY

Mock objects can, indeed, provide a way to achieve the three goals that were defined at the beginning of this chapter, namely:

- focused tests

- independent tests, and

- fast tests.

We looked at several reasons for using mocks, and the tradeoffs of four different mocking techniques: coding them from scratch by hand, coding them by hand using the MockObjects framework, stubbing them out using MockMaker, and finally automatically creating them (most easily, but with the biggest performance hit and most constraints) using EasyMock.

Mock objects are a fairly young concept. New tools and techniques are continually being developed. EasyMock is one of the recent developments in this area. It makes it fast, easy, and cheap to take full advantage of mocks. There are no extra classes to create and maintain, and the mock-related code is part of the test which uses it. We will use EasyMock extensively in our approach to test-driving user interfaces later in this book.

There are still cases where you might want to build a mock class by hand (likely using the MockObjects framework). Even then you can get a head start by using a tool like MockMaker to generate the skeletal mock class for you. You can then add custom behavior.

I'll close this chapter with a slight warning: Mocks are great, and can be invaluable at times, but don't overuse them or become overly reliant on them. They are but one tool in our bag of tricks, and we have many others.

## Stubs, Fakes, and Mocks

I've talked about *Mocks* in this chapter. Technically, there are three concepts that are commonly referred to as *mocks*:

**Stubs** A class with methods that do nothing. They simply are there to allow the system to compile and run.

**Fakes** A class with methods that return a fixed value or values that can either be hardcoded or set programmatically.

**Mocks** A class in which you can set expectations regarding what methods are calls, with what parameters, how often, etc. You can also set return values for various calling situations. A mock will also provide a way to verify that the expectations were met.

# Chapter 8

# DEVELOPING A GUI TEST-FIRST

Using TDD to develop the Graphical User Interface (GUI) of an application is tricky. Part of the problem is that GUIs are, by definition, graphical. In this chapter we look at ways to test GUI components programmatically, and ways to minimize what is required.

There are several approaches that can be taken when developing the GUI test-first. We will illustrate them using the same approach we used in Chapter 7: define a common example and apply each approach to it.

## THE EXAMPLE

The example we will be working with in this chapter will be the first bit of GUI for the project we'll be working through later in the book. Specifically, we need a GUI to a movie list with the ability to add new movies.

First, we'll brainstorm and decide what it should look like. We need the following components:

1. a list of movies

2. a text field in which to enter the name of a new movie

3. a button to indicate that we would like to add the movie we entered in the text field.

The result of this brainstorming is the sketch shown in Figure 8.1.

We're intentionally limiting ourselves to a very simple GUI example in this chapter—only what suffices to explore techniques for developing GUIs test-first. In later chapters we will see these techniques applied to the development of more elaborate interfaces.

For the purposes of the examples we will assume that this is the interface that we use to create a mock to which the GUI class talks:

```
public interface MovieListEditor {
  Vector getMovies();
  void add(String string);
  void delete(int i);
}
```

We'll examine several alternative approaches, starting with the simpler ones and moving to the more elegant, flexible ones. We'll end the survey by considering the alternative which we'll make use of later in the book.

**Figure 8.1** GUI sketch.

## THE AWT ROBOT

Though for our purposes it is unworkable, the AWT Robot approach does deserve mention, if for no other reason than it's often mentioned when people talk about testing GUIs.

The **Robot** is for programmatically feeding key and mouse events to an application. The problem is that it deals with pixel locations, not components. This is at the wrong level for automated programmer tests. Future changes to the production GUI code could too easily break our test code. **Robot** could be used for automating customer tests, though. It could be used either programmatically or using a capture and replay approach.

That's it for **Robot**.

## BRUTE FORCE

The first approach we will explore is to give our tests direct access to the visual components in the GUI. We can do this in one of several ways:

1. make them public instance variables so that the test can access them directly

2. provide an accessor for each component so that the test can get hold of them

3. make the test class an inner class of the class that creates the GUI

4. use reflection to gain access to the components

All of these approaches have the drawback that the components cannot be local to a method; they must be instance variables. Also, all but the last require extra production code that is used only for testing.

Since I learned Object Oriented Programming in a Smalltalk environment, I find the idea of making instance variables public unthinkable. This rules out option one. Also, I like to keep my test code separate from production code, so I avoid option three as well. The last option is very overhead intensive to do *manually*. We'll explore some frameworks later in this chapter that make use of reflection, but hide the details.

That leaves the second approach: adding accessors for the components.

Keep in mind that the code was developed incrementally: enough new test to fail, followed by enough new code to pass. During development, both the code and the tests were refactored as needed. Notice how the tests are in two TestCase classes. Notice the different setUp() methods.

---

As we discuss more fully in the JUnit chapter, TestCase is a mechanism to group tests that rely on the same fixture, not tests that happen to use the same class. When we need a different fixture, we should create a new TestCase class. As you add tests, add them to the TestCase that maintains the fixture that they require.

---

Given that preamble, here's the test code. First we have a TestCase that verifies that the required components are present. Notice how we've used EasyMock. For this test we aren't concerned with the interaction of the GUI with the underlying object (i.e., the mock) so we've used niceControlFor() which provides default implementations for all of the methods in MovieListEditor.

```
public class TestWidgets extends TestCase {
  private MockControl control;
  private MovieListEditor mockEditor;
  private MovieListWindow window;


  protected void setUp() {
    control = EasyMock.niceControlFor(MovieListEditor.class);
    mockEditor = (MovieListEditor) control.getMock();
    control.activate();
    window = new MovieListWindow(mockEditor);
    window.init();
    window.show();
  }

  public void testList() {
    JList movieList = window.getMovieList();
    assertNotNull("Movie list should be non null", movieList);
    assertTrue("Movie list should be showing", movieList.isShowing());
  }

  public void testField() {
    JTextField movieField = window.getMovieField();
    assertNotNull("Movie field should be non null", movieField);
    assertTrue("Movie field should be showing", movieField.isShowing());
  }
```

```java
public void testAddButton() {
  JButton addButton = window.getAddButton();
  assertNotNull("Add button should be non null", addButton);
  assertTrue("Add button should be showing", addButton.isShowing());
  assertEquals("Add button should be labeled \"Add\"",
               "Add",
               addButton.getText());
}

public void testDeleteButton() {
  JButton deleteButton = window.getDeleteButton();
  assertNotNull("Delete button should be non null", deleteButton);
  assertTrue("Delete button should be showing", deleteButton.isShowing());
  assertEquals("Delete button should be labeled \"Delete\"",
               "Delete",
               deleteButton.getText());
}
}
```

The other TestCase tests for correct operation of the GUI and uses a more involved
mock. Here we build the mock in each test method, setting different method call
expectations and return values in each. Note, however, the common mock creation
code in setUp().

```java
public class TestOperation extends TestCase {
  private static final String LOST_IN_SPACE = "Lost In Space";
  private Vector movieNames;
  private MovieListWindow window;
  private MockControl control = null;
  private MovieListEditor mockEditor = null;


  protected void setUp() {
    movieNames = new Vector() {
      { add("Star Wars"); add("Star Trek"); add("Stargate"); }
    };
    window = null;

    MockControl control = EasyMock.controlFor(MovieListEditor.class);
    MovieListEditor mockEditor = (MovieListEditor) control.getMock();
  }
  public void testMovieList() {
    mockEditor.getMovies();
    control.setReturnValue(movieNames, 1);

    control.activate();

    MovieListWindow window = new MovieListWindow(mockEditor);
    window.init();
    window.show();
```

```
      JList movieList = window.getMovieList();
      ListModel movieListModel = movieList.getModel();
      assertEquals("Movie list is the wrong size",
                   movieNames.size(),
                   movieListModel.getSize());

      for (int i = 0; i < movieNames.size(); i++) {
        assertEquals("Movie list contains bad name",
                     movieNames.get(i),
                     movieListModel.getElementAt(i));
      }

      control.verify();
    }
    public void testAdd() {
      Vector movieNamesWithAddition = new Vector(movieNames);
      movieNamesWithAddition.add(LOST_IN_SPACE);

      mockEditor.getMovies();
      control.setReturnValue(movieNames, 1);

      mockEditor.add(LOST_IN_SPACE);
      control.setVoidCallable(1);

      mockEditor.getMovies();
      control.setReturnValue(movieNamesWithAddition, 1);

      control.activate();

      MovieListWindow window = new MovieListWindow(mockEditor);
      window.init();
      window.show();

      JTextField movieField = window.getMovieField();
      movieField.setText(LOST_IN_SPACE);

      JButton addButton = window.getAddButton();
      addButton.doClick();

      JList movieList = window.getMovieList();
      ListModel movieListModel = movieList.getModel();
      assertEquals("Movie list is the wrong size after add",
                   movieNamesWithAddition.size(),
                   movieListModel.getSize());

      assertEquals("Movie list doesn't contain new name",
                   LOST_IN_SPACE,
                   movieListModel.getElementAt(movieNames.size()));

      control.verify();
    }
    public void testDelete() {
      Vector movieNamesWithDeletion = new Vector(movieNames);
      movieNamesWithDeletion.remove(1);
```

```
            mockEditor.getMovies();
            control.setReturnValue(movieNames, 1);

            mockEditor.delete(1);
            control.setVoidCallable(1);

            mockEditor.getMovies();
            control.setReturnValue(movieNamesWithDeletion, 1);

            control.activate();

            MovieListWindow window = new MovieListWindow(mockEditor);
            window.init();
            window.show();

            JList movieList = window.getMovieList();
            movieList.setSelectedIndex(1);

            JButton deleteButton = window.getDeleteButton();
            deleteButton.doClick();

            ListModel movieListModel = movieList.getModel();
            assertEquals("Movie list is the wrong size after delete",
                        movieNamesWithDeletion.size(),
                        movieListModel.getSize());

            control.verify();
        }
    }
```

The GUI class is below, with a screen shot of the resulting window shown in Figure 8.2.

```
    public class MovieListWindow extends JFrame {
        private JList movieList;
        private JButton addButton;
        private MovieListEditor myEditor;
        private JTextField movieField;
        private JButton deleteButton;

        public MovieListWindow(MovieListEditor anEditor) {
            super();
            myEditor = anEditor;
        }
        public JList getMovieList() {
            return movieList;
        }
        public JTextField getMovieField() {
            return movieField;
        }
        public JButton getAddButton() {
            return addButton;
        }
```

```java
    public JButton getDeleteButton() {
      return deleteButton;
    }

    public void init() {
      setLayout();
      initMovieList();
      initMovieField();
      initAddButton();
      initDeleteButton();
      pack();
    }

    private void setLayout() {
      getContentPane().setLayout(new FlowLayout());
    }

    private void initMovieList() {
      movieList = new JList(getMovies());
      JScrollPane scroller = new JScrollPane(movieList);
      getContentPane().add(scroller);
    }

    private void initMovieField() {
      movieField = new JTextField(16);
      getContentPane().add(movieField);
    }

    private void initAddButton() {
      addButton = new JButton("Add");
      addButton.addActionListener(new ActionListener() {
        public void actionPerformed(ActionEvent e) {
          myEditor.add(movieField.getText());
          movieList.setListData(getMovies());
        }
      });
      getContentPane().add(addButton);
    }

    private void initDeleteButton() {
      deleteButton = new JButton("Delete");
      deleteButton.addActionListener(new ActionListener() {
        public void actionPerformed(ActionEvent e) {
          myEditor.delete(movieList.getSelectedIndex());
          movieList.setListData(getMovies());
        }
      });
      getContentPane().add(deleteButton);
    }
```

```
private Vector getMovies() {
  Vector movies = myEditor.getMovies();
  return (movies == null) ? new Vector() : movies;
}
}
```

**Figure 8.2** The resulting GUI.

## JFCUNIT

Now let's try a similar but more elegant solution that doesn't require us to explicitly make the GUI class internals (components) accessible. JFCUnit also takes care of the threading issues involved with testing Swing code that is driven by events that are processed by the AWT thread. It automatically blocks the AWT thread while each test is run and unblocks it afterwards. As well, by calling **awtSleep()**, JFCUnit gives you the ability to unblock the AWT thread within a test and allows it to process any events that the test has placed in the queue. Once all events have been processed, the AWT thread is again blocked and your test continues. One way or another, control is given back to the test (and the AWT thread is blocked) after a specified period of time. You can set this period of time using the **setSleepTime()** method.

JFCUnit also provides a helper class named, aptly, **JFCTestHelper**. This class provides a variety of methods you can use to find various parts of the GUI being tested, to track what windows are open, and to clean up any open/showing windows.

### The JFCUnit API

Let's have a look at the APIs for these classes before tackling the example. These are the two main classes that provide you with the functionality required to test Swing

GUIs. There are also an assortment of support classes for encapsulating event data that we will use in conjunction with the methods below.

## junit.extensions.jfcunit.JFCTestCase

Here's the API that you have access to by virtue of extending JFCTestCase.

**awtSleep()** suspends the test, for no longer than the specified sleep time (the default or that set by setSleepTime()), allowing the AWT thread to run and process UI events that are in its queue.

**awtSleep(long sleepTime)** is equivalent to calling setSleepTime(sleepTime) followed by awtSleep(). This means that subsequent calls to awtSleep() will use sleepTime as the maximum sleep time.

**resetSleepTime()** resets the awtSleep() maximum sleep time to the default.

**setSleepTime(long time)** sets the maximum time (in milliseconds) for which awtSleep() will sleep.

**sleep(long delay)** suspends the test for *at least* delay milliseconds, allowing the AWT thread to run.

## junit.extensions.jfcunit.JFCTestHelper

We generally want to create an instance of JFCTestHelper in the JFCTestCase's setUp() method since it will typically be needed in all tests. The major methods of JFCTest Helper are listed below. Consult the JFCUnit documentation for details.

**cleanUp()** can be used in the tearDown() method to close and dispose of any windows left open when a test fails partway through.

**disposeWindow()** can be used to destroy a window.

**enterClickAndLeave()** generates appropriate events to click on a component.

**enterDragAndLeave()** generates appropriate events to drag and drop a component.

**enterDropDownClickAndLeave()** generates appropriate events to make a selection from a combo box.

**enterJListClickAndLeave()** generates appropriate events to make a selection from a list.

**findComponent()** finds a specific type of component.

**findNamedComponent()** finds a component with a specific name.

**getMessageFromJDialog()** gets the message displayed in a dialog box.

**getShowingDialogs()** gets all visible dialogs, using various selection criteria.

**getShowingJFileChooser()** finds a FileChooser being shown by a specific window.

**getShowingJFileChoosers()** finds all FileChoosers being shown by a specific window.

**getWindow()** gets a window that is showing and has a specific title.

**getWindows()** gets all currently visible windows, with various selection criteria.

**sendKeyAction()** sends KeyPressed, KeyTyped, and KeyReleased events to a component.

**sendString()** sends a series of key events to a component to simulate the typing in of a string.

## Tackling the Example

Our test classes aren't too different with JFCUnit than without it. The main differences are in how we access the GUI components. Using JFCUnit we don't need direct access to them. Instead, we use the **JFCTestHelper** class to find them for us. Since the GUI is simple, we have only a single instance of some classes of components (i.e., one list, and one field) so we can find them by class and not worry about naming them. To find the buttons we can either request all the buttons and search the resulting collection for the instance we want, or we can name them. Here, we'll do the latter. Note that the search-based approach can be a better solution if we are adding tests to an existing GUI for which we don't have (or can't change) the source code (and hence, don't know or can't set the widget names).

```java
public class TestWidgets extends JFCTestCase {
  private JFCTestHelper helper;
  private MockControl control;
  private MovieListEditor mockEditor;
  private Window window;

  protected void setUp() throws Exception {
    super.setUp();
    helper = new JFCTestHelper();
    control = EasyMock.niceControlFor(MovieListEditor.class);
    mockEditor = (MovieListEditor) control.getMock();
    control.activate();
    MovieListWindow.start(mockEditor);
    window = helper.getWindow("Movie List");
  }

  protected void tearDown() throws Exception {
    super.tearDown();
    helper.cleanUp(this);
  }

  public void testList() {
    JList movieList = (JList)helper.findComponent(JList.class, window, 0);
    assertNotNull("Movie list should be non null", movieList);
    assertTrue("Movie list should be showing", movieList.isShowing());
  }

  public void testField() {
    JTextField movieField =
    (JTextField)helper.findComponent(JTextField.class,
                            window,
                            0);
    assertNotNull("Movie field should be non null", movieField);
    assertTrue("Movie field should be showing", movieField.isShowing());
  }
```

```
    public void testAddButton() {
      JButton addButton =
 (JButton)helper.findNamedComponent("addButton",
                                    window,
                                    0);

     assertNotNull("Add button should be non null", addButton);
     assertTrue("Add button should be showing", addButton.isShowing());
     assertEquals("Add button should be labeled \"Add\"",
                  "Add",
                  addButton.getText());


    }
    public void testDeleteButton() {
      JButton deleteButton =
 (JButton)helper.findNamedComponent("deleteButton",
                                    window,
                                    0);

     assertNotNull("Delete button should be non null", deleteButton);
     assertTrue("Delete button should be showing", deleteButton.isShowing());
     assertEquals("Delete button should be labeled \"Delete\"",
                  "Delete",
                  deleteButton.getText());


    }
  }
```

There are more differences in the TestOperation class. Notice how we are now manipulating the GUI components at a higher level by providing events to them, rather than directly manipulating their internal state.

```
  public class TestOperation extends JFCTestCase {
    private static final String LOST_IN_SPACE = "Lost In Space";
    private Vector movieNames = null;
    private Window window = null;

    private JFCTestHelper helper;

    protected void setUp() throws Exception {
      super.setUp();
      helper = new JFCTestHelper();
      movieNames = new Vector() {
        { add("Star Wars"); add("Star Trek"); add("Stargate"); }
      };
    }

    protected void tearDown() throws Exception {
      super.tearDown();
      helper.cleanUp(this);
    }
```

```
public void testMovieList() throws JFCTestException {
  MockControl control = EasyMock.controlFor(MovieListEditor.class);
  MovieListEditor mockEditor = (MovieListEditor) control.getMock();

  mockEditor.getMovies();
  control.setReturnValue(movieNames, 1);

  control.activate();

  MovieListWindow.start(mockEditor);
  window = helper.getWindow("Movie List");

  JList movieList = (JList)helper.findComponent(JList.class, window, 0);
  ListModel movieListModel = movieList.getModel();
  assertEquals("Movie list is the wrong size",
               movieNames.size(),
               movieListModel.getSize());

  for (int i = 0; i < movieNames.size(); i++) {
    assertEquals("Movie list contains bad name",
                 movieNames.get(i),
                 movieListModel.getElementAt(i));
  }

  control.verify();
}
public void testAdd() throws JFCTestException, Exception {
  Vector movieNamesWithAddition = new Vector(movieNames);
  movieNamesWithAddition.add(LOST_IN_SPACE);
  MockControl control = EasyMock.controlFor(MovieListEditor.class);
  MovieListEditor mockEditor = (MovieListEditor) control.getMock();

  mockEditor.getMovies();
  control.setReturnValue(movieNames, 1);

  mockEditor.add(LOST_IN_SPACE);
  control.setVoidCallable(1);

  mockEditor.getMovies();
  control.setReturnValue(movieNamesWithAddition, 1);

  control.activate();

  MovieListWindow.start(mockEditor);
  window = helper.getWindow("Movie List");

  JTextField movieField =
  (JTextField)helper.findComponent(JTextField.class,
                                   window,
                                   0);

  movieField.requestFocus();
  helper.sendString(this, movieField, LOST_IN_SPACE);
```

```
        JButton addButton =
        (JButton)helper.findNamedComponent("addButton",
                                    window,
                                    0);
        addButton.doClick();

        JList movieList = (JList)helper.findComponent(JList.class, window, 0);
        ListModel movieListModel = movieList.getModel();
        assertEquals("Movie list is the wrong size after add",
                movieNamesWithAddition.size(),
                movieListModel.getSize());

        assertEquals("Movie list doesn't contain new name",
                LOST_IN_SPACE,
                movieListModel.getElementAt(movieNames.size()));

      control.verify();
    }
    public void testDelete() throws JFCTestException, Exception {
      Vector movieNamesWithDeletion = new Vector(movieNames);
      movieNamesWithDeletion.remove(1);

      MockControl control = EasyMock.controlFor(MovieListEditor.class);
      MovieListEditor mockEditor = (MovieListEditor) control.getMock();

      mockEditor.getMovies();
      control.setReturnValue(movieNames, 1);

      mockEditor.delete(1);
      control.setVoidCallable(1);

      mockEditor.getMovies();
      control.setReturnValue(movieNamesWithDeletion, 1);

      control.activate();

      MovieListWindow.start(mockEditor);
      window = helper.getWindow("Movie List");

      JList movieList = (JList)helper.findComponent(JList.class, window, 0);
      movieList.setSelectedIndex(1);

      JButton deleteButton =
      (JButton)helper.findNamedComponent("deleteButton",
                                    window,
                                    0);
      deleteButton.doClick();

      ListModel movieListModel = movieList.getModel();
      assertEquals("Movie list is the wrong size after delete",
                movieNamesWithDeletion.size(),
                movieListModel.getSize());

      control.verify();
    }
  }
```

Finally, here's the GUI class. It is almost identical to what we had before, except for the component access methods that we don't need.

```java
package com.saorsa.tddbook.samples.gui.jfcunit;

import java.awt.FlowLayout;
import java.awt.event.ActionEvent;
import java.awt.event.ActionListener;
import java.util.Vector;
import javax.swing.*;


public class MovieListWindow extends JFrame {
  private MovieListEditor myEditor = null;
  private JList movieList = null;
  private JTextField movieField = null;

  public MovieListWindow(MovieListEditor anEditor) {
    super();
    myEditor = anEditor;
  }

  public void init() {
    setTitle("Movie List");
    setLayout();
    initMovieList();
    initMovieField();
    initAddButton();
    initDeleteButton();
    pack();
  }

  private void setLayout() {
    getContentPane().setLayout(new FlowLayout());
  }

  private void initMovieList() {
    movieList = new JList(getMovies());
    JScrollPane scroller = new JScrollPane(movieList);
    getContentPane().add(scroller);
  }

  private void initMovieField() {
    movieField = new JTextField(16);
    getContentPane().add(movieField);
  }
```

```
private void initAddButton() {
  JButton addButton = new JButton("Add");
  addButton.setName("addButton");
  addButton.addActionListener(new ActionListener() {
    public void actionPerformed(ActionEvent e) {
      myEditor.add(movieField.getText());
      movieList.setListData(getMovies());
    }
  });
  getContentPane().add(addButton);
}

private void initDeleteButton() {
  JButton deleteButton = new JButton("Delete");
  deleteButton.setName("deleteButton");
  deleteButton.addActionListener(new ActionListener() {
    public void actionPerformed(ActionEvent e) {
      myEditor.delete(movieList.getSelectedIndex());
      movieList.setListData(getMovies());
    }
  });
  getContentPane().add(deleteButton);
}

private Vector getMovies() {
  Vector movies = myEditor.getMovies();
  return (movies == null) ? new Vector() : movies;
}

public static void start(MovieListEditor anEditor) {
  MovieListWindow window = new MovieListWindow(anEditor);
  window.init();
  window.show();
}
}
```

# JEMMY

Jemmy is from the NetBeans world where it takes the form of a module that plugs into the NetBeans platform. The developers of Jemmy made a wise decision and made Jemmy capable of being used in a stand-alone fashion, independent of NetBeans. In fact, Jemmy can be used directly from a standard JUnit TestCase. We'll look at how Jemmy is structured and used, then put it into practice in our example.

## How it works

Jemmy works a bit differently than JFCUnit. Using Jemmy, you create *operators* that wrap a corresponding Swing object.

Each component in the Swing API has a corresponding Operator class in the Jemmy API.

Before creating operators for individual components, you should create one for the main window of the GUI you are testing, for example:

JFrameOperator mainWindow = new JFrameOperator("Movie List");

Now, to find the *Add* button from the example, we create a JButtonOperator in the window we found with a specific label text:

JButtonOperator addButton = new JButtonOperator(mainWindow, "Add");

For most operators there are a variety of constructors. Using JButtonOperator as an example, we'll look at them below. With the exception of the first case, all constructors have an initial parameter that is the operator for a parent (recursively) container (e.g., the main window JFrame).

**JButtonOperator(JButton b)**  creates an operator that wraps the given JButton.

**JButtonOperator(ContainerOperator cont, ComponentChooser chooser, int index)** searches through all JButtons contained by cont, filtering them using chooser, and creates an operator for the index$^{th}$ one (zero based) that is found.

**JButtonOperator(ContainerOperator cont, ComponentChooser chooser)** searches through JButtons contained by cont, filtering them using chooser, and creates an operator for the first one found.

**JButtonOperator(ContainerOperator cont, String text, int index)** searches through all JButtons contained by cont and creates an operator for the index$^{th}$ one (zero based) that has text as its label text.

**JButtonOperator(ContainerOperator cont, String text)** searches through all JButtons contained by cont and creates an operator for the first one that has text as its label text.

**JButtonOperator(ContainerOperator cont, int index)** creates an operator for the index$^{th}$ one (zero based) JButton contained by cont

**JButtonOperator(ContainerOperator cont)**  creates an operator for the first JButton contained by cont

One approach that's useful when we are test-driving a GUI is to give every component a unique name (using setName()). Then we can use a ComponentChooser that searches for a given name. The chooser will look something like:

```
public class NameBasedChooser implements ComponentChooser {
  private String name;

  public NameBasedChooser(String componentName) {
    name = componentName;
  }

  public boolean checkComponent(Component aComponent) {
    String theName = aComponent.getName();
    return (theName != null) && theName.equals(name);
  }
```

```
    public String getDescription() {
      return "Matches Components named \"" + name + "\"";
    }
}
```

Here's an example of how we can use it:

```
JListOperator movieList =
        new JListOperator(mainWindow, new NameBasedChooser("movieList"));
```

As you can see, the work of finding components is done in the Jemmy operator constructors. A result of this is that our test code is very clean... a single line of overhead for each component we want to use. Additionally, the operator constructors throw TimeoutExpiredException if the requested component cannot be found in a reasonable period of time. JUnit will catch these and fail if they are thrown. This means that we don't need to verify that the desired component was found as we did in JFCUnit. This simplifies our tests even more.

Once we have operators for the components we need to use, we can use those operators to access and manipulate those components. Each operator provides methods that match those of the wrapped component and forwards calls as appropriate.

Although simple to use, the Jemmy API is large and involved. To make it easier to learn and use, there are a few simple ideas to keep in mind:

- Find components by constructing an appropriate operator with the information required to find what you need.

- Operator constructors throw an exception that will cause the test to fail if a required component isn't present, so you don't need to check the result.

- Most component methods are present in the operators and are forwarded through to the component.

---

The application being accessed through Jemmy has to be run in the same JVM as the code that uses Jemmy. One way to accomplish this is to launch the GUI being tested in the setUp() method.

---

## The Example

Rather than go through the same exercise again with Jemmy, since it is quite similar to the JFCUnit example, I will simply present the Jemmy-based tests that result in the comparable UI code.

```
public class TestOperation extends TestCase {

    private static final String LOST_IN_SPACE = "Lost In Space";
    private Vector movieNames = null;
    private JFrameOperator mainWindow = null;
```

```java
protected void setUp() throws Exception {
  super.setUp();
  movieNames = new Vector();
  movieNames.add("Star Wars");
  movieNames.add("Star Trek");
  movieNames.add("Stargate");
}

protected void tearDown() throws Exception {
  super.tearDown();
  mainWindow.dispose();
}

public void testMovieList() {
  MockControl control = EasyMock.controlFor(MovieListEditor.class);
  MovieListEditor mockEditor = (MovieListEditor) control.getMock();

  mockEditor.getMovies();
  control.setReturnValue(movieNames, 1);

  control.activate();

  MovieListWindow.start(mockEditor);
  mainWindow = new JFrameOperator("Movie List");

  JListOperator movieList = new JListOperator(mainWindow);
  ListModel movieListModel = movieList.getModel();
  assertEquals("Movie list is the wrong size",
               movieNames.size(),
               movieListModel.getSize());

  for (int i = 0; i < movieNames.size(); i++) {
    assertEquals("Movie list contains bad name",
                 movieNames.get(i),
                 movieListModel.getElementAt(i));
  }

  control.verify();
}

public void testAdd() {

  Vector movieNamesWithAddition = new Vector(movieNames);
  movieNamesWithAddition.add(LOST_IN_SPACE);
  MockControl control = EasyMock.controlFor(MovieListEditor.class);
  MovieListEditor mockEditor = (MovieListEditor) control.getMock();

  mockEditor.getMovies();
  control.setReturnValue(movieNames, 1);

  mockEditor.add(LOST_IN_SPACE);
  control.setVoidCallable(1);

  mockEditor.getMovies();
  control.setReturnValue(movieNamesWithAddition, 1);

  control.activate();

  MovieListWindow.start(mockEditor);
  mainWindow = new JFrameOperator("Movie List");
```

```
JTextFieldOperator movieField = new JTextFieldOperator(mainWindow);
movieField.enterText(LOST_IN_SPACE);

JButtonOperator addButton = new JButtonOperator(mainWindow, "Add");
addButton.doClick();

JListOperator movieList = new JListOperator(mainWindow);
ListModel movieListModel = movieList.getModel();
assertEquals("Movie list is the wrong size after add",
             movieNamesWithAddition.size(),
             movieListModel.getSize());

assertEquals("Movie list doesn't contain new name",
             LOST_IN_SPACE,
             movieListModel.getElementAt(movieNames.size()));

control.verify();
}
public void testDelete() {
  Vector movieNamesWithDeletion = new Vector(movieNames);
  movieNamesWithDeletion.remove(1);

  MockControl control = EasyMock.controlFor(MovieListEditor.class);
  MovieListEditor mockEditor = (MovieListEditor) control.getMock();

  mockEditor.getMovies();
  control.setReturnValue(movieNames, 1);

  mockEditor.delete(1);
  control.setVoidCallable(1);

  mockEditor.getMovies();
  control.setReturnValue(movieNamesWithDeletion, 1);

  control.activate();

  MovieListWindow.start(mockEditor);
  mainWindow = new JFrameOperator("Movie List");

  JListOperator movieList = new JListOperator(mainWindow);
  movieList.clickOnItem(1, 1);

  JButtonOperator deleteButton = new JButtonOperator(mainWindow, "Delete");
  deleteButton.doClick();

  ListModel movieListModel = movieList.getModel();
  assertEquals("Movie list is the wrong size after delete",
               movieNamesWithDeletion.size(),
               movieListModel.getSize());

  control.verify();
  }
}
```

Let's have a look at Figure 8.3: testAdd() in operation. It shows the typical sequence of a Jemmy-based test:

1. Open the application window being tested.

2. Create the top level JFrameOperator.

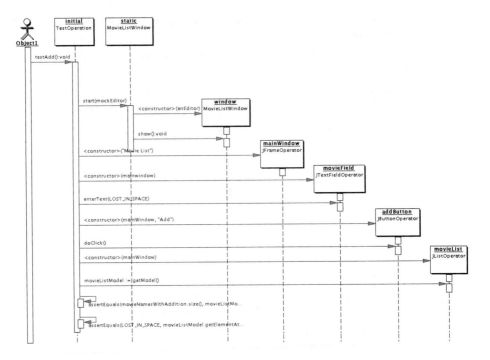

**Figure 8.3** Sequence diagram for the Jemmy part of testing add().

3. Create operators for the fields involved in the test, manipulating them as required (entering text, making selections, etc.) to set the required state.

4. Create operators for the required command component(s), in this case, a **JButton**.

5. Perform the action, e.g., clicking on the button.

6. Check the results.

## ULTRA-THIN GUI

When you practice TDD, you generally end up with your model well-encapsulated. When you get around to adding a GUI, you find that all you need are components that make calls into the model... exactly what the rules of good OO design tell you you should have. This makes test-driven development of the GUI either trivial or beside the point.

   This is the traditional approach to dealing with the GUI in a TDD context. It is still a fairly valid option. If you make the GUI as thin as possible, then user interaction simply delegates to a domain object and other components simply provide a getter/setter to get/set their value. All the action happens in the domain objects. There is no logic in the GUI and so nothing that needs testing. The domain class can be tested (through TDD) as any other. In fact, it should be already.

   We can combine this approach with one of the previous ones to put functional tests in place for the GUI as well. You could mock the domain class that responds to and controls the GUI to behave in a specific way, although you will need to use more than EasyMock since the user action handlers will almost always need to query or control the GUI components. Recall that mocks generated using EasyMock are passive. They can not do anything other than maintain and verify expectations and provide return values. To mock the domain classes you will need to have the mock query and/or manipulate the appropriate components in response to user action (e.g., clicking the *Add* button calls **add()** in the model which should query the data fields, and update the listbox).

One way to approach this is to use what Mike Feathers has called *making a humble dialog*[14].

We'll have a closer look at this method, for several reasons:

- It is more in line with the philosophy of Test-Driven Development.

- It results in an extremely thin GUI that is essentially just a view.

- No special tools are required since all processing and computation is done in a non-GUI class where it can easily be test-driven using standard tools.

- I prefer it.

OK, we start with one simple test: Given a collection of movie names, fill in the listbox in the GUI.

```
public class TestGUI extends TestCase {

  public void testList() {
    Vector movieNames = new Vector() {
      { add("Star Wars"); add("Star Trek"); add("Stargate"); }
    };
    MockControl control = EasyMock.controlFor(MovieEditorView.class);
    MovieEditorView mockView = (MovieEditorView)control.getMock();

    mockView.setMovieNames(movieNames);
    control.setVoidCallable();

    control.activate();

    MovieListEditor editor = new MovieListEditor(mockView);
    editor.setMovieNames(movieNames);

    control.verify();
  }
}
```

This is another good summary view of the TDD process. We write one simple test, with nothing else written. That test, while simple, drives the creation of an interface and a class. To support the above test, we need to create a couple of things.

First, the view interface that we are mocking:

```
public interface MovieListEditorView {
  void setMovieNames(Vector movieNames);
}
```

Next, the class that does the work:

```
public class MovieListEditor {
  private MovieListEditorView myView;

  public MovieListEditor(MovieListEditorView aView) {
    myView = aView;
  }
  public void setMovieNames(Vector movieNames) {
    myView.setMovieNames(movieNames);
  }
}
```

Notice how we do the simplest thing. The setMovieNames() method simply sends its argument on to the view. It doesn't save it anywhere. That isn't needed to pass the test, so we don't do it.

Now we add another test, this one for the *adding a movie* operation. In the process, we noticed the need for a common fixture, so we refactored that into a setUp() method. Here's the test case now:

```
public class TestGUI extends TestCase {
  private Vector movieNames = null;
  private MockControl control = null;
  private MovieListEditorView mockView = null;

  protected void setUp() {
    movieNames = new Vector() {
      { add("Star Wars"); add("Star Trek"); add("Stargate"); }
    };
    control = EasyMock.controlFor(MovieListEditorView.class);
    mockView = (MovieListEditorView)control.getMock();
  }

  public void testList() {
    mockView.setMovieNames(movieNames);
    control.setVoidCallable(1);

    control.activate();

    MovieListEditor editor = new MovieListEditor(mockView);
    editor.setMovieNames(movieNames);

    control.verify();
  }
  public void testAdding() {
    String LOST_IN_SPACE = "Lost In Space";
    Vector movieNamesWithAddition = new Vector(movieNames);

    mockView.setMovieNames(movieNames);
    control.setVoidCallable(1);
```

```
        mockView.getNewName();
        control.setReturnValue(LOST_IN_SPACE, 1);

        mockView.setMovieNames(movieNamesWithAddition);
        control.setVoidCallable(1);

        control.activate();

        MovieListEditor editor = new MovieListEditor(mockView);
        editor.setMovieNames(movieNames);
        editor.add();

        control.verify();
      }
    }
```

We need to add a method to the interface (**String getNewName()**), and an **add()** method to the editor class. We also need to save the list of movie names.

Here's the new version of the class:

```
    public class MovieListEditor {
      private MovieListEditorView myView;
      private Vector myNames = null;

      public MovieListEditor(MovieListEditorView aView) {
        myView = aView;
      }

      public void setMovieNames(Vector movieNames) {
        myNames = movieNames;
        myView.setMovieNames(movieNames);
      }

      public void add() {
        String newMovieName = myView.getNewName();
        myNames.add(newMovieName);
        myView.setMovieNames(myNames);
      }
    }
```

Figure 8.4 shows the sequence diagram for the **add()** method we just wrote. While this is a very simple example, we can see the clean separation of the interface and the application. The user clicks on the add button, which is part of the interface, which simply delegates to the **MovieListEditor**. The interaction with the interface is very simple: get the contents of a field and set the contents of a list.

In making the new test (**testAdding()**) work, notice how we simply added code without regard for the already existing code. Also notice the duplication between **set-MovieNames()** and **add()**. How can we refactor that away?

First, look at **setMovieNames()**. See how we store the argument in **myNames**, then send the argument to the view? Recall that in getting **testAdding()** working we added the assignment to save the names. Now we clean up. We start by noting that by the time we sent the argument to the view, we've already saved it in **myNames**. We've just found a smaller bit of duplication. To get rid of it, we can send the saved value of the

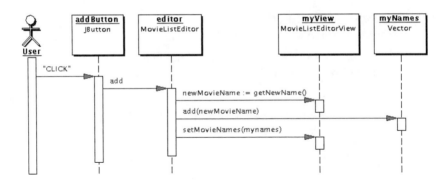

**Figure 8.4** Sequence diagram for MovieListEditor.add().

argument rather than the argument itself. Compile and run the tests. Green bar! Now
setMovieNames() is:

```
public void setMovieNames(Vector movieNames) {
  myNames = movieNames;
  myView.setMovieNames(myNames);
}
```

Now, look at add(). See how it sends myNames to the view as well? Let's extract
that line into a separate method:

```
private void updateNamesInView() {
  myView.setMovieNames(myNames);
}
```

Notice how we made the extracted method private? That's a good habit to develop. The
rationale is that extracted methods aren't part of the external behavior, they support it.
Therefore, they shouldn't be made public. If it turns out later that they are useful to another class or a subclass, then they can be changed to public or protected, respectively.
Until then, leave them private.

The add() method is also changed to use the extracted method:

```
public void add() {
  String newMovieName = myView.getNewName();
  myNames.add(newMovieName);
  updateNamesInView();
}
```

Compile and test. Green bar. The next step is to use the new method in setMovie
Names():

```
public void setMovieNames(Vector movieNames) {
  myNames = movieNames;
  updateNamesInView();
}
```

Compile and test. Green bar. Now on to deleting.
First, a test:

```
public void testDeleting() {
  Vector movieNamesWithDeletion = new Vector(movieNames);
  movieNamesWithDeletion.remove(1);

  mockView.setMovieNames(movieNames);
  control.setVoidCallable(1);

  mockView.getSelection();
  control.setReturnValue(1, 1);

  mockView.setMovieNames(movieNamesWithDeletion);
  control.setVoidCallable(1);

  control.activate();

  MovieListEditor editor = new MovieListEditor(mockView);
  editor.setMovieNames(movieNames);
  editor.delete();

  control.verify();
}
```

Notice how we are making the operations of the editor very simple: add() and
delete()... no parameters, returning nothing. These are just actions forwarded directly
from the GUI, which is then queried for its state as necessary. This, coupled with using
an interface to define the GUI, gives us very good separation between the domain code
and the GUI. This separation is worth striving for, and this approach helps a great deal
in achieving it.

Next, make the test pass as simply as possible:

```
public void delete() {
  int index = myView.getSelection();
  myNames.remove(index);
  updateNamesInView();
}
```

Time to clean up. OK, nothing to do this time. Since the updateNamesInView()
method was already there, we just used it when writing delete(). We could have explicitly written the call to update the view, then refactored to replace it with the update
method, but why? We've done that duplication elimination already, and we learned
something in the process.

Now we have to create a real GUI to use in place of the mock. Notice that with this
degree of separation it will be very thin, and very simple, since it is almost completely
passive.

In implementing the GUI we discover an oversight. It needs to know about the
editor so that it can delegate to it. We haven't done this yet since we were driving the
editor from the tests, not the mock view. But this is simple enough to add. We just
need a method to set the editor. For the test with the mock it doesn't really matter
since the calls that the GUI would be making in response to button clicks are coming
from the test itself. Here's the new method in the interface:

```
void setEditor(MovieListEditor anEditor);
```

Where is the best place to call this? The constructor of MovieListEditor is a good
choice:

```
public MovieListEditor(MovieListEditorView aView) {
  myView = aView;
  myView.setEditor(this);
}
```

To accommodate this call being made to the mock in the tests, we need to set up
the mock to accept it with any argument value. We can do this using the setDefault-
VoidCallable() method on the mock control. And since this requirement applies to all
of the tests, we can put it in setUp() after creating the mock. Here's the new version of
setUp(); notice the last two lines:

```
protected void setUp() {
  movieNames = new Vector() {
    { add("Star Wars"); add("Star Trek"); add("Stargate"); }
  };

  control = EasyMock.controlFor(MovieListEditorView.class);
  mockView = (MovieListEditorView)control.getMock();
  mockView.setEditor(null);
  control.setDefaultVoidCallable();
}
```

Now, with these tweaks made, we can write the GUI code. It is very much like the
previous version, except simpler. Notice that it is mostly just building the GUI. Other
than that there are just accessors and mutators for component contents, and enough
code to delegate user actions to the associated editor.

```java
public class SwingMovieListEditorView extends JFrame
                              implements MovieListEditorView {
  private JTextField movieField = null;
  private JList movieList = null;
  private MovieListEditor myEditor;

  public SwingMovieListEditorView() {
    super();
  }

  public void setEditor(MovieListEditor anEditor) {
    myEditor = anEditor;
  }

  public void setMovieNames(Vector movieNames) {
    movieList.setListData(movieNames);
  }

  public String getNewName() {
    return movieField.getText();
  }

  public int getSelection() {
    return movieList.getSelectedIndex();
  }

  public void init() {
    setLayout();
    initMovieList();
    initMovieField();
    initAddButton();
    initDeleteButton();
    pack();
  }

  private void setLayout() {
    getContentPane().setLayout(new FlowLayout());
  }

  private void initMovieList() {
    movieList = new JList(new Vector());
    JScrollPane scroller = new JScrollPane(movieList);
    getContentPane().add(scroller);
  }

  private void initMovieField() {
    movieField = new JTextField(16);
    getContentPane().add(movieField);
  }
```

```
    private void initAddButton() {
      JButton addButton = new JButton("Add");
      addButton.addActionListener(new ActionListener() {
        public void actionPerformed(ActionEvent e) {
          myEditor.add();
        }
      });
      getContentPane().add(addButton);
    }

    private void initDeleteButton() {
      JButton deleteButton = new JButton("Delete");
      deleteButton.addActionListener(new ActionListener() {
        public void actionPerformed(ActionEvent e) {
          myEditor.delete();
        }
      });
      getContentPane().add(deleteButton);
    }
}
```

Note that we could use any of the earlier GUI-oriented techniques to test-drive the
creation of the GUI in this execution as well. For this simple example it would have
been overkill. In Part III we'll see how that approach works.

## SUMMARY

In this chapter we've explored approaches to test-driving the development of a graphical
user interface. At one extreme was a brute force approach, which required that the tests
have direct access to the components making up the GUI. This is very coupled, and
requires a significant amount of overhead in the GUI classes. At the other end of
the spectrum was an elegant, flexible, two-stage approach. In that we separated the
user interface into two layers: one containing the logic of the user interaction, and one
containing the presentation code.

Using the latter technique, we can test-drive very simple, well decoupled interfaces.
Using a mocked view in place of a real GUI component we can design and develop the
logical layer of the user interface, which can be used as the basis of any sort of interface:
Swing, Web, or whatever is the fad of the day. In fact, it can easily, and cheaply, support
multiple presentation layers.

When using JFCUnit or Jemmy we can drive the actual Swing-based GUI component. This approach (using Jemmy) will be put into practice in Part III of this book.
Jemmy has several advantages, including not needing any extra helper utilities and
being useful for adding tests to existing GUI components.

Part III

# A JAVA PROJECT: TEST-DRIVEN END TO END

This is a practical book. With that in mind, we'll now explore and learn TDD in the context of a real project. By the time you get to this point in the book you should know enough background and be familiar enough with the tools and techniques that you can undertake test-driving an application.

We start off by defining the project in XP fashion:

- an overall vision,

- a set of user stories, and

- a set of tasks into which the stories have been decomposed.

That is the purpose of Chapter 9. Each of the remaining chapters in this part of the book will cover the development of a single story. Sections within each chapter will focus on a specific task within the story.

I've written this part of the book as though I were sitting with you, the reader, and working side-by-side on the project. The style is intentionally a little more casual and conversational. I've tried to make you feel as though you are here with me as I write. You have to provide your own coffee, though.

The code shown here is real. It was copied directly from the IDE. Sometimes we make mistakes or oversights that we then catch, sometimes they get caught later. It's not perfect, but it doesn't have to be. It does have to be understandable and malleable, though. The final code is available at the companion Web site [URL 65].

So, let's get to it!

# Chapter 9

# THE PROJECT

*Give wings to my propension and cut off*
*All fears attending on so dire a project.*

*- Troiles and Cressida, Act 2 Scene 2*
*William Shakespeare*

## OVERVIEW

This part of the book is written around the Test-Driven Development of a single project: an application to help keep track of movies you would like to see and help in choosing a movie to see.

The following chapters are an annotated walk through the development of the application. It's real code; how it was really written. I wrote this part of the book as the code was being written. Code was copied and pasted directly from Eclipse into Emacs in *real time*. So sometimes you'll see things that aren't quite right. In the last chapter of this part I'll talk a bit about what might have been done differently.

This project was done using eXtreme Programming, so requirements are written as user stories. However, the stories are ordered with a linear path through the project in mind, rather than by some measure of business value of importance to a customer. The stories are then decomposed into tasks. Once you are at the task level, it makes little difference how you got there. I feel very strongly that, while it is a cornerstone of XP, TDD can be used in many development processes. The caveat is that Big Design Up Front (BDUF) conflicts with TDD, so you do need to be using a fairly agile process that lets you evolve the design organically. In particular, you need to be practicing an agile approach to modeling and design (see Appendix B).

As we work on each task, we'll start by sketching out what tests we'll want to see passing. These tests are identified at the beginning of the task as we tackle each one. For your convenience, a full list of these tests is provided in Chapter 20, with references to where each is defined and implemented. At times we'll discover more tests as we work. These are taken as they come and no extra effort is made to make them stand out.

First, we start with a vision statement for the project.

**Project Vision:**   Make it easy to keep track of movies you want to see. Provide support for ratings, reviews, recommendations, etc., to help in deciding what to watch.

## USER STORIES AND TASKS

Now we'll look at the user stories that specify what the system has to do. At the same time we'll also look at how the stories break down into tasks. Since this isn't a book about XP per se, we won't examine this process. If you want to learn more about XP, see [6], [8], [URL 11], and [URL 12]

**Story 1. *Movie List***

Provide a way to keep a list of movies and a way to add movies to it. Ordering of the list isn't a concern.

> **Task 1-1.** Make a container for movies with a way to add to it. Doesn't have to be ordered or sorted.

> **Task 1-2.** Make a GUI that shows a list of movies. List order is just what is in the underlying collection. List should scroll as required.

> **Task 1-3.** Provide a text field and "Add" button for adding movies to the list via the GUI.

**Story 2. *Movies Can Be Renamed***

Provide a way to rename movies that are in the list.

> **Task 2-1.** Allow the movie name to be changed.

> **Task 2-2.** On the GUI, selecting a movie fills in the text field with its name. An "Update" button will update the movie name with the contents of the field.

**Story 3. *Movies Are Unique***

A movie appears only once in the list; the names are unique and case-insensitive. Attempts to add a duplicate should fail and result in an error.

> **Task 3-1.** Enforce uniqueness of movies during add and update operations. Attempts to add or rename with the same name as an existing movie should raise an exception.

> **Task 3-2.** The GUI provides an error message dialog when a non-unique add or rename is attempted.

**Story 4. *Ratings***

Movies each have a single, editable rating.

> **Task 4-1.** Add support for a single rating to Movie. Support the concept of an unrated movie.

> **Task 4-2.** Show the rating in the GUI, next to the movie name.

> **Task 4-3.** Allow the rating to be edited.

**Story 5. *Categories***

Movies belong to a category; categories such as *Horror*, *Comedy*, etc.

> **Task 5-1.** Add support for a movie to have a single category, from a fixed list of alternatives.

> **Task 5-2.** Show the category in the GUI. There should be a field that gets filled in when a movie is selected.

**Task 5-3.** Allow the category of a movie to be changed by selecting it from a fixed list of possibilities.

**Story 6.** *Filter on Category*

Filter the movies in the list by category. There needs to be a way to select the category to show, including ALL.

**Task 6-1.** Given a category, ask the movie list for a list of its movies that belong to that category.

**Task 6-2.** Get the entire list using an ALL category.

**Task 6-3.** Add a combo box to the GUI to select a category. When a category is selected, update the list to include only movies of that category.

**Task 6-4.** When the list is filtered, changing a movie to a different category should remove it from the list.

**Story 7.** *Persistence*

Movie data is persistent across application sessions.

**Task 7-1.** Write movie collection to a flat text file.

**Task 7-2.** Provide, in the GUI, the capability to save the movie collection to a specific file.

**Task 7-3.** Provide, in the GUI, the capability to save the movie collection to the same file it was previously saved to.

**Task 7-4.** Read a movie collection from a flat text file.

**Task 7-5.** Provide, in the GUI, the capability to load the movie collection from a file.

**Story 8.** *Sorting*

In the GUI, allow the movie list to be sorted by selecting from a set of options on a menu. Two orderings are required: ascending by name, and descending by rating.

**Task 8-1.** Create the ability to compare two movies based on either name (ascending order) or rating (descending order). This is needed for sorting.

**Task 8-2.** Add the capability to ask a MovieList to provide its list sorted on a specific attribute, for the moment this is one of name or rating.

**Task 8-3.** Add sorting capabilities to MovieListEditor.

**Task 8-4.** Add a *View* menu to the GUI with an option for each attribute that can be sorted on. Selecting one of them results in the visible movie list being sorted by that attribute.

**Story 9.** *Multiple Ratings*

Movies can have more than one rating, each with an identified source. Selecting a movie should show all of its ratings. There should also be a way to add a rating. A movie's displayed rating should now be the average of all of its individual ratings.

**Task 9-1.** Add support for multiple ratings rather than just one. Provide access to the average of all the ratings.

**Task 9-2.** Create a class to represent the source for a rating. Keep in mind that a single source can have many ratings, but not the reverse.

**Task 9-3.** Revamp the persistence capabilities to handle the changes to the rating structure.

**Task 9-4.** In the GUI, show a list of all ratings for the selected movie.

**Task 9-5.** In the GUI, provide a way to add a rating to the selected movie. Be sure to handle an empty source and map it to *Anonymous*.

**Task 9-6.** The single-rating field no longer serves any purpose. Remove it and update the system appropriately.

**Story 10.** *Reviews*

Movies can have a review attached to each rating. If there is a review there must be a source.

**Task 10-1.** Add support for a single review to Rating.

**Task 10-2.** Add support to persistence for saving reviews.

**Task 10-3.** Add support to persistence for loading reviews.

**Task 10-4.** Add support to the GUI to display reviews.

**Task 10-5.** Add support to the GUI to enter a review as part of adding a rating.

# Chapter 10

# MOVIE LIST

*Provide a way to keep a list of movies and a way to add movies to it.*
*Ordering of the list isn't a concern.*

## MAKE A MOVIE CONTAINER

*Make a container for movies with a way to add to it. Doesn't have to be ordered or sorted.*

### The First Test

We begin, of course, with a single test. What should that test be? Well, it needs to be something simple since there is absolutely no code yet. How do we figure out what the first test should be? Look at the task. We need to keep a list of movies. Should we write a test for a movie? Let's not get ahead of ourselves. The task doesn't say much about movies. It just says that we have some and we want some place to keep them. The *some place to keep them* is the focus of the task, and should be our focus as well.

OK, so we want a test of something that holds movies. What should we test? Look back at the tips at the end of Chapter 4. Can we get ideas from that? You bet! How about *Test the simple stuff first*, specifically, *empty collection or null object behavior*. OK, let's start with a test for an empty list of movies. Now that we've gotten a start we can come up with more tests that we'll need for this task:

**Test 1.** An empty list should have a size of zero.

**Test 2.** Adding a movie to an empty list should result in a list with a size of one.

**Test 3.** Adding two movies to an empty list should result in a list with a size of two.

**Test 4.** If we add a movie to a list, we should be able to ask if it's there and receive a positive response. Conversely, we should receive a negative response when we ask about a movie that we haven't added.

### Test 1: An empty list should have a size of zero.

Here it is, with the basic overhead. Notice that we've paid attention to another tip: we've included a **main()** method.

---

Eclipse provides a wizard for creating test cases. One of the options is to automatically include exactly the main method we would like to have.

```
public class TestMovieList extends TestCase {

  public void testEmptyListSize() {
    MovieList emptyList = new MovieList();
    assertEquals("Size of empty movie list should be 0.", 0, emptyList.size());
  }

  public static void main(String[] args) {
    junit.textui.TestRunner.run(TestMovieList.class);
  }
}
```

This is about as simple as it gets. We create a new instance of MovieList, and assert that it contains zero movies.

Try compiling... it won't. We need to add some code stubs to make it compile. Let's look at what we've written and get a list of assumptions we've made.

Another feature of Eclipse is the flagging of situations which prevent code from compiling, and generally providing a list of possible corrections. Choose from the list to make it happen.
Interestingly, the indicator used is a yellow light in the margin.

What we find is the class **MovieList** and the method **MovieList.size()**. We need to create the class and the method. Remember, all we are trying to do at this point is to get the test compiling. We do the absolute minimum that will accomplish that. With that in mind, here's what we get:

```
public class MovieList {

  public int size() {
    return 0;
  }
}
```

That's it. Our test compiles now. Try running it. It passes. What! Aren't we supposed to have a failing test first? Generally, yes. In Smalltalk, and other similar languages, yes. However, in a strongly typed language like Java, if we define a method that returns something (an int in this case) we *must* provide a return value. No wonder XP and TDD evolved in the Smalltalk world. What do we return? The simplest thing. That would be **0**, **false**, or **null** depending on the return type of the method. Since the **size()** method returns an **int**, we have it return **0**. It just so happens that **0** is the size of an empty **MovieList**. It also just so happens that this is exactly what we would have done to get the text to pass.

Is there any duplication that needs cleaning up? No. Any refactoring that has to be done? No. OK, next test.

## Test 2: Adding a movie to an empty list should result in a list with a size of one.

This test is a bit more involved, so let's slow down and look at building it one step at a time. We typically won't go this slowly, but it's worth doing it once at the beginning so that you can see how a test is built up from nothingness.

First, we need the skeleton:

```
public void testSizeAfterAddingOne() {
}
```

The significant thing here is the method name. What are we going to test? The method name should indicate that. It should say something meaningful to us when we look at the test results. It should communicate intent to someone else who is reading the tests. Looking at the list of test methods should be equivalent to looking at the table of contents in a "How to use this system" manual.

Our next step is to decide what the test will be, that is, what assertion(s) we need. Since we are testing the size of the list after the addition of one movie, it makes sense to check that the movie list reports its size as 1 afterwards. So now the test is:

```
public void testSizeAfterAddingOne() {
  assertEquals("Size of one item list should be 1.", 1, oneItemList.size());
}
```

Notice that we use

  a) assertEquals, and

  b) a message in the assertion.

It's a good thing.

Next, we consider what needs to be done to set things up for the assertion. We need an instance of **MovieList** called **oneItemList** to which we've added a single movie. Let's add that to the test:

```
public void testSizeAfterAddingOne() {
  oneItemList.add(starWars);
  assertEquals("Size of one item list should be 1.", 1, oneItemList.size());
}
```

OK, now we need to define **oneItemList**:

```
public void testSizeAfterAddingOne() {
  MovieList oneItemList = new MovieList();
  oneItemList.add(starWars);
  assertEquals("Size of one item list should be 1.", 1, oneItemList.size());
}
```

The variable **starWars** has to be defined next. What is it? It's being stored in a MovieList, so it must be a Movie. Make it so:

```
public void testSizeAfterAddingOne() {
  Movie starWars = new Movie();
  MovieList oneItemList = new MovieList();
  oneItemList.add(starWars);
  assertEquals("Size of one item list should be 1.", 1, oneItemList.size());
}
```

This all looks good, but we're still missing **Movie**. We need to create a class now:

```
public class Movie {
}
```

Now we see that we need an **add()** method in **MovieList**. All we are worried about at the moment is getting our test to compile, so write the simplest stub possible:

```
public void add(Movie movieToAdd) {
}
```

Since this doesn't return anything, all we need is an empty method. Now everything compiles. Run the test. Red bar! Specifically, JUnit reports:

```
Size of one item list should be 1. expected:<1> but was:<0>
```

Oh no! Wait a minute, we want to see that red bar. It's good at this point, as long as it's only the new test that is failing (i.e., we haven't broken anything that used to work). This is the case (**testEmptyList** still works), so we're happy since we've written just enough test to fail. Now we need to write just enough code to pass. Onward!

Our test expects MovieList.size() to return 1 after MovieList.add() has been called. Let's consider the simplest thing that could possibly work. Could we have Movie-List.size() return 1? No, that would break TestMovieList.testEmptyListSize(). We need to return 1 after MovieList.add() has been called. Let's try capturing that information:

```
public void add(Movie movieToAdd) {
  numberOfMovies = 1;
}
```

If we think ahead we can see that this is too simple... Ha! Caught you! Don't look ahead. Solve the problem at hand. Break the rules to get it working. That's the TDD mantra.

OK, we need some support for that, specifically, an instance variable, **numberOf-Movies**, so we add it to MovieList:

```
private int numberOfMovies = 0;
```

Now we need to use this new information in order to return the expected value:

```
public int size() {
   return numberOfMovies;
}
```

Compile and run the tests... green bar! Now we check to see if it introduced duplication. No. Anything smells? Nothing really bad. The implementation of MovieList.add() smells a bit...that constant being assigned to numberOfMovies is suspicious. Nothing obvious to do about it now. We'll wait until we know more.

## Test 3: Adding two movies to an empty list should result in a list with a size of two.

We've tested the base case (an empty list) and the first inductive case (a list with one thing in it). Time to take the inductive leap. We know it works for zero and one, so if we get it working for 2, then we can reasonably assume it will work for anything.

We write another test, this time testing that we can add two movies and the size is returned as 2:

```
public void testSizeAfterAddingTwo() {
   Movie starWars = new Movie();
   Movie starTrek = new Movie();
   MovieList twoItemList = new MovieList();
   twoItemList.add(starWars);
   twoItemList.add(starTrek);
   assertEquals("Size of a two item list should be 2.", 2, twoItemList.size());
}
```

Of course this fails. Each call to add() simply sets the size to 1. The solution is obvious: increment the size (i.e., the numberOfMovies instance variable) each time add() is called. Let's make that change:

```
public void add(Movie movieToAdd) {
   numberOfMovies++;
}
```

Compile. Test. Green bar. Nothing to clean up.

I can hear you thinking, "Wait a minute! We're not doing anything with the Movie instances that are passed in to add()!" No. We're not. We don't have a test that requires it. Maybe it's time we did.

## Refactoring Tests

Before we continue with more tests, let's look at what we have so far:

```
public class TestMovieList extends TestCase {

  public void testEmptyListSize() {
    MovieList emptyList = new MovieList();
    assertEquals("Size of empty movie list should be 0.", 0, emptyList.size());
  }

  public void testSizeAfterAddingOne() {
    Movie starWars = new Movie();
    MovieList oneItemList = new MovieList();
    oneItemList.add(starWars);
    assertEquals("Size of one item list should be 1.", 1, oneItemList.size());
  }

  public void testSizeAfterAddingTwo() {
    Movie starWars = new Movie();
    Movie starTrek = new Movie();
    MovieList twoItemList = new MovieList();
    twoItemList.add(starWars);
    twoItemList.add(starTrek);
    assertEquals("Size of a two item list should be 2.", 2, twoItemList.size());
  }

  public static void main(String[] args) {
    junit.textui.TestRunner.run(TestMovieList.class);
  }
}
```

Notice a couple of things:

- We use an instance of MovieList in each test, each time creating it using new MovieList().

- We use some instances of Movie in a couple of the tests.

In short, we have some duplication in our tests. Furthermore, that duplication is in setting up fixtures for the tests. Let's refactor that duplicated code into a setUp() method.

For instructional purposes, we'll go through the process step by step.

We'll start by making an instance variable for each local that is part of a fixture. The Movie instances are easy since we have some common names already. The MovieList instance is a bit more complex because we use a different name in each test. My approach is to generalize them to movieList. So we add the following instance variables:

```
private MovieList movieList = null;
private Movie starWars = null;
private Movie starTrek = null;
```

Note that we didn't do anything to the test methods yet, they are still using local variables in each fixture. We have to be even more cautious when refactoring test code because we don't have a test suite backing us up. We do have the fact that the tests run successfully, so as we make changes, they should still run.

Our next step is to add a **setUp()** method and initialize the new instance variables:

```
protected void setUp() {
    movieList = new MovieList();
    starWars = new Movie();
    starTrek = new Movie();
}
```

Everything still works. Now, one by one, we'll replace the local variables with our new fixture. We compile and test after each step. First we'll replace **starWars**. The test methods are now:

```
public void testSizeAfterAddingOne() {
    MovieList oneItemList = new MovieList();
    oneItemList.add(starWars);
    assertEquals("Size of one item list should be 1.", 1, oneItemList.size());
}

public void testSizeAfterAddingTwo() {
    Movie starTrek = new Movie();
    MovieList twoItemList = new MovieList();
    twoItemList.add(starWars);
    twoItemList.add(starTrek);
    assertEquals("Size of a two item list should be 2.", 2, twoItemList.size());
}
```

Likewise, we'll replace **starTrek** in the third test:

```
public void testSizeAfterAddingTwo() {
    MovieList twoItemList = new MovieList();
    twoItemList.add(starWars);
    twoItemList.add(starTrek);
    assertEquals("Size of a two item list should be 2.", 2, twoItemList.size());
}
```

Finally, we tackle the **MovieList** instance. We work one method at a time, moving it to use the new instance variable. Using Eclipse with its built-in refactoring, we can simply rename the local variable to **movieList**, compile and test, remove the local variable, and compile and test a final time. We'll just step through working on testEmptyListSize().

So, rename the local variable to **movieList**:

```
public void testEmptyListSize() {
    MovieList movieList = new MovieList();
    assertEquals("Size of empty movie list should be 0.", 0, movieList.size());
}
```

Then remove the local:

```
public void testEmptyListSize() {
  assertEquals("Size of empty movie list should be 0.", 0, movieList.size());
}
```

Now we do the same to the other two tests and end up with:

```
public void testSizeAfterAddingOne() {
  movieList.add(starWars);
  assertEquals("Size of one item list should be 1.", 1, movieList.size());
}

public void testSizeAfterAddingTwo() {
  movieList.add(starWars);
  movieList.add(starTrek);
  assertEquals("Size of a two item list should be 2.", 2, movieList.size());
}
```

Not only is the duplication removed, but we have less code!

## Test 4: If we add a movie to a list, we should be able to ask if it's there and receive a positive response. Conversely, we should receive a negative response when we ask about a movie that we haven't added.

Due to the previous tests, we have the basic scaffolding in place. We have a Movie class, a MovieList class, and a basic concept of adding to the list and finding out how many things we have added. The next step is to get back the things we've added. Here's the next test:

```
public void testContents() {
  movieList.add(starWars);
  movieList.add(starTrek);
  assertTrue("List should contain starWars.", movieList.contains(starWars));
  assertTrue("List should contain starTrek.", movieList.contains(starTrek));
  assertFalse("List should not contain stargate.", movieList.contains(stargate));
}
```

To get this to compile we need to stub a contains() method in MovieList:

```
public boolean contains(Movie movieToCheckFor) {
  return false;
}
```

It compiles, and fails with:

```
List should contain starWars.
```

Of course it fails, for two reasons:

1. MovieList doesn't *contain* anything; we've been ignoring the objects passed into the add() method.

2. The contains() method just returns false.

Now, let's do something about that. First, we'll do something with the arguments to add(). We want to capture and accumulate the arguments to add(). The simplest way to do this is to toss them into a Collection of some sort. For lack of a good reason not to, we'll use an ArrayList.

First, we need an instance variable. Notice that we declare it as a Collection and instantiate an ArrayList. By using the most abstract interface possible, we commit the least:

```
private Collection movies = new ArrayList();
```

We need to take the argument to add() and put it in the ArrayList:

```
public void add(Movie movieToAdd) {
    numberOfMovies++;
    movies.add(movieToAdd);
}
```

---

**You only want to have one test failing at a time—ever!**

---

Notice that we didn't remove the line that increments numberOfMovies. If we had, the tests that do work would stop. When we're working in this fashion (replacing functionality that works) we leave in the old code until we have made sure that the new code works the same way, that is, it has to pass all the tests that the old code did.

Now, movies contains all the Movie instances that have been passed in through add(), so we should be able to change size() to return the number of objects in movies:

```
public int size() {
    return movies.size();
}
```

This is the critical change. Up to now our changes have been building parallel functionality in the background. The new code wasn't being relied on. This change uses the new code instead of the old. We compile and test. All of our previous tests still pass. Excellent! We can now clean up the old code. What do we do with the old code? Throw it out! Don't comment it out... trash it. You won't need it again, and if you ever do it's safely in your source control system.

> When you replace old code with new, resulting in dead code (i.e., code that isn't used anymore), delete it. Also, make sure you are integrating continuously (well, at least as frequently as you can) so that you always have a fine granularity history of the project in case you do need to get something back.

After being cleaned up, here's MovieList:

```
public class MovieList {
  private Collection movies = new ArrayList();

  public int size() {
    return movies.size();
  }
  public void add(Movie movieToAdd) {
    movies.add(movieToAdd);
  }
  public boolean contains(Movie movieToCheckFor) {
    return false;
  }
}
```

Now we can turn our attention to the contains() method. Since we have all of the movies in a Collection, this is easy—we can just delegate to movies for the containment check:

```
public boolean contains(Movie movieToCheckFor) {
  return movies.contains(movieToCheckFor);
}
```

Compile, test, green bar!

Are there any opportunities to refactor? Actually, yes. Have a look at our TestCase:

```
public class TestMovieList extends TestCase {
  private MovieList movieList = null;
  private Movie starWars = null;
  private Movie starTrek = null;
  private Movie stargate = null;

  protected void setUp() {
    movieList = new MovieList();
    starWars = new Movie();
    starTrek = new Movie();
    stargate = new Movie();
  }
  public void testEmptyListSize() {
    assertEquals("Size of empty movie list should be 0.", 0, movieList.size());
  }
```

```
    public void testSizeAfterAddingOne() {
      movieList.add(starWars);
      assertEquals("Size of one item list should be 1.", 1, movieList.size());
    }

    public void testSizeAfterAddingTwo() {
      movieList.add(starWars);
      movieList.add(starTrek);
      assertEquals("Size of a two item list should be 2.", 2, movieList.size());
    }

    public void testContents() {
      movieList.add(starWars);
      movieList.add(starTrek);
      assertTrue("List should contain starWars.", movieList.contains(starWars));
      assertTrue("List should contain starTrek.", movieList.contains(starTrek));
      assertFalse("List should not contain stargate.", movieList.contains(stargate));
    }

    public static void main(String[] args) {
      junit.textui.TestRunner.run(TestMovieListWithEmptyList.class);
    }
  }
```

Have a close look at testSizeAfterAddingTwo() and testContents(). Both start with the statements:

```
    movieList.add(starWars);
    movieList.add(starTrek);
```

Oh dear! Duplication. Yes, but it's more than that, though. Those two tests are using an extension of the fixture that setUp() is building. This is bad. The solution is simple, however: we must extract those two tests along with their fixture into a new TestCase. Here it is:

```
public class TestMovieListWithTwoMovies extends TestCase {
  private MovieList movieList = null;
  private Movie starWars = null;
  private Movie starTrek = null;
  private Movie stargate = null;

  protected void setUp() {
    starWars = new Movie();
    starTrek = new Movie();
    stargate = new Movie();
    movieList = new MovieList();
    movieList.add(starWars);
    movieList.add(starTrek);
  }

  public void testSizeAfterAddingTwo() {
    assertEquals("Size of a two item list should be 2.", 2, movieList.size());
  }
```

```
public void testContents() {
  assertTrue("List should contain starWars.", movieList.contains(starWars));
  assertTrue("List should contain starTrek.", movieList.contains(starTrek));
  assertFalse("List should not contain stargate.", movieList.contains(stargate));
}

public static void main(String[] args) {
  junit.textui.TestRunner.run(TestMovieListWithTwoMovies.class);
}
}
```

One last change here is to rename testSizeAfterAddingTwo() to be clearer. Notice how its current name includes a description of the fixture. This is a smell that indicates that a TestCase should be split. A better name would be testSize().

We can also see that the two tests that remain in TestMovieListWithEmptyList use slightly different fixtures: testEmptyListSize() uses an empty list, while testSizeAfterAddingOne() uses a list with one item. Again, the test names describe the fixtures. Let's split them into separate classes and rename them accordingly. The two classes that result are:

```
public class TestEmptyMovieList extends TestCase {
  private MovieList movieList = null;

  protected void setUp() {
    movieList = new MovieList();
  }

  public void testSize() {
    assertEquals("Size of empty movie list should be 0.", 0, movieList.size());
  }

  public static void main(String[] args) {
    junit.textui.TestRunner.run(TestMovieListWithEmptyList.class);
  }
}

public class TestMovieListWithOneMovie extends TestCase {
  private MovieList movieList = null;
  private Movie starWars = null;

  protected void setUp() {
    starWars = new Movie();
    movieList = new MovieList();
    movieList.add(starWars);
  }

  public void testSize() {
    assertEquals("Size of one item list should be 1.", 1, movieList.size());
  }

  public static void main(String[] args) {
    junit.textui.TestRunner.run(TestMovieListWithOneMovie.class);
  }
}
```

There, much cleaner and clearer.

Now that we have more than one TestCase in the package, we should create a TestSuite containing them so that we can run all the tests together. As we create new TestCases we will add them to the suite. Here's the initial form of the suite:

```
public class AllTests extends TestSuite {

  public static void main(String[] args) {
    junit.textui.TestRunner.run(AllTests.class);
  }


  public static Test suite() {
    TestSuite suite = new TestSuite("Test for com.saorsa.nowplaying.tests");
    suite.addTest(new TestSuite(TestMovieListWithEmptyList.class));
    suite.addTest(new TestSuite(TestMovieListWithOneMovie.class));
    suite.addTest(new TestSuite(TestMovieListWithTwoMovies.class));
    return suite;
  }
}
```

Notice that Movie is an empty class. That's all we've needed so far. We know there will need to be some instance variables and methods in Movie, but we don't have any need for them yet. When we have a test that requires them, we'll add them. Until then it's just speculation, and we won't add anything on speculation.

# MAKE A MOVIE LIST GUI

*Make a GUI that shows a list of movies. List order is just what is in the underlying collection. List should scroll as required.*

Now we'll add a user interface to what we have so far. For this task all we need is to display a list of movies. We are going to tackle this in two phases: the logic, and the presentation.

Here's a list of tests we think we'll need:

**Test 5.** The logical layer should send the appropriate list of movies to the view for display.

**Test 6.** The GUI should have a listbox and should display a list of movies in it as requested.

## Test 5: The logical layer should send the appropriate list of movies to the view for display.

We will use the humble dialog approach described in Chapter 8 to drive the development of the GUI. This task is pretty simple: we just need to display the list.

Here's the test for the interface model class's ability to display a list:

```
public class TestGUI extends TestCase {
  private MockControl control = null;
  private MovieListEditorView mockView = null;
  private Vector movies = null;
  private Movie starWars = null;
  private Movie starTrek = null;
  private Movie stargate = null;
  private MovieList movieList;

  protected void setUp() {
    starWars = new Movie();
    starTrek = new Movie();
    stargate = new Movie();

    movies = new Vector();
    movies.add(starWars);
    movies.add(starTrek);
    movies.add(stargate);

    movieList = new MovieList();
    movieList.add(starWars);
    movieList.add(starTrek);
    movieList.add(stargate);
  }

  public void testList() {
    control = EasyMock.controlFor(MovieListEditorView.class);
    mockView = (MovieListEditorView)control.getMock();
    mockView.setMovies(movies);
    control.setVoidCallable(1);
    control.activate();
    MovieListEditor editor = new MovieListEditor(movieList, mockView);
    control.verify();
  }
}
```

What are we testing here? We want a class that will sit between a **MovieList** and the interface (whatever that might be) for the purposes of presenting and editing the movie list. We'll call this new class **MovieListEditor**. We'll use EasyMock to mock the interface so that we can easily check that the editor object is using it properly. This test just checks that when a **MovieListEditor** is asked to manage the display and editing of a **MovieList**, it sends the expected collection of movies to the interface for display.

The setUp() method creates a few movies, and uses them to build a **Vector** and a **MovieList**. The **Vector** is equal to the one that should be sent to the display by the **MovieListEditor** being tested.

Once the mock is set up, the test creates a **MovieListEditor**. We pass the constructor everything it needs to do its job, specifically, the **MovieList** to be edited and the interface object (in this case, a mock).

Try to compile. As expected, it doesn't. We need to create the class MovieListEditor:

```
public class MovieListEditor {
  public MovieListEditor(MovieList movieList, MovieListEditorView aView) {
  }
}
```

We also need to create the interface being mocked:

```
public interface MovieListEditorView {
  void setMovies(Vector movies);
}
```

This interface is fine the way it is, but MovieListEditor needs some work before the test will pass. Fortunately, it doesn't take much to get the test to pass:

```
public MovieListEditor(MovieList movieList, MovieListEditorView aView) {
  aView.setMovies(new Vector(movieList.getMovies()));
}
```

Now we can build a real interface to use in place of the mock in order to actually run the application.

## Test 6: The GUI should have a listbox and should display a list of movies in it as requested.

We will use Jemmy to drive the development of the actual GUI layer. Mostly, we will be concerned with functional issues, not aesthetic ones. For this task all we need is a window with a list box that shows the names of the movies in the underlying MovieList.

Here's our Jemmy-based test case (most of it is setup, the actual test just grabs the list elements and checks them):

```
public class TestSwingMovieListEditorView extends TestCase {

  private JFrameOperator mainWindow;
  private Vector movies = null;
  private Movie starWars = null;
  private Movie starTrek = null;
  private Movie stargate = null;
  private MovieList movieList = null;

  protected void setUp() throws Exception {
    super.setUp();
    SwingMovieListEditorView.start();
    starWars = new Movie("Star Wars");
    starTrek = new Movie("Star Trek");
    stargate = new Movie("Stargate");
```

```
    movies = new Vector();
    movies.add(starWars);
    movies.add(starTrek);
    movies.add(stargate);

    movieList = new MovieList();
    movieList.add(starWars);
    movieList.add(starTrek);
    movieList.add(stargate);
  }

protected void tearDown() throws Exception {
  super.tearDown();
  mainWindow.dispose();
}

public void testListContents() {
  mainWindow = new JFrameOperator("Movie List");
  MovieListEditor editor =
    new MovieListEditor(movieList,
                        (SwingMovieListEditorView)mainWindow.getWindow());

  JListOperator movieList = new JListOperator(mainWindow);
  ListModel listModel = movieList.getModel();
  assertEquals("Movie list is the wrong size",
               movies.size(),
               listModel.getSize());
  for (int i = 0; i < movies.size(); i++) {
    assertEquals("Movie list contains bad movie at index " + i,
                 movies.get(i),
                 listModel.getElementAt(i));
  }
}
```

Using this to drive the creation of the GUI we end up with:

```
public class SwingMovieListEditorView extends JFrame
                                implements MovieListEditorView {
  private JList movieList = null;

  public SwingMovieListEditorView() {
    super();
  }


  public void setMovies(Vector movies) {
    movieList.setListData(movies);
  }
```

```
public void init() {
  setTitle("Movie List");
  getContentPane().setLayout(new FlowLayout());
  movieList = new JList(new Vector());
  JScrollPane scroller = new JScrollPane(movieList,
          ScrollPaneConstants.VERTICAL_SCROLLBAR_ALWAYS,
          ScrollPaneConstants.HORIZONTAL_SCROLLBAR_NEVER);
  getContentPane().add(scroller);
  pack();
}
public static void start() {
  SwingMovieListEditorView window = new SwingMovieListEditorView();
  window.init();
  window.show();
}
}
```

## Visual Inspection

Now that we have a real GUI we have something to look at. Notice how quickly we've gotten to the point of having something on the screen. Not much, mind you, but something. Something to look at. Something to show the customer. Something *real*.

So let's have a look (see Figure 10.1). Oh dear! There's the window. There's the scrollpane. Instead of the list of movies we'd expect, there's list of object identifiers. The test tells us that the movies that should be in the list box are, indeed, there. So, what's wrong?

Look at the code for Movie:

```
public class Movie {
}
```

Well, that's the problem. There's nothing to be displayed. The items are in the list but there's nothing to render. We need to give Movie something to identify it that can be placed in the list box. Now it's time for you to sit back smugly and say that you said it should have had a name from the start. I thought so, too, but it wasn't needed until

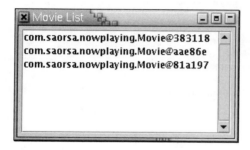

**Figure 10.1** Initial movie list application GUI.

now. We both knew that it would be eventually. Now it is, so now we'll do something about it. But, we add no code without a failing test that requires it. So...

```
public class TestMovie extends TestCase {

  public void testMovieName() {
    Movie starWars = new Movie("Star Wars");
    assertEquals("starWars should have name \"Star Wars\".",
                 "Star Wars",
                 starWars.getName());
  }

  public static void main(String[] args) {
    junit.textui.TestRunner.run(TestMovie.class);
  }
}
```

That looks good, but it causes our previous tests to fail because they used the default constructor (e.g., starWars = new Movie();). We can either add a default constructor, or we can fix the other tests. My opinion is that we fix the other tests rather than incur code debt. Why is this code debt? Because we've just made the default constructor obsolete. Now that each Movie has a name that is set in the constructor, can you imagine a use for a Movie without a name? Me neither. Do we do it now or after we get the new test running? Now. Those tests will fail with errors if we don't. That will violate our goal of only having one test failing at a time.

So, we go back and bring the tests up to date. (We won't include the code here, as the change is so simple: you just need to change the default constructor calls to ones taking a movie name.) All of the code in the book is available online anyway [URL 65].

Now we're back to testMovieName(). We need a getName() method that returns the name. The simplest thing that will make this test pass is:

```
public String getName() {
  return "Star Wars";
}
```

Green bar. Now we have to clean up by refactoring to remove duplication. The duplication is the string literal "Star Wars". It's being passed into the constructor and returned by getName(). To remove the duplication we can store the value that is passed in and return that:

```
public class Movie {
  private String name;

  public Movie(String aName) {
    name = aName;
  }
  public String getName() {
    return name;
  }
}
```

Green bar, still. We're finished with the tweak to Movie. Let's have another look at the GUI again. Same thing. We need a way for the list box to get the name from each Movie. We could write a customer renderer, or we could add a **toString()** method. Guess what's simpler? You got it, we'll go with **toString()**. But first a test:

```
public void testToString() {
  Movie starWars = new Movie("Star Wars");
  assertEquals("starWars should have toString of \"Star Wars\".",
             "Star Wars",
             starWars.toString());
}
```

Sniff, sniff. I smell some duplication. Take a moment to refactor the **starWars** creation into **setUp()**. The result is:

```
public class TestMovie extends TestCase {
  private Movie starWars = null;

  protected void setUp() {
    starWars = new Movie("Star Wars");
  }

  public void testMovieName() {
    assertEquals("starWars should have name \"Star Wars\".",
               "Star Wars",
               starWars.getName());
  }

  public void testToString() {
    assertEquals("starWars should have toString of \"Star Wars\".",
               "Star Wars",
               starWars.toString());
  }

  public static void main(String[] args) {
    junit.textui.TestRunner.run(TestMovie.class);
  }

}
```

The two tests look a lot alike, but they do test different methods, and **toString()** may not always be the same as **getName()**. YAGNI (You Ain't Gonna Need It)? My choice is to leave it as is.

Anyway, we go on to implement Movie.**toString()** to get to the green bar:

```
public String toString() {
  return name;
}
```

This is very similar to **getName**. Should we refactor and have **toString()** delegate to **getName()**? Maybe. For now I won't. In time we may not even need **toString()**.

How's the GUI look now? Have a look at Figure 10.2. That's more like it. Now we're done. And that finishes off the task. High five! Snack time!

**Figure 10.2** Working movie list application GUI.

## ADD A MOVIE IN THE GUI

*Provide a text field and "Add" button for adding movies to the list via the GUI.*

**Test 7.** When the logical layer is asked to add a movie, it should request the required data from the view and update the movie list to include a new movie based on the data provided.

**Test 8.** The GUI should have a field for the movie name and an add button. It should answer the contents of the name field when asked, and request that the logical layer add a movie when the add button is pushed.

To add a movie to the list, we go back to our *humble dialog* approach and revisit TestGUI.

### Test 7: When the logical layer is asked to add a movie, it should request the required data from the view and update the movie list to include a new movie based on the data provided.

Here's the test for adding a movie:

```
public void testAdding() {
    String LOST_IN_SPACE = "Lost In Space";
    Movie lostInSpace = new Movie(LOST_IN_SPACE);
    Vector moviesWithAddition = new Vector(movies);
    moviesWithAddition.add(lostInSpace);

    control = EasyMock.controlFor(MovieListEditorView.class);
    mockView = (MovieListEditorView)control.getMock();

    mockView.setMovies(movies);
    control.setVoidCallable(1);

    mockView.getNewName();
    control.setReturnValue(LOST_IN_SPACE, 1);
```

```
    mockView.setMovies(moviesWithAddition);
    control.setVoidCallable(1);

    control.activate();

    MovieListEditor editor = new MovieListEditor(movieList, mockView);
    editor.add();

    control.verify();
  }
```

Before this will compile we need to add getNewName() to MovieListEditorView:

```
  public interface MovieListEditorView {
    void setMovies(Vector movies);
    String getNewName();
  }
```

Compile, run, red bar.

Before we turn to making the test work, notice the duplication in setting up the control and mock between this and our previous test. Let's start by refactoring that into setUp(). We won't show the updated code here just for that change... watch for it later.

Now let's get back to our green bar. The failure we're getting is an EasyMock expectation failure on verify (i.e., found by the verify() call):

```
method call getNewName():
          calls expected: 1,
          received: 0
method call setMovies([Star Wars,
                       Star Trek,
                       Stargate,
                       Lost In Space]):
          calls expected: 1,
          received: 0
```

Looking at the testAdding() method we can see that the first expected call to set the initial movie list was satisfied, but that the expectations to get the name of the movie to add and to set the larger movie list were not satisfied. Let's take them one at a time.

We'll start with the expected call to getNewName. The task says to add a text field in which the user can enter the name of the movie to be added. So in the add() method of MovieListEditor we need to get the contents of that field using getNewName. To do this we need access to the MovieListEditorView that was passed into the constructor. This means we need to store it in an instance variable. So MovieListEditor is now:

```
  public class MovieListEditor {
    private MovieListEditorView view;

    public MovieListEditor(MovieList movieList, MovieListEditorView aView) {
      view = aView;
      view.setMovies(new Vector(movieList.getMovies()));
    }
```

```
  public void add() {
    view.getNewName();
  }
}
```

That satisfies the expected call to getNewName(). Now to set the new list value. Notice that getNewName() is set up to return the name of the movie to be added. If we use that returned value to create a new Movie which we add to the list, which we then pass to the view with setMovies(), we just might get to the green bar again! Let's try it:

```
  public void add() {
    Movie newMovie = new Movie(view.getNewName());
  }
```

OK, we need the MovieList that was passed to the constructor. We'll have to save it somewhere:

```
  public MovieListEditor(MovieList movieList, MovieListEditorView aView) {
    movies = movieList;
    view = aView;
    view.setMovies(new Vector(movies.getMovies()));
  }
```

Now we can use movies in add():

```
  public void add() {
    Movie newMovie = new Movie(view.getNewName());
    movies.add(newMovie);
    view.setMovies(new Vector(movies.getMovies()));
  }
```

That should do it. Let's see. Red bar!?! OK, what's the failure?

```
Unexpected method call setMovies([Star Wars,
                                 Star Trek,
                                 Stargate,
                                 Lost In Space])
```

Hmm... wasn't it just failing because that call wasn't being made? Now we're making it and it's complaining that the call wasn't expected. Consider what's happening under the covers. If we dig through the EasyMock and MockObjects code, we find that the expected and actual arguments to the expected method calls are compared using equals(). Our argument is an instance of Vector and Vector.equals() compares elements pairwise using equals(). What does equals() mean for Movie? We haven't defined Movie.equals() so it's using what it inherits from Object, which considers two objects equal if they are the same physical object.

Looking at our code we see that we created a Movie in the test and another in MovieListEditor.add() which are getting compared. So, there's the problem. We just

need to add an equals() method to Movie. As always, we start with a test, this one in
TestMovie:

```
public void testEquals() {
  final Movie a = new Movie("Star Wars");
  final Movie b = new Movie("Star Wars");
  final Movie c = new Movie("Star Trek");
  final Movie d = new Movie("Star Wars") {};
  new EqualsTester(a, b, c, d);
}
```

Here are the equals() and hashCode() methods:

```
public boolean equals(Object o) {
  if (o == this) return true;
  if (o == null) return false;
  if (o.getClass() != this.getClass()) return false;
  Movie otherMovie = (Movie)o;
  return name.equals(otherMovie.name);
}
```

```
public int hashCode() {
  return name.hashCode();
}
```

OK. That finishes off the logic part of the interface change. Now we'll turn our
attention to the Swing-based view and TestSwingMovieListEditorView. Before we start
we need to add a stub for the method we added to the interface:

```
public String getNewName() {
  return "";
}
```

## Test 8: The GUI should have a field for the movie name and an add button. It should answer the contents of the name field when asked, and request that the logical layer add a movie when the add button is pushed.

We begin by writing a test for the add operation:

```
public void testAdding() {
  String LOST_IN_SPACE = "Lost In Space";
  Movie lostInSpace = new Movie(LOST_IN_SPACE);
  movies.add(lostInSpace);

  mainWindow = new JFrameOperator("Movie List");
  MovieListEditor editor =
    new MovieListEditor(movieList,
                    (SwingMovieListEditorView)mainWindow.getWindow());
```

```
JTextFieldOperator newMovieField = new JTextFieldOperator(mainWindow);
newMovieField.enterText(LOST_IN_SPACE);

JButtonOperator addButton = new JButtonOperator(mainWindow, "Add");
addButton.doClick();

JListOperator movieList = new JListOperator(mainWindow);
ListModel listModel = movieList.getModel();
assertEquals("Movie list is the wrong size", movies.size(), listModel.getSize());
for (int i = 0; i < movies.size(); i++) {
  assertEquals("Movie list contains bad movie at index " + i,
               movies.get(i),
               listModel.getElementAt(i));
}
}
```

When we run this we get a red bar. There's no **JTextField** component in the interface yet, so new **JTextFieldOperator(mainWindow)** is failing. We need to add the text field in the init() method:

```
JTextField movieField = new JTextField(16);
getContentPane().add(movieField);
```

Now our test is failing because the button can't be found. We need to add that to the interface (don't forget, it's found by name):

```
JButton addButton = new JButton("Add");
getContentPane().add(addButton);
```

Compile and run again. Still a red bar:

```
Movie list is the wrong size expected:<4> but was:<3>
```

Structurally, the components we need are there. Now we just need to hook the add button to the add() method of **MovieListEditor**. Adding an **ActionListener** to the button is easy enough. The problem is what should it do? We don't have an instance of **MovieListEditor**. The way the code is now, we create a view and hand that in to the **MovieListEditor** constuctor. We can add a call there to the supplied view in order to tell it what editor instance it's hooked up to. To support that we'll need several things:

- a method (let's call it **setEditor()**) in the Swing-based view
- a matching method declaration in the view interface
- an instance variable in the Swing-based view to store the editor

Here's the updated interface:

```
public interface MovieListEditorView {
  void setMovies(Vector movies);
  String getNewName();
  void setEditor(MovieListEditor anEditor);
}
```

And here are the additions to SwingMovieListEditorView:

```
private MovieListEditor myEditor = null;

public void setEditor(MovieListEditor anEditor) {
  myEditor = anEditor;
}
```

Now we can add the call to setEditor() to the MovieListEditor constructor:

```
public MovieListEditor(MovieList movieList, MovieListEditorView aView) {
  movies = movieList;
  view = aView;
  view.setMovies(new Vector(movies.getMovies()));
  view.setEditor(this);
}
```

Now we can add the ActionListener to our add button:

```
addButton.addActionListener(new ActionListener() {
  public void actionPerformed(ActionEvent e) {
    myEditor.add();
  }
});
```

One more thing remaining to get to the green bar. Recall that we had to stub get-
NewName() because we had added it to the interface to support adding in MovieListEditor. Now we need to make it real. In the process we need to store the field component
in an instance variable so that it is accessible:

```
public String getNewName() {
  return movieField.getText();
}
```

Green bar! Time to clean up. The first thing that I see is that the SwingMovieList
EditorView.init() method has gotten rather large. What do you think? It's doing several
things:

- setting the title
- setting the layout manager
- creating all the components

Let's use Extract Method to pull those different functions out, compiling and rerunning the tests after each extraction. Here's the result:

```
public void init() {
  setTitle();
  setLayout();
  initList();
  initField();
  initAddButton();
  pack();
}

private void setTitle() {
  setTitle("Movie List");
}

private void setLayout() {
  getContentPane().setLayout(new FlowLayout());
}

private void initList() {
  movieList = new JList(new Vector());
  JScrollPane scroller = new JScrollPane(movieList,
          ScrollPaneConstants.VERTICAL_SCROLLBAR_ALWAYS,
          ScrollPaneConstants.HORIZONTAL_SCROLLBAR_NEVER);
  getContentPane().add(scroller);
}

private void initField() {
  movieField = new JTextField(16);
  getContentPane().add(movieField);
}

private void initAddButton() {
  JButton addButton = new JButton("Add");
  addButton.addActionListener(new ActionListener() {
    public void actionPerformed(ActionEvent e) {
      myEditor.add();
    }
  });
  getContentPane().add(addButton);
}
```

Now that we have the Swing GUI working and refactored, we need to run all of our tests. Uh oh! The tests in TestGUI are failing! A quick look at the trace tells us that the mock view is getting an unexpected call to setEditor(). We need to add an expectation for this call that doesn't care what the argument is. We can do this by adding the following to the end of TestGUI.setUp():

```
mockView.setEditor(null);
control.setDefaultVoidCallable();
```

There, rerunning the tests gives us a green bar again.

# RETROSPECTIVE

In this chapter we've implemented the first story—taking the system from nothing to a list of named movies with a way to add new movies, as well as a GUI. Some things we designed and built from the start, while other things we didn't do until we had a need. There was no *requirement* to have an equals() method in Movie, but we needed it to support an argument expectation. No doubt we'll need it at some point, but we didn't bother to consider it until we had an immediate, concrete need.

In addition to test-driving the core logic of the growing application, we implemented a simple GUI to expose the functionality we built. This is an important point. It's imperative to develop the system in as many wide-ranging slices as possible. Even after the first story you should have something to show.

# Chapter 11

# MOVIES CAN BE RENAMED

*Provide a way to rename movies that are in the list.*

## SUPPORT MOVIE NAME EDITING

*Allow the movie name to be changed.*

So far we have the class Movie that has a name. When we construct an instance, we supply a name and we can retrieve the name with the getName() method. For this task we need a way to set the name of a Movie after it has been constructed.

Now, a question comes to mind: "Can we have a movie without a name?" Ask the customer... "No, every movie has a name." We need to capture that in a test!

**Test 9.** Changing the name of a movie results in it using the new name hereafter.

**Test 10.** A movie can't be constructed with a null name.

**Test 11.** A movie can't be constructed with an empty name.

**Test 12.** A movie can't be renamed to a null name.

**Test 13.** A movie can't be renamed to an empty name.

Before starting, run the tests to give us confidence. Green bar. Then let's go.

### Test 9: Changing the name of a movie results in it using the new name hereafter.

As always, we start with a test, which we will add to TestMovie:

```
public void testRenaming() {
  String newName = "Star Trek";
  Movie aMovie = new Movie("Star Wars");
  aMovie.rename(newName);
  assertEquals("Renaming should change the name.",
            newName,
            aMovie.getName());
}
```

Next, we get it to compile. We need to add a rename() method to Movie:

```
public void rename(String newName) {
}
```

Everything compiles. Run the tests (we can just run **TestMovie** at the moment). Red bar. Our new test failed. Good. Now we add enough code to **rename()** to pass the test. Easy enough:

```
public void rename(String newName) {
  name = newName;
}
```

Green bar.

## Test 10: A movie can't be constructed with a null name.

First, we'll add tests for the constructor to verify that it won't accept empty or null names. One test at a time, first let's test with null. Constructing a **Movie** with a null name should throw an **IllegalArgumentException**. If nothing is thrown, the test should fail. If an unexpected exception is thrown, JUnit will notice and the test will fail. Here's the test:

```
public void testNullName() {
  try {
    new Movie(null);
    fail("null name should have thrown IllegalArgumentException.");
  } catch (IllegalArgumentException ex) {
  }
}
```

As expected, it fails. We need to add a check for a **null** argument to the constructor:

```
public Movie(String aName) {
  if (aName == null) {
    throw new IllegalArgumentException("null Movie name");
  }
  name = aName;
}
```

## Test 11: A movie can't be constructed with an empty name.

The next test is for constructing with an empty name. As before, we want an **IllegalArgumentException** to be thrown:

```
public void testEmptyName() {
  try {
    new Movie("");
    fail("empty name should have thrown IllegalArgumentException.");
  } catch (IllegalArgumentException ex) {
  }
}
```

Compile, run, red. Add an empty name check:

```
public Movie(String aName) {
  if (aName == null) {
    throw new IllegalArgumentException("null Movie name");
  }
  if (aName.length() == 0) {
    throw new IllegalArgumentException("empty Movie name");
  }
  name = aName;
}
```

That takes care of the constructor.

## Test 12: A movie can't be renamed to a null name.

Now for our newly added renaming capability. Again, one test at a time:

```
public void testNullRename() {
  Movie aMovie = new Movie("Star Wars");
  try {
    aMovie.rename(null);
    fail("null rename should have thrown IllegalArgumentException.");
  } catch (IllegalArgumentException ex) {
  }
}
```

Now get it to pass:

```
public void rename(String newName) {
  if (newName == null) {
    throw new IllegalArgumentException("null Movie name");
  }
  name = newName;
}
```

Green bar. Compare what we just did to what we did earlier to the constructor. The duplication jumps out. Let's clean that up by extracting the common text for null into a separate method and calling it from both the constructor and rename():

```
public Movie(String aName) {
  checkNull(aName);
  if (aName.length() == 0) {
    throw new IllegalArgumentException("empty Movie name");
  }
  name = aName;
}
```

```
public void rename(String newName) {
  checkNull(newName);
  name = newName;
}

private void checkNull(String newName) throws IllegalArgumentException {
  if (newName == null) {
    throw new IllegalArgumentException("null Movie name");
  }
}
```

Compile, test, green. Excellent! Next, the "renaming with an empty name" test:

## Test 13: A movie can't be renamed to an empty name.

```
public void testEmptyRename() {
  Movie aMovie = new Movie("Star Wars");
  try {
    aMovie.rename("");
    fail("empty rename should have thrown IllegalArgumentException.");
  } catch (IllegalArgumentException ex) {
  }
}
```

And make it work:

```
public void rename(String newName) {
  checkNull(newName);
  if (newName.length() == 0) {
    throw new IllegalArgumentException("empty Movie name");
  }
  name = newName;
}
```

Again, we have duplication in the empty name check between the constructor and rename(). As we did before, we will extract the empty name check into a separate method:

```
public Movie(String aName) {
  checkNull(aName);
  checkEmpty(aName);
  name = aName;
}

public void rename(String newName) {
  checkNull(newName);
  checkEmpty(newName);
  name = newName;
}
```

```
    private void checkEmpty(String newName) throws IllegalArgumentException {
      if (newName.length() == 0) {
        throw new IllegalArgumentException("empty Movie name");
      }
    }
```

OK. We're finished with that, and with this task.

# MOVIE RENAME GUI

> *On the GUI, selecting a movie fills in the text field with its name. An*
> *"Update" button will update the movie name with the contents of the field.*

Now we must make the newly added rename capability available on the GUI. The task calls for two things:

1. selecting a movie will put its name in the text field

2. clicking an *Update* button that will cause the selected movie to be renamed with what is in the text field.

Here are the required tests:

**Test 14.** Indicating, to the logical layer, that a selection is made from the list causes the view to be given a value for the name field, that is, the selected movie's name.

**Test 15.** Selecting from the list causes the name field to be filled in with the selected movie's name.

**Test 16.** When an update is requested, the selected movie is renamed to whatever is answered by the view as the new name.

**Test 17.** When the update button is pushed, the selected movie is renamed to whatever is in the name field.

Let's tackle them one at a time, in the order above. First, we need a test for filling in the text field with the name of the selected movie. As before, we will work at the logic level first, then the GUI.

## Test 14: Indicating, to the logical layer, that a selection is made from the list causes the view to be given a value for the name field, that is, the selected movie's name.

```
    public void testSelecting() {
      mockView.setMovies(movies);
      control.setVoidCallable(1);

      mockView.setNewName("Star Trek");
      control.setVoidCallable(1);

      control.activate();

      MovieListEditor editor = new MovieListEditor(movieList, mockView);
      editor.select(1);

      control.verify();
    }
```

We need to stub two methods to get this to compile. First, we need to add setNew-Name() to MovieListEditorView:

```
void setNewName(String string);
```

Second, we need to add select() to MovieListEditor:

```
public void select(int i) {
}
```

Now it compiles and fails: the expected call to setNewName() didn't happen. That needs to happen in response to calling select() on the MovieListEditor. So we add enough to select() to get the test to pass:

```
public void select(int i) {
  view.setNewName("Star Trek");
}
```

Green bar! But look at that string literal. Yuck! That duplicates the name of the second movie in the list we set up. Let's get it from there:

```
public void select(int i) {
  view.setNewName(movies.getMovie(i).getName());
}
```

In order to get this to compile we need to add getMovie() to MovieList:

```
public Movie getMovie(int i) {
  return null;
}
```

Oops! That breaks our test. But it's the null that getMovie() is returning that is causing the problem. We'll have to expand on that:

```
public Movie getMovie(int i) {
  return (Movie) movies.get(i);
}
```

OK, our test is working again. Just to be sure, let's add to our test. We'll make it select another movie in the list and make sure that that name is sent to the view:

```
public void testSelecting() {
  mockView.setMovies(movies);
  control.setVoidCallable(1);

  mockView.setNewName("Star Trek");
  control.setVoidCallable(1);
```

```
      mockView.setNewName("Star Wars");
      control.setVoidCallable(1);

      control.activate();

      MovieListEditor editor = new MovieListEditor(movieList, mockView);
      editor.select(1);
      editor.select(0);

      control.verify();
   }
```

Compile, run, green bar. That verifies that the work we just did really does work for the general case. Now we're done with the logical layer; time to turn our attention to the GUI.

## Test 15: Selecting from the list causes the name field to be filled in with the selected movie's name.

This will be fairly simple since it doesn't involve adding additional components. Here's the test (in TestGUI):

```
   public void testSelecting() {
      mainWindow = new JFrameOperator("Movie List");
      MovieListEditor editor =
         new MovieListEditor(movieList,
                             (SwingMovieListEditorView)mainWindow.getWindow());
      JListOperator movieList = new JListOperator(mainWindow);
      movieList.clickOnItem(1, 1);

      JTextFieldOperator newMovieField = new JTextFieldOperator(mainWindow);
      assertEquals("wrong text from selection.",
                   "Star Trek",
                   newMovieField.getText());
   }
```

First, we need to add setNewName() to SwingMovieListEditorView to conform to the change in the interface MovieListEditorView:

```
   public void setNewName(String newName) {
   }
```

Now it compiles, and fails. We need to add some code to hook up list selection to the underlying logic (while we're there and dealing with selection, we'll set the selection mode):

```
private void initList() {
  movieList = new JList(new Vector());
  movieList.setSelectionMode(ListSelectionModel.SINGLE_SELECTION);
  movieList.addListSelectionListener(new ListSelectionListener() {
    public void valueChanged(ListSelectionEvent e) {
      myEditor.select(movieList.getSelectedIndex());
    }
  });
  JScrollPane scroller = new JScrollPane(movieList,
        ScrollPaneConstants.VERTICAL_SCROLLBAR_ALWAYS,
        ScrollPaneConstants.HORIZONTAL_SCROLLBAR_NEVER);
  getContentPane().add(scroller);
}
```

Compile, run, red bar. One more thing to do. We need to fill in the setNewName method so that it puts its argument into the text field:

```
public void setNewName(String newName) {
  movieField.setText(newName);
}
```

Compile, run, green bar! Now we need to add the *Update* button.

## Test 16: When an update is requested, the selected movie is renamed to whatever is answered by the view as the new name.

We will start back at the logic layer with a test:

```
public void testUpdating() {
  Vector newMovies = new Vector();
  newMovies.add(starWars);
  newMovies.add(new Movie("Star Trek I"));
  newMovies.add(stargate);

  mockView.setMovies(movies);
  control.setVoidCallable(1);

  mockView.setNewName("Star Trek");
  control.setVoidCallable(1);

  mockView.getNewName();
  control.setReturnValue("Star Trek I", 1);

  mockView.setMovies(newMovies);
  control.setVoidCallable(1);

  control.activate();
```

```
        MovieListEditor editor = new MovieListEditor(movieList, mockView);
        editor.select(1);
        editor.update();

        control.verify();
    }
```

To compile we need to add a stub to MovieListEditor:

```
    public void update() {
    }
```

The test fails due to the expected calls to getNewName() and setMovies() not happening. This is hardly surprising since update() does nothing. Let's add some code to it:

```
    public void update() {
      if (selectedMovie != null) {
        selectedMovie.rename(view.getNewName());
        view.setMovies(new Vector(movies.getMovies()));
      }
    }
```

We haven't defined selectedMovie yet. We can just grab the Movie whose name we fetch in select (keeping in mind that we will get calls of select(-1) due to the way JList works):

```
    private Movie selectedMovie;

    public void select(int i) {
      if (i == -1) {
        selectedMovie = null;
      } else {
        selectedMovie = movies.getMovie(i);
        view.setNewName(selectedMovie.getName());
      }
    }
```

You will find that there is a significant amount of code that you will write in GUI classes that isn't strictly test-driven. This is, in my opinion, an unavoidable aspect of developing a GUI. The code I'm referring to is the framework-related details. An example here is handling list selections with index -1 denoting the clearing of all selection, dealing with layout managers, and other visual aspects of the interface. These things are the subject of other types of testing that don't relate strictly to the functional aspects of the application. At the functional level, all we really care about is that the required components are present and that they operate as required. Once the tests are in place, you can tweak the visual aspects, confident that you are not breaking the functionality. It's a lot like optimization: get it right, then make it look good.

Now it compiles, and we get a green bar!

## Test 17: When the update button is pushed, the selected movie is renamed to whatever is in the name field.

Now we can move on to the Swing layer. This will involve adding a new button for updating. Here's the test (notice the click on the 0th list item to reset the text field):

```
public void testUpdating() {
  mainWindow = new JFrameOperator("Movie List");
  MovieListEditor editor =
      new MovieListEditor(movieList,
          (SwingMovieListEditorView) mainWindow.getWindow());

  JListOperator movieList = new JListOperator(mainWindow);
  movieList.clickOnItem(1, 1);

  JTextFieldOperator newMovieField = new JTextFieldOperator(mainWindow);
  newMovieField.enterText("Star Trek I");

  JButtonOperator updateButton = new JButtonOperator(mainWindow, "Update");
  updateButton.doClick();

  movieList.clickOnItem(0, 1);
  movieList.clickOnItem(1, 1);
  assertEquals("Movie should have been renamed.",
              "Star Trek I",
              newMovieField.getText());
}
```

This compiles, but fails, because there isn't an update button in the GUI yet. We add it:

```
public void init() {
  setTitle();
  setLayout();
  initList();
  initField();
  initAddButton();
  initUpdateButton();
  pack();
}

private void initUpdateButton() {
  JButton updateButton = new JButton("Update");
  getContentPane().add(updateButton);
}
```

Now the test fails due to an assertion failure: the name isn't being changed. We next need to hook up the update button to the underlying editor:

```
updateButton.addActionListener(new ActionListener() {
  public void actionPerformed(ActionEvent e) {
    myEditor.update();
  }
});
```

Green bar! Now have a look. Is there anything that needs to be cleaned up?

In MovieListEditor there is some duplication between methods that update the movie list on the interface, specifically, the line:

```
view.setMovies(new Vector(movies.getMovies()));
```

This appears in three different methods; time to refactor, to be sure. We'll use Extract Method to put it in its own method:

```
private void updateMovieList() {
  view.setMovies(new Vector(movies.getMovies()));
}
```

In each method where that line occurred we'll replace it by a call to update-MovieList(); for example:

```
public void update() {
  if (selectedMovie != null) {
    selectedMovie.rename(view.getNewName());
    updateMovieList();
  }
}
```

One last thing we should do is add a main() method to our Swing GUI class so that we can run our application stand-alone:

```
public static void main(String[] args) {
  SwingMovieListEditorView window = new SwingMovieListEditorView();
  window.init();
  window.show();
  MovieList list = new MovieList();
  MovieListEditor editor = new MovieListEditor(list, window);
}
```

Now there's some duplication between this method and start() in the same class:

```
public static void start() {
  SwingMovieListEditorView window = new SwingMovieListEditorView();
  window.init();
  window.show();
}
```

Since, in this case, all of the code in start() is included in main(), we can replace those lines in main() with a call to start() if we have start() return the window it creates:

```
public static SwingMovieListEditorView start() {
  SwingMovieListEditorView window = new SwingMovieListEditorView();
  window.init();
  window.show();
  return window;
}
```

```
public static void main(String[] args) {
  SwingMovieListEditorView window = SwingMovieListEditorView.start();
  MovieList list = new MovieList();
  MovieListEditor editor = new MovieListEditor(list, window);
}
```

Compile, run all the tests, green bar. No worries!

## RETROSPECTIVE

In this chapter we've added a small bit of functionality to the system: the ability to rename a movie. This extends to the GUI where we can now select a movie in the list, edit its name, and update it.

# Chapter 12

# MOVIES ARE UNIQUE

> *A movie appears only once in the list; the names are unique and case-insensitive. Attempts to add a duplicate should fail and result in an error.*

Now that we're getting the hang of this, we'll pick up the pace a bit.

## MOVIES ARE UNIQUE

> *Enforce uniqueness of movies during add and update operations. Attempts to add or rename with the same name as an existing movie should raise an exception.*

This task adds a bit of error detection/prevention functionality to what we did in the last chapter: it disallows movies with duplicate names.

**Test 18.** Attempting to add a duplicate movie throws an exception and leaves the list unchanged.

**Test 19.** Asking the movielist to rename a movie results in its name being changed.

**Test 20.** Asking the logical layer to add a duplicate movie causes it to inform the presentation layer that the operation would result in a duplicate.

**Test 21.** Asking the logical layer to update a movie that would result in a duplicate causes it to inform the presentation layer that the operation would result in a duplicate.

**Test 22.** Trying to add a movie that is the same as one in the list results in the display of a "Duplicate Movie" error dialog.

**Test 23.** Trying to rename a movie to the name of one in the list results in the display of a "Duplicate Movie" error dialog.

First, we'll tackle adding a new Movie that is the same as one in the list.

## Test 18: Attempting to add a duplicate movie throws an exception and leaves the list unchanged.

The test we're about to write needs to start with a populated list. OK, that should go into the fixture. All the TestCases we have so far have a sepcific fixture that serves their tests. The biggest fixture has two movies in it. Is this enough? I'd like something a bit bigger... say, three movies. Should we try to do this with TestMovieListWithTwoMovies, or should we create a new TestCase (aka fixture)? When in doubt, create a new fixture.

Here's the test and new fixture:

```
public class TestMovieListWithPopulatedList extends TestCase {
  private MovieList movieList = null;
  private Movie starWars = null;
  private Movie starTrek = null;
  private Movie stargate = null;

  protected void setUp() throws DuplicateMovieException {
    starWars = new Movie("Star Wars");
    starTrek = new Movie("Star Trek");
    stargate = new Movie("Stargate");

    movieList = new MovieList();
    movieList.add(starWars);
    movieList.add(starTrek);
    movieList.add(stargate);
  }
  public void testAddingDuplicate() throws DuplicateMovieException {
    movieList.add(starWars);
    movieList.add(starTrek);
    Movie duplicate = new Movie(starTrek.getName());
    try {
      movieList.add(duplicate);
      fail("Adding duplicate Movie should throw DuplicateMovieException");
    } catch (DuplicateMovieException ex) {
      assertEquals("Failed add of duplicate shouldn't chage the list size.",
                   2,
                   movieList.size());
    }
  }
}
```

To compile this test, we need to create a class, DuplicateMovieException, as well as indicate that MovieList.add() throws this new exception. This, in turn, requires that everything that calls MovieList.add() has to be updated to reflect the fact that a DuplicateMovieException could be thrown.

First, we verify that the test fails. It does—good. Here's the extended MovieList.add() method that lets the test pass:

```
public void add(Movie movieToAdd) throws DuplicateMovieException {
  if (this.contains(movieToAdd)) {
    throw new DuplicateMovieException(movieToAdd.getName());
  }
  movies.add(movieToAdd);
}
```

## Test 19: Asking the movielist to rename a movie results in its name being changed.

Next, we'll move to renaming. It's a bit different because renaming was written with the focus on a specific Movie in isolation. Now we are considering renaming in the context of a MovieList. So, we need to work at the MovieList level. That will require some sort of *rename* method in that class. But we can't do that without a test requiring it. We now need to digress for a short while to take care of that:

```java
public void testRenaming() {
  final String newName = "StarTrek I";
  movieList.rename(starTrek, newName);
  assertEquals("name should be different after renaming",
               newName,
               starTrek.getName());
}
```

To get this to pass, we need to add rename() to MovieList:

```java
public void rename(Movie aMovie, String newName)  {
  aMovie.rename(newName);
}
```

OK, now we're ready to add the test for renaming a duplicate:

```java
public void testRenamingDuplicate() {
  try {
    movieList.rename(starTrek, "Star Wars");
    fail("Renaming to a duplicate should throw DuplicateMovieException");
  } catch (DuplicateMovieException ex) {

    assertEquals("Failed rename shouldn't change list size.",
                 3,
                 movieList.size());

    assertEquals("Failed rename shouldn't change the name.",
                 "Star Trek",
                 starTrek.getName());
  }
}
```

This test requires that MovieList.rename() be marked as throwing DuplicateMovieException. When we do that, this test compiles, but our previous one won't. We need to take that **throws** clause into account. The simplest thing to do is ripple it and let JUnit handle it as an error. That's exactly what we would want to happen.

Now everything compiles and we have a red bar! The failure is because the rename is succeeding when it shouldn't. We need to add code to MovieList.rename() to throw a DuplicateMovieException when a rename would result in a duplicate movie:

```
public void rename(Movie aMovie, String newName)
            throws DuplicateMovieException {
  Movie potentialMovie = new Movie(aMovie);
  potentialMovie.rename(newName);
  if (this.contains(potentialMovie)) {
    throw new DuplicateMovieException(newName);
  }
  aMovie.rename(newName);
}
```

The approach we've used is to create a copy of the movie to be renamed, rename it, and check for the result in the MovieList. To do that, we need to add a copy constructor to Movie. But first we need a test (in TestMovie):

```
public void testCopyConstructor() {
  Movie copyOfStarWars = new Movie(starWars);
  assertNotSame("A copy should not be the same as the original.",
                starWars,
                copyOfStarWars);

  assertEquals("A copy should be equal to the original.",
               starWars,
               copyOfStarWars);
}
```

And now we'll add the copy constructor:

```
public Movie(Movie original) {
  name = original.name;
}
```

Something interesting happened. In TestMovie.testNullName() the constructor call, new Movie(null), no longer compiles since it's ambiguous. It could be a reference to either constructor. It needs to be tweaked to attach type information to the null:

```
public void testNullName() {
  String nullString = null;
  try {
    new Movie(nullString);
    fail("null name should have thrown IllegalArgumentException.");
  } catch (IllegalArgumentException ex) {
  }
}
```

OK, everything compiles and testCopyConstructor() passes. We have a copy constructor in place for Movie now, so we can go back to our renaming test. Green bar there as well. Run AllTests... green bar.

We should revisit the GUI rename code we wrote earlier and bring it up to spec in regards to routing the renaming through MovieList rather than calling Movie.rename() directly. All that needs to be changed is MovieListEditor.update(). Because we have tests in place, we can make changes and immediately see if they work. Here's the updated method:

```
public void update() {
  if (selectedMovie != null) {
    movies.rename(selectedMovie, view.getNewName());
    updateMovieList();
  }
}
```

This won't compile until we deal with the DuplicateMovieException that can be thrown by MovieList.rename(). Because there is no test to require anything more advanced, we'll just ignore it:

```
public void update() {
  if (selectedMovie != null) {
    try {
      movies.rename(selectedMovie, view.getNewName());
      updateMovieList();
    } catch (DuplicateMovieException e) {
    }
  }
}
```

OK, we're ready to move on to the next task.

## ERROR MESSAGE ON NON-UNIQUENESS

*The GUI provides an error message dialog when a non-unique add or rename is attempted.*

Now we need to percolate the *rename would cause a duplicate* error up through the GUI. As usual, we will start at the logic layer.

### Test 20: Asking the logical layer to add a duplicate movie causes it to inform the presentation layer that the operation would result in a duplicate.

We need to add a test for a duplicate addition:

```
public void testDuplicateCausingAdd() {
  mockView.setMovies(movies);
  control.setVoidCallable(1);

  mockView.getNewName();
  control.setReturnValue("Star Wars", 1);
```

```
        mockView.duplicateException("Star Wars");
        control.setVoidCallable(1);

        control.activate();

        MovieListEditor editor = new MovieListEditor(movieList, mockView);
        editor.add();

        control.verify();
    }
```

We need to add a duplicateException method to the MovieListEditorView interface that will take a String indicating the potential duplicate name:

```
    public interface MovieListEditorView {
      void setMovies(Vector movies);
      String getNewName();
      void setEditor(MovieListEditor anEditor);
      void setNewName(String string);
      void duplicateException(String string);
    }
```

The compiler tells us that MovieListEditor.add() can throw DuplicateMovieException which needs handling. Well, we don't want to handle it in the test case; it's what should be causing the call to duplicateException. Let's revisit MovieListEditor.add():

```
    public void add() throws DuplicateMovieException {
      Movie newMovie = new Movie(view.getNewName());
      movies.add(newMovie);
      updateMovieList();
    }
```

It just ripples the exception upward. It needs to handle it by informing the view of the problem. And we know how, because we figured that out when we wrote the test: it has to call duplicateException():

```
    public void add() {
      Movie newMovie = new Movie(view.getNewName());
      try {
        movies.add(newMovie);
        updateMovieList();
      } catch (DuplicateMovieException e) {
        view.duplicateException(newMovie.getName());
      }
    }
```

Green bar. Can we clean anything up? Yes, we get the name from the view twice in add(). Let's pull that out into a local variable:

```
public void add() {
  String newName = view.getNewName();
  Movie newMovie = new Movie(newName);
  try {
    movies.add(newMovie);
    updateMovieList();
  } catch (DuplicateMovieException e) {
    view.duplicateException(newName);
  }
}
```

## Test 21: Asking the logical layer to update a movie that would result in a duplicate causes it to inform the presentation layer that the operation would result in a duplicate.

We need a similar test for updating that would cause a duplicate:

```
public void testDuplicateCausingUpdate() {
  mockView.setMovies(movies);
  control.setVoidCallable(1);

  mockView.setNewName("Star Trek");
  control.setVoidCallable(1);

  mockView.getNewName();
  control.setReturnValue("Star Wars", 1);

  mockView.duplicateException("Star Wars");
  control.setVoidCallable(1);

  control.activate();

  MovieListEditor editor = new MovieListEditor(movieList, mockView);
  editor.select(1);
  editor.update();

  control.verify();
}
```

Red bar. EasyMock is complaining that it got an extra call to:

```
setMovies([Star Wars, Star Trek, Stargate])
```

This indicates that the rename was not performed (same movie names), but that the error was ignored. Recall that we needed to handle the exception in MovieListEditor.update(). Let's revisit that:

```
public void update() {
  if (selectedMovie != null) {
    try {
      movies.rename(selectedMovie, view.getNewName());
      updateMovieList();
    } catch (DuplicateMovieException e) {
    }
  }
}
```

It's just ignoring the exception. That's no longer the simplest thing that could possibly work. We need to do something. We need to pass the information on to the view that there was a problem so that it can inform the user:

```
public void update() {
  if (selectedMovie != null) {
    try {
      movies.rename(selectedMovie, view.getNewName());
      updateMovieList();
    } catch (DuplicateMovieException e) {
      view.duplicateException(view.getNewName());
    }
  }
}
```

But that doesn't work since it's doing two calls to view.getNewName() when the mock only expected one.

This is a problem that can occur when you are using mocks: overspecification. Do we really care that we call getNewName() an extra time? Not really. It shouldn't cause the test to fail. We could have specified the mock differently, setting up a default expectation for the call to getNewName(). See page 167 for more information.

Anyway, this is the same situation that we encountered earlier, so we can extract the getNewName() call into a local variable, which is clearer. The result is:

```
public void update() {
  if (selectedMovie != null) {
    String newName = view.getNewName();
    try {
      movies.rename(selectedMovie, newName);
      updateMovieList();
```

```
        } catch (DuplicateMovieException e) {
          view.duplicateException(newName);
        }
      }
    }
```

Green bar. On to the Swing GUI. The first thing we notice is that SwingMovieList
EditorView doesn't compile since MovieListEditor.add() no longer throws DuplicateMovie-
Exception. We can remove the try-catch wrapper around the call to add():

```
    private void initAddButton() {
      JButton addButton = new JButton("Add");
      addButton.addActionListener(new ActionListener() {
        public void actionPerformed(ActionEvent e) {
          myEditor.add();
        }
      });
      getContentPane().add(addButton);
    }
```

## Test 22: Trying to add a movie that is the same as one in the list results in the display of a "Duplicate Movie" error dialog.

Now, a test for a bad add:

```
    public void testDuplicateCausingAdd() {
      mainWindow = new JFrameOperator("Movie List");
      MovieListEditor editor =
        new MovieListEditor(movieList,
          (SwingMovieListEditorView) mainWindow.getWindow());

      JTextFieldOperator newMovieField = new JTextFieldOperator(mainWindow);
      newMovieField.enterText(starWars.getName());

      JButtonOperator addButton = new JButtonOperator(mainWindow, "Add");
      addButton.pushNoBlock();

      JDialogOperator messageDialog = new JDialogOperator("Duplicate Movie");
      JLabelOperator message = new JLabelOperator(messageDialog);
      assertEquals("Wrong message text",
              "That would result in a duplicate Movie.",
              message.getText());
      JButtonOperator okButton = new JButtonOperator(messageDialog, "OK");
      okButton.doClick();

      JListOperator movieList = new JListOperator(mainWindow);
      ListModel listModel = movieList.getModel();
      assertEquals("Movie list is the wrong size",
              movies.size(),
              listModel.getSize());
```

```
for (int i = 0; i < movies.size(); i++) {
  assertEquals(
    "Movie list contains bad movie at index " + i,
    movies.get(i),
    listModel.getElementAt(i));
  }
}
```

Getting this test to pass requires filling in the duplicateException() method in the GUI class:

```
public void duplicateException(String duplicateName) {
  JOptionPane.showMessageDialog(this,
                "That would result in a duplicate Movie.",
                "Duplicate Movie",
                JOptionPane.ERROR_MESSAGE);

}
```

Notice that since the expected error dialog is modal, we need to use the pushNoBlock() method in JButtonOperator rather than doClick() as we have up until now. If we don't, doClick() wouldn't return until the user manually dismissed the dialog. By then, the dialog would be gone and the next step in the test (finding the dialog) would fail.

## Test 23: Trying to rename a movie to the name of one in the list results in the display of a "Duplicate Movie" error dialog.

The test for a bad update is similar:

```
public void testDuplicateCausingUpdate() {
  mainWindow = new JFrameOperator("Movie List");
  MovieListEditor editor =
      new MovieListEditor(movieList,
          (SwingMovieListEditorView) mainWindow.getWindow());

  JListOperator movieList = new JListOperator(mainWindow);
  movieList.clickOnItem(1, 1);

  JTextFieldOperator newMovieField = new JTextFieldOperator(mainWindow);
  newMovieField.enterText(starWars.getName());

  JButtonOperator updateButton = new JButtonOperator(mainWindow, "Update");
  updateButton.pushNoBlock();

  JDialogOperator messageDialog = new JDialogOperator("Duplicate Movie");
  JLabelOperator message = new JLabelOperator(messageDialog);
  assertEquals("Wrong message text",
              "That would result in a duplicate Movie.",
              message.getText());
```

```
    JButtonOperator okButton = new JButtonOperator(messageDialog, "OK");
    okButton.doClick();

    ListModel listModel = movieList.getModel();
    assertEquals("Movie list is the wrong size",
                 movies.size(),
                 listModel.getSize());

    for (int i = 0; i < movies.size(); i++) {
      assertEquals("Movie list contains bad movie at index " + i,
                   movies.get(i),
                   listModel.getElementAt(i));
    }
  }
}
```

Green bar right away. Is that odd? No, since it's testing the same reaction to a bad update as we just implemented for a bad add.

Take a minute to look at the tests we just added. They are very similar. We can refactor some of that commonality out by extracting a couple of methods for the message dialog check and the check that the list is unchanged. The result is:

```
public void testDuplicateCausingAdd() {
  mainWindow = new JFrameOperator("Movie List");
  MovieListEditor editor =
      new MovieListEditor(movieList,
          (SwingMovieListEditorView) mainWindow.getWindow());

  JTextFieldOperator newMovieField = new JTextFieldOperator(mainWindow);
  newMovieField.enterText(starWars.getName());

  JButtonOperator addButton = new JButtonOperator(mainWindow, "Add");
  addButton.pushNoBlock();

  checkDuplicateExceptionDialog();

  JListOperator movieList = new JListOperator(mainWindow);
  checkListIsUnchanged(movieList);
}

public void testDuplicateCausingUpdate() {
  mainWindow = new JFrameOperator("Movie List");
  MovieListEditor editor =
      new MovieListEditor(movieList,
          (SwingMovieListEditorView) mainWindow.getWindow());

  JListOperator movieList = new JListOperator(mainWindow);
  movieList.clickOnItem(1, 1);

  JTextFieldOperator newMovieField = new JTextFieldOperator(mainWindow);
  newMovieField.enterText(starWars.getName());

  JButtonOperator updateButton = new JButtonOperator(mainWindow, "Update");
  updateButton.pushNoBlock();
```

```
      checkDuplicateExceptionDialog();
      checkListIsUnchanged(movieList);
   }

   private void checkListIsUnchanged(JListOperator movieList) {
      ListModel listModel = movieList.getModel();
      assertEquals("Movie list is the wrong size",
                   movies.size(),
                   listModel.getSize());

      for (int i = 0; i < movies.size(); i++) {
         assertEquals("Movie list contains bad movie at index " + i,
                      movies.get(i),
                      listModel.getElementAt(i));
      }
   }

   private void checkDuplicateExceptionDialog() {
      JDialogOperator messageDialog = new JDialogOperator("Duplicate Movie");
      JLabelOperator message = new JLabelOperator(messageDialog);
      assertEquals("Wrong message text",
                   "That would result in a duplicate Movie.",
                   message.getText());

      JButtonOperator okButton = new JButtonOperator(messageDialog, "OK");
      okButton.doClick();
   }
```

Looking more at this test case, we notice that the code at the beginning of almost every test is identical:

```
   mainWindow = new JFrameOperator("Movie List");
   MovieListEditor editor =
       new MovieListEditor(
          movieList,
          (SwingMovieListEditorView) mainWindow.getWindow());
```

We can pull that out and put it in setUp():

```
   protected void setUp() throws Exception {
      super.setUp();
      SwingMovieListEditorView.start();
      starWars = new Movie("Star Wars");
      starTrek = new Movie("Star Trek");
      stargate = new Movie("Stargate");

      movies = new Vector();
      movies.add(starWars);
      movies.add(starTrek);
      movies.add(stargate);

      movieList = new MovieList();
      movieList.add(starWars);
      movieList.add(starTrek);
      movieList.add(stargate);
```

```
    mainWindow = new JFrameOperator("Movie List");
    editor = new MovieListEditor(movieList,
                            (SwingMovieListEditorView) mainWindow.getWindow());
}
```

Now those two lines can be removed from each of the tests. This cleans things up nicely.

## RETROSPECTIVE

In this chapter we added some error checking. Specifically, we checked whether an add or rename operation will result in a duplicate movie in the list. If not, the action is performed, otherwise, a **DuplicateMovieException** is thrown. This percolates to the GUI where an error dialog is presented to the user. Since this is a modal dialog, we had to use **pushNoBlock()** rather than **doClick()** in Jemmy to click the *Add* and *Update* buttons.

# Chapter 13

# RATINGS

*Movies each have a single, editable rating.*

## ADD A SINGLE RATING TO MOVIE

*Add support for a single rating to Movie. Support the concept of an unrated movie.*

This is a straightforward task; we're simply adding a piece of information to a class. Note that the task does not require changing the rating.

**Test 24.** An unrated movie answers negative when asked if it is rated.

**Test 25.** A rated movie answers positive when asked if it is rated, and it can answer its rating when asked.

**Test 26.** Asking an unrated movie for its rating throws an exception.

We'll start with the test for unrated movies.

## Test 24: An unrated movie answers negative when asked if it is rated.

```
public void testUnrated() {
    assertFalse("starWars should be unrated.", starWars.hasRating());
}
```

To pass this test we add Movie.hasRating():

```
public boolean hasRating() {
    return false;
}
```

## Test 25: A rated movie answers positive when asked if it is rated, and it can answer its rating when asked.

Now we write a test for a movie with a rating. Here's the start of the test:

```
public void testRatedMovie() {
    assertTrue("fotr should be rated.", fotr.hasRating());
    assertEquals("fotr should be rated at 5.", 5, fotr.getRating());
}
```

Now we need to answer the question, "How does a movie get a rating?" There are two reasonable answers to this:

1. by a constructor, and/or

2. using a mutator (e.g., setRating()).

Since we have no requirement yet to be able to change a movie's rating, let's go with the first option. We will add another constructor that takes a rating in addition to a name. Our test is:

```
public void testRatedMovie() {
  Movie fotr = new Movie("Fellowship of the Ring", 5);
  assertTrue("fotr should be rated", fotr.hasRating());
  assertEquals("fotr should be rated at 5.", 5, fotr.getRating());
}
```

Now we have to add a constructor and a getRating() method to Movie to get the test to compile:

```
public Movie(String aName, int aRating) {
  this(aName);
}

public int getRating() {
  return 5;
}
```

Now, of course, hasRating() always returns false which causes the first assert to fail. We could go in baby steps, but by now we're feeling more confident and experienced so we'll take a bigger step. What needs to be done? It's pretty obvious that we should grab the rating that is passed to the constructor, store it somewhere, and use that to determine the value returned from hasRating() and getRating(). Now the question is, "What does it mean for a movie to be unrated?" A valid rating is between 0 and 5, inclusive. The simplest thing is to assign -1 to denote *unrated*. Here's the changed code in Movie:

```
private int rating;

public Movie(String aName) {
  this(aName, −1);
}

public Movie(Movie original) {
  name = original.name;
  rating = original.rating;
}
```

```
public Movie(String aName, int aRating) {
  checkNull(aName);
  checkEmpty(aName);
  name = aName;
  rating = aRating;
}

public boolean hasRating() {
  return rating > −1;
}

public int getRating() {
  return rating;
}
```

Our tests all pass now. Can we refactor anything? I don't think so. One thing that would be nice to do would be to move rating from being an int to an object of some sort. In the future, maybe, when we need it. For now, however, an int works fine.

## Test 26: Asking an unrated movie for its rating throws an exception.

Next, we want to throw an exception if an unrated Movie is asked for its rating:

```
public void testUnratedException() {
  try {
    starWars.getRating();
    fail("getRating() of an unrated Movie should throw UnratedException.");
  } catch (UnratedException ex) {
    assertEquals("UnratedException should identify the movie.",
                 starWars.getName(),
                 ex.getMessage());
  }
}
```

This requires us to add an exception class, UnratedException, and have it thrown by Movie.getRating(). The code changes are simple enough. The fallout from this is that now testRatedMovie() doesn't compile since it doesn't handle UnratedException. We simply make the test method throw it on to JUnit and all is well. Well, everything compiles. When we run the tests we get a red bar—that is expected and desired. Now we can add the code to make it green again:

```
public int getRating() throws UnratedException {
  if (hasRating()) {
    return rating;
  } else {
    throw new UnratedException(name);
  }
}
```

## SHOW THE RATING IN THE GUI

*Show the rating in the GUI, next to the movie name.*

Now we need the rating on the GUI. This is all in the presentation layer since the movie list is given a list of movies. This means that we have nothing to do at the logic level (i.e., MovieListEditor) and we can move directly to the Swing classes. After getting more information about what is desired/possible/easy, it is decided that we will display an *N of 5* star indicator to the left of the movie name in the list. This will require a custom renderer for the list. We can easily write tests for this. We'll need a new test case, TestCustomListRenderer.

**Test 27.** When asked for the renderer component, the renderer returns itself.

**Test 28.** When given a movie to render, the resulting test and rating image corresponds to the movie being rendered.

**Test 29.** When rendering an unselected item, the renderer uses its list's unselected colors.

**Test 30.** When rendering a selected item, the renderer uses its list's selected colors.

We'll need an instance of the renderer to test, a JList to pass in, and a couple of Movies to test with. Let's start by creating a fixture:

```
private Movie fotr = null;
private Movie starTrek = null;
private CustomMovieListRenderer renderer = null;
private JList list = null;

protected void setUp() {
  fotr = new Movie("Fellowship of The Ring", 5);
  starTrek = new Movie("Star Trek", 3);
  renderer = new CustomMovieListRenderer();
  list = new JList();
}
```

We'll work simply, testing one behavior at a time.

## Test 27: When asked for the renderer component, the renderer returns itself.

To start, the rendering method should return the renderer itself:

```
public void testReturnsSelf() {
  Component result = renderer.getListCellRendererComponent(list,
                                                           fotr,
                                                           1,
                                                           false,
                                                           false);

  assertSame("getListCellRendererComponent should return self.",
             renderer,
             result);
}
```

This needs just the basic rendering method:

```
public Component getListCellRendererComponent(JList list,
                                              Object value,
                                              int index,
                                              boolean isSelected,
                                              boolean cellHasFocus) {
    return this;
}
```

## Test 28: When given a movie to render, the resulting test and rating image corresponds to the movie being rendered.

The next step is to make sure the text and rating image is getting set properly:

```
public void testContents() {
    renderer.getListCellRendererComponent(list, fotr, 1, false, false);
    assertEquals("Text should be " + fotr.getName(),
                 fotr.getName(),
                 renderer.getText());

    assertSame("Icon should be 5 stars.",
               CustomMovieListRenderer.iconForRating(5),
               renderer.getIcon());

    renderer.getListCellRendererComponent(list, starTrek, 1, true, false);
    assertEquals("Text should be " + starTrek.getName(),
                 starTrek.getName(),
                 renderer.getText());

    assertSame("Icon should be 3 stars.",
               CustomMovieListRenderer.iconForRating(3),
               renderer.getIcon());
}
```

Here's the new rendering method:

```
public Component getListCellRendererComponent(JList list,
                                              Object value,
                                              int index,
                                              boolean isSelected,
                                              boolean cellHasFocus) {
    Movie movieToRender = (Movie) value;
    setText(movieToRender.getName());
```

```
if (movieToRender.hasRating()) {
  try {
    setIcon(ratingIcons[movieToRender.getRating() + 1]);
  } catch (UnratedException ex) {}
} else {
  setIcon(ratingIcons[0]);
}
return this;
}
```

To support this we need some icons where we can get at them based on the rating. We'll do this with a static variable on the renderer:

```
private static ImageIcon[] ratingIcons =
  {
    new ImageIcon("images/no-rating.gif"),
    new ImageIcon("images/zero-stars.gif"),
    new ImageIcon("images/one-star.gif"),
    new ImageIcon("images/two-stars.gif"),
    new ImageIcon("images/three-stars.gif"),
    new ImageIcon("images/four-stars.gif"),
    new ImageIcon("images/five-stars.gif")
  };

public static ImageIcon iconForRating(int rating) {
  return ratingIcons[rating];
}
```

## Test 29: When rendering an unselected item, the renderer uses its list's unselected colors.

Next, we need to deal with the colors. First, the unselected colors:

```
public void testUnSelectedColors() {
  list.setBackground(Color.BLUE);
  list.setForeground(Color.RED);
  list.setSelectionBackground(Color.RED);
  list.setSelectionForeground(Color.BLUE);
  renderer.getListCellRendererComponent(list, fotr, 1, false, false);

  assertEquals("Unselected background should be blue.",
              Color.BLUE,
              renderer.getBackground());

  assertEquals("Unselected foreground should be red.",
              Color.RED,
              renderer.getForeground());
}
```

And the new renderer method to pass it:

```
public Component getListCellRendererComponent(JList list,
                                              Object value,
                                              int index,
                                              boolean isSelected,
                                              boolean cellHasFocus) {
    Movie movieToRender = (Movie) value;
    setBackground(list.getBackground());
    setForeground(list.getForeground());
    setText(movieToRender.getName());

    if (movieToRender.hasRating()) {
      try {
        setIcon(ratingIcons[movieToRender.getRating() + 1]);
      } catch (UnratedException ex) {}
    } else {
      setIcon(ratingIcons[0]);
    }
    return this;
}
```

## Test 30: When rendering a selected item, the renderer uses its list's selected colors.

And, finally, selected colors:

```
public void testSelectedColors() {
  list.setBackground(Color.BLUE);
  list.setForeground(Color.RED);
  list.setSelectionBackground(Color.RED);
  list.setSelectionForeground(Color.BLUE);
  renderer.getListCellRendererComponent(list, fotr, 1, true, false);

  assertEquals("Selected background should be bluered.",
              Color.RED,
              renderer.getBackground());

  assertEquals("Selected foreground should be redblue.",
              Color.BLUE,
              renderer.getForeground());
}
```

And the code to pass it:

```
public Component getListCellRendererComponent(JList list,
                                              Object value,
                                              int index,
                                              boolean isSelected,
                                              boolean cellHasFocus) {
    Movie movieToRender = (Movie) value;
```

```
    if (isSelected) {
      setBackground(list.getSelectionBackground());
      setForeground(list.getSelectionForeground());
    } else {
      setBackground(list.getBackground());
      setForeground(list.getForeground());
    }

    setText(movieToRender.getName());
    if (movieToRender.hasRating()) {
      try {
        setIcon(ratingIcons[movieToRender.getRating() + 1]);
      } catch (UnratedException ex) {
      }
    } else {
      setIcon(ratingIcons[0]);
    }
    return this;
  }
```

Green bar all the way. We should refactor the code that sets the list colors into setUp(). Here's the new version of the affected code:

```
  protected void setUp() {
    fotr = new Movie("Fellowship of The Ring", 5);
    starTrek = new Movie("Star Trek", 3);
    renderer = new CustomMovieListRenderer();
    list = new JList();

    list.setBackground(Color.BLUE);
    list.setForeground(Color.RED);
    list.setSelectionBackground(Color.RED);
    list.setSelectionForeground(Color.BLUE);
  }

  public void testUnSelectedColors() {
    renderer.getListCellRendererComponent(list, fotr, 1, false, false);
    assertEquals("Unselected background should be blue.",
                 Color.BLUE,
                 renderer.getBackground());

    assertEquals("Unselected foreground should be red.",
                 Color.RED,
                 renderer.getForeground());
  }

  public void testSelectedColors() {
    renderer.getListCellRendererComponent(list, fotr, 1, true, false);
    assertEquals("Selected background should be red.",
                 Color.RED,
                 renderer.getBackground());
```

```
        assertEquals("Selecetd foreground should be blue.",
                Color.BLUE,
                renderer.getForeground());
}
```

Now all we need to do is use this renderer in the Swing GUI. Figure 13.1 shows the new version of the GUI, and here's the updated code:

```
private void initList() {
  movieList = new JList(new Vector());
  movieList.setSelectionMode(ListSelectionModel.SINGLE_SELECTION);
  movieList.setCellRenderer(new CustomMovieListRenderer());
  movieList.addListSelectionListener(new ListSelectionListener() {
    public void valueChanged(ListSelectionEvent e) {
      myEditor.select(movieList.getSelectedIndex());
    }
  });

  JScrollPane scroller =
    new JScrollPane(
      movieList,
      ScrollPaneConstants.VERTICAL_SCROLLBAR_ALWAYS,
      ScrollPaneConstants.HORIZONTAL_SCROLLBAR_NEVER);
  getContentPane().add(scroller);
}
```

**Figure 13.1** GUI with ratings.

## EDIT THE RATING

*Allow the rating to be edited.*

For this task, we'll need the following tests:

**Test 31.** Selecting a movie updates the rating in the GUI.

**Test 32.** Updating a movie changes its rating if a different rating was selected for it.

**Test 33.** Selecting a movie from the list updates the displayed rating.

**Test 34.** Updating a movie in the GUI changes its rating if a different rating was selected for it, and updates the display accordingly.

We'll start by adding some ratings to TestMovieListEditor's fixture:

```
starWars = new Movie("Star Wars", 5);
starTrek = new Movie("Star Trek", 3);
stargate = new Movie("Stargate");
```

## Test 31: Selecting a movie updates the rating in the GUI.

Next we'll extend testSelecting() to check that a selection in the movie list causes an update of the rating:

```
public void testSelecting() {
    mockView.setMovies(movies);
    control.setVoidCallable(1);

    mockView.setNewName("Star Wars");
    control.setVoidCallable(1);
    mockView.setNewRating(6);
    control.setVoidCallable(1);

    mockView.setNewName("Star Trek");
    control.setVoidCallable(1);
    mockView.setNewRating(4);
    control.setVoidCallable(1);

    mockView.setNewName("Stargate");
    control.setVoidCallable(1);
    mockView.setNewRating(0);
    control.setVoidCallable(1);

    control.activate();

    MovieListEditor editor = new MovieListEditor(movieList, mockView);
    editor.select(0);
    editor.select(1);
    editor.select(2);

    control.verify();
}
```

The first step to getting to a green bar again is to add a method to the MovieList EditorView interface:

```
public interface MovieListEditorView {
  void setMovies(Vector movies);
  String getNewName();
  void setEditor(MovieListEditor anEditor);
  void setNewName(String string);
  void duplicateException(String string);
  void setNewRating(int i);
}
```

Next, we need to add to MovieListEditor.select() to set the rating as well as the name:

```
public void select(int i) {
  if (i == -1) {
    selectedMovie = null;
  } else {
    selectedMovie = movies.getMovie(i);
    view.setNewName(selectedMovie.getName());

    try {
      view.setNewRating(selectedMovie.getRating() + 1);
    } catch (UnratedException e) {
      view.setNewRating(0);
    }
  }
}
```

Now we see that several tests are failing due to the additional (and unexpected) calls to setNewRating(). We can either add expectations to these tests or have them ignore those calls. We'll do the latter since it's the simplest thing that will work. We just need to add the following line to the beginning of each failing test:

```
mockView.setNewRating(0);
control.setDefaultVoidCallable();
```

Upon looking over the code, I feel that some renaming is in order. The method for getting and setting the name and rating fields are misleading. Let's change them as so: getNewName() changes to getNameField(). For brevity, we'll just show the interface:

```
public interface MovieListEditorView {
  void setMovies(Vector movies);
  String getNameField();
  void setEditor(MovieListEditor anEditor);
  void setNameField(String string);
  void duplicateException(String string);
  void setRatingField(int i);
}
```

## Test 32: Updating a movie changes its rating if a different rating was selected for it.

Now for the flip side of editing the rating...updating the movie behind it. We'll start by extending testUpdating() by adding ratings to the Movies we create and adding expectations for calls to setRatingField() and getRatingField():

```java
public void testUpdating() {
  Vector newMovies = new Vector();
  newMovies.add(starWars);
  newMovies.add(new Movie("Star Trek I", 5));
  newMovies.add(stargate);

  mockView.setMovies(movies);
  control.setVoidCallable(1);

  mockView.setNameField("Star Trek");
  control.setVoidCallable(1);
  mockView.setRatingField(4);
  control.setVoidCallable();

  mockView.getNameField();
  control.setReturnValue("Star Trek I", 1);
  mockView.getRatingField();
  control.setReturnValue(6, 1);

  mockView.setMovies(newMovies);
  control.setVoidCallable(1);

  control.activate();

  MovieListEditor editor = new MovieListEditor(movieList, mockView);
  editor.select(1);
  editor.update();

  control.verify();
}
```

To get to green, we have to do some work on MovieListEditor.update(). We'll add a line that sets the rating of the selected Movie if it can be renamed successfully:

```java
public void update() {
  if (selectedMovie != null) {
    String newName = view.getNameField();

    try {
      movies.rename(selectedMovie, newName);
      selectedMovie.setRating(view.getRatingField());
      updateMovieList();
    } catch (DuplicateMovieException e) {
      view.duplicateException(newName);
    }
  }
}
```

Now we need to add a setRating() method to Movie. We won't test-drive that, as it will be a simple mutator and it will be tested indirectly. In fact, I won't even bother showing it here. Most IDEs will have a way to generate accessors and mutators for instance variables.

Green bar. Now we can turn to the Swing layer. We can take the same approach to editing the rating as to editing the name: When a movie is selected, use a field to edit its value. In this case, since the range is constrained, we'll use a combo box.

We'll start by adding some ratings to the fixture:

```
starWars = new Movie("Star Wars", 5);
starTrek = new Movie("Star Trek", 3);
stargate = new Movie("Stargate");
```

Green bar. All the tests still work. We can continue.

## Test 33: Selecting a movie from the list updates the displayed rating.

We'll start with a test to check that selecting a movie in the list sets the rating selection combo box to the appropriate value:

```
public void testSelectUpdatesRating() {
    JListOperator movieList = new JListOperator(mainWindow);
    JComboBoxOperator ratingCombo = new JComboBoxOperator(mainWindow);

    movieList.clickOnItem(0, 1);
    assertEquals("wrong rating from selecting starWars.",
                 6,
                 ratingCombo.getSelectedIndex());

    movieList.clickOnItem(1, 1);
    assertEquals("wrong rating from selecting starTrek.",
                 4,
                 ratingCombo.getSelectedIndex());

    movieList.clickOnItem(2, 1);
    assertEquals("wrong rating from selecting stargate.",
                 0,
                 ratingCombo.getSelectedIndex());
}
```

Now we need to make it pass. We need a combo box in the GUI and methods to set and get its value:

```
private JComboBox ratingField = null;

public void setRatingField(int i) {
    ratingField.setSelectedIndex(i);
}
```

```
public int getRatingField() {
  return ratingField.getSelectedIndex();
}

public void init() {
  setTitle();
  setLayout();
  initList();
  initField();
  initRatingCombo();
  initAddButton();
  initUpdateButton();
  pack();
}

private void initRatingCombo() {
  ratingField = new JComboBox(CustomMovieListRenderer.icons());
  getContentPane().add(ratingField);
}
```

Green bar. OK. We talk to the customer. We need to be able to select a movie, change the rating, and click update. We try it. Uh oh. We get the *duplicate movie* message. Hmmm... think think... talk talk... what we need to do is raise that error only if the update makes the selected movie equal to a **different** movie in the list.

We need to go back to TestMovieListEditor and create a test to drive that behavior:

```
public void testUpdatingWithSameName() {
  Vector newMovies = new Vector();
  newMovies.add(starWars);
  newMovies.add(new Movie("Star Trek", 5));
  newMovies.add(stargate);

  mockView.setMovies(movies);
  control.setVoidCallable(1);

  mockView.setNameField("Star Trek");
  control.setVoidCallable(1);
  mockView.setRatingField(4);
  control.setVoidCallable();

  mockView.getNameField();
  control.setReturnValue("Star Trek", 1);
  mockView.getRatingField();
  control.setReturnValue(6, 1);

  mockView.setMovies(newMovies);
  control.setVoidCallable(1);

  control.activate();

  MovieListEditor editor = new MovieListEditor(movieList, mockView);
  editor.select(1);
  editor.update();
```

```
      control.verify();
    }
```

Now we can tweak the MovieListEditor.update() method to make the bar green again:

```
public void update() {
  if (selectedMovie != null) {
    String newName = view.getNameField();
    if (selectedMovie.getName().equals(newName)) {
      updateMovie();
    } else {

      try {
        movies.rename(selectedMovie, newName);
        updateMovie();
      } catch (DuplicateMovieException e) {
        view.duplicateException(newName);
      }
    }
  }
}

private void updateMovie() {
  selectedMovie.setRating(view.getRatingField() - 1);
  updateMovieList();
}
```

Notice that we did some refactoring while we were there.

## Test 34: Updating a movie in the GUI changes its rating if a different rating was selected for it, and updates the display accordingly.

Now back to the Swing GUI. We need a test that selects a movie, changes the rating, and updates:

```
public void testUpdateRating() {
  JListOperator movieList = new JListOperator(mainWindow);
  JComboBoxOperator ratingCombo = new JComboBoxOperator(mainWindow);
  movieList.clickOnItem(0, 1);
  ratingCombo.setSelectedIndex(4);

  JButtonOperator updateButton = new JButtonOperator(mainWindow, "Update");
  updateButton.pushNoBlock();
  movieList.clickOnItem(1, 1);
  movieList.clickOnItem(0, 1);
  assertEquals("updating should have changed rating.",
               4,
               ratingCombo.getSelectedIndex());
}
```

Green bar. Life is good. Finally, Figure 13.2 shows the current state of the GUI.

**Figure 13.2** GUI with editable ratings.

## RETROSPECTIVE

We've done a few things in this chapter. One interesting thing was developing a custom list cell renderer test-first. We've also extended our Jemmy testing repertoire by adding combo boxes.

# Chapter 14

# CATEGORIES

*Movies belong to a category; categories such as* Horror, Comedy, *etc.*

## ADD A CATEGORY

*Add support for a movie to have a single category, from a fixed list of alternatives.*

To add support for categories through the application we will want these tests:

**Test 35.** A movie that hasn't explicitly been given a category should answer that it is uncategorized when asked for its category.

**Test 36.** If a movie is given a category when it is created, it answers that when asked for its category.

**Test 37.** Trying to create a movie with an invalid category (i.e., not from the predefined set) throws an exception.

We begin by adding support for a category to Movie. Notice that the fleshed out task description mentions that the categories are from a fixed list. That means that the category of a movie can't be just anything (like an arbitrary string), but has to be picked from a fixed set of alternatives. So let's pick an initial list to work with: *Science Fiction, Drama, Comedy, Horror, Western,* and *Fantasy.* We will also need an *Uncategorized* setting.

## Test 35: A movie that hasn't explicitly been given a category should answer that it is uncategorized when asked for its category.

We'll start with the last case, since it doesn't require actually setting the category of a Movie:

```
public void testUncategorized() {
  assertEquals("starWars should be uncategorized.",
               "Uncategorized",
               starWars.getCategory());
}
```

Getting to green bar by doing the simplest thing results in:

```
public String getCategory() {
  return "Uncategorized";
}
```

## Test 36: If a movie is given a category when it is created, it answers that when asked for its category.

Now, when we are testing for the other categories, we need a way to set the category of a Movie. The simplest thing is to add a constructor that takes a category string. So here is the test:

```
public void testScienceFiction() {
    Movie alien = new Movie("Alien", "Science Fiction");
    assertEquals("alien should be Science Fiction.",
                "ScienceFiction",
                alien.getCategory());
}
```

We know we'll have to store the category value and return it from getCategory(), so let's take a bigger step and just do it. And here's the new code:

```
private String category = null;

public Movie(String aName, String aCategory) {
    this(aName, −1);
    category = aCategory;
}

public Movie(Movie original) {
    name = original.name;
    rating = original.rating;
    category = original.category;
}

public String getCategory() {
    return (category != null) ? category : "Uncategorized";
}
```

Green bar. The constructors of Movie are proliferating, so let's make a more general one and retrofit our tests to use it:

```
public Movie(String aName, String aCategory, int aRating) {
    checkNull(aName);
    checkEmpty(aName);
    name = aName;
    category = (aCategory != null) ? aCategory : "Uncategorized";
    rating = aRating;
}
```

While we're at it we notice that some refactoring can be applied to TestMovie. We do that as well, removing unneeded instance creation from the tests and using starWars that is created in setUp().

## Exercises

1.  Refactor TestMovie to use a single Constructor Method that we just added to Movie.

*Answer on p. 521*

2.  Refactor the tests again, this time removing the unneeded Movie creation.

*Answer on p. 523*

## Test 37: Trying to create a movie with an invalid category (i.e., not from the predefined set) throws an exception.

Now, we need to enforce the constraint that only a fixed set of alternatives can be used:

```
public void testBadCategory() {
  try {
    Movie alien = new Movie("Alien", "SciFi", −1);
    fail("Bad category accepted");
  } catch (IllegalArgumentException ex) {
  }
}
```

So how do we constrain the category values to a closed, fixed set of alternatives? We could use guard statements and the string comparison:

```
public Movie(String aName, String aCategory, int aRating) {
  checkNull(aName);
  checkEmpty(aName);
  checkCategory(aCategory);
  name = aName;
  category = (aCategory != null) ? aCategory : "Uncategorized";
  rating = aRating;
}

private void checkCategory(String aCategory) {
  if (aCategory == null) return;
  if (aCategory.equals("Uncategorized")) return;
  if (aCategory.equals("Science Fiction")) return;
  if (aCategory.equals("Horror")) return;
  throw new IllegalArgumentException("Bad category: " + aCategory);
}
```

This smells! Imagine changing the spelling of a category once we have a large, complex system built. We could refactor the string literals to constants and use them everywhere:

```
public static final String UNCATEGORIZED = "Uncategorized";
public static final String SCIFI = "Science Fiction";
public static final String HORROR = "Horror";
```

```
public Movie(String aName, String aCategory, int aRating) {
  checkNull(aName);
  checkEmpty(aName);
  checkCategory(aCategory);
  name = aName;
  category = (aCategory != null) ? aCategory : UNCATEGORIZED;
  rating = aRating;
}

private void checkCategory(String aCategory) {
  if (aCategory == null) return;
  if (aCategory.equals(UNCATEGORIZED)) return;
  if (aCategory.equals(SCIFI)) return;
  if (aCategory.equals(HORROR)) return;
  throw new IllegalArgumentException("Bad category: " + aCategory);
}
```

The corresponding version of the tests look like:

```
public void testUncategorized() {
  assertEquals("starWars should be uncategorized.",
            Movie.UNCATEGORIZED,
            starWars.getCategory());
}

public void testScienceFiction() {
  Movie alien = new Movie("Alien", Movie.SCIFI, -1);
  assertEquals("alien should be Science Fiction.",
            Movie.SCIFI,
            alien.getCategory());
}
```

This still has a smell. It would be nice to refactor this in a way that would let us leverage Java to enforce the constraints for us. We can do that by refactoring to a type-safe enumeration. Joshua Kerievsky discusses this refactoring in [29].

First, we create the type-safe enumeration class:

```
public class Category {
  private String name = null;

  private Category(String categoryName) {
    name = categoryName;
  }

  public static final Category UNCATEGORIZED = new Category("Uncategorized");
  public static final Category SCIFI = new Category("Science Fiction");
  public static final Category HORROR = new Category("Horror");
}
```

Next, we update the related tests. One advantage of using a type-safe enumeration is that we no longer need to test for bad values; the compiler enforces that for us. Here are the remaining tests:

```
public void testUncategorized() {
  assertEquals("starWars should be uncategorized.",
              Category.UNCATEGORIZED,
              starWars.getCategory());
}

public void testScienceFiction() {
  Movie alien = new Movie("Alien", Category.SCIFI, −1);
  assertEquals("alien should be Science Fiction.",
              Category.SCIFI,
              alien.getCategory());
}
```

And, finally, here are the affected bits of **Movie** (note that the string constants have been deleted):

```
private Category category = Category.UNCATEGORIZED;

public Movie(String aName, Category aCategory, int aRating) {
  checkNull(aName);
  checkEmpty(aName);
  name = aName;
  category = (aCategory != null) ? aCategory : Category.UNCATEGORIZED;
  rating = aRating;
}

public Category getCategory() {
  return category;
}
```

Now we can go back to the customer and get a list of the categories that should be supported and add them to **Category**.

## Exercises

**3.**    The customer identified these categories: *Science Fiction, Horror, Comedy, Western, Drama, Fantasy, Kids, Adult, Mystery, Thriller.* Add these to **Category**.  *Answer on p. 526*

## SHOW THE CATEGORY IN THE GUI

*Show the category in the GUI. There should be a field that gets filled in when a movie is selected.*

Now that we have categories supported in **Movie**, we can add support for them to the interface layers. We'll start with these tests:

**Test 38.** Telling the logical layer that a movie is selected causes the presentation layer to be told the category to display.

**Test 39.** Selecting a movie in the GUI causes the category field to be updated.

To get the category to reflect on the interface, we'll start, as usual, with **MovieListEditor**.

## Test 38: Telling the logical layer that a movie is selected causes the presentation layer to be told the category to display.

We start by extending testSelecting:

```
public void testSelecting() {
  mockView.setMovies(movies);
  control.setVoidCallable(1);

  mockView.setNameField(starWars.getName());
  control.setVoidCallable(1);
  mockView.setRatingField(6);
  control.setVoidCallable(1);
  mockView.setCategoryField(Category.SCIFI);
  control.setVoidCallable(1);

  mockView.setNameField(starTrek.getName());
  control.setVoidCallable(1);
  mockView.setRatingField(4);
  control.setVoidCallable(1);
  mockView.setCategoryField(Category.SCIFI);
  control.setVoidCallable(1);

  mockView.setNameField(stargate.getName());
  control.setVoidCallable(1);
  mockView.setRatingField(0);
  control.setVoidCallable(1);
  mockView.setCategoryField(Category.SCIFI);
  control.setVoidCallable(1);

  mockView.setNameField(theShining.getName());
  control.setVoidCallable(1);
  mockView.setRatingField(3);
  control.setVoidCallable(1);
  mockView.setCategoryField(Category.HORROR);
  control.setVoidCallable(1);

  control.activate();

  MovieListEditor editor = new MovieListEditor(movieList, mockView);
  editor.select(0);
  editor.select(1);
  editor.select(2);
  editor.select(3);

  control.verify();
}
```

To support this, we have to update setUp() as well. Note: We don't need to create a new fixture (which would require a new TestCase), but the current fixture needs to be more complete. Here it is:

```
protected void setUp() throws DuplicateMovieException {
  starWars = new Movie("Star Wars", Category.SCIFI, 5);
  starTrek = new Movie("Star Trek", Category.SCIFI, 3);
  stargate = new Movie("Stargate", Category.SCIFI, -1);
  theShining = new Movie("The Shining", Category.HORROR, 2);

  movies = new Vector();
  movies.add(starWars);
  movies.add(starTrek);
  movies.add(stargate);
  movies.add(theShining);

  movieList = new MovieList();
  movieList.add(starWars);
  movieList.add(starTrek);
  movieList.add(stargate);
  movieList.add(theShining);

  control = EasyMock.controlFor(MovieListEditorView.class);
  mockView = (MovieListEditorView)control.getMock();

  mockView.setEditor(null);
  control.setDefaultVoidCallable();
}
```

Now we have the test. Let's make it compile and get to the red bar as quickly as we can. We need to add a setCategoryField() method to MovieListEditorView. Now we have the red bar we were aiming for.

## Exercises

**4.**   Extend setCategoryField() to make testSelecting() pass.

**5.**   What problem does this cause? Why? Fix it.

*Answer on p. 526*

*Answer on p. 527*

Green bar! To the Swing interface layer.

## Test 39: Selecting a movie in the GUI causes the category field to be updated.

First, we need a test that checks that selecting updates the category field as expected:

```
public void testSelectUpdatesCategory() {
  JListOperator movieList = new JListOperator(mainWindow);
  JTextFieldOperator categoryField = new JTextFieldOperator(mainWindow,
                                                    "category");

  movieList.clickOnItem(0, 1);
  assertEquals("wrong category from selecting starWars.",
            Category.SCIFI.toString(),
            categoryField.getText());
```

```
    movieList.clickOnItem(3, 1);
    assertEquals("wrong category from selecting theShining.",
              Category.HORROR.toString(),
              categoryField.getText());

    movieList.clickOnItem(1, 1);
    assertEquals("wrong category from selecting starTrek.",
              Category.SCIFI.toString(),
              categoryField.getText());
}
```

Now we need to add a JTextField for displaying the category:

```
    private JTextField categoryField = null;

    public void setCategoryField(Category aCategory) {
      categoryField.setText(aCategory.toString());
    }
    public void init() {
      setTitle();
      setLayout();
      initList();
      initNameField();
      initRatingCombo();
      initCategoryField();
      initAddButton();
      initUpdateButton();
      pack();
    }
    private void initCategoryField() {
      categoryField = new JTextField(16);
      categoryField.setText("category");
      getContentPane().add(categoryField);
    }
```

Green bar. Next.

## Exercises

*Answer
on p. 529*    **6.**    We used the toString() method to get the value for the category field, as well
           as the value from the expected **Category** to compare against the field contents.
           What's the problem that we have with the system in its current state? (Hint:
           look at **Category**.) Fix it.

## ADD A SELECTION OF CATEGORY

*Allow the category of a movie to be changed by selecting it from a fixed list
of possibilities.*

For this task we need only be concerned with the interface layers. Here's our list of
tests:

**Test 40.** Telling the logical layer to update and providing it with data that indicates a category change results in the GUI layer being given a new set of movies with that change reflected.

**Test 41.** Selecting a movie from the list, changing the value of the category, and pressing Update updates the data for that movie. When that movie is selected again, the new category is displayed.

Here we go, then. As usual, we'll start at the logical layer.

## Test 40: Telling the logical layer to update and providing it with data that indicates a category change results in the GUI layer being given a new set of movies with that change reflected.

For this test we can extend TestMovieListEditor.testUpdating() to check that the movie category gets changed:

```
public void testUpdating() {
    Vector newMovies = new Vector();
    newMovies.add(starWars);
    newMovies.add(new Movie("Star Trek I", Category.COMEDY, 5));
    newMovies.add(stargate);
    newMovies.add(theShining);

    mockView.setMovies(movies);
    control.setVoidCallable(1);

    mockView.setNameField("Star Trek");
    control.setVoidCallable(1);
    mockView.setRatingField(4);
    control.setVoidCallable();
    mockView.setCategoryField(Category.SCIFI);
    control.setVoidCallable(1);

    mockView.getNameField();
    control.setReturnValue("Star Trek I", 1);
    mockView.getRatingField();
    control.setReturnValue(6, 1);
    mockView.getCategoryField();
    control.setReturnValue(Category.COMEDY, 1);

    mockView.setMovies(newMovies);
    control.setVoidCallable(1);

    control.activate();

    MovieListEditor editor = new MovieListEditor(movieList, mockView);
    editor.select(1);
    editor.update();

    control.verify();
}
```

Getting this to compile requires the addition of getCategoryField() to the MovieList EditorView interface:

```
public interface MovieListEditorView {
  void setMovies(Vector movies);
  String getNameField();
  void setEditor(MovieListEditor anEditor);
  void setNameField(String string);
  void duplicateException(String string);
  void setRatingField(int i);
  int getRatingField();
  void setCategoryField(Category aCategory);
  Category getCategoryField();
}
```

Now to get a green bar. We'll start by updating MovieListEditor.updateMovie() to fetch the category from the view and use that to set the category of the selected Movie:

```
private void updateMovie() {
  selectedMovie.setRating(view.getRatingField() − 1);
  selectedMovie.setCategory(view.getCategoryField());
  updateMovieList();
}
```

This in turn requires a setCategory() mutator in Movie, which we won't bother showing here. Next, we need to add an expectation to testUpdatingWithSameName() for the call to getCategoryField(). OK. Green bar!

## Exercises

*Answer
on p. 529*
**7.**    Make the required changes to Movie and TestMovieListEditor.

## Test 41: Selecting a movie from the list, changing the value of the category, and pressing Update updates the data for that movie. When that movie is selected again, the new category is displayed.

Now that we've finished with the logic layer for this task, we can turn to the Swing layer. We'll start by adding a test for updating the category:

```
public void testUpdateCategory() {
  JListOperator movieList = new JListOperator(mainWindow);
  JComboBoxOperator categoryCombo =
      new JComboBoxOperator(mainWindow,
                          Category.UNCATEGORIZED.toString());
  movieList.clickOnItem(0, 1);
  categoryCombo.setSelectedIndex(2);

  JButtonOperator updateButton = new JButtonOperator(mainWindow, "Update");
  updateButton.pushNoBlock();
  movieList.clickOnItem(1, 1);
  movieList.clickOnItem(0, 1);
  assertEquals("updating should have changed category.",
            Category.HORROR,
            categoryCombo.getSelectedItem());
}
```

First, we need to change the category field to a combo box:

```
private JComboBox categoryField = null;

public void setCategoryField(Category aCategory) {
  categoryField.setSelectedItem(anObject)(aCategory);
}

public Category getCategoryField() {
  return (Category) categoryField.getSelectedItem();
}

private void initCategoryField() {
  categoryField = new JComboBox(Category.categories());
  categoryField.setSelectedItem(Category.UNCATEGORIZED);
  getContentPane().add(categoryField);
}
```

This requires some slight changes to Category to collect and fetch all the defined categories:

```
private static Vector allCategories = new Vector();

private Category(String categoryName) {
  name = categoryName;
  allCategories.add(this);
}

public static Vector categories() {
  return (Vector) allCategories.clone();
}
```

OK, that gets our new test to pass, but we've broken our earlier testSelectUpdatesCategory test. It needs to be rewritten to use a combo box for the category field:

```
public void testSelectUpdatesCategory() {
  JListOperator movieList = new JListOperator(mainWindow);
  JComboBoxOperator categoryField =
      new JComboBoxOperator(mainWindow,
                            Category.UNCATEGORIZED.toString());

  movieList.clickOnItem(0, 1);
  assertEquals("wrong category from selecting starWars.",
               Category.SCIFI,
               categoryField.getSelectedItem());

  movieList.clickOnItem(3, 1);
  assertEquals("wrong category from selecting theShining.",
               Category.HORROR,
               categoryField.getSelectedItem());
```

```
movieList.clickOnItem(1, 1);
assertEquals("wrong category from selecting starTrek.",
             Category.SCIFI,
             categoryField.getSelectedItem());
```
}

Green bar! We're done. Figure 14.1 shows the current GUI.

**Figure 14.1** GUI with categories.

## RETROSPECTIVE

There wasn't much that was really new in this chapter. We did make use of a type-safe enumeration to encapsulate a closed, fixed set of alternative values. There's a good discussion of this pattern in [10], and one of the refactorings in [29] deals with replacing a type with a type-safe enumeration.

# Chapter 15

# FILTER ON CATEGORY

*Filter the movies in the list by category. There needs to be a way to select the category to show, including ALL.*

## GET A SUBLIST BASED ON CATEGORY

*Given a category, ask the movie list for a list of its movies that belong to that category.*

Now we need to have MovieList generate sublists based on categories. Here are some tests:

**Test 42.** Requesting a sublist filtered on a specific category answers a list containing all movies of that category, and only those movies.

Let's start by setting up a fixture with a MovieList containing a selection of movies with various categories and another MovieList containing just fantasy movies:

```
protected void setUp() throws Exception {
    starWars = new Movie("Star Wars", Category.SCIFI, 5);
    starTrek = new Movie("Star Trek", Category.SCIFI, 3);
    stargate = new Movie("Stargate", Category.SCIFI, -1);
    theShining = new Movie("The Shining", Category.HORROR, 2);
    carrie = new Movie("Carrie", Category.HORROR, 3);
    fotr = new Movie("The Fellowship of The Ring", Category.FANTASY, 5);
    redOctober = new Movie("The Hunt For Red October", Category.THRILLER, 3);
    congo = new Movie("Congo", Category.THRILLER, 3);
    princessBride = new Movie("The Princess Bride", Category.FANTASY, 5);

    movieList.add(starWars);
    movieList.add(starTrek);
    movieList.add(stargate);
    movieList.add(theShining);
    movieList.add(carrie);
    movieList.add(fotr);
    movieList.add(redOctober);
    movieList.add(congo);
    movieList.add(princessBride);

    fantasyList = new MovieList();
    fantasyList.add(fotr);
    fantasyList.add(princessBride);
}
```

## Test 42: Requesting a sublist filtered on a specific category answers a list containing all movies of that category, and only those movies.

```
public void testSubsets() {
    assertEquals("wrong FANTASY sublist.",
                 fantasyList,
                 movieList.categorySublist(Category.FANTASY));
}
```

To get this compiled we need to add a stub for MovieList.categorySublist():

```
public Object categorySublist(Category category) {
    return null;
}
```

Compile, run, red bar. Now to make it green. But first, consider the failure message:

```
wrong FANTASY sublist.
    expected:<com.saorsa.nowplaying.MovieList@d5550d>
    but was:<null>
```

That doesn't tell us much other than something was expected, but nothing was provided. The instance identifier of the expected MovieList is essentially unreadable, and generally meaningless. We can make that more useful by adding a reasonable toString() to MovieList:

```
wrong FANTASY sublist.
    expected:<["The Fellowship of The Ring" "The Princess Bride"]>
    but was:<null>
```

## Exercises

*Answer on p. 530*

**8.**    Write a toString() method for MovieList.

OK, back to the pursuit of the green bar. The simplest thing is to make a new MovieList and selectively add movies to it that match the filter criteria, in this case, a category. We'll move a bit faster this time and skip the *fake it* step. I can imagine a time when we might want something more elaborate, possibly using a Decorator pattern where you could decorate a MovieList with multiple filters and/or sorters. Such a possibility is shown in Figure 15.1. This would involve a class structure something like that shown in Figure 15.2. For now, though, the simplest thing will suffice:

```
public MovieList category(Category aCategory) {
    MovieList filteredList = new MovieList();
    Iterator movieIterator = movies.iterator();

    while (movieIterator.hasNext()) {
        Movie aMovie = (Movie)movieIterator.next();
```

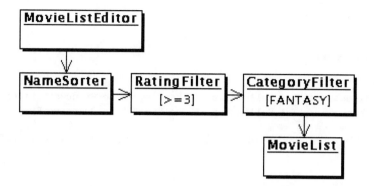

**Figure 15.1** Example of decorator style filters.

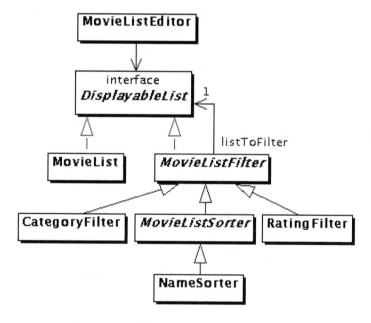

**Figure 15.2** Classes for decorator style filters.

```
if (aMovie.isOfCategory(aCategory)) {
  try {
    filteredList.add(aMovie);
  } catch (DuplicateMovieException e) {
  }
 }
}
```

```
    return filteredList;
  }
```

The bar's still red:

```
wrong FANTASY sublist.
  expected:<["The Fellowship of The Ring" "The Princess Bride"]>
  but was:<["The Fellowship of The Ring" "The Princess Bride"]>
```

Looks like we need an **equals()** method for MovieList. Sure enough, so we'll write one.

## Exercises

*Answer
on p. 530*
**9.**    Write an **equals()** method for MovieList. Start by adding a test to TestMovieList-WithPopulatedList.

That does it—green bar! Now beef up the test to check for other subsets:

```
public void testSubsets() {
  assertEquals("wrong FANTASY sublist.",
                 fantasyList,
                 movieList.categorySublist(Category.FANTASY));

  assertEquals("wrong SCIFI sublist.",
                 scifiList,
                 movieList.categorySublist(Category.SCIFI));

  assertEquals("wrong HORROR sublist.",
                 horrorList,
                 horrorList.categorySublist(Category.HORROR));

  assertEquals("wrong THRILLER sublist.",
                 thrillerList,
                 movieList.categorySublist(Category.THRILLER));
}
```

## Exercises

*Answer
on p. 531*
**10.**    Extend the fixture to support this test.

## SUPPORT AN ALL CATEGORY

*Get the entire list using an ALL category.*

We can now ask a MovieList to return a sublist for a given category. The story requires that we be able to fetch the entire list for the *ALL* category. Here's the test:

**Test 43.** Asking for a subset for the ALL category answers the original list.

# Test 43: Asking for a subset for the ALL category answers the original list.

```
public void testAllSubset() {
  assertEquals("All subset should equal the full list.",
              movieList,
              movieList.categorySublist(Category.ALL));
}
```

To compile we need to add an **ALL** instance to **Category**:

```
public static final Category ALL = new Category("All");
```

Red bar. Now we need to update categorySublist() to handle the **ALL** category:

```
public MovieList categorySublist(Category aCategory) {
  if (aCategory.equals(Category.ALL)) {
    return this;
  }

  MovieList filteredList = new MovieList();
  Iterator movieIterator = movies.iterator();
  while (movieIterator.hasNext()) {
    Movie aMovie = (Movie)movieIterator.next();

    if (aMovie.isOfCategory(aCategory)) {
      try {
        filteredList.add(aMovie);
      } catch (DuplicateMovieException e) {
      }
    }
  }
  return filteredList;
}
```

Green bar. That was an easy one!

# ADD A CATEGORY SELECTOR TO THE GUI

*Add a combo box to the GUI to select a category. When a category is selected, update the list to include only movies of that category.*

Now another GUI task. We need to extend the GUI logic layer to handle category changes and respond by filtering the displayed list of movies.

**Test 44.** When the logical layer is told to filter on a specific category, the presentation layer is given a new list to display containing movies for the specified category.

**Test 45.** Telling the logical layer to select a specific movie in a filtered list rather than the complete list from actually selects the appropriate movie, in spite of being selected from a sublist.

**Test 46.** Telling the logical layer to update a specific movie in a filtered list rather than from the complete list actually updates the appropriate movie properly.

**Test 47.** A rename performed in the context of the logical layer is done in the underlying full list; that is, potential duplicates in the full list are detected.

**Test 48.** Selecting a category to filter on in the GUI causes the displayed list of movies to update accordingly.

Since we need movies with assorted categories, we'll start by creating a new **TestCase** to hold a more elaborate fixture, rather than extending the one we have:

```java
public class TestMovieListEditorWithCategoryFiltering extends TestCase {
    private MockControl control = null;
    private MovieListEditorView mockView = null;

    private Movie starWars = null;
    private Movie starTrek = null;
    private Movie stargate = null;
    private Movie theShining = null;
    private Movie carrie = null;
    private Movie fotr = null;
    private Movie redOctober = null;
    private Movie congo = null;
    private Movie princessBride = null;

    private MovieList movieList = null;
    private MovieList fantasyList = null;
    private MovieList scifiList = null;
    private MovieList thrillerList = null;
    private MovieList horrorList = null;

    private Vector movies = null;
    private Vector fantasyMovies = null;
    private Vector horrorMovies = null;
    private Vector thrillerMovies = null;
    private Vector scifiMovies = null;

    protected void setUp() throws Exception {
        super.setUp();
        starWars = new Movie("Star Wars", Category.SCIFI, 5);
        starTrek = new Movie("Star Trek", Category.SCIFI, 3);
        stargate = new Movie("Stargate", Category.SCIFI, -1);
        theShining = new Movie("The Shining", Category.HORROR, 2);
        carrie = new Movie("Carrie", Category.HORROR, 3);
        fotr = new Movie("The Fellowship of The Ring", Category.FANTASY, 5);
        redOctober = new Movie("The Hunt For Red October", Category.THRILLER, 3);
        congo = new Movie("Congo", Category.THRILLER, 3);
        princessBride = new Movie("The Princess Bride", Category.FANTASY, 5);

        movieList = new MovieList();
        movieList.add(starWars);
        movieList.add(starTrek);
        movieList.add(stargate);
        movieList.add(theShining);
        movieList.add(carrie);
        movieList.add(fotr);
        movieList.add(redOctober);
        movieList.add(congo);
        movieList.add(princessBride);
        movies = new Vector(movieList.getMovies());
```

```
        scifiList = new MovieList();
        scifiList.add(starWars);
        scifiList.add(starTrek);
        scifiList.add(stargate);
        scifiMovies = new Vector(scifiList.getMovies());

        thrillerList = new MovieList();
        thrillerList.add(redOctober);
        thrillerList.add(congo);
        thrillerMovies = new Vector(thrillerList.getMovies());

        horrorList = new MovieList();
        horrorList.add(theShining);
        horrorList.add(carrie);
        horrorMovies = new Vector(horrorList.getMovies());

        fantasyList = new MovieList();
        fantasyList.add(fotr);
        fantasyList.add(princessBride);
        fantasyMovies = new Vector(fantasyList.getMovies());

        control = EasyMock.controlFor(MovieListEditorView.class);
        mockView = (MovieListEditorView)control.getMock();
        mockView.setEditor(null);
        control.setDefaultVoidCallable();
    }
}
```

## Test 44: When the logical layer is told to filter on a specific category, the presentation layer is given a new list to display containing movies for the specified category.

We need a test that will start with the entire list, select a category, then select the ALL category to get the entire list back. Here's the test:

```
public void testCategoryFiltering() {
    mockView.setMovies(movies);
    control.setVoidCallable(1);

    mockView.setMovies(scifiMovies);
    control.setVoidCallable(1);

    mockView.setMovies(movies);
    control.setVoidCallable(1);

    control.activate();

    MovieListEditor editor = new MovieListEditor(movieList, mockView);
    editor.filterOnCategory(Category.SCIFI);
    editor.filterOnCategory(Category.ALL);

    control.verify();
}
```

Add a stub for filterOnCategory() to get to the red bar. It fails because the stub does nothing; specifically, it does not cause a corresponding call to setMovies(). We need to fill it in:

```
public void filterOnCategory(Category category) {
  filteredMovies = movies.categorySublist(category);
  updateMovieList();
}
```

We also need to add a field to hold the filtered movie list, filteredMovies, to maintain and use to fill the list in the view.

## Exercises

*Answer*
*on p. 532*
**11.**    Make the required updates to add filteredMovies.

Green bar.

## Test 45: Telling the logical layer to select a specific movie in a filtered list rather than the complete list from actually selects the appropriate movie, in spite of being selected from a sublist.

The next test verifies that selecting a movie in a filtered list is really selecting the appropriate movie:

```
public void testSelecting() {
  mockView.setMovies(movies);
  control.setVoidCallable(1);
  mockView.setMovies(fantasyMovies);
  control.setVoidCallable(1);

  mockView.setNameField(fotr.getName());
  control.setVoidCallable(1);
  mockView.setRatingField(6);
  control.setVoidCallable(1);
  mockView.setCategoryField(Category.FANTASY);
  control.setVoidCallable(1);

  control.activate();

  MovieListEditor editor = new MovieListEditor(movieList, mockView);
  editor.filterOnCategory(Category.FANTASY);
  editor.select(0);

  control.verify();
}
```

When we run it, it fails. We need to look at MovieListEditor.select(). There we see that movie selection is still dealing with the underlying movie list, not the filtered one. We need to change that:

```
public void select(int i) {
  if (i == −1) {
    selectedMovie = null;
  } else {
    selectedMovie = filteredMovies.getMovie(i);
    view.setNameField(selectedMovie.getName());
    view.setCategoryField(selectedMovie.getCategory());
    try {
      view.setRatingField(selectedMovie.getRating() + 1);
    } catch (UnratedException e) {
      view.setRatingField(0);
    }
  }
}
```

That does it.

# Test 46: Telling the logical layer to update a specific movie in a filtered list rather than from the complete list actually updates the appropriate movie properly.

Another test to make sure that the existing functionality still works ok:

```
public void testUpdating() throws UnratedException {
  mockView.setMovies(movies);
  control.setVoidCallable(1);
  mockView.setMovies(fantasyMovies);
  control.setVoidCallable(2);

  mockView.setNameField(princessBride.getName());
  control.setVoidCallable(1);
  mockView.setRatingField(6);
  control.setVoidCallable(1);
  mockView.setCategoryField(Category.FANTASY);
  control.setVoidCallable(1);

  mockView.getNameField();
  control.setReturnValue(princessBride.getName(), 1);
  mockView.getRatingField();
  control.setReturnValue(2, 1);
  mockView.getCategoryField();
  control.setReturnValue(Category.FANTASY, 1);
  control.activate();
```

```
MovieListEditor editor = new MovieListEditor(movieList, mockView);
editor.filterOnCategory(Category.FANTASY);
editor.select(1);
editor.update();
control.verify();
assertEquals("princessBride should have been changed to rating of 1.",
          1,
          princessBride.getRating());
}
```

Green bar. That's good. One more test and I'll be happy.

## Test 47: A rename performed in the context of the logical layer is done in the underlying full list; that is, potential duplicates in the full list are detected.

This one will test that renames are being done in the context of the master list, not the filtered one. We'll do this by selecting a sublist and renaming one of the movies in it to be a duplicate of a movie not in the sublist. This should cause an error:

```
public void testDuplicateCausingUpdate() {
    mockView.setMovies(movies);
    control.setVoidCallable(1);
    mockView.setMovies(fantasyMovies);
    control.setVoidCallable(1);

    mockView.setNameField(princessBride.getName());
    control.setVoidCallable(1);
    mockView.setRatingField(6);
    control.setVoidCallable(1);
    mockView.setCategoryField(Category.FANTASY);
    control.setVoidCallable(1);

    mockView.getNameField();
    control.setReturnValue(starWars.getName(), 1);
    mockView.duplicateException("Star Wars");
    control.setVoidCallable(1);
    control.activate();

    MovieListEditor editor = new MovieListEditor(movieList, mockView);
    editor.filterOnCategory(Category.FANTASY);
    editor.select(1);
    editor.update();

    control.verify();
}
```

It runs fine. Now I'm confident.

As usual, we need to extend category selection to the Swing GUI. Like the last test, we'll create a new fixture/TestCase, very similar to the last.

## Test 48: Selecting a category to filter on in the GUI causes the displayed list of movies to update accordingly.

Here's the test:

```
public void testCategoryFiltering() {
    JListOperator movieList = new JListOperator(mainWindow);
    JComboBoxOperator categoryCombo =
        new JComboBoxOperator(mainWindow,
                              Category.ALL.toString());

    categoryCombo.setSelectedItem(Category.FANTASY);
    ListModel fantasyListModel = movieList.getModel();
    assertEquals("Fantasy list is the wrong size",
                 fantasyMovies.size(),
                 fantasyListModel.getSize());

    for (int i = 0; i < fantasyMovies.size(); i++) {
      assertEquals("Fantasy list contains bad movie at index " + i,
                   fantasyMovies.get(i),
                   fantasyListModel.getElementAt(i));
    }

    categoryCombo.setSelectedItem(Category.THRILLER);
    ListModel thrillerListModel = movieList.getModel();
    assertEquals("Thriller list is the wrong size",
                 thrillerMovies.size(),
                 thrillerListModel.getSize());

    for (int i = 0; i < thrillerMovies.size(); i++) {
      assertEquals("Thriller list contains bad movie at index " + i,
                   thrillerMovies.get(i),
                   thrillerListModel.getElementAt(i));
    }

    categoryCombo.setSelectedItem(Category.ALL);
    ListModel allListModel = movieList.getModel();
    assertEquals("Movie list is the wrong size",
                 movies.size(),
                 allListModel.getSize());

    for (int i = 0; i <movies.size(); i++) {
      assertEquals("Movie list contains bad movie at index " + i,
                   movies.get(i),
                   allListModel.getElementAt(i));
    }
  }
}
```

This immediately gives us a red bar since there is no combo box for selecting the category on which to filter. That's easy enough to add:

```
public void init() {
  setTitle();
  setLayout();
  initCategoryFilterField();
  initList();
  initNameField();
  initRatingCombo();
  initCategoryField();
  initAddButton();
  initUpdateButton();
  pack();
}

private void initCategoryFilterField() {
  categoryField = new JComboBox(Category.categories());
  categoryField.setSelectedItem(Category.ALL);
  getContentPane().add(categoryField);
}
```

Now we get a red bar due to the listbox not getting updated when the category filter setting changes. We need to add a selection handler to the new combo box:

```
private void initCategoryFilterField() {
  JComboBox categoryFilterField = new JComboBox(Category.categories());
  categoryFilterField.setSelectedItem(Category.ALL);
  categoryFilterField.addActionListener(new ActionListener() {
    public void actionPerformed(ActionEvent e) {
      JComboBox source = (JComboBox)e.getSource();
      myEditor.filterOnCategory((Category)source.getSelectedItem());
    }
  });
  getContentPane().add(categoryFilterField);
}
```

Green bar. That does it.

## HANDLE CHANGING A MOVIE'S CATEGORY

*When the list is filtered, changing a movie to a different category should remove it from the list.*

This task lies completely in the logic layer of the GUI. One simple test is all that is required.

**Test 49.** Changing the category of a movie in a filtered list causes that movie to be removed from the list. If that category is filtered on, that movie will be in the list.

Here it is:

## Test 49: Changing the category of a movie in a filtered list causes that movie to be removed from the list. If that category is filtered on, that movie will be in the list.

```
public void testChangingCategory() {
    Vector newFantasyMovies = new Vector();
    newFantasyMovies.add(fotr);
    Vector comedyMovies = new Vector();
    comedyMovies.add(princessBride);

    mockView.setMovies(movies);
    control.setVoidCallable(1);
    mockView.setMovies(fantasyMovies);
    control.setVoidCallable(1);

    mockView.setNameField(princessBride.getName());
    control.setVoidCallable(1);
    mockView.setRatingField(6);
    control.setVoidCallable(1);
    mockView.setCategoryField(Category.FANTASY);
    control.setVoidCallable(1);

    mockView.getNameField();
    control.setReturnValue(princessBride.getName(), 1);
    mockView.getRatingField();
    control.setReturnValue(6, 1);
    mockView.getCategoryField();
    control.setReturnValue(Category.COMEDY, 1);

    mockView.setMovies(newFantasyMovies);
    control.setVoidCallable(1);
    mockView.setMovies(comedyMovies);
    control.setVoidCallable(1);

    control.activate();
    MovieListEditor editor = new MovieListEditor(movieList, mockView);
    editor.filterOnCategory(Category.FANTASY);
    editor.select(1);
    editor.update();
    editor.filterOnCategory(Category.COMEDY);
    control.verify();
}
```

The test fails because after changing the category on *The Princess Bride* to COM-
EDY, it is still in the list. We need to extend update() in MovieListEditor to refresh the
filtered list.

And how do we do that? The filtered list is just a MovieList with no retention of
the filtering criteria. The simplest thing that could work is to regenerate the filtered
list on each update:

```
private void updateMovie() {
  selectedMovie.setRating(view.getRatingField() − 1);
  selectedMovie.setCategory(view.getCategoryField());
  filterOnCategory(filterCategory);
}
```

To support this we need a field to hold the current **Category** on which to filter:

```
private Category filterCategory = Category.ALL;
```

The test still fails since we're not maintaining the value in the new field yet. Let's take care of that:

```
public void filterOnCategory(Category category) {
  filterCategory = category;
  filteredMovies = movies.categorySublist(filterCategory);
  updateMovieList();
}
```

Green bar. Time to clean up.

The use of filterOnCategory() is confusing. It's called from the GUI when the filter category is changed, and from updateMovie() whenever the update button is pushed. There is no reason to set the filter category if it hasn't changed, so we should extract the common behavior into a separate method and call that from updateMovie(). We'll also call it from filterOnCategory() after setting filterCategory. Here's the new code:

```
private void updateMovie() {
  selectedMovie.setRating(view.getRatingField() − 1);
  selectedMovie.setCategory(view.getCategoryField());
  updateAndDisplayFilteredMovies();
}

public void filterOnCategory(Category category) {
  filterCategory = category;
  updateAndDisplayFilteredMovies();
}

private void updateAndDisplayFilteredMovies() {
  filteredMovies = movies.categorySublist(filterCategory);
  updateMovieList();
}
```

The bar's still green, so we're done here. Before we're happy, though, we have to run all the tests. We get a green bar on **AllTests** but the Swing tests have some failures. We investigate and find that the problem is the search for the rating combo box. Before we added the category filter combo box, the rating combo box was the first one returned by default when Jemmy was asked for a JComboBoxOperator. Now life is more complex. It's time to add a bit of infrastructure; specifically, we will add a

name to each component and search for them by name. To do this, we need to create
a ComponentChooser subclass (part of Jemmy) to do the name checking. We will use
this chooser for finding components. Here it is:

```
public class NameBasedChooser implements ComponentChooser {
  private String name;

  public NameBasedChooser(String componentName) {
    name = componentName;
  }
  public boolean checkComponent(Component aComponent) {
    String theName = aComponent.getName();
    return (theName != null) && theName.equals(name);
  }
  public String getDescription() {
    return "Matches Components named \"" + name + "\"";
  }
}
```

Now we add names to our Swing components:

```
private void initCategoryFilterField() {
  JComboBox categoryFilterField = new JComboBox(Category.categories());
  categoryFilterField.setName("categoryFilter");
  //...
}

private void initCategoryField() {
  categoryField = new JComboBox(Category.categories());
  categoryField.setName("category");
  //...
}
private void initRatingCombo() {
  ratingField = new JComboBox(CustomMovieListRenderer.icons());
  ratingField.setName("rating");
  //...
}
private void initUpdateButton() {
  JButton updateButton = new JButton("Update");
  updateButton.setName("update");
  //...
}
private void initAddButton() {
  JButton addButton = new JButton("Add");
  addButton.setName("add");
  //...
}
```

```
private void initNameField() {
  movieField = new JTextField(16);
  movieField.setName("name");
  //...
}

private void initList() {
  movieList = new JList(new Vector());
  movieList.setName("movieList");
  //...
}
```

Finally, we use our new **NameBasedChooser** in the Swing tests. For example:

```
public void testUpdateRating() {
  JListOperator movieList =
      new JListOperator(mainWindow, new NameBasedChooser("movieList"));
  JComboBoxOperator ratingCombo =
      new JComboBoxOperator(mainWindow, new NameBasedChooser("rating"));
  movieList.clickOnItem(0, 1);
  ratingCombo.setSelectedIndex(0);


  JButtonOperator updateButton =
      new JButtonOperator(mainWindow, new NameBasedChooser("update"));
  updateButton.pushNoBlock();
  movieList.clickOnItem(1, 1);
  movieList.clickOnItem(0, 1);
  assertEquals("updating should have changed rating.",
               0,
               ratingCombo.getSelectedIndex());
}
```

OK, all is green, all is good. Now we're confident that we are finished.

## INTERFACE CLEANUP

The GUI has been gradually getting more complex as we've added functionality to the application. It's time to go back and rework the layout as we've outgrown the simple **FlowLayout** that we've been using. Figure 15.3 shows the current state of the GUI.

We will start by splitting the GUI into three panes:

1. a list pane for the category filter combo and the movie list,

2. a detail pane for the information about the new/selected movie, and

3. a button pane for the buttons.

For each pane we will use a **BoxLayout**—the button pane will be laid out horizontally, while the other panes will be vertical. The panes themselves will be laid out by a vertical **BoxLayout**. Here's the updated GUI creation code:

**Figure 15.3** The current FlowLayout-based GUI.

```
public void init() {
  setTitle();
  setLayout();
  getContentPane().add(initListPane());
  getContentPane().add(initDetailPane());
  getContentPane().add(initButtonPane());
  pack();
}

private JPanel initListPane() {
  JPanel listPane = new JPanel();
  listPane.setLayout(new BoxLayout(listPane, BoxLayout.Y_AXIS));
  listPane.setBorder(BorderFactory.createEmptyBorder(10, 10, 10, 10));
  listPane.add(initCategoryFilterField());
  listPane.add(Box.createRigidArea(new Dimension(0, 5)));
  listPane.add(initList());
  return listPane;
}

private JPanel initDetailPane() {
  JPanel detailPane = new JPanel();
  detailPane.setLayout(new BoxLayout(detailPane, BoxLayout.Y_AXIS));
  detailPane.setBorder(BorderFactory.createEmptyBorder(1, 10, 10, 10));
  detailPane.add(initNameField());
  detailPane.add(Box.createRigidArea(new Dimension(0, 5)));
  detailPane.add(initRatingCombo());
  detailPane.add(Box.createRigidArea(new Dimension(0, 5)));
  detailPane.add(initCategoryField());
  return detailPane;
}
```

```
private JPanel initButtonPane() {
  JPanel buttonPane = new JPanel();
  buttonPane.setLayout(new BoxLayout(buttonPane, BoxLayout.X_AXIS));
  buttonPane.setBorder(BorderFactory.createEmptyBorder(1, 10, 10, 10));
  buttonPane.add(initAddButton());
  buttonPane.add(Box.createRigidArea(new Dimension(5, 0)));
  buttonPane.add(initUpdateButton());
  return buttonPane;
}
```

The component initialization methods are tweaked to return the component rather than add it to the main window. Here's an example:

```
private JComboBox initCategoryField() {
  categoryField = new JComboBox(Category.categories());
  categoryField.setName("category");
  categoryField.setSelectedItem(Category.UNCATEGORIZED);
  return categoryField;
}
```

That's all there is to it. The result is shown in Figure 15.4.

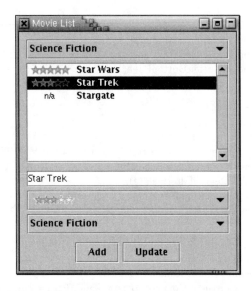

**Figure 15.4** The current nested BoxLayout-based GUI.

## RETROSPECTIVE

We started off by considering possible solutions to the problem of presenting a filtered list to the user. We explored one model that used the Decorator pattern to compose filters. In the end we decided that that was overkill at the moment, and did something much simpler.

We did more work on the interface to support category filtering. In the process we moved to a more sophisticated way of having Jemmy find components. We finished off by refactoring the structure of the GUI, using a more elaborate layout approach by that of nested BoxLayouts.

There's a bit of a smell to the code. It feels like MovieListEditor knows too much about the filtering of the list. Maybe that knowledge should be extracted into a class that sits between the MovieListEditor and the MovieList. That's starting to sound like the decorator-based solution we thought about at the beginning of this chapter. I'll resist pursuing that now. If we get pushed farther in that direction, we'll have to stop and do some big refactoring to move forward. Stay tuned.

# Chapter 16

# PERSISTENCE

*Movie data is persistent across application sessions.*

We need to persist data. After some discussion, it was decided that the way in which the data was stored didn't matter much... the choice is ours. Since our data is structurally very simple, we'll use a simple solution: a flat ASCII file.

## WRITE TO A FLAT FILE

*Write movie collection to a flat text file.*

Java has a lovely IO abstraction facility that we will use to decouple our persistence facility from physical files: streams. Not only does this make our design cleaner, but it also makes writing tests easier. Here are the tests we'll want:

**Test 50.** Writing an empty list to a stream writes nothing.

**Test 51.** Writing a list of one movie should write that movie to the stream in the format <name> | <category> | <rating>.

**Test 52.** Writing a list containing several movies writes each movie to the stream, one per line, in the format of the previous test.

Our first task is to write a MovieList to a Stream. We begin, of course, with a test. Where should the test go? My feeling is that since we are starting on a new area of functionality we should start with a new fixture.

## Test 50: Writing an empty list to a stream writes nothing.

The first test will be for writing an empty MovieList:

```
public void testWritingEmptyList() {
  StringWriter destination = new StringWriter();
  MovieList emptyList = new MovieList();
  emptyList.writeTo(destination);
  assertEquals("Writing an empty list should produce nothing.",
          "",
          destination.toString());
}
```

To get this to compile, we need the MovieList.writeTo() class:

```
public void writeTo(Writer destination) {
}
```

With this in place, the test compiles and, somewhat surprisingly, passes. Maybe it shouldn't be so surprising. Writing an empty list results in empty output. Currently, writeTo() does nothing at all, so the output is empty.

The next test will require us to do some real programming.

## Test 51: Writing a list of one movie should write that movie to the stream in the format <name> | <category> | <rating>.

```
public void testWritingOneMovie() throws Exception {
    String starWarsOutput = "Star Wars|Science Fiction|4\n";
    StringWriter destination = new StringWriter();
    MovieList movieList = new MovieList();
    Movie starWars = new Movie("Star Wars", Category.SCIFI, 4);
    movieList.add(starWars);

    movieList.writeTo(destination);
    assertEquals("Wrong output from writing a single movie list.",
                starWarsOutput,
                destination.toString());
}
```

Notice how we've made a design decision while specifying the test. We've defined and specified the file format that will be used to store our movie data.

Red bar right away! Now we implement MovieList.writeTo() as simply as we can get away with.

```
public void writeTo(Writer destination) throws IOException {
    if (size() > 0) {
        Movie movieToWrite = getMovie(0);
        destination.write(movieToWrite.getName());
        destination.write('|');
        destination.write(movieToWrite.getCategory().toString());
        destination.write('|');

        try {
            destination.write(Integer.toString(movieToWrite.getRating()));
        } catch (UnratedException ex) {
            destination.write("-1");
        }
        destination.write('\n');
        destination.flush();
    }
}
```

This is about as simple as we can get. Well, ok...we could have written a string literal. The test only requires that the first (and only) movie in the collection is written, so that's all we write code to do. Notice that we need the if (size() > 0) check to keep testWritingEmptyList() passing.

Green, but not yet clean. First, look at the two tests. We can rename emptyList and extract a fixture to setUp().

## Exercises

**12.**    Extract the fixture code from the two tests into setUp().                *Answer on p. 532*

Now let's turn our attention to MovieList.writeTo(). The way we have MovieList dealing with the internal details of Movie stinks of **Inappropriate Intimacy**. That code should be moved to Movie where the structural details can be encapsulated. First, we will extract the Movie writing code to a separate method, then move it to Movie. First to extract it:

```java
public void writeTo(Writer destination) throws IOException {
  if (size() > 0) {
    Movie movieToWrite = getMovie(0);
    writeMovieTo(movieToWrite, destination);
    destination.flush();
  }
}

public void writeMovieTo(Movie movieToWrite, Writer destination)
          throws IOException {
  destination.write(movieToWrite.getName());
  destination.write('|');
  destination.write(movieToWrite.getCategory().toString());
  destination.write('|');

  try {
    destination.write(Integer.toString(movieToWrite.getRating()));
  } catch (UnratedException ex) {
    destination.write("-1");
  }
  destination.write('\n');
}
```

Now move it to Movie. In MovieList:

```java
public void writeTo(Writer destination) throws IOException {
  if (size() > 0) {
    Movie movieToWrite = getMovie(0);
    movieToWrite.writeTo(destination);
    destination.flush();
  }
}
```

And in Movie:

```
public void writeTo(Writer destination) throws IOException {
  destination.write(getName());
  destination.write('|');
  destination.write(getCategory().toString());
  destination.write('|');

  try {
    destination.write(Integer.toString(getRating()));
  } catch (UnratedException ex) {
    destination.write("-1");
  }
  destination.write('\n');
}
```

## Test 52: Writing a list containing several movies writes each movie to the stream, one per line, in the format of the previous test.

Now we need a test for writing multiple Movies:

```
public void testWritingMultipleMovies() throws Exception {
  String expectedResult = "Star Wars|Science Fiction|4\n" +
                          "The Princess Bride|Fantasy|5\n";
  Movie starWars = new Movie("Star Wars", Category.SCIFI, 4);
  Movie princessBride = new Movie("The Princess Bride", Category.FANTASY, 5);
  movieList.add(starWars);
  movieList.add(princessBride);
  movieList.writeTo(destination);
  assertEquals("Wrong output from writing multiple movies.",
               expectedResult,
               destination.toString());
}
```

This test fails, which drives us to generalize MovieList.writeTo() to write the entire collection of Movies:

```
public void writeTo(Writer destination) throws IOException {
  Iterator movieIterator = movies.iterator();
  while (movieIterator.hasNext()) {
    Movie movieToWrite = (Movie) movieIterator.next();
    movieToWrite.writeTo(destination);
  }
  destination.flush();
}
```

Green! Now there's a bit of cleanup to do on Movie.writeTo(): we should extract the writing of the separator to its own method. This is because:

- we can name it and make clear what it is doing, and

- it will encapsulate the separator character.

Here's the new code:

```
public void writeTo(Writer destination) throws IOException {
  destination.write(getName());
  writeSeparator(destination);
  destination.write(getCategory().toString());
  writeSeparator(destination);

  try {
    destination.write(Integer.toString(getRating()));
  } catch (UnratedException ex) {
    destination.write("-1");
  }
  destination.write('\n');
}
private void writeSeparator(Writer destination) throws IOException {
  destination.write('|');
}
```

There—green and clean!

## SAVE-AS IN GUI

*Provide, in the GUI, the capability to save the movie collection to a specific file.*

For the GUI, we will start with the "Save As" functionality. We are ordering our tasks so that we do this task before simply saving since that needs to be a place to which the list was previously saved (or, as we will see, from which it was loaded). Here are the tests:

**Test 53.** Telling the logical layer to "save–as" causes it to ask the presentation layer to specify a file into which it writes the movie list.

**Test 54.** Selecting "Save As" from the "File" menu prompts for a file using the standard file chooser. The list is written into the selected file.

**Test 55.** If the file selection is cancelled, nothing is written to any file.

### Test 53: Telling the logical layer to "save–as" causes it to ask the presentation layer to specify a file into which it writes the movie list.

```
public void testSaving() throws Exception {
  String expected = "Star Wars|Science Fiction|5\n" +
                    "Star Trek|Science Fiction|3\n" +
                    "Stargate|Science Fiction|-1\n" +
                    "The Shining|Horror|2\n";

  File outputFile = File.createTempFile("testSaveAs", ".dat");
  outputFile.deleteOnExit();
  mockView.setMovies(movies);
  control.setVoidCallable(1);
  mockView.getFile("*.dat");
  control.setReturnValue(outputFile, 1);
  control.activate();
```

```
MovieListEditor editor = new MovieListEditor(movieList, mockView);
editor.saveAs();
control.verify();
assertFileEquals("Saved file ", expected, outputFile);
}

private void assertFileEquals(String message, String expected, File outputFile)
    throws Exception {

assertEquals(message + "is wrong size.",
                expected.length(),
                outputFile.length());

FileReader reader = new FileReader(outputFile);
for (int charIndex = 0; charIndex < expected.length(); charIndex++) {
  char characterRead = (char)reader.read();
  assertEquals(message + "has wrong character at index " + charIndex + ".",
                expected.charAt(charIndex),
                characterRead);
}
}
```

## Exercises

*Answer*
*on p. 533*  **13.**    Add the method stubs and declarations we need in order to get the test compiling.

We fail because the mock isn't getting the expected call to **getFile()**. Let's add some code to MovieListEditor.saveAs():

```
public void saveAs() {
  File outputFile = view.getFile("*.dat");
}
```

Now the failure is due to the saved file having a size of 0. We need to add more code to write out the list to the specified file:

```
public void saveAs() throws IOException {
  File outputFile = view.getFile("*.dat");
  FileWriter writer = new FileWriter(outputFile);
  movies.writeTo(writer);
  writer.close();
}
```

That does it. Before we move on, there is some refactoring we should do to our tests. I'd like to extract the file-oriented tests into a separate test case since it's inherently different than the rest of the tests. However, we need an extension of the existing fixture. Do we duplicate the fixture? Do we extend the existing test case? No to both: Duplication is to be avoided as much as possible, and if we extend a test case, we inherit all of its tests, which isn't what we want. The solution is to extract the fixture into a common, abstract superclass and extend it as required in the subclasses. So here's the superclass that houses the common fixture:

```
public abstract class CommonTestMovieListEditor extends TestCase {
  protected MockControl control = null;
  protected MovieListEditorView mockView = null;
  protected Vector movies = null;
  protected Movie starWars = null;
  protected Movie starTrek = null;
  protected Movie stargate = null;
  protected Movie theShining = null;
  protected MovieList movieList = null;

  protected void setUp() throws Exception {
    starWars = new Movie("Star Wars", Category.SCIFI, 5);
    starTrek = new Movie("Star Trek", Category.SCIFI, 3);
    stargate = new Movie("Stargate", Category.SCIFI, -1);
    theShining = new Movie("The Shining", Category.HORROR, 2);

    movies = new Vector();
    movies.add(starWars);
    movies.add(starTrek);
    movies.add(stargate);
    movies.add(theShining);

    movieList = new MovieList();
    movieList.add(starWars);
    movieList.add(starTrek);
    movieList.add(stargate);
    movieList.add(theShining);

    control = EasyMock.controlFor(MovieListEditorView.class);
    mockView = (MovieListEditorView)control.getMock();

    mockView.setEditor(null);
    control.setDefaultVoidCallable();
  }
}
```

Our previous test case is the same except that now it extends CommonTestMovie-ListEditor and doesn't have a fixture (i.e., no instance variables or setUp() method). We create a new TestCase for the file-related tests and move the testSaving() and assert-FileEquals() to it:

```
public class TestMovieListEditorFileOperations extends CommonTestMovieListEditor {
  private String expected;
  private File outputFile;

  protected void setUp() throws Exception {
    super.setUp();
    expected = "Star Wars|Science Fiction|5\n" +
               "Star Trek|Science Fiction|3\n" +
               "Stargate|Science Fiction|-1\n" +
               "The Shining|Horror|2\n";
    outputFile = File.createTempFile("testSaveAs", ".dat");
    outputFile.deleteOnExit();
  }
```

```
public void testSaving() throws Exception {
  mockView.setMovies(movies);
  control.setVoidCallable(1);
  mockView.getFile("*.dat");
  control.setReturnValue(outputFile, 1);
  control.activate();

  MovieListEditor editor = new MovieListEditor(movieList, mockView);
  editor.saveAs();
  assertFileEquals("Saved file ", expected, outputFile);
  control.verify();
}

private void assertFileEquals(String message, String expected, File outputFile)
    throws Exception {
  assertEquals(message + "is wrong size.",
              expected.length(),
              outputFile.length());
  FileReader reader = new FileReader(outputFile);
  for ( int charIndex = 0; charIndex < expected.length(); charIndex++) {
    char characterRead = (char)reader.read();
    assertEquals(message + "has wrong character at " + charIndex + ".",
                expected.charAt(charIndex),
                characterRead);
  }
}

public static void main(String[] args) {
  junit.textui.TestRunner.run(TestMovieListEditorFileOperations.class);
}
}
```

## Test 54: Selecting "Save As" from the "File" menu prompts for a file using the standard file chooser. The list is written into the selected file.

Now to add support for the *save as* functionality to the Swing GUI. We're going to gear down for a bit and take some smaller steps again. Here's the start of the test:

```
public void testSaving() {
  FileAssert.assertSize("Saved list has wrong size.",
                        savedText.length(),
                        outputFile);
  FileAssert.assertEquals("Saved file", savedText, outputFile);
}
```

Notice that we've started with what we want to be true, written as assertions. Also notice that we're using a class that doesn't exist yet: FileAssert. Out next step is to create that class and the methods in it that we call. The code for those asserts are derived from the assertFileEquals() method that we wrote for a previous test. Before we go farther with this test, we'll revisit that previous one to refactor and extract the file-related assertion method into a helper class. We're doing this because we see utility in having those assertions generally available, not buried in a TestCase.

First, extract the method into a separate class:

```
public class FileAssert extends Assert {
  public static void assertFileEquals(String message, String expected, File outputFile)
      throws Exception {
    assertEquals(message + "is wrong size.",
                 expected.length(),
                 outputFile.length());
    FileReader reader = new FileReader(outputFile);
    for ( int charIndex = 0; charIndex < expected.length(); charIndex++) {
      char characterRead = (char)reader.read();
      assertEquals(message + "has wrong character at " + charIndex + ".",
                   expected.charAt(charIndex),
                   characterRead);
    }
  }
}
```

Next, we change the test that called the original version so that it calls this version:

```
public void testSaving() throws Exception {
  mockView.setMovies(movies);
  control.setVoidCallable(1);
  mockView.getFile("*.dat");
  control.setReturnValue(outputFile, 1);
  control.activate();

  MovieListEditor editor = new MovieListEditor(movieList, mockView);
  editor.saveAs();
  FileAssert.assertFileEquals("Save As-ed file ", expected, outputFile);
  control.verify();
}
```

Green. Now we can delete the original copy in TestMovieListEditorFileOperations. Still green. This method was fine as a helper method, but now it smells like it's doing too much. Let's split up the size and content checks:

```
public class FileAssert extends Assert {

  public static void assertFileEquals(String message, String expected, File outputFile)
      throws Exception {
    assertSize(message, expected.length(), outputFile);
    assertEquals(message, expected, outputFile);
  }

  public static void assertEquals(String message, String expected, File outputFile)
      throws FileNotFoundException, IOException {
    FileReader reader = new FileReader(outputFile);
    for (int charIndex = 0; charIndex < expected.length(); charIndex++) {
      char characterRead = (char)reader.read();
      assertEquals(message + "has wrong character at " + charIndex + ".",
                   expected.charAt(charIndex),
                   characterRead);
    }
  }
}
```

```
    public static void assertSize(String message, int expectedSize, File outputFile) {
        assertEquals(message + "is wrong size.", expectedSize, outputFile.length());
    }
}
```

Compile, test, green! The message handling is messy; let's clean that up so that the two nested asserts act more like the built-in ones:

```
public class FileAssert extends Assert {

    public static void assertFileEquals(String message, String expected, File outputFile)
            throws Exception {
        assertSize(message + "is wrong size.", expected.length(), outputFile);
        assertEquals(message + "has wrong contents.", expected, outputFile);
    }

    public static void assertEquals(String message, String expected, File outputFile)
            throws FileNotFoundException, IOException {
        FileReader reader = new FileReader(outputFile);
        for (int charIndex = 0; charIndex < expected.length(); charIndex++) {
            char characterRead = (char)reader.read();
            assertEquals(message + " at index: " + charIndex,
                         expected.charAt(charIndex),
                         characterRead);
        }
    }

    public static void assertSize(String message, int expectedSize, File outputFile) {
        assertEquals(message, expectedSize, outputFile.length());
    }
}
```

Still green. The next step is to rewrite the original test method to use the two new asserts:

```
public void testSaving() throws Exception {
    mockView.setMovies(movies);
    control.setVoidCallable(1);
    mockView.getFile("*.dat");
    control.setReturnValue(outputFile, 1);
    control.activate();

    MovieListEditor editor = new MovieListEditor(movieList, mockView);
    editor.saveAs();
    FileAssert.assertSize("Save As-ed file has wrong size.",
                          expected.length(),
                          outputFile);
    FileAssert.assertEquals("Save As-ed file has wrong contents ",
                            expected,
                            outputFile);
    control.verify();
}
```

It still gives us a green bar, so we can delete assertFileEquals(). Everything is still green, so we're done. Now we can go back to the Swing test we were writing, with the required assertions written and available. The next thing we need to do is build the fixture that we'll need. This involves creating the list of movies that we will be saving, the expected contents of the saved file, a file to save to, a running view, and a MovieListEditor instance:

```
protected void setUp() throws Exception {
  SwingMovieListEditorView.start();
  movieList = new MovieList();
  movieList.add(new Movie("Star Wars", Category.SCIFI, 5));
  movieList.add(new Movie("Star Trek", Category.SCIFI, 3));
  movieList.add(new Movie("Stargate", Category.SCIFI, -1));


  savedText = "Star Wars|Science Fiction|5\n" +
              "Star Trek|Science Fiction|3\n" +
              "Stargate|Science Fiction|-1\n";

  outputFile = File.createTempFile("testSaving", ".dat");
  outputFile.deleteOnExit();

  mainWindow = new JFrameOperator("Movie List");
  editor = new MovieListEditor(movieList,
                     (SwingMovieListEditorView)mainWindow.getWindow());
}
```

Now we have a compiling test with fixture and assertions in place. As expected, it fails. Now we need to add to the test to manipulate the GUI to set things up for the assertions. This is fairly simple in this case. We just need to select *Save As...* from the *File* menu, and enter the name of the temporary file we created in the filename field in the resulting FileChooser dialog:

```
public void testSaving() throws Exception {
  JMenuBarOperator menubar = new JMenuBarOperator(mainWindow);
  JMenuOperator fileMenu = new JMenuOperator(menubar, "File");
  fileMenu.push();
  JMenuItemOperator saveAsItem = new JMenuItemOperator(mainWindow,
                                                     "Save As...");


  saveAsItem.pushNoBlock();
  JFileChooserOperator fileChooser = new JFileChooserOperator();
  fileChooser.setSelectedFile(outputFile);
  JButtonOperator saveButton = new JButtonOperator(fileChooser, "Save");
  saveButton.push();

  FileAssert.assertSize("Saved list has wrong size.",
                   savedText.length(),
                       FileAssert.assertEquals("Saved file", savedText, outputFile);
}
```

This fails immediately when trying to find the menu bar, and we don't have one yet. Let's add a menu bar to our GUI:

```
public void init() {
  setTitle();
  setLayout();
  setJMenuBar(initMenuBar());
  //...
}

private JMenuBar initMenuBar() {
  JMenuBar menuBar = new JMenuBar();
  JMenu fileMenu = new JMenu("File");
  menuBar.add(fileMenu);
  JMenuItem saveAsItem = new JMenuItem("Save As...");
  fileMenu.add(saveAsItem);
  return menuBar;
}
```

Now the test gets to the point of waiting for the JFileChooser. What causes the file chooser to open? Remember that the saveAs() method in MovieListEditor called getFile() on its view. That's what should use a JFileChooser to get a File from the user. Furthermore, the *Save As...* menu item should cause the saveAs() method to be called on the editor. Here's the menu item handler:

```
saveAsItem.addActionListener(new ActionListener() {
  public void actionPerformed(ActionEvent e) {
    try {
      myEditor.saveAs();
    } catch (IOException ex) {
      // TODO: deal with this
    }
  }});
```

And the implementation of getFile():

```
public File getFile(String pattern) {
  int returnVal = fileChooser.showSaveDialog(this);
  if (returnVal == JFileChooser.APPROVE_OPTION) {
    return fileChooser.getSelectedFile();
  } else {
    return null;
  }
}
```

Green. Notice how we are handling the cancelling of the file chooser dialog: we return null to the editor. It's time to revisit MovieListEditor's saveAs() method to account for this. But first, of course, a test that will fail because we aren't handling with getFile() returning null when the file chooser is cancelled.

## Test 55: If the file selection is cancelled, nothing is written to any file.

```
public void testCancelledSaving() throws Exception {
    mockView.setMovies(movies);
    control.setVoidCallable(1);
    mockView.getFile();
    control.setReturnValue(null, 1);
    control.activate();


    MovieListEditor editor = new MovieListEditor(movieList, mockView);
    assertFalse("Editor should not have saved.", editor.saveAs());
    control.verify();
}
```

This fails with an error: a NullPointerException is thrown when it tries to create a FileWriter around null. Something else we've done is expect a **boolean** value to be returned from saveAs() indicating whether saving took place successfully. It would be a good idea to take advantage of this in our earlier testSaving() in TestMovieListEditorFileOperations.

## Exercises

**14.**   Make the required change to TestMovieListEditorFileOperations.testSaving().    *Answer
on p. 533*

We'll fix it and get back to green by checking for **null** being returned from **getFile()** (and returning the appropriate value):

```
public boolean saveAs() throws IOException {
    File outputFile = view.getFile();
    if (outputFile == null) {
        return false;
    }


    FileWriter writer = new FileWriter(outputFile);
    movies.writeTo(writer);
    writer.close();
    return true;
}
```

Now, for completeness, we'll go back to the Swing-based tests and add a **testCancelledSave()** for the GUI level:

```
public void testCancelledSaving() throws Exception {
    JMenuBarOperator menubar = new JMenuBarOperator(mainWindow);
    JMenuOperator fileMenu = new JMenuOperator(menubar, "File");
    fileMenu.push();
    JMenuItemOperator saveAsItem = new JMenuItemOperator(mainWindow,
                                                          "Save As...");
    saveAsItem.pushNoBlock();
    JFileChooserOperator fileChooser = new JFileChooserOperator();
    fileChooser.setSelectedFile(outputFile);
    JButtonOperator cancelButton = new JButtonOperator(fileChooser, "Cancel");
    cancelButton.push();
    FileAssert.assertSize("Saved list has wrong size.", 0, outputFile);
}
```

This also tests that we can select a file in the file chooser and cancel. It verifies that
nothing happens to the file.

## SAVE IN GUI

*Provide, in the GUI, the capability to save the movie collection to the same
file it was previously saved to.*

We took it slowly for the last task since there were a few new ideas involved. Now
we'll pick it up a bit since this task requires only a refinement of what we've done so far
on this story. Specifically, we need to add the ability to resave to the same file without
asking the user for a filename again.

**Test 56.** Telling the logical layer to "Save" causes it to save the current list to the
same file as the previous "Save As" operation.

**Test 57.** Selecting "Save" from the "File" menu causes the list to be written into the
previously selected file.

Since the required setup for testing this involves what we've already done for testing
the *Save As* functionality, we'll extend the **testSaving()** tests.

## Test 56: Telling the logical layer to "Save" causes it to save the current list to the same file as the previous "Save As" operation.

We'll start in TestMovieListEditorFileOperations:

```
public void testSaving() throws Exception {
  mockView.setMovies(movies);
  control.setVoidCallable(1);
  mockView.getFile();
  control.setReturnValue(outputFile, 1);
  mockView.getNameField();
  control.setReturnValue(fotr.getName(), 1);
  mockView.getCategoryField();
  control.setReturnValue(fotr.getCategory(), 1);
  mockView.getRatingField();
  control.setReturnValue(fotr.getRating() + 1, 1);
  mockView.setMovies(extendedMovies);
  control.setVoidCallable(1);
  control.activate();

  MovieListEditor editor = new MovieListEditor(movieList, mockView);
  assertTrue("Editor should have saved", editor.saveAs());

  FileAssert.assertSize("Save As-ed file has wrong size.",
                        expected.length(),
                        outputFile);

  FileAssert.assertEquals("Save As-ed file has wrong contents ",
                          expected,
                          outputFile);
  editor.add();
  assertTrue("Editor should have resaved", editor.save());
  FileAssert.assertEquals("Saved file ", extendedExpected, outputFile);
  control.verify();
}
```

Here we've added to the test to add a movie to the list, resave it, and verify the result. To support this, we need to extend the fixture:

```
fotr = new Movie("The Fellowship of The Ring", Category.FANTASY, 5);
extendedExpected = expected + "The Fellowship of The Ring|Fantasy|5\n";
extendedMovies = new Vector(movies);
extendedMovies.add(fotr);
```

Add the required stub for MovieListEditor.save() and give it a try:

```
public boolean save() {
  return false;
}
```

Of course it fails because save() doesn't do anything yet. Most notably, it just returns false. We need to write some code for save():

```
public boolean save() {
  if (outputFile == null) {
    return false;
  }

  FileWriter writer = new FileWriter(outputFile);
  movies.writeTo(writer);
  writer.close();
  return true;
}
```

To make this compile we need to have an instance variable for outputFile. Add it, compile, and run the tests. It still fails because we don't initialize the outputFile instance variable. We'll do this in saveAs(); we need to use the new instance variable rather than the local we had before:

```
public boolean saveAs() throws IOException {
  outputFile = view.getFile();
  if (outputFile == null) {
    return false;
  }

  FileWriter writer = new FileWriter(outputFile);
  movies.writeTo(writer);
  writer.close();
  return true;
}
```

Now the test fails because the resulting file is wrong. Hmm... that seems unlikely. Everything looks good. Run the test in the debugger (set a breakpoint on entry to MovieListEditor.save()) and we find that the Movie that got added is uncategorized and unrated. Hmm... a quick look at MovieListEditor.add() reveals the problem. It was creating a movie with just a name. Ponder, ponder, scratch, scratch...oh, yes. Our thought was to create a template movie to probe for a duplicate. We missed going back and filling in the rest of the data. A quick look at the test for adding (which was written when we had only a name) shows that the mock has no expectations regarding the category and rating being fetched during an add. Not a nice feeling, discovering that—but it happens. Because we are practicing TDD, we have a better chance of finding that sort of thing early.

First things first, though. We'll fix add() to get our current test passing:

```
public void add() {
  String newName = view.getNameField();
  Movie newMovie = new Movie(newName,
                             view.getCategoryField(),
                             view.getRatingField());
```

```
    try {
      movies.add(newMovie);
      updateMovieList();
    } catch (DuplicateMovieException e) {
      view.duplicateException(newName);
    }
  }
```

Rerun the test. Green. It's not clean yet.

## Exercises

**15.** Fix the add() related tests in TestMovieListEditor.

*Answer on p. 534*

Now to clean up MovieListEditor. If we compare save() and saveAs() we see that other than the initial fetch of outputFile in saveAs(), they are identical. That's an easy cleanup: we just have to have saveAs() set outputFile and call save():

```
    public boolean saveAs() throws IOException {
      outputFile = view.getFile();
      return save();
    }
```

Green and clean!

## Test 57: Selecting "Save" from the "File" menu causes the list to be written into the previously selected file.

The next step is to do something very similar to the GUI testSaving(). But first we'll do some damage control and fix up the add-related GUI tests which we see are also out of date. Actually, I'll make that an exercise for you.

## Exercises

**16.** Fix up the add related tests in TestSwingMovieListEditorView.

*Answer on p. 535*

Here's the new testSaving() GUI test:

```
    public void testSaving() throws Exception {
      JMenuBarOperator menubar = new JMenuBarOperator(mainWindow);
      JMenuOperator fileMenu = new JMenuOperator(menubar, "File");
      fileMenu.push();

      JMenuItemOperator saveAsItem =
            new JMenuItemOperator(mainWindow,
                          new NameBasedChooser("saveas"));
      saveAsItem.pushNoBlock();
      JFileChooserOperator fileChooser = new JFileChooserOperator();
      fileChooser.setSelectedFile(outputFile);
      JButtonOperator saveButton = new JButtonOperator(fileChooser, "Save");
      saveButton.push();
```

```
        FileAssert.assertSize("Save-Ased list has wrong size.",
                            savedText.length(),
                            outputFile);
        FileAssert.assertEquals("Save-Ased file", savedText, outputFile);

        JTextFieldOperator newMovieField =
                new JTextFieldOperator(mainWindow,
                                    new NameBasedChooser("name"));
        newMovieField.enterText(theShining.getName());

        JComboBoxOperator ratingCombo =
                new JComboBoxOperator(mainWindow,
                                    new NameBasedChooser("rating"));
        ratingCombo.setSelectedIndex(theShining.getRating() + 1);

        JComboBoxOperator categoryCombo =
                new JComboBoxOperator(mainWindow,
                                    new NameBasedChooser("category"));
        categoryCombo.setSelectedIndex(2);

        JButtonOperator addButton =
                new JButtonOperator(mainWindow,
                                    new NameBasedChooser("add"));
        addButton.doClick();

        fileMenu.push();
        JMenuItemOperator saveItem =
                new JMenuItemOperator(mainWindow,
                                    new NameBasedChooser("save"));
        saveItem.push();

        FileAssert.assertSize("Saved list has wrong size.",
                            extendedSavedText.length(),
                            outputFile);

        FileAssert.assertEquals("Saved file",
                            extendedSavedText,
                            outputFile);
    }
```

We need to also extend the fixture somewhat:

```
    theShining = new Movie("The Shining", Category.HORROR, 2);
    extendedSavedText = savedText + "The Shining|Horror|2\n";
```

This compiles but fails because there is no *Save* item. Easy enough to add:

```
    priate JMenuBar initMenuBar() {
      JMenuBar menuBar = new JMenuBar();
      JMenu fileMenu = new JMenu("File");
      menuBar.add(fileMenu);
```

```
      JMenuItem saveAsItem = new JMenuItem("Save As. . .");
      saveAsItem.setName("saveas");
      saveAsItem.addActionListener(new ActionListener() {
        public void actionPerformed(ActionEvent e) {
          try {
            myEditor.saveAs();
          } catch (IOException ex) {
            // TODO: deal with this
          }
        }});
      fileMenu.add(saveAsItem);

      JMenuItem saveItem = new JMenuItem("Save");
      saveItem.setName("save");
      fileMenu.add(saveItem);
      return menuBar;
    }
```

Now the test fails because the file is not being updated. We next need to call **save()** in the associated MovieListEditor in response to the *Save* item being selected:

```
    private JMenuBar initMenuBar() {
      JMenuBar menuBar = new JMenuBar();
      JMenu fileMenu = new JMenu("File");
      menuBar.add(fileMenu);

      JMenuItem saveAsItem = new JMenuItem("Save As. . .");
      saveAsItem.setName("saveas");
      saveAsItem.addActionListener(new ActionListener() {
        public void actionPerformed(ActionEvent e) {
          try {
            myEditor.saveAs();
          } catch (IOException ex) {
            // TODO: deal with this
          }
        }});
      fileMenu.add(saveAsItem);

      JMenuItem saveItem = new JMenuItem("Save");
      saveItem.setName("save");
      saveItem.addActionListener(new ActionListener() {
        public void actionPerformed(ActionEvent e) {
          try {
            myEditor.save();
          } catch (IOException ex) {
            // TODO: deal with this
          }
        }});
      fileMenu.add(saveItem);
      return menuBar;
    }
```

The test now runs green. However, initMenuBar has grown too large and is starting to smell. A couple of Extract Method applications (one to each JMenuItem setup) will take care of it:

```java
private JMenuBar initMenuBar() {
  JMenuBar menuBar = new JMenuBar();
  JMenu fileMenu = new JMenu("File");
  menuBar.add(fileMenu);
  fileMenu.add(initSaveAsItem());
  fileMenu.add(initSaveItem());
  return menuBar;
}

private JMenuItem initSaveAsItem() {
  JMenuItem saveAsItem = new JMenuItem("Save As...");
  saveAsItem.setName("saveas");
  saveAsItem.addActionListener(new ActionListener() {
    public void actionPerformed(ActionEvent e) {
      try {
        myEditor.saveAs();
      } catch (IOException ex) {
        // TODO: deal with this
      }
    }});
  return saveAsItem;
}

private JMenuItem initSaveItem() {
  JMenuItem saveItem = new JMenuItem("Save");
  saveItem.setName("save");
  saveItem.addActionListener(new ActionListener() {
    public void actionPerformed(ActionEvent e) {
      try {
        myEditor.save();
      } catch (IOException ex) {
        // TODO: deal with this
      }
    }});
  return saveItem;
}
```

OK. Green and clean! There's still some duplication in the menu item creation and setup code, but that's largely unavoidable in GUI construction code where you are creating multiples of the same type of component.

## READ FROM A FLAT FILE

*Read a movie collection from a flat text file.*

This task requires us to add support for reading a previously written MovieList back into the system.

**Test 58.** Reading from an empty stream results in an empty list of movies.

**Test 59.** Reading from a stream containing the data for a single movie results in a list containing the single movie.

**Test 60.** Reading from a stream containing the data for several movies results in a list containing those movies.

We'll start with reading a MovieList from a Reader. This is a different style of test than the writing tests and will need a different fixture, so we need a new TestCase.

## Test 58: Reading from an empty stream results in an empty list of movies.

We start simply—with a test for reading an empty list:

```
public class TestMovieListReading extends TestCase {
  private String emptyString;

  protected void setUp() throws Exception {
    emptyString = "";
  }
  public void testReadingEmptyList() {
    Reader reader = new StringReader(emptyString);
    MovieList movies = MovieList.readFrom(reader);
    assertEquals("Empty list shouldn't have entries.", 0, movies.size());
  }
  public static void main(String[] args) {
    junit.textui.TestRunner.run(TestMovieListReading.class);
  }
}
```

To make this compile, we need to stub MovieList.read() in the simplest way possible:

```
public static MovieList readFrom(Reader reader) {
  return null;
}
```

The test now redbars with a NullPointerException because the stub returns null.

---

*While we make a practice of writing initial stubs to return the simplest thing (i.e., 0, false, null, etc.), it's generally frowned on to return null in real code if that would cause you to have code similar to:*

```
SomeClass anObject = someMethod();
if (anObject != null) {
  anObject.doSomething();
}
```

*In this case, you should return what's called a null object. Examples of this include empty collections.*

---

So, we rewrite the stub to return an empty MovieList:

```
public static MovieList readFrom(Reader reader) {
  return new MovieList();
}
```

Green.

## Test 59: Reading from a stream containing the data for a single movie results in a list containing the single movie.

The next test will be to read a single movie. We start simply by verifying that exactly one Movie was read:

```
public void testReadingOneMovie() throws Exception {
  Reader reader = new StringReader(oneMovieString);
  MovieList movies = MovieList.readFrom(reader);
  assertEquals("Reading a one movie list should result in a one item list.",
              1,
              movies.size());
}
```

We need to add the string being read to the fixture:

```
oneMovieString = "Star Wars|Science Fiction|4\n";
```

Now we need to write some code to read exactly one Movie. We will take a similar approach to the one we ended up with in the writing code: We will delegate the reading of a Movie to the Movie class:

```
public static MovieList readFrom(Reader reader) throws DuplicateMovieException {
  BufferedReader bufferedReader = new BufferedReader(reader);
  MovieList newList = new MovieList();
  Movie newMovie = Movie.readFrom(bufferedReader);

  if (newMovie != null) {
    newList.add(newMovie);
  }
  return newList;
}
```

Notice the interface design we've done while writing this method. We've decided that if a Movie can't be read, null is returned instead of a Movie instance. We need this (and the conditional addition to the list) in order to keep the previous test from failing. The standard stub for Movie.readFrom() satisfies this:

```
public static Movie readFrom(Reader reader) {
  return null;
}
```

Next, we need to implement code to actually read a Movie:

```
public static Movie readFrom(BufferedReader reader) throws IOException {
  String oneLine = reader.readLine();
  if (oneLine == null) {
    return null;
  }

  StringTokenizer tokenizedLine = new StringTokenizer(oneLine, DELIMITER);
  try {
    String name = tokenizedLine.nextToken();
    Category category = Category.getCategoryNamed(tokenizedLine.nextToken());
    int rating = Integer.parseInt(tokenizedLine.nextToken());
    return new Movie(name, category, rating);
  } catch (NoSuchElementException ex) {
    throw new IOException("Badly formatted movie collection");
  }
}
```

We need to convert from the name of a category (that of the stored Movie) to an instance of the Category class. We can't just create an instance with the name because Category is a type-safe enum and as such has a constraint set of instances. If you recall, this is enforced by having a private constructor. So we need a static method in Category to return the instance corresponding to a name. This is simply a matter of using a map to store a mapping between the names and the instances:

```
public class Category {
  private static Map categoriesByName = new HashMap();

  //...

  private Category(String categoryName) {
    name = categoryName;
    categoriesByName.put(name, this);
    allCategories.add(this);
  }
  //...
}
```

And adding the lookup method:

```
public static Category getCategoryNamed(String categoryName) {
  Category theCategory = (Category)categoriesByName.get(categoryName);
  return (theCategory == null) ? Category.UNCATEGORIZED : theCategory;
}
```

Now we can compile everything (most notably Movie.readFrom()) and run the tests: green bar!

Next, we have to extend the test to make sure that the Movie that was read was what was expected:

```
public void testReadingOneMovie() throws Exception {
   Reader reader = new StringReader(oneMovieString);
   MovieList movies = MovieList.readFrom(reader);

   assertEquals("Reading a one movie list should result in a one item list.",
               1,
               movies.size());
   Movie theMovieRead = movies.getMovie(0);
   assertEquals("Read movie has wrong name.",
               "Star Wars",
               theMovieRead.getName());

   assertEquals("Read movie has wrong category.",
               Category.SCIFI,
               theMovieRead.getCategory());

   assertEquals("Read movie has wrong rating.",
               4,
               theMovieRead.getRating());
}
```

Green bar. We just had to be sure. Also, this will guard us against unintentional changes to the behavior of the reading code in the future.

## Test 60:  Reading from a stream containing the data for several movies results in a list containing those movies.

We now need a test to drive the reading of a collection of multiple Movies:

```
public void testReadingMultipleMovie() throws Exception {
   Reader reader = new StringReader(multiMovieString);
   MovieList movies = MovieList.readFrom(reader);
   assertEquals("Reading a multiple movie list should result in 3 items.",
               3,
               movies.size());
}
```

As before, we need to extend the fixture:

```
multiMovieString = oneMovieString +
                  "Star Trek|Science Fiction|3\n" +
                  "Stargate|Science Fiction|-1\n";
```

Compile, run, red bar. Of course it fails; it only reads the first movie. Now we need to add just enough code to make it read as many movies as are present. We only need to work on the readFrom() method of MovieList:

```
public static MovieList readFrom(Reader reader)
      throws DuplicateMovieException, IOException {
   BufferedReader bufferedReader = new BufferedReader(reader);
   MovieList newList = new MovieList();
```

```
      for (Movie newMovie = Movie.readFrom(bufferedReader);
            newMovie != null;
            newMovie = Movie.readFrom(bufferedReader)) {
         newList.add(newMovie);
      }
      return newList;
   }
```

That does it. Green.

## LOAD IN GUI

*Provide, in the GUI, the capability to load the movie collection from a file.*

**Test 61.** With the list empty, telling the logical layer to load from a file that contains data for a set of movies results in the list containing those movies.

**Test 62.** Choosing "Load" from the "File" menu and selecting a file containing a specific set of movie data causes the corresponding movies to be placed in the list.

**Test 63.** With a set of movies loaded, cancelling the load of a different set leaves the originally loaded set unchanged.

Now we move up a level and add loading capabilities to the MovieListEditor.

### Test 61: With the list empty, telling the logical layer to load from a file that contains data for a set of movies results in the list containing those movies.

Our first test starts with an empty list, loads a file, and verifies that the expected list was sent to the view:

```
      public void testLoading() {
         mockView.setMovies(emptyMovies);
         control.setVoidCallable(1);
         mockView.getFileToLoad();
         control.setReturnValue(inputFile, 1);

         mockView.setMovies(movies);
         control.setVoidCallable(1);
         control.activate();

         MovieListEditor editor = new MovieListEditor(new MovieList(), mockView);
         assertTrue("Editor should have loaded.", editor.load());

         control.verify();
      }
```

After adding the required fixture and stubs, we get a red bar due to the false returned by the stub load(). Let's fake it and have load() return true. The bar's still red, but we have a more helpful failure:

```
      junit.framework.AssertionFailedError:
        EasyMock for interface com.saorsa.nowplaying.MovieListEditorView:
        Expectation failure on verify:
          method call getFileToLoad():
```

```
      calls expected: 1,
      received: 0
method call setMovies([Star Wars,Star Trek,Stargate,The Shining]):
      calls expected: 1,
      received: 0
```

Now we can go to work on implementing load():

```
public boolean load()
    throws FileNotFoundException, IOException, DuplicateMovieException {
  File inputFile = view.getFileToLoad();
  if (inputFile == null) {
    return false;
  }


  FileReader reader = new FileReader(inputFile);
  movies = MovieList.readFrom(reader);
  filterOnCategory(Category.ALL);
  return true;
}
```

OK, now the test fails with:

```
junit.framework.AssertionFailedError:
  EasyMock for interface com.saorsa.nowplaying.MovieListEditorView:
  method call setMovies([]):
      calls expected: 1,
      received: 2
```

We haven't provided any data to be loaded, so load() results in an empty list. This is good, but not what we're interested in testing here.

Hmm. This is starting to look like a completely different fixture. Maybe we should split TestMovieListEditorFileOperations into two test cases, one for saving, and one for loading.

## Exercises

*Answer*
*on p. 536*

**17.**   Do the split: TestMovieListEditorFileOperations into TestMovieListEditorSaving and TestMovieListEditorLoading.

Now let's provide some data to load by setting up the input file in setUp():

```
movieList.writeTo(new FileWriter(inputFile));
```

That does it. Green bar.

To finish off we take loading to the GUI.

## Test 62: Choosing "Load" from the "File" menu and selecting a file containing a specific set of movie data causes the corresponding movies to be placed in the list.

### Exercises

**18.**    In looking at adding another test to TestSwingMovieListEditorFileOperations, we     *Answer*
notice that we have some code debt. The *Rule of Three* has kicked in. This is     *on p. 537*
the third test, and as we think about it we see that there are a few lines of code
duplicated in each test. Time to refactor. What do we need to do?

So, here's the first test:

```
public void testLoading() {
  JMenuItemOperator loadItem =
          new JMenuItemOperator(mainWindow, "Open...");
  loadItem.pushNoBlock();


  JFileChooserOperator fileChooser = new JFileChooserOperator();
  fileChooser.setSelectedFile(inputFile);
  JButtonOperator loadButton = new JButtonOperator(fileChooser, "Open");
  loadButton.push();


  JListOperator movieList =
      new JListOperator(mainWindow, new NameBasedChooser("movieList"));
  ListModel listModel = movieList.getModel();
  assertEquals("Movie list is the wrong size", 4,  listModel.getSize());
}
```

The first thing we need to do is add a stub for getFileToLoad():

```
public File getFileToLoad() {
  return null;
}
```

If we're calling this method getFileToLoad(), it makes sense to rename getFile() to get-
FileToSave(). It's just a rename, so we won't spend any more time or text on it. Just
remember that it appears in an interface and several mocks as well.

Next, we need to add an *Open* option to the *File* menu (in SwingMovieListEditorView). Since the format of this will be almost identical to the two existing menu
items, we'll take a big step and just do it:

```
private JMenuBar initMenuBar() {
  JMenuBar menuBar = new JMenuBar();
  JMenu fileMenu = new JMenu("File");
  menuBar.add(fileMenu);
  fileMenu.add(initOpenItem());
  fileMenu.add(initSaveAsItem());
  fileMenu.add(initSaveItem());
  return menuBar;
}

private JMenuItem initOpenItem() {
  JMenuItem openItem = new JMenuItem("Open...");
  openItem.setName("open");
  openItem.addActionListener(new ActionListener() {
    public void actionPerformed(ActionEvent e) {
      try {
        myEditor.load();
      } catch (Exception ex) {
        // TODO: deal with this
      }
    }});
  return openItem;
}
```

Now the test is looking for a file chooser. Time to fill in getFileToLoad():

```
public File getFileToLoad() {
  int returnVal = fileChooser.showOpenDialog(this);
  if (returnVal == JFileChooser.APPROVE_OPTION) {
    return fileChooser.getSelectedFile();
  } else {
    return null;
  }
}
```

Green!

## Test 63: With a set of movies loaded, cancelling the load of a different set leaves the originally loaded set unchanged.

```
public void testCancelledLoading() {
  JMenuItemOperator openItem =
          new JMenuItemOperator(mainWindow, new NameBasedChooser("open"));
  openItem.pushNoBlock();

  JFileChooserOperator fileChooser = new JFileChooserOperator();
  fileChooser.setSelectedFile(inputFile);
  JButtonOperator loadButton = new JButtonOperator(fileChooser, "Cancel");
  loadButton.push();
```

```
    JListOperator movieList =
        new JListOperator(mainWindow, new NameBasedChooser("movieList"));
    ListModel listModel = movieList.getModel();
    assertEquals("Movie list is the wrong size", 3,  listModel.getSize());
}
```

Green and clean enough! Time to move on.

## RETROSPECTIVE

In this chapter we added persistence to our application. We did it in the simplest way that could possibly work: a plain ASCII file, one movie per line, with movie instance variables separated by a delimiter character. This is basically the same as a Comma Separated Value file except that commas could reasonably appear in a movie title, so we chose something more unlikely. This let us avoid having to do something like wrap movie titles in quote characters.

In the process, we've added a *File* menu to the GUI. Figure 16.1 shows it.

**Figure 16.1** The new *File* menu.

Maybe later we will have need for structured storage or even a relational database. But that is *maybe* and *later*—YAGNI. We did what was barely sufficient for today. Maybe we won't need anything more. "But," you say, "there's a story for it." So... we may not get to that. The customer might decide that they don't need it; the project may be cancelled before then. Things change. Don't make things more complex than you have to... until you have to. That's one of the secrets of simple design.

# Chapter 17

# SORTING

*In the GUI, allow the movie list to be sorted by selecting from a set of options on a menu. Two orderings are required: ascending by name, and descending by rating.*

The first step is to start with the innermost *stuff*. In this case, we are talking about the user being able to sort the list of movies they see. As we peel off the layers of the onion, we pass through the GUI layer being able to change the order of the displayed list, the MovieListEditor updating its view's list in response to a change in the sorting requirements, the sorting of a MovieList, and finally we arrive at comparing two Movies. Now we'll back out through the layers, testing and implementing as we go.

## COMPARE MOVIES

*Create the ability to compare two movies based on either name (ascending order) or rating (descending order). This is needed for sorting.*

The first step, at the innermost layer, is adding the ability to compare two Movies. We'll use the standard Java approach to this. Since, in this case, we need to be able to sort on different attributes (i.e., name and rating), making Movie implement Comparable doesn't suffice. We will need to create a Comparator for each ordering we need. Here are the tests:

**Test 64.** Comparing two movies with the same name, based on name, should answer 0.

**Test 65.** Comparing two movies, the first having a lexically smaller name, based on name, should answer a negative integer.

**Test 66.** Comparing two movies, the first having a lexically greater name, based on name, should answer a positive integer.

**Test 67.** Comparing two movies with the same rating, based on rating, should answer 0.

**Test 68.** Comparing two movies, the first having a lower rating, based on rating, should answer a negative integer.

**Test 69.** Comparing two movies, the first having a higher rating, based on rating, should answer a positive integer.

**Test 70.** For the purposes of comparison, an unrated movie always has a lower rating.

Let's start with ordering by name. Here's a test:

## Test 64: Comparing two movies with the same name, based on name, should answer 0.

```
public void testCompareSame() {
    Movie starTrek = new Movie("Star Trek", Category.SCIFI, 3);
    Movie anotherStarTrek = new Movie("Star Trek", Category.SCIFI, 3);
    MovieNameComparator comparatorToTest = new MovieNameComparator();
    assertEquals("Comparing equal movies should return 0.",
                 0,
                 comparatorToTest.compare(starTrek, anotherStarTrek));
}
```

Create a stub for MovieNameComparator:

```
public class MovieNameComparator implements Comparator {
    public MovieNameComparator() {
        super();
    }

    public int compare(Object o1, Object o2) {
        return 0;
    }
}
```

Compile, run, green! The test is expecting 0 to be returned, which is what the stub does. The next test will drive us to generalize.

## Test 65: Comparing two movies, the first having a lexically smaller name, based on name, should answer a negative integer.

```
public void testCompareBefore() {
    Movie starTrek = new Movie("Star Trek", Category.SCIFI, 3);
    Movie alien = new Movie("Alien", Category.SCIFI, 5);
    MovieNameComparator comparatorToTest = new MovieNameComparator();
    assertTrue("Comparing a lesser movie should return < 0.",
               comparatorToTest.compare(alien, starTrek) < 0);
}
```

This test, of course, fails. This is good (have I emphasized this enough?) because it lets us drive the implementation. Now we need to do some work on MovieNameComparator.compareTo(). Since we are ordering by name, and name is a String, and String implements Comparable, it makes sense to delegate the comparison to the name:

```
public int compare(Object o1, Object o2) {
    return ((Movie)o1).getName().compareTo(((Movie)o2).getName());
}
```

Green. Now let's do some refactoring. First, we've introduced some duplication in the test class. We can extract a common fixture:

```
protected void setUp() {
  starTrek = new Movie("Star Trek", Category.SCIFI, 3);
  comparatorToTest = new MovieNameComparator();
}
```

Next, have a look at compare(). Something smells very obtuse and ugly. Let's clean it up by extracting some explaining variables, running the tests after each change. Here's the end result:

```
public int compare(Object o1, Object o2) {
  Movie firstMovie = (Movie)o1;
  Movie secondMovie = (Movie)o2;
  String nameOfFirstMovie = firstMovie.getName();
  String nameOfSecondMovie = secondMovie.getName();
  return nameOfFirstMovie.compareTo(nameOfSecondMovie);
}
```

There, that's better. Next, a test to confirm the remaining class of comparison.

## Test 66: Comparing two movies, the first having a lexically greater name, based on name, should answer a positive integer.

```
public void testCompareAfter() {
  Movie starWars = new Movie("Star Wars", Category.SCIFI, 4);
  assertTrue("Comparing a greater movie should return > 0.",
             comparatorToTest.compare(starWars, starTrek) > 0);
}
```

As expected, this passes right away. Next, let's look at the other ordering we need: by rating. This is very similar to what we've just done. The only twist is that the ordering is descending rather than ascending. First, the fixture:

```
public class TestMovieComparingByRating extends TestCase {
  private MovieRatingComparator comparatorToTest = null;
  private Movie starTrek = null;

  protected void setUp() throws Exception {
    starTrek = new Movie("Star Trek", Category.SCIFI, 3);
    comparatorToTest = new MovieRatingComparator();
  }

  public static void main(String[] args) {
    junit.textui.TestRunner.run(TestMovieComparingByRating.class);
  }
}
```

And now, each of the tests. We'll just go through them one after another, since they're so similar to what we just did.

## Test 67: Comparing two movies with the same rating, based on rating, should answer 0.

```
public void testCompareSame() {
    Movie anotherStarTrek = new Movie("Star Trek", Category.SCIFI, 3);
    assertEquals("Comparing equally rated movies should return 0.",
                 0,
                 comparatorToTest.compare(starTrek, anotherStarTrek));
}
```

## Test 68: Comparing two movies, the first having a lower rating, based on rating, should answer a negative integer.

```
public void testCompareBefore() {
    Movie alien = new Movie("Alien", Category.SCIFI, 5);
    assertTrue("Comparing a higher rated movie should return < 0.",
               comparatorToTest.compare(alien, starTrek) < 0);
}
```

## Test 69: Comparing two movies, the first having a higher rating, based on rating, should answer a positive integer.

```
public void testCompareAfter() {
    Movie starshipTroopers = new Movie("Starship troopers", Category.SCIFI, 1);
    assertTrue("Comparing a lower rated movie should return > 0.",
               comparatorToTest.compare(starshipTroopers, starTrek) > 0);
}
```

## Test 70: For the purposes of comparison, an unrated movie always has a lower rating.

Here's the only difference: With ratings we have the concept of an unrated movie; we didn't have a corresponding *unnamed movie* to deal with earlier.

```
public void testComparingWithUnrated() {
    Movie jurassicPark = new Movie("Jurassic Park", Category.SCIFI, -1);
    assertTrue("Comparing with an unrated movie should return > 0.",
               comparatorToTest.compare(jurassicPark, starTrek) > 0);
}
```

And, here's the comparator:

```
public class MovieRatingComparator implements Comparator {
    public MovieRatingComparator() {
        super();
    }
```

```
      public int compare(Object o1, Object o2) {
        Movie firstMovie = (Movie)o1;
        Movie secondMovie = (Movie)o2;
        int ratingOfFirstMovie = firstMovie.getRawRating();
        int ratingOfSecondMovie = secondMovie.getRawRating();
        return ratingOfSecondMovie − ratingOfFirstMovie;
      }
    }
```

Notice that we reference a new accessor, Movie.getRawRating(). This method doesn't throw an UnratedMovieException if the movie has no rating. Instead, it returns -1, the value indicating an unrated Movie. This works perfectly with our comparison method: unrated Movies compare as the lowest rating value.

Now we have a way of determining two orderings on a list of Movies. The next step is to use that to provide MovieList with the capability of sorting.

## SORT A MOVIELIST

*Add the capability to ask a MovieList to provide its list sorted on a specific attribute, for the moment this is one of name or rating.*

Sorting is different than the category filtering we did earlier. It doesn't change the number of items, it only changes their order. With that in mind, let's approach this by making sorting an in-place operation. By that I mean that we will ask a MovieList to sort itself, and it will (potentially) modify the order of its items.

**Test 71.** Sorting an empty list has no effect on it.

**Test 72.** Sorting a list, by name, that is already sorted has no effect on it.

**Test 73.** Sorting a list, by name, that is in reverse order puts it in order.

**Test 74.** Sorting a list, by rating, that is already sorted has no effect on it.

**Test 75.** Sorting a list, by rating, that is in reverse order puts it in order.

**Test 76.** Sorting a list, by rating, that has duplicates puts it in order; the duplicates being in their original order relative to one another.

**Test 77.** Sorting a randomly ordered list by name puts it in order, by name.

**Test 78.** Sorting a randomly ordered list by rating puts it in order, by name.

We'll tackle name sorting first. We start simply with what it means to sort an empty list.

## Test 71: Sorting an empty list has no effect on it.

```
    public void testSortingEmptyList() {
      emptyList.sortUsing(nameComparator);
      assertEquals("Sorting a empty list shouldn't change its size.",
                   0,
                   emptyList.size());
    }
```

To make this pass we need to stub sortUsing():

```
public void sortUsing(Comparator aComparator) {
}
```

Not much, but it is enough to make the test compile, and pass.

The next test isn't much different. It tests that sorting an already sorted list doesn't change the order.

## Test 72: Sorting a list, by name, that is already sorted has no effect on it.

```
public void testSortingSortedListByName() throws DuplicateMovieException {
  Vector sortedMovies = new Vector();

  sortedMovies.add(new Movie("A", Category.SCIFI, 5));
  sortedMovies.add(new Movie("B", Category.SCIFI, 4));
  sortedMovies.add(new Movie("C", Category.SCIFI, 3));
  sortedMovies.add(new Movie("D", Category.SCIFI, 2));
  sortedMovies.add(new Movie("E", Category.SCIFI, 1));
  sortedMovies.add(new Movie("F", Category.SCIFI, 0));
  sortedMovies.add(new Movie("G", Category.SCIFI, -1));

  MovieList sortedList = new MovieList();
  Iterator i = sortedMovies.iterator();
  while (i.hasNext()) {
    sortedList.add((Movie) i.next());
  }

  sortedList.sortUsing(nameComparator);
  assertEquals("Sorting should not change size.",
                sortedMovies.size(),
                sortedList.size());

  Iterator original = sortedMovies.iterator();
  Iterator sorted = sortedList.iterator();

  while (original.hasNext()) {
    assertEquals("Sorted list should stay sorted when sorted.",
                  original.next(),
                  sorted.
}
```

To compile we need to add iterator() to MovieList. We'll skip the stub stage and go right to the real implementation since it's so obvious: it should return an iterator over the underlying collection:

```
public Iterator iterator() {
  return movies.iterator();
}
```

Now it compiles and passes. When we wrote the test we added a lot of fixture code. Let's take a moment to move that to setUp() to make the test cleaner and clearer. Now we have:

```
public void testSortingSortedListByName() throws DuplicateMovieException {
  sortedList.sortUsing(nameComparator);
  assertEquals("Sorting should not change size.",
               sortedMovies.size(),
               sortedList.size());


  Iterator original = sortedMovies.iterator();
  Iterator sorted = sortedList.iterator();
  while (original.hasNext()) {
    assertEquals("Sorted list should stay sorted when sorted.",
                 original.next(),
                 sorted.next());
  }
}
```

## Exercises

**19.**    What does the fixture look like?

*Answer on p. 537*

The next test will take a reverse ordered list, sort it, and verify that it has been sorted.

## Test 73: Sorting a list, by name, that is in reverse order puts it in order.

```
public void testSortingReverseSortedListByName() {
  reversedList.sortUsing(nameComparator);
  Iterator original = sortedMovies.iterator();
  Iterator sorted = reversedList.iterator();
  while (original.hasNext()) {
    assertEquals("Reversed list should be sorted when sorted.",
                 original.next(),
                 sorted.next());
  }
}
```

Next, we need a reversed list. The straightforward way to do this is something like:

```
reversedList = new MovieList();
int numberOfMovies = sortedMovies.size();
for (int i = 0; i < numberOfMovies; i++) {
  reversedList.add((Movie)sortedMovies.get(numberOfMovies - (i + 1)));
}
```

If we're doing that we might as well incorporate the construction of the sorted list we used in the last test. So now we have:

```
sortedList = new MovieList();
reversedList = new MovieList();
int numberOfMovies = sortedMovies.size();
for (int i = 0; i < numberOfMovies; i++) {
  reversedList.add((Movie)sortedMovies.get(numberOfMovies - (i + 1)));
  sortedList.add((Movie)sortedMovies.get(i));
}
```

OK. Now we compile and get a red bar because the result of sorting the list isn't sorted. Now it's time to actually do something about sorting a MovieList. The good thing is that the Java Collection framework provides what we need to do this. That's why we started off with a task to build Comparators:

```
public void sortUsing(Comparator aComparator) {
  Collections.sort(movies, aComparator);
}
```

Green!

We need to clean up the tests a bit, though. The most recent test introduced some duplication, specifically, the code that tests that a MovieList is in sorted order. We can use Extract Method to take care of that:

```
public void testSortingSortedListByName() throws Exception {
  sortedList.sortUsing(nameComparator);
  checkThatListIsSorted("Sorted list should stay sorted when sorted.",
                        sortedList);
}

public void testSortingReverseSortedListByName() {
  reversedList.sortUsing(nameComparator);
  checkThatListIsSorted("Reversed list should be sorted when sorted.",
                        reversedList);
}

private void checkThatListIsSorted(String message, MovieList listToCheck) {
  assertEquals("Sorting shouldn't change list size.",
               sortedMovies.size(),
               listToCheck.size());
  Iterator original = sortedMovies.iterator();
  Iterator sorted = listToCheck.iterator();
  while (original.hasNext()) {
    assertEquals(message, original.next(), sorted.next());
  }
}
```

There, that cleans things up nicely. Next, we need to take care of sorting a MovieList based on rating. This will be very similar to what we just did, so as we did in the first task, we'll show it all in one step here, even though we did it one test at a time.

## Test 74: Sorting a list, by rating, that is already sorted has no effect on it.

```
public void testSortingSortedListByRating() throws Exception {
  sortedList.sortUsing(ratingComparator);
  checkThatListIsSorted("Sorted list should stay sorted when sorted.",
                        sortedList);
}
```

## Test 75: Sorting a list, by rating, that is in reverse order puts it in order.

```
public void testSortingReverseSortedListByRating() {
  reversedList.sortUsing(ratingComparator);
  checkThatListIsSorted("Reversed list should be sorted when sorted.",
                        reversedList);
}
```

As expected, everything works. We already have the Comparators working as well as the basic sorting mechanism. Using a different (but tested) Comparator should work without any problems.

Hmmm...that seemed too easy. Let's try another test. Movie names are unique, but ratings aren't. Let's write a test that takes a list with duplicate ratings and sorts it.

## Test 76: Sorting a list, by rating, that has duplicates puts it in order; the duplicates being in their original order relative to one another.

```
public void testSortingListWithDuplicatesByRating() throws Exception {
  Movie unratedMovie = new Movie("Unrated", Category.SCIFI, -1);
  sortedList.add(unratedMovie);
  sortedMovies.add(unratedMovie);
  sortedList.sortUsing(ratingComparator);
  checkThatListIsSorted("List with duplicates has bad ordering.",
                        sortedList);
}
```

Green bar. I'm still not confident enough. I want to see it sorting a jumbled list, using both Comparators. First, a tweak to the fixture:

```
protected void setUp() throws Exception {
  //...
  jumbledList = new MovieList();
  Vector movies = new Vector(sortedMovies);
  for (int i = sortedMovies.size(); i > 0; i--) {
    int index = (int) Math.floor((Math.random() * movies.size()));
    jumbledList.add((Movie)movies.get(index));
    movies.remove(index);
  }
  //...
}
```

## Test 77: Sorting a randomly ordered list by name puts it in order, by name.

```
public void testSortingJumbledListByName() throws Exception {
  jumbledList.sortUsing(nameComparator);
  checkThatListIsSorted("Jumbled list should now be sorted by name.",
                        jumbledList);
}
```

## Test 78: Sorting a randomly ordered list by rating puts it in order, by name.

```
public void testSortingJumbledListByRating() throws Exception {
  jumbledList.sortUsing(ratingComparator);
  checkThatListIsSorted("Jumbled list should now be sorted by rating.",
                        jumbledList);
}
```

We've shown the addition to the fixture already factored to setUp(), but remember that we would have started off with it in testSortingJumbledListByName(), then extracted it into setUp() when we needed the same thing in testSortingJumbledListByRating.

That passes all the tests. I'm finally confident enough to move on. I do mean all the tests. The AllTests suite is getting bigger:

```
public class AllTests extends TestSuite {
  public static void main(String[] args) {
    junit.textui.TestRunner.run(AllTests.class);
  }

  public static Test suite() {
    TestSuite suite = new TestSuite("Test for com.saorsa.nowplaying.tests");
    suite.addTest(new TestSuite(TestCustomListRenderer.class));
    suite.addTest(new TestSuite(TestMovie.class));

    suite.addTest(new TestSuite(TestMovieComparingByName.class));
    suite.addTest(new TestSuite(TestMovieListEditor.class));
    suite.addTest(new TestSuite(TestMovieListEditorLoading.class));
    suite.addTest(new TestSuite(TestMovieListEditorSaving.class));

    suite.addTest(new TestSuite(TestMovieListEditorWithCategoryFiltering.class));
    suite.addTest(new TestSuite(TestMovieListReading.class));
    suite.addTest(new TestSuite(TestMovieListSorting.class));
    suite.addTest(new TestSuite(TestEmptyMovieList.class));
    suite.addTest(new TestSuite(TestMovieListWithOneMovie.class));
    suite.addTest(new TestSuite(TestMovieListWithTwoMovies.class));

    suite.addTest(new TestSuite(TestMovieListWithMixedList.class));
    suite.addTest(new TestSuite(TestMovieListWithPopulatedList.class));
    suite.addTest(new TestSuite(TestMovieListWriting.class));
    return suite;
  }
}
```

# ASK A MOVIELISTEDITOR FOR SORTED LISTS

*Add sorting capabilities to MovieListEditor.*

In the last task we did all the work required to show that the sorting capabilities work in the various situations. For this task, we just need to test that MovieListEditor responds properly to a request to sort the list. Actually, one test might suffice:

**Test 79.** Asking the logical layer to sort its list causes the associated view's list to be updated to one that is in order (order depends on what is being sorted on).

First, the extended fixture:

```
public class TestMovieListEditorSorting extends CommonTestMovieListEditor {
  private Vector sortedMovies;

  protected void setUp() throws Exception {
    super.setUp();
    sortedMovies = new Vector();
    sortedMovies.add(starTrek);
    sortedMovies.add(starWars);
    sortedMovies.add(stargate);
    sortedMovies.add(theShining);
  }

  public static void main(String[] args) {
    junit.textui.TestRunner.run(TestMovieListEditorSorting.class);
  }

}
```

Now for the test.

## Test 79: Asking the logical layer to sort its list causes the associated view's list to be updated to one that is in order (order depends on what is being sorted on).

```
public void testSorting() {
  mockView.setMovies(movies);
  control.setVoidCallable(1);
  mockView.setMovies(sortedMovies);
  control.setVoidCallable(1);
  control.activate();
  MovieListEditor editor = new MovieListEditor(movieList, mockView);
  editor.sortUsing(new MovieNameComparator());
  control.verify();
}
```

Add an empty stub for MovieListEditor.sortUsing() and run it. This, of course, fails because sortUsing() does nothing. We need it to sort the list and update the display:

```
public void sortUsing(Comparator aComparator) {
  movies.sortUsing(aComparator);
  updateAndDisplayFilteredMovies();
}
```

Green bar! That was simple. There's a lesson here that reinforces and validates the way we've been working: Do the real work in the model without worrying about any sort of user interface. You will spend most of your time there, and it's the easiest part of a system to write good tests for. It also keeps the interface layers as thin as possible. This, in turn, makes it easier to replace the interface with something else. Splitting the interface into operation and presentation layers helps too.

## ADD A WAY TO SORT TO THE GUI

*Add a* View *menu to the GUI with an option for each attribute that can be sorted on. Selecting one of them results in the visible movie list being sorted by that attribute.*

The last task for the sorting story is to add access to the new sorting capabilities to the Swing GUI.

**Test 80.** Selecting "Sort by name" from the "View" menu causes the displayed list to be sorted by name.

**Test 81.** Selecting "Sort by rating" from the "View" menu causes the displayed list to be sorted by rating.

Since this is conceptually different than our previous GUI tests, and requires a slightly different fixture, we'll create a new TestCase:

```
public class TestSwingMovieListEditorViewSorting extends TestCase {
  private MovieList movieList;
  private Movie starWars;
  private Movie starTrek;
  private Movie stargate;
  private Movie theShining;
  private Vector movies;
  private JFrameOperator mainWindow;
  private MovieListEditor editor;
  private Vector sortedMovies;
  private JMenuBarOperator menubar;
  private JMenuOperator viewMenu;

  protected void setUp() throws Exception {
    super.setUp();
    SwingMovieListEditorView.start();
    stargate = new Movie("Stargate", Category.SCIFI, −1);
    theShining = new Movie("The Shining", Category.HORROR, 2);
    starWars = new Movie("Star Wars", Category.SCIFI, 5);
    starTrek = new Movie("Star Trek", Category.SCIFI, 3);
```

```
        movies = new Vector();
        movies.add(stargate);
        movies.add(theShining);
        movies.add(starWars);
        movies.add(starTrek);

        sortedMovies = new Vector();
        sortedMovies.add(starTrek);
        sortedMovies.add(starWars);
        sortedMovies.add(stargate);
        sortedMovies.add(theShining);

        movieList = new MovieList();
        movieList.add(stargate);
        movieList.add(theShining);
        movieList.add(starWars);
        movieList.add(starTrek);

        mainWindow = new JFrameOperator("Movie List");
        editor = new MovieListEditor(movieList,
                          (SwingMovieListEditorView)mainWindow.getWindow());

        menubar = new JMenuBarOperator(mainWindow);
        viewMenu = new JMenuOperator(menubar, "View");
        viewMenu.push();
    }

    protected void tearDown() throws Exception {
        super.tearDown();
        mainWindow.dispose();
    }
}
```

## Test 80: Selecting "Sort by name" from the "View" menu causes the displayed list to be sorted by name.

```
    public void testSortingByName() {
        JMenuItemOperator sortByNameItem =
              new JMenuItemOperator(mainWindow,
                                new NameBasedChooser("sortByName"));
        sortByNameItem.push();

        JListOperator movieList =
              new JListOperator(mainWindow,
                            new NameBasedChooser("movieList"));
        ListModel listModel = movieList.getModel();
        assertEquals("Movie list is the wrong size", sortedMovies.size(),
                  listModel.getSize());

        for (int i = 0; i < sortedMovies.size(); i++) {
          assertEquals("Movie list contains bad movie at index " + i,
                      sortedMovies.get(i),
                      listModel.getElementAt(i));
        }
    }
}
```

This fails with an error when looking for the *View* menu. We need to add it to the GUI:

```
private JMenuBar initMenuBar() {
  //...
  JMenu viewMenu = new JMenu("View");
  menuBar.add(viewMenu);
  viewMenu.add(initSortByNameItem());
  return menuBar;
}

private JMenuItem initSortByNameItem() {
  JMenuItem sortByNameItem = new JMenuItem("Sort by name");
  sortByNameItem.setName("sortByName");
  return sortByNameItem;
}
```

Now we see a failure due to the list not being sorted after the *Sort by name* menu item is selected. To deal with this, we need to add an action listener which will forward the request to the associated editor:

```
sortByNameItem.addActionListener(new ActionListener() {
  public void actionPerformed(ActionEvent e) {
    myEditor.sortUsing(new MovieNameComparator());
  }});
```

Green.

## Test 81: Selecting "Sort by rating" from the "View" menu causes the displayed list to be sorted by rating.

Now we do the same for *Sort by rating*. Here's the test:

```
protected void setUp() throws Exception {
  //...
  ratingSortedMovies = new Vector();
  ratingSortedMovies.add(starWars);
  ratingSortedMovies.add(starTrek);
  ratingSortedMovies.add(theShining);
  ratingSortedMovies.add(stargate);
  //...
}

public void testSortingByRating() {
  JMenuItemOperator sortByRatingItem =
      new JMenuItemOperator(mainWindow,
                              new NameBasedChooser("sortByRating"));
  sortByRatingItem.push();

  JListOperator movieList =
      new JListOperator(mainWindow,
                          new NameBasedChooser("movieList"));
```

```
      ListModel listModel = movieList.getModel();
      assertEquals("Movie list is the wrong size",
                  ratingSortedMovies.size(),
                  listModel.getSize());

    for (int i = 0; i < ratingSortedMovies.size(); i++) {
      assertEquals("Movie list contains bad movie at index " + i,
                  ratingSortedMovies.get(i),
                  listModel.getElementAt(i));
    }
  }
```

And here's the new menu item code to make it pass (done in one bigger step):

```
  private JMenuBar initMenuBar() {
    //...
    viewMenu.add(initSortByRatingItem());
    //...
  }

  private JMenuItem initSortByRatingItem() {
    JMenuItem sortByRatingItem = new JMenuItem("Sort by rating");
    sortByRatingItem.setName("sortByRating");
    sortByRatingItem.addActionListener(new ActionListener() {
      public void actionPerformed(ActionEvent e) {
        myEditor.sortUsing(new MovieRatingComparator());
      }});
    return sortByRatingItem;
  }
```

## RETROSPECTIVE

Working on this story illustrated how most of the work can (and should) be done in the guts of the application. Sometimes this is called the *model* or *problem domain* code. Do all you can there, and put good, well-crafted interfaces in place. This makes it easy, and sometimes trivial, to expose new functionality in the interface layer(s).

The new GUI features are shown in Figures 17.1 and 17.2.

**Figure 17.1** The GUI showing sorting by name.

**Figure 17.2** The GUI showing sorting by rating.

# Chapter 18

# MULTIPLE RATINGS

*Movies can have more than one rating, each with an identified source. Selecting a movie should show all of its ratings. There should also be a way to add a rating. A movie's displayed rating should now be the average of all of its individual ratings.*

Here's an interesting story that extends an earlier one. We've previously added a rating to Movie; now we have to extend that to handle multiple ratings and report the average. Furthermore, we need to be able to identify the source of each rating. We'll take it one step at a time.

## MULTIPLE RATINGS

*Add support for multiple ratings rather than just one. Provide access to the average of all the ratings.*

The first task is simply to support more than one rating value, and provide access to an average. Also, we have to maintain the current behavior (i.e., keep all the existing tests passing) unless it is overridden by the new behavior. For example, setRating() doesn't make sense anymore.

**Test 82.** Constructing a Movie with no arguments creates an unrated Movie.

**Test 83.** Add a single rating to an unrated movie. Asking for the average rating answers the rating just added.

**Test 84.** Add several ratings: 3, 5, and 4. Asking for the average rating answers 4.

**Test 85.** Add several ratings: 3, 5, 5, and 3. Asking for the average rating answers 4.

**Test 86.** Writing movies uses for format: <name> | <category> | <total rating> | <number of ratings>.

**Test 87.** Reading movies uses for format: <name> | <category> | <total rating> | <number of ratings>.

For simplicity, we'll add our new tests to TestMovie.

## Test 82: Constructing a Movie with no arguments creates an unrated Movie.

```
public void testUnratedConstructor() {
  Movie starTrek = new Movie("Star Trek", Category.SCIFI);
  try {
    starTrek.getRating();
    fail("Getting rating of an unrated Movie should throw UnratedMovieException");
  } catch (UnratedException ex) {
  }
}
```

Simply chaining to the more general constructor will get this working:

```
public Movie(String name, Category category) {
  this(name, category, −1);
}
```

## Test 83: Add a single rating to an unrated movie. Asking for the average rating answers the rating just added.

```
public void testAddingOneRating() throws Exception {
  Movie starTrek = new Movie("Star Trek", Category.SCIFI);
  starTrek.addRating(3);
  assertEquals("Bad average rating of 1.", 3, starTrek.getRating());
}
```

We need a stub addRating():

```
public void addRating(int aRating) {
}
```

This causes the test to fail, throwing an UnratedException. Let's have addRating() do something:

```
public void addRating(int aRating) {
  rating = aRating;
}
```

Green. Hmm...we have some common fixture in the two tests that should be refactored out. But it's not used by the previous tests in TestMovie, and what's more, the new tests don't use the existing fixture. We need to create a new TestCase to correspond with the new fixture:

```
public class TestMovieRatings extends TestCase {

  public void testUnratedConstructor() {
    Movie starTrek = new Movie("Star Trek", Category.SCIFI);
    try {
      starTrek.getRating();
      fail("Getting rating of an unrated Movie should throw UnratedMovieException");
    } catch (UnratedException ex) {
    }
  }
```

```
        public void testAddingOneRating() throws Exception {
          Movie starTrek = new Movie("Star Trek", Category.SCIFI);
          starTrek.addRating(3);
          assertEquals("Bad average rating of 1.", 3, starTrek.getRating());
        }
        public static void main(String[] args) {
          junit.textui.TestRunner.run(TestMovieRatings.class);
        }
      }
```

Run it to make sure it works as it should (i.e., both tests should pass). Good. Now we can refactor the fixture into a **setUp()** method.

## Exercises

**20.** Do the extraction of the fixture.

*Answer on p. 538*

We can see the inductive testing pattern emerging:

1. test the basis case (no rating)
2. test the next simplest case (one rating)
3. test the general case (more than 1 rating)

## Test 84: Add several ratings: 3, 5, and 4. Asking for the average rating answers 4.

To test the general case, let's try adding three ratings:

```
      public void testAddingThreeRatings() throws Exception {
        starTrek.addRating(3);
        starTrek.addRating(5);
        starTrek.addRating(4);
        assertEquals("Bad average rating after adding 3, 5, and 4.",
                     4,
                     starTrek.getRating());
      }
```

Red bar! Good, now we have some work to do. The failure is:

```
junit.framework.AssertionFailedError:
  Bad average rating after adding 3, 5, and 4.
  expected:<5>
  but was:<4>
```

Let's try the simplest thing that could possibly work:

```
      public void addRating(int aRating) {
        if (rating == −1) {
          rating = aRating;
        } else {
          rating = (rating + aRating) / 2;
        }
      }
```

Green. Nice. Not an overly elegant solution, but it works...for now. Let's try a few other tests. Remember that averaging integers involves rounding. That can cause trouble if we don't do it right. Let's try another test with some other numbers, some that might cause some problems.

## Test 85: Add several ratings: 3, 5, 5, and 3. Asking for the average rating answers 4.

```
public void testAddingThreeOtherRatings() throws Exception {
    starTrek.addRating(3);
    starTrek.addRating(5);
    starTrek.addRating(5);
    starTrek.addRating(3);
    assertEquals("Bad average rating after adding 3, 5, 5, and 3.",
                 4,
                 starTrek.getRating());
}
```

This fails:

```
junit.framework.AssertionFailedError:
  Bad average rating after adding 3, 5, 5, and 3.
  expected:<4>
  but was:<3>
```

What's going on? Let's do some math:

$$(3+5+5+3)/4 \quad = \quad 4$$
$$(((((3+5)/2)+5)/2)+3)/2 \quad = \quad 3$$

There, this test brings to light a rounding error. Our simple implementation has the potential to make a rounding error each time a rating is added. This is compounded with each rating. We can do one of three things:

1. Keep the running average as a floating point, rounding only when the average rating is requested (and even then, only rounding the value that is returned, not the stored average).

2. Store all ratings, taking all into account when the average is requested.

3. Keep track of a running total and a count of the number of ratings the total represents. Calculate the average when asked to, from those two items.

What's the simplest? I'll go with the third option:

```
public void addRating(int aRating) {
    if (rating == -1) {
        rating = aRating;
    } else {
        rating += aRating;
    }
    numberOfRatings++;
}
```

```
    public int getRating() throws UnratedException {
      if (hasRating()) {
        return rating / numberOfRatings;
      } else {
        throw new UnratedException(name);
      }
    }
  }
```

Green. Now let's look at what we have when a Movie is unrated: numberOfRatings == 0. Before, we were using a special value of rating (specifically -1) as a flag for that state. That's never a pretty solution, and now we have an opportunity to improve it. We have to start running all the tests for this part because we want our changes to preserve existing behavior. Here's the new version of the effected methods:

```
  public class Movie {
    //...
    private int rating = 0;

    //...
    private int numberOfRatings = 0;

    public Movie(Movie original) {
      name = original.name;
      rating = original.rating;
      numberOfRatings = original.numberOfRatings;
      category = original.category;
    }

    public Movie(String aName, Category aCategory, int aRating) {
      checkNull(aName);
      checkEmpty(aName);
      name = aName;
      category = (aCategory != null) ? aCategory : Category.UNCATEGORIZED;
      if (aRating > -1) {
        rating = aRating;
        numberOfRatings = 1;
      }
    }
    //...
    public boolean hasRating() {
      return numberOfRatings > 0;
    }

    public int getRating() throws UnratedException {
      if (hasRating()) {
        return rating / numberOfRatings;
      } else {
        throw new UnratedException(name);
      }
    }
  }
```

```
public void setRating(int newRating) {
  rating = newRating;
  numberOfRatings = 1;
}
//...
public int getRawRating() {
  return hasRating() ? (rating / numberOfRatings) : −1;
}
public void addRating(int aRating) {
  if (rating == −1) {
    rating = aRating;
  } else {
    rating += aRating;
  }
  numberOfRatings++;
}
}
```

The next item to work on is reading and writing. Here we are changing the behavior so we need to go back to the tests, and add support for the rating count.

## Test 86: Writing movies uses for format: <name> | <category> | <total rating> | <number of ratings>.

Here's the changed code of the two affected tests in TestMovieListWriting:

```
public void testWritingOneMovie() throws Exception {
  String starWarsOutput = "Star Wars|Science Fiction|4|1\n";
  /...
}
```

```
public void testWritingMultipleMovies() throws Exception {
  String expectedResult = "Star Wars|Science Fiction|4|1\n" +
                          "The Princess Bride|Fantasy|5|1\n";
  //...
}
```

These two tests now fail since Movie doesn't write out its rating counter. Here's the new Movie.writeTo() method that will get these tests to pass:

```
public void writeTo(Writer destination) throws IOException {
  destination.write(name);
  writeSeparator(destination);
  destination.write(getCategory().toString());
  writeSeparator(destination);
  destination.write(Integer.toString(rating));
  writeSeparator(destination);
  destination.write(Integer.toString(numberOfRatings));
  destination.write('\n');
}
```

## Test 87: Reading movies uses for format: <name> | <category> | <total rating> | <number of ratings>.

We do the same thing with reading. First the tests, really just the fixture, to force the calculation of an average... thus requiring the reading of the total and count:

```java
public class TestMovieListReading extends TestCase {
  //...

  protected void setUp() throws Exception {
    emptyString = "";
    oneMovieString = "Star Wars|Science Fiction|8|2\n";
    //...
  }
  //...
}
```

This causes a failure as Movie.readFrom() only reads the total, which it takes as the rating itself. We must update that method as so:

```java
public static Movie readFrom(BufferedReader reader) throws IOException {
  String oneLine = reader.readLine();
  if (oneLine == null) {
    return null;
  }

  StringTokenizer tokenizedLine = new StringTokenizer(oneLine, DELIMITER);
  try {
    String name = tokenizedLine.nextToken();
    Category category = Category.getCategoryNamed(tokenizedLine.nextToken());
    int rating = Integer.parseInt(tokenizedLine.nextToken());
    int count = Integer.parseInt(tokenizedLine.nextToken());
    return new Movie(name, category, rating, count);

  } catch (NoSuchElementException ex) {
    throw new IOException("Badly formatted movie collection");
  }
}
```

Notice how we need a new constructor to create the new Movie. We shouldn't need it elsewhere, so we make it private:

```java
private Movie(String name, Category category, int rating, int count) {
  this(name, category, rating);
  numberOfRatings = count;
}
```

Green again! It feels a little *hacky* to me, though. We'll have to keep an eye on this. A quick run of all the (non-Swing) tests shows one failure in TestMovieListEditorSaving(). Running Swing tests yields a similar failure.

## Exercises

**21.** What is the problem, and how do we fix it?

*Answer on p. 538*

Now all the tests pass and we can move on.

# RATING SOURCE

*Create a class to represent the source for a rating. Keep in mind that a single source can have many ratings, but not the reverse.*

We have implemented multiple ratings, and the averaging of them. Now we will turn to the task of attaching a source (e.g., *The New York Times*) to each rating. What should this source look like? Should it be a new class? Or can we get away with a simple string? For now, all we know is that we need to attach to each rating an indication of *where* it came from. For now, at least, we can get by with a string.

So, here are our tests:

**Test 88.** A rating without a specified source should be anonymous.

**Test 89.** If we add a rating with a source to a movie, we should be able to later retrieve the source associated with the rating.

And now, down to work.

## Test 88: A rating without a specified source should be anonymous.

From discussions with the customer, we learn that we need to be able to support anonymous ratings. That fits nicely with our work so far, and gives us a good place to start:

```java
public void testAnonymousRating() throws Exception {
    Movie starWars = new Movie("Star Wars", Category.SCIFI);
    starWars.addRating(5);
    Iterator ratingIterator = starWars.ratings();
    assertTrue("There should be a rating.", ratingIterator.hasNext());

    Rating theRating = (Rating)ratingIterator.next();
    assertEquals("Bad Rating value.", 5, theRating.getValue());
    assertEquals("The rating should be anonymous.",
                "Anonymous",
                theRating.getSource());

    assertFalse("There should only be one rating.", ratingIterator.hasNext());
    assertEquals("bad average rating.", 5, starWars.getRating());
}
```

Two stubs are needed to make this compile. First, a **ratings()** method for **Movie**:

```java
public Iterator ratings() {
    return null;
}
```

Second, a Rating class:

```
public class Rating {
  public int getValue() {
    return 0;
  }

  public String getSource() {
    return "";
  }
}
```

The test now fails with a **NullPointerException** due to the null returned by **ratings()**. Now we need to do something more here. What should it be? Do we feel we know enough to be confident taking a larger step? Why not? We can always roll back to where we are now if it doesn't work out.

We know that we want to accumulate a list of ratings, so we can add that to **addRating()**. We'll start by adding an instance variable to hold the list:

```
private List ratings = null;
```

Next, we need to initialize **ratings** in the constructors:

```
public Movie(Movie original) {
  //...
  ratings = new ArrayList(original.ratings);
}

public Movie(String aName, Category aCategory, int aRating) {
    checkNull(aName);
    checkEmpty(aName);
    name = aName;
    category = (aCategory != null) ? aCategory : Category.UNCATEGORIZED;
    ratings = new ArrayList();

    if (aRating > -1) {
      rating = aRating;
      numberOfRatings = 1;
      ratings.add(new Rating(aRating));
    }
}
```

To support this, we need to flesh out **Rating** a bit:

```
public class Rating {
  private int value;
  private String source;
```

```
    public Rating(int aRating) {
      value = aRating;
      source = "Anonymous";
    }
    public int getValue() {
      return value;
    }
    public String getSource() {
      return source;
    }
  }
```

Next, we need to extend addRating():

```
  public void addRating(int aRating) {
    if (rating == −1) {
      rating = aRating;
    } else {
      rating += aRating;
    }
    numberOfRatings++;
    ratings.add(new Rating(aRating));
  }
```

Now we can implement Movie.ratings():

```
  public Iterator ratings() {
    return ratings.iterator();
  }
```

Green. Have we introduced any duplication? Yes—have a look at these two lines in addRating():

```
    numberOfRatings++;
    ratings.add(new Rating(aRating));
```

Furthermore, notice in the constructors for Movie that either numberOfRatings == 0 and ratings is empty, or numberOfRatings == 1 and ratings contains one Rating. So the value of numberOfRatings is always the same as the size of ratings. We can replace all queries as to the value of numberOfRatings with ratings.size().

In doing this, we find ourselves looking at setRating() in Movie:

```
  public void setRating(int newRating) {
    rating = newRating;
    numberOfRatings = 1;
  }
```

A quick *senders* check tells us that this is only used in updateMovie(), which in turn is only called from the interface code. We have two choices here:

1. we can update setRating() to handle the ratings list, or

2. we can ignore it for now, and deal with it when we get to the interface tasks.

We'll opt for the latter. The crux of the matter is that setRating() is a leftover from the single-rating system. We are in the process of changing that to a multiple-rating system so, in all likelihood, setRating() will become obsolete anyway. Since it has no impact on what we are currently focused on, we can ignore it for now. It would be a good idea, however, to add a short comment to the method to note what we decided about it. Something similar to this will suffice:

```
// needs consideration to move to multi-rating when we work on the interface
```

Another potential problem is the constructor:

```
private Movie(String name, Category category, int rating, int count) {
  this(name, category, rating);
  numberOfRatings = count;
}
```

This constructor is only used by readFrom(), so it would appear that a similar argument applies: it doesn't affect what we are doing at the moment, so we'll defer worrying about it until we renovate the persistence code. Let's see what happens when we run AllTests. The reading test fails. That means we need to fix that constructor now. We'll have to add multiple copies of the given rating. Note that this isn't strictly correct, since the total of the list of ratings does equal the stored total. Oh well. It passes all the current tests, and it's a side issue at the moment. It'll do. YAGNI.

```
private Movie(String name, Category category, int rating, int count) {
  this(name, category, rating);
  numberOfRatings = count;
  ratings = new ArrayList();
  for (int i = 0; i < count; i++) {
    ratings.add(new Rating(rating));
  }
}
```

OK, now let's finish the job and remove numberOfRatings (after confirming that the tests all pass). Green. One more thing we notice during this exercise: the method hasRating() is now:

```
public boolean hasRating() {
  return ratings.size() > 0;
}
```

We can rewrite that in a way that communicates the intent much better:

```
public boolean hasRating() {
  return !ratings.isEmpty();
}
```

Also, we can simplify addRating() to:

```
public void addRating(int aRating) {
  rating += aRating;
  ratings.add(new Rating(aRating));
}
```

Everything still passes. Now we need a test for a rating with an identified source.

### Test 89: If we add a rating with a source to a movie, we should be able to later retrieve the source associated with the rating.

```
public void testRatingWithSource() {
  starWars.addRating(5, "NY Times");
  Iterator ratingIterator = starWars.ratings();
  Rating theRating = (Rating)ratingIterator.next();

  assertEquals("Bad Rating value.", 5, theRating.getValue());
  assertEquals("The rating should be the NY Times.",
               "NY Times",
               theRating.getSource());
}
```

We need a new addRating() method in Movie to add a rating with a known source. We start with a simple stub that does nothing except give us the desired red bar. Now we can add code to it:

```
public void addRating(int aRating, String aRatingSource) {
  rating += aRating;
  ratings.add(new Rating(aRating, aRatingSource));
}
```

This, in turn, requires a new Rating constructor:

```
public Rating(int aRating, String aRatingSource) {
  value = aRating;
  source = aRatingSource;
}
```

OK, green!

Now we can eliminate some duplication we've added. First, look back at the two addRating() methods:

```
public void addRating(int aRating) {
  rating += aRating;
  ratings.add(new Rating(aRating));
}
```

```
public void addRating(int aRating, String aRatingSource) {
  rating += aRating;
  ratings.add(new Rating(aRating, aRatingSource));
}
```

These are much the same, the only difference being the construction of the **Rating**. If we extract the common parts to a new method, we end up with:

```
private void primAddRating(Rating ratingToAdd) {
  rating += ratingToAdd.getValue();
  ratings.add(ratingToAdd);
}

public void addRating(int aRating) {
  primAddRating(new Rating(aRating));
}

public void addRating(int aRating, String aRatingSource) {
  primAddRating(new Rating(aRating, aRatingSource));
}
```

OK, let's look at the two constructors for **Rating**:

```
public Rating(int aRating) {
  value = aRating;
  source = "Anonymous";
}

public Rating(int aRating, String aRatingSource) {
  value = aRating;
  source = aRatingSource;
}
```

We can rewrite the first one to chain to the more general one, like this:

```
public Rating(int aRating) {
  this(aRating, "Anonymous");
}
```

We still have duplication lurking in the total rating that is being maintained. We need to remove it. In most cases, this is simply a matter of removing the reference to **rating**, since it is used in parallel with the **ratings** collection. In the cases where it is used in a calculation, we need to do a bit more work. The obvious case is **getRating()**. This becomes:

```
public int getRating() throws UnratedException {
  if (hasRating()) {
    return calculateAverageRating();
  } else {
    throw new UnratedException(name);
  }
}
```

```
public int getRawRating() {
  if (hasRating()) {
     return calculateAverageRating();
  } else {
    return −1;
  }
}

private int calculateAverageRating() {
  int acc = 0;
  Iterator ratingIterator = ratings.iterator();
  while (ratingIterator.hasNext()) {
    Rating aRating = (Rating) ratingIterator.next();
    acc += aRating.getValue();
  }
  return acc / ratings.size();
}
```

The setRating() method needs some attention as well, but only a bit. The significant thing is that to maintain the current behavior we need a single rating after calling it. We can do this by throwing out the current set of ratings (recall that this method is a leftover from the single-rating system and will be gone once the GUI is updated to handle multiple ratings):

```
public void setRating(int newRating) {
  ratings = new ArrayList();
  addRating(newRating);
}
```

The final issue is persistence. We had hoped this could be ignored until we upgraded it to handle multiple ratings, but we want to clean up the code now. We could just go ahead and leave the persistence-related tests failing until we revamp the whole area. That could work, but it's not a good idea to have failing tests lying around. Recall that one of the guidelines is to only ever have one failing test... the one you are actively working with. So writeTo() becomes:

```
public void writeTo(Writer destination) throws IOException {
  destination.write(name);
  writeSeparator(destination);
  destination.write(getCategory().toString());
  writeSeparator(destination);

  int ratingToWrite = 0;
  if (hasRating()) {
    ratingToWrite = calculateTotalRating();
  } else {
    ratingToWrite = 0;
  }
  destination.write(Integer.toString(ratingToWrite));
```

```
        writeSeparator(destination);
        destination.write(Integer.toString(ratings.size()));
        destination.write('\n');
    }
```

To get the required calculateTotalRating() method we can extract it from calculateAverageRating(), as so:

```
    private int calculateAverageRating() {
      int totalRating = calculateTotalRating();
      return totalRating / ratings.size();
    }

    private int calculateTotalRating() {
      int acc = 0;
      Iterator ratingIterator = ratings.iterator();

      while (ratingIterator.hasNext()) {
        Rating aRating = (Rating) ratingIterator.next();
        acc += aRating.getValue();
      }
      return acc;
    }
```

Now we have only one reading-related test failing: testReadingOneMovie. The problem is related to the constructor used:

```
    private Movie(String name, Category category, int rating, int count) {
      this(name, category, rating);
      ratings = new ArrayList();

      for (int i = 0; i < count; i++) {
        ratings.add(new Rating(rating));
      }
    }
```

We faked it before, now we need to do a better job of faking it. Let's think. We are given the total desired rating value, and the number of ratings that have to add up to that total. What if we did:

```
    private Movie(String name, Category category, int rating, int count) {
      this(name, category);
      ratings = new ArrayList();

      if (count > 0) {
        int singleRating = rating / count;
        int lastRating = rating - (singleRating * (count - 1));

        for (int i = 0; i < count - 1; i++) {
          addRating(singleRating);
        }
        addRating(lastRating);
      }
    }
```

Try it, compile, run the tests. Green. All right!

We just need to finish cleaning out the **rating** instance variable, and we're done. The core code is completely converted to using multiple ratings.

## REVISED PERSISTENCE

*Revamp the persistence capabilities to handle the changes to the rating structure.*

The core of the system is using multiple ratings throughout. Now it's time to upgrade the persistence capabilities. Until now, a flat text file has sufficed to store our data. Now that each **Movie** has an arbitrarily sized collection of **Ratings**, we need something more structured. We could develop our own file format to handle this, but it's easier and more standard to useXML. We could have used XML from the beginning almost as easily, but it would have been overkill if we didn't have a real reason for it... which we didn't.

We'll adopt the following XML format:

```
<movielist>
    <movie name = "name" category = "category">
        <ratings>
            <rating value="value" source="source" />
            . . .
        </ratings>
    </movie>
    . . .
</movielist>
```

**Test 90.** Writing an empty list outputs an empty <movielist> pair.

**Test 91.** Writing a list containing one movie outputs in the adopted XML format.

**Test 92.** Writing a list containing one movie with multiple ratings outputs in the adopted XML format.

**Test 93.** Writing a list containing multiple movies outputs in the adopted XML format.

**Test 94.** Reading an empty <movielist> pair results in an empty list.

**Test 95.** Reading an appropriate XML stream containing a single movie definition results in a list containing the single movie defined in the stream.

**Test 96.** Reading an appropriate XML stream containing more than one movie definition results in a list containing the movies defined in the stream.

Since we are moving to a more structured storage solution, and it requires more overhead, we'll move the reading and writing (i.e., the persistence) to a class specializing in that functionality.

### Writing the new format

We'll start by tossing out the existing version of **TestMovieListWriting** and writing a new test for the new storage format. Since we're using XML, let's use the xmlUnit that Tim Bacon told us about in Chapter 5. Here's the new **TestCase**. Notice that we've started out with a small fixture. Based on previous experience, we know we'll need it, and XMLUnit does need some setup:

```
public class TestMovieListWriting extends XMLTestCase {
  private StringWriter destination = null;
  private MovieListWriter writer = null;
  private MovieList movieList = null;

  public TestMovieListWriting(String name) {
      super(name);
  }

  protected void setUp() {
    String parser ="org.apache.xerces.jaxp.DocumentBuilderFactoryImpl";
    XMLUnit.setControlParser(parser);
    XMLUnit.setTestParser(parser);
    destination = new StringWriter();
    writer = new XMLMovieListWriter(destination);
    movieList = new MovieList();
  }
}
```

## Test 90: Writing an empty list outputs an empty <movielist> pair.

And here's the new version of the test for writing an empty MovieList:

```
public void testWritingEmptyList() throws Exception {
  writer.write(movieList);
  assertXMLEqual("Writing an empty list should produce empty <movielist>.",
            "<movielist></movielist>",
            destination.toString());
}
```

This one simple test, with its fixture, lays out the design of the saving system, as shown in Figure 18.1. This corresponds to the following stubs:

```
public interface MovieListWriter {
  void write(MovieList movieList);
}

public class XMLMovieListWriter implements MovieListWriter {
  public XMLMovieListWriter(Writer destination) {
  }

  public void write(MovieList movieList){
  }
}
```

With these stubs in place, we can compile and run the test, which fails with an XML validation error:

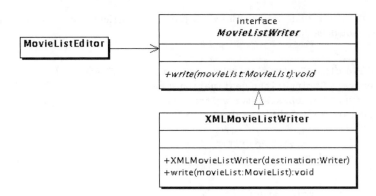

**Figure 18.1** The design of the *Saving* system.

```
org.xml.sax.SAXParseException:
  The root element is required in a well-formed document.
```

There is no root element, since we are not outputting XML... in fact, we're not outputting anything yet. Let's start by faking it (note that we need to add the throws clause to MovieListWriter.write() as well):

```
public void write(MovieList movieList) throws IOException {
  destination.write("<movielist></movielist>");
  destination.flush();
}
```

That works fine. Now to drive moving from faking to making we need another test.

## Test 91: Writing a list containing one movie outputs in the adopted XML format.

```
public void testWritingOneMovie() throws Exception {
  String starWarsOutput = "<movielist>" +
                        "<movie name = \"Star Wars\"" +
                            "category = \"Science Fiction\">" +
                          "<ratings>" +
                            "<rating value=\"4\" " +
                                "source=\"NY Times\" />" +
                          "</ratings>" +
                        "</movie>" +
                    "</movielist>";

  Movie starWars = new Movie("Star Wars", Category.SCIFI);
  starWars.addRating(4, "NY Times");
  movieList.add(starWars);
  writer.write(movieList);
```

```
    assertXMLEqual("Wrong output from writing a single movie list.",
                    starWarsOutput,
                    destination.toString());
  }
```

When we run this, the call to assertXMLEqual fails. We need to move from *faking it* to *making it...* at least a bit. To pass this test we need:

```
public void write(MovieList movieList) throws IOException{
  destination.write("<movielist>");

  if (movieList.size()> 0) {
    Movie movieToWrite = (Movie)movieList.getMovie(0);
    destination.write("<movie name=\"");
    destination.write(movieToWrite.getName());
    destination.write("\" category=\"");
    destination.write(movieToWrite.getCategory().toString());
    destination.write("\">");

    destination.write("<ratings>");
    Iterator ratingIterator = movieToWrite.ratings();

    if (ratingIterator.hasNext()) {
      Rating ratingToWrite = (Rating)ratingIterator.next();
      destination.write("<rating value=\"");
      destination.write(Integer.toString(ratingToWrite.getValue()));
      destination.write("\" source=\"");
      destination.write(ratingToWrite.getSource());
      destination.write("\" />");
    }

    destination.write("</ratings>");
    destination.write("</movie>");
  }

  destination.write("</movielist>");
  destination.flush();
}
```

Well... it passes the test. It is pretty smelly, though. Let's start by extracting some methods. First, we'll pull out the body of the inner conditional that outputs a rating:

```
public void write(MovieList movieList) throws IOException{
  destination.write("<movielist>");

  if (movieList.size()> 0) {
    Movie movieToWrite = (Movie)movieList.getMovie(0);
    destination.write("<movie name=\"");
    destination.write(movieToWrite.getName());
    destination.write("\" category=\"");
    destination.write(movieToWrite.getCategory().toString());
    destination.write("\">");
    destination.write("<ratings>");
```

```
      Iterator ratingIterator = movieToWrite.ratings();
      if (ratingIterator.hasNext()) {
        writeRating((Rating)ratingIterator.next());
      }

      destination.write("</ratings>");
      destination.write("</movie>");
    }

    destination.write("</movielist>");
    destination.flush();
  }
  private void writeRating(Rating ratingToWrite) throws IOException {
    destination.write("<rating value=\"");
    destination.write(Integer.toString(ratingToWrite.getValue()));
    destination.write("\" source=\"");
    destination.write(ratingToWrite.getSource());
    destination.write("\" />");
  }
```

Next, we can extract the body of the outer conditional:

```
  public void write(MovieList movieList) throws IOException{
    destination.write("<movielist>");

    if (movieList.size()> 0) {
      Movie movieToWrite = (Movie)movieList.getMovie(0);
      writeMovie(movieToWrite);
    }

    destination.write("</movielist>");
    destination.flush();
  }
  private void writeMovie(Movie movieToWrite) throws IOException {
    destination.write("<movie name=\"");
    destination.write(movieToWrite.getName());
    destination.write("\" category=\"");
    destination.write(movieToWrite.getCategory().toString());
    destination.write("\">");
    destination.write("<ratings>");

    Iterator ratingIterator = movieToWrite.ratings();
    if (ratingIterator.hasNext()) {
      writeRating((Rating)ratingIterator.next());
    }

    destination.write("</ratings>");
    destination.write("</movie>");
  }
```

This is much cleaner and will be easier to work with as we add more tests to drive the development. Here's the next test, one for multiple ratings.

## Test 92: Writing a list containing one movie with multiple ratings outputs in the adopted XML format.

```
public void testWritingOneMovieWithMultipleratings() throws Exception {
String starWarsOutput = "<movielist>" +
                    "<movie name = \"Star Wars\"" +
                        "category = \"Science Fiction\">" +
                    "<ratings>" +
                        "<rating value=\"4\" " +
                                "source=\"NY Times\" />" +

                        "<rating value=\"5\" " +
                                "source=\"Jason\" />" +
                    "</ratings>" +

                    "</movie>" +
                "</movielist>";

Movie starWars = new Movie("Star Wars", Category.SCIFI);
starWars.addRating(4, "NY Times");
starWars.addRating(5, "Jason");
movieList.add(starWars);
writer.write(movieList);

assertXMLEqual("Wrong output from writing a single movie list.",
            starWarsOutput,
            destination.toString());
}
```

This fails because we're only outputting the first rating. We need to generalize this. It's simply a matter of changing the if to while:

```
private void writeMovie(Movie movieToWrite) throws IOException {
  //..
  Iterator ratingIterator = movieToWrite.ratings();
  while (ratingIterator.hasNext()) {
    writeRating((Rating)ratingIterator.next());
  }
  //..
}
```

The next test will use multiple movies.

## Test 93: Writing a list containing multiple movies outputs in the adopted XML format.

```
public void testWritingMultipleMovies() throws Exception {
String expectedResult = "<movielist>" +
                    "<movie name = \"Star Wars\"" +
                        "category = \"Science Fiction\">" +
                    "<ratings>" +
                        "<rating value=\"4\" " +
                                "source=\"NY Times\" />" +
```

```
                        "<rating value=\"5\" " +
                            "source=\"Jason\" />" +
                    "</ratings>" +
                "</movie>" +
                "<movie name = \"The Princess Bride\"" +
                        "category = \"Fantasy\">" +
                    "<ratings>" +
                        "<rating value=\"5\" " +
                            "source=\"Kent\" />" +
                        "<rating value=\"5\" " +
                            "source=\"Ron\" />" +
                    "</ratings>" +
                "</movie>" +
            "</movielist>";
    Movie starWars = new Movie("Star Wars", Category.SCIFI);
    starWars.addRating(4, "NY Times");
    starWars.addRating(5, "Jason");

    Movie princessBride = new Movie("The Princess Bride", Category.FANTASY);
    princessBride.addRating(5, "Kent");
    princessBride.addRating(5, "Ron");

    movieList.add(starWars);
    movieList.add(princessBride);
    writer.write(movieList);

    assertXMLEqual("Wrong output from writing a multiple movie list.",
                expectedResult,
                destination.toString());
}
```

Similar to the previous test, this fails because only the first movie is getting output. Again, we must generalize, this time changing the other conditional to a loop:

```
public void write(MovieList movieList) throws IOException{
    //...
    Iterator movieIterator = movieList.iterator();
    while (movieIterator.hasNext()) {
        writeMovie((Movie)movieIterator.next());
    }
    //...
}
```

This code is pretty ugly and the intent is lost in the multitude of destination.write() calls. We can use java.text.MessageFormat to clean it up some, and clarify the intent:

```
private MessageFormat ratingFormat =
        new MessageFormat("<rating value=\"{0,number,integer}\" " +
                        "source=\"{1}\" />");
private MessageFormat movieFormat =
        new MessageFormat("<movie name=\"{0}\" category=\"{1}\">");
```

```
      private void writeMovie(Movie movieToWrite) throws IOException {
        Object[] args = { movieToWrite.getName(),
                          movieToWrite.getCategory().toString() };
        destination.write(movieFormat.format(args));

        Iterator ratingIterator = movieToWrite.ratings();
        destination.write("<ratings>");
        while (ratingIterator.hasNext()) {
          writeRating((Rating)ratingIterator.next());
        }

        destination.write("</ratings>");
        destination.write("</movie>");
      }

      private void writeRating(Rating ratingToWrite) throws IOException {
        Object[] args = { new Integer(ratingToWrite.getValue()),
                          ratingToWrite.getSource() };
        destination.write(ratingFormat.format(args));
      }
    }
```

The writeMovie() method is still a bit long, don't you think? Let's extract the code that writes the ratings:

```
    private void writeMovie(Movie movieToWrite) throws IOException {
      Object[] args = { movieToWrite.getName(),
                        movieToWrite.getCategory().toString() };
      destination.write(movieFormat.format(args));
      writeRatings(movieToWrite);
      destination.write("</movie>");
    }

    private void writeRatings(Movie movieToWrite) throws IOException {
      Iterator ratingIterator = movieToWrite.ratings();
      destination.write("<ratings>");
      while (ratingIterator.hasNext()) {
        writeRating((Rating)ratingIterator.next());
      }
      destination.write("</ratings>");
    }
```

There, much nicer. The next step is to remove all of the previous writing-related code from MovieList and Movie.

Finally, we need to fix the writing-related code in MovieListEditor to use the new writing code. We'll start by updating the tests. We need to convert them to expect XML output.

## Exercises

**22.** Convert TestMovieListEditorSaving as required.

**23.** Update MovieListEditor.save() to make it work.

*Answer on p. 539*

*Answer on p. 542*

## Reading the new format

Now we must turn to reading. As before, we'll replace the old version of TestMovieList-Reading with a new, XML-based version. We know we'll need a similar fixture, so we'll convert the existing one as a starting point:

```
public class TestMovieListReading extends XMLTestCase {
    private String emptyString = null;
    private String oneMovieString = null;
    private String multiMovieString = null;
    private String oneMoviePrefix = null;


    public TestMovieListReading(String name) {
      super(name);
    }

    protected void setUp() throws Exception {
      emptyString = "<movielist></movielist>";
      oneMoviePrefix = "<movielist>" +
                      "<movie name=\"Star Wars\" " +
                          "category=\"Science Fiction\">" +
                        "<ratings>" +
                          "<rating value=\"3\" " +
                                  "source=\"Dave\" />" +
                          "<rating value=\"5\" " +
                                  "source=\"Jason\" />" +
                        "</ratings>" +
                      "</movie>";

      oneMovieString= oneMoviePrefix + "</movielist>";
      multiMovieString = oneMoviePrefix +
                      "<movie name=\"Star Trek\" " +
                          "category=\"Science Fiction\">" +
                        "<ratings>" +
                          "<rating value=\"3\" " +
                              "source=\"Anonymous\" />" +
                        "</ratings>" +
                      "</movie>" +
                      "<movie name=\"Stargate\" " +
                          "category=\"Science Fiction\">" +
                        "<ratings></ratings>" +
                      "</movie>" +
                    "</movielist>";

    }
  }
```

Next, we need a starting point. It makes sense to follow the path we did the first time, so we'll start with a test for reading an empty list.

## Test 94: Reading an empty <movielist> pair results in an empty list.

```
public void testReadingEmptyList() throws Exception {
  Reader reader = new StringReader(emptyString);
  MovieList movies = new XMLMovieListReader(reader).read();
  assertEquals("Empty list shouldn't have entries.", 0, movies.size());
}
```

We need some stubs. We'll follow the same structure as we did when we designed the writer: a general interface, and a concrete implemention to handle reading XML:

```
public interface MovieListReader {
  MovieList read();
}
```

```
public class XMLMovieListReader implements MovieListReader {
  private Reader source;

  public XMLMovieListReader(Reader reader) {
    source = reader;
  }
  public MovieList read() {
    return null;
  }
}
```

Now we can compile and run the test. It fails with a NullPointerException because stubbed read to return null. Now we can fake it:

```
public MovieList read() {
  return new MovieList();
}
```

The next test requires reading a single Movie, driving the code toward something real.

## Test 95: Reading an appropriate XML stream containing a single movie definition results in a list containing the single movie defined in the stream.

```
public void testReadingOneMovie() throws Exception {
  Reader reader = new StringReader(oneMovieString);
  MovieList movies = new XMLMovieListReader(reader).read();
  assertEquals("Reading a one movie list should result in a one item list.",
               1,
               movies.size());

  Movie theMovieRead = movies.getMovie(0);
  assertEquals("Read movie has wrong name.",
               "Star Wars",
               theMovieRead.getName());
```

```
        assertEquals("Read movie has wrong category.",
                    Category.SCIFI,
                    theMovieRead.getCategory());

        assertEquals("Read movie has wrong rating.",
                    4,
                    theMovieRead.getRating());

        Iterator ratingIterator = theMovieRead.ratings();
        assertTrue("Read movie should have ratings.",
                    ratingIterator.hasNext());

        Rating firstRating = (Rating)ratingIterator.next();
        assertEquals("First rating has wrong value",
                    3,
                    firstRating.getValue());

        assertEquals("First rating has bad source",
                    "Dave",
                    firstRating.getSource());

        assertTrue("Read movie should have two ratings.",
                    ratingIterator.hasNext());
        Rating secondRating = (Rating)ratingIterator.next();

        assertEquals("Second rating has wrong value",
                    5,
                    secondRating.getValue());

        assertEquals("Second rating has bad source",
                    "Jason",
                    secondRating.getSource());
        assertFalse("Read movie should have only two ratings.",
                    ratingIterator.hasNext());
    }
```

That's a rather long test, but it really just crawls through the structure that was read and verifies that all is as expected. This, of course, fails since we faked **read()**, and it simply returns an empty **MovieList**. Let's start by adding the code required to set up and use JDOM to process the XML data:

```
public MovieList read() throws IOException {
  SAXBuilder builder = new SAXBuilder();
  Document theMovielistDocument;

  try {
    theMovielistDocument = builder.build(source);
  } catch (JDOMException e) {
    throw new IOException(e.getMessage());
  }

  MovieList theNewList = processDocument(theMovielistDocument);
  return theNewList;
}

private MovieList processDocument(Document theMovielistDocument) {
  return new MovieList();
}
```

This still fails in the same place, because even though we are now processing the input, we still just return an empty MovieList. This is a good sign, though, because it does mean that our input XML is valid, and is being processed. Next, we need to process it and build our objects from the resulting document. Let's do that a small bit at a time, working our way through the tests as we do. First, we need to get the right number of Movies:

```
private MovieList processDocument(Document theMovielistDocument)
        throws DuplicateMovieException {
    MovieList newMovieList = new MovieList();
    Element movielistElement = theMovielistDocument.getRootElement();

    List movies = movielistElement.getChildren();
    Iterator movieElementIterator = movies.iterator();
    while (movieElementIterator.hasNext()) {
        Element movieElement = (Element) movieElementIterator.next();

        String name = movieElement.getAttributeValue("name");
        String categoryName = movieElement.getAttributeValue("category");
        Category category = Category.getCategoryNamed(categoryName);

        Movie newMovie = new Movie(name, category);
        newMovieList.add(newMovie);
    }
    return newMovieList;
}
```

Now the test gets to the check of the average rating. This fails due to an UnratedException being thrown. This tells us that one movie is being read and the name and category are correct. Next, we'll add code to process the ratings:

```
private MovieList processDocument(Document theMovielistDocument)
        throws DuplicateMovieException {
    //...
    Movie newMovie = new Movie(name, category);

    Element ratingsElement = movieElement.getChild("ratings");
    List ratings = ratingsElement.getChildren();
    Iterator ratingIterator = ratings.iterator();

    while (ratingIterator.hasNext()) {
        Element ratingElement = (Element) ratingIterator.next();
        int value;

        try {
            value = ratingElement.getAttribute("value").getIntValue();
        } catch (DataConversionException e) {
            throw new IOException(e.getMessage());
        }
```

```
        String source = ratingElement.getAttributeValue("source");
        newMovie.addRating(value, source);
      }
      newMovieList.add(newMovie);
    }
    return newMovieList;
  }
```

Green! Now we need to refactor to clean up the mess. We'll extract the processing of movies and ratings, resulting in:

```
  private MovieList processDocument(Document theMovielistDocument)
          throws DuplicateMovieException {
    MovieList newMovieList = new MovieList();
    Element movielistElement = theMovielistDocument.getRootElement();

    List movies = movielistElement.getChildren();
    Iterator movieElementIterator = movies.iterator();

    while (movieElementIterator.hasNext()) {
      Element movieElement = (Element) movieElementIterator.next();
      newMovieList.add(processMovie(movieElement));
    }
    return newMovieList;
  }
  private Movie processMovie(Element movieElement) throws IOException {
    String name = movieElement.getAttributeValue("name");
    String categoryName = movieElement.getAttributeValue("category");
    Category category = Category.getCategoryNamed(categoryName);

    Movie newMovie = new Movie(name, category);
    Element ratingsElement = movieElement.getChild("ratings");
    List ratings = ratingsElement.getChildren();
    Iterator ratingIterator = ratings.iterator();

    while (ratingIterator.hasNext()) {
      Element ratingElement = (Element) ratingIterator.next();
      newMovie.addRating(processRating(ratingElement));
    }
    return newMovie;
  }
  private Rating processRating(Element ratingElement) throws IOException {
    int value;
    try {
      value = ratingElement.getAttribute("value").getIntValue();
    } catch (DataConversionException e) {
      throw new IOException(e.getMessage());
    }
    String source = ratingElement.getAttributeValue("source");
    return new Rating(value, source);
  }
```

Note that we had to rename Movie.primAddRating() to addRating() and change its visibility to public. You may sometimes (I won't go as far as to say *often*) find that methods that are the result of refactoring eventually become useful as part of the public interface of the class.

That takes care of reading a single movie. Next, we need to test the reading of multiple movies.

## Test 96: Reading an appropriate XML stream containing more than one movie definition results in a list containing the movies defined in the stream.

```
public void testReadingMultipleMovie() throws Exception {
    Reader reader = new StringReader(multiMovieString);
    MovieList movies = new XMLMovieListReader(reader).read();
    assertEquals("Reading a multiple movie list should result in 3 items.",
            3,
            movies.size());
}
```

This compiles and passes without a hitch. Notice that since we already have a test that verifies that a movie can be read properly, all we need to do here is verify that a collection can be read.

Now we can move up a level and upgrade the reading-related MovieListEditor tests. Very little changes in the test, just the creation of the test file in setUp():

```
new XMLMovieListWriter(new FileWriter(inputFile)).write(movieList);
```

The test fails with a file format exception, since MovieListEditor is using the previous reading code. We need to change its load() method to use the new code:

```
public boolean load()
        throws FileNotFoundException, IOException, DuplicateMovieException {
    File inputFile = view.getFileToLoad();
    if (inputFile == null) {
        return false;
    }

    FileReader reader = new FileReader(inputFile);
    movies = new XMLMovieListReader(reader).read();
    filterOnCategory(Category.ALL);
    return true;
}
```

There—green bar. Now run AllTests to be sure—green bar. The last step is to remove the readFrom() methods from Movie and MovieList. Run AllTests again for safety and we're done.

Now a couple of tweaks to the Swing tests. First, TestSwingMovieListEditorFileOperations needs to extend XMLTestCase. Next, the test data:

```java
protected void setUp() throws Exception {
    //...
    String textPrefix = "<movielist>" +
                        "<movie name=\"Star Wars\" " +
                            "category=\"Science Fiction\">" +
                        "<ratings>" +
                            "<rating value=\"5\" " +
                                "source=\"Anonymous\" />" +
                        "</ratings>" +
                    "</movie>" +

                        "<movie name=\"Star Trek\" " +
                            "category=\"Science Fiction\">" +
                        "<ratings>" +
                            "<rating value=\"3\" " +
                                "source=\"Anonymous\" />" +
                        "</ratings>" +
                    "</movie>" +

                        "<movie name=\"Stargate\" " +
                            "category=\"Science Fiction\">" +
                        "<ratings></ratings>" +
                    "</movie>";
    savedText = textPrefix + "</movielist>";
    extendedSavedText = textPrefix + "<movie name=\"The Shining\" " +
                                "category=\"Horror\">" +
                        "<ratings>" +
                            "<rating value=\"2\" " +
                                "source=\"Anonymous\" />" +
                        "</ratings>" +
                    "</movie>" +
                    "</movielist>";
    //...
}
```

The other change is to the comparison code in testSaving():

```java
public void testSaving() throws Exception {
    //...
    saveButton.push();
    assertXMLEqual("Save-Ased file has wrong contents.",
                savedText,
                contentsOf(outputFile));

    //...
    saveItem.push();
    assertXMLEqual("Resaved file has wrong contents.",
                extendedSavedText,
                contentsOf(outputFile));
}
```

```
private String contentsOf(File aFile) throws IOException {
  FileInputStream fstream = new FileInputStream(aFile);
  int size = fstream.available();
  byte[] buffer = new byte[size];
  fstream.read(buffer);
  return new String(buffer);
}
```

And that's it. Green all the way.

# SHOW MULTIPLE RATINGS IN THE GUI

*In the GUI, show a list of all ratings for the selected movie.*

To show all of a movie's ratings we need to add a list to the GUI in which to show them. For now, we'll leave the existing rating combo in place so that we don't break the add and update tests. We'll take care of that in a later task.

This task doesn't require any new tests; we need to update to use the new storage format, though.

## In the Logical Layer

First, we'll work on the MovieListEditor. We need to extend the test testSelecting() in TestMovieListEditor:

```
public void testSelecting() {
  //...
  mockView.setNameField(starWars.getName());
  //...
  mockView.setRatings(starWars.getRatings());
  control.setVoidCallable(1);

  mockView.setNameField(starTrek.getName());
  //...
  mockView.setRatings(starTrek.getRatings());
  control.setVoidCallable(1);

  mockView.setNameField(stargate.getName());
  //...
  mockView.setRatings(stargate.getRatings());
  control.setVoidCallable(1);

  mockView.setNameField(theShining.getName());
  //...
  mockView.setRatings(theShining.getRatings());
  control.setVoidCallable(1);
  //...
}
```

All we had to add was the expectations for a call to setRatings() corresponding to each selected movie. This fails because those calls are not being made. A simple addition to MovieListEditor.select() does the job (the call to setRatings()):

```
public void select(int i) {
  if (i == -1) {
    selectedMovie = null;
  } else {
    selectedMovie = filteredMovies.getMovie(i);
    view.setNameField(selectedMovie.getName());
    view.setCategoryField(selectedMovie.getCategory());
    view.setRatings(selectedMovie.getRatings());

    try {
      view.setRatingField(selectedMovie.getRating() + 1);
    } catch (UnratedException e) {
      view.setRatingField(0);
    }
  }
}
```

Now testSelecting() passes, but three other tests fail because they were not expecting the setRatings() call. Instead of editing them to expect it, we can have their mock view ignore those calls. This is reasonable as they aren't performing tests related to the ratings. There are a handful of tests that need the following lines added at the beginning:

```
mockView.setRatings(null);
control.setDefaultVoidCallable();
```

That's all we need to do here.

## In the Swing Layer

The first test we will update is testSelectUpdatesRating() in TestSwingMovieListEditorView. The new version is as follows (notice the addition of a second rating to star-Wars):

```
public void testSelectUpdatesRating() {
{
  starWars.addRating(4, "Dave");
  JListOperator movieList =
      new JListOperator(mainWindow, new NameBasedChooser("movieList"));
  JListOperator ratingsList =
      new JListOperator(mainWindow, new NameBasedChooser("ratings"));

  movieList.clickOnItem(0, 1);
  verifyRatings(ratingsList, starWars);
  movieList.clickOnItem(1, 1);
  verifyRatings(ratingsList, starTrek);
  movieList.clickOnItem(2, 1);
  verifyRatings(ratingsList, stargate);
}
```

```
private void verifyRatings(JListOperator ratingsList, Movie aMovie) {
  ListModel listModel = ratingsList.getModel();
  Iterator ratingIterator = aMovie.ratings();
  int i = 0;

  while (ratingIterator.hasNext()) {
    Rating aRating = (Rating) ratingIterator.next();
    assertEquals("Expected rating not displayed",
                 aRating,
                 listModel.getElementAt(i));
    i++;
  }
  assertEquals("Wrong number of ratings displayed", i, listModel.getSize());
}
```

This, of course, fails because we don't have a list of ratings in the GUI yet. That's easy to fix in SwingMovieListEditorView:

```
private JPanel initDetailPane() {
  JPanel detailPane = new JPanel();
  //...

  detailPane.add(initRatingList());
  detailPane.add(Box.createRigidArea(new Dimension(0, 5)));
  detailPane.add(initCategoryField());
  return detailPane;
}

// ...

private JScrollPane initRatingList() {
  ratingList = new JList(new Vector());
  ratingList.setName("ratings");
  ratingList.setSelectionMode(ListSelectionModel.SINGLE_SELECTION);

  JScrollPane scroller =
        new JScrollPane(ratingList,
                        ScrollPaneConstants.VERTICAL_SCROLLBAR_ALWAYS,
                        ScrollPaneConstants.HORIZONTAL_SCROLLBAR_NEVER);
  return scroller;
}
```

Now the test fails when checking the ratings since nothing is being done with the new list box. We need to add some code to setRatings() to take care of that:

```
public void setRatings(Vector newRatings) {
  ratingList.setListData(newRatings);
}
```

That makes it work. For aesthetic reasons, we'd like to use the same format as we did in the movie list, namely, the rating star icons followed by the text. We'll do something similar to what we did in Chapter 13. We've done this before, so we'll skip the details here, showing only the results. Here's the test case:

```java
public class TestRatingRenderer extends TestCase {
  private JList list;
  private Rating fiveStars;
  private RatingRenderer renderer;
  private Rating threeStars;

  protected void setUp() {
    fiveStars = new Rating(5, "Dave");
    threeStars = new Rating(3, "Jason");
    renderer = new RatingRenderer();
    list = new JList();
    list.setBackground(Color.BLUE);
    list.setForeground(Color.RED);
    list.setSelectionBackground(Color.RED);
    list.setSelectionForeground(Color.BLUE);
  }

  public void testReturnsSelf() {
    Component result = renderer.getListCellRendererComponent(list,
                                                      fiveStars,
                                                      1,
                                                      false,
                                                      false);
    assertSame("getListCellRendererComponent should return self.", renderer,
            result);
  }

  public void testContents() {
    renderer.getListCellRendererComponent(list, fiveStars, 1, false, false);
    assertEquals("Bad text.", fiveStars.getSource(), renderer.getText());
    assertSame("Icon should be 5 stars.",
            RatingRenderer.iconForRating(5),
            renderer.getIcon());
    renderer.getListCellRendererComponent(list, threeStars, 1, true, false);
    assertEquals("Bad text.", threeStars.getSource(), renderer.getText());
    assertSame("Icon should be 3 stars.",
            RatingRenderer.iconForRating(3),
            renderer.getIcon());
  }

  public void testUnSelectedColors() {
    renderer.getListCellRendererComponent(list, fiveStars, 1, false, false);
    assertEquals("Unselected background should be blue.", Color.BLUE,
              renderer.getBackground());
    assertEquals("Unselected foreground should be red.", Color.RED,
              renderer.getForeground());
  }

  public void testSelectedColors() {
    renderer.getListCellRendererComponent(list, fiveStars, 1, true, false);
    assertEquals("Selected background should be red.", Color.RED,
              renderer.getBackground());
    assertEquals("Selecetd foreground should bo blue.", Color.BLUE,
              renderer.getForeground());
  }
```

```
        public static void main(String[] args) {
          junit.textui.TestRunner.run(TestRatingRenderer.class);
        }
      }
```

And here's the code for the renderer:

```
  public class RatingRenderer extends JLabel implements ListCellRenderer {
    private static ImageIcon[] ratingIcons = {
      new ImageIcon("images/zero-stars.gif"),
      new ImageIcon("images/one-star.gif"),
      new ImageIcon("images/two-stars.gif"),
      new ImageIcon("images/three-stars.gif"),
      new ImageIcon("images/four-stars.gif"),
      new ImageIcon("images/five-stars.gif")
    };

    public RatingRenderer(String text, Icon icon,
                                    int horizontalAlignment) {
      super(text, icon, horizontalAlignment);
    }

    public RatingRenderer(String text, int horizontalAlignment) {
      super(text, horizontalAlignment);
    }

    public RatingRenderer(String text) {
      super(text);
    }

    public RatingRenderer(Icon image, int horizontalAlignment) {
      super(image, horizontalAlignment);
    }

    public RatingRenderer(Icon image) {
      super(image);
    }

    public RatingRenderer() {
      super();
    }
    public static ImageIcon[] icons() {
      return ratingIcons;
    }
    public static ImageIcon iconForRating(int rating) {
      return ratingIcons[rating];
    }
    public Component getListCellRendererComponent(JList list,
                                            Object value,
                                            int index,
                                            boolean isSelected,
                                            boolean cellHasFocus) {
      Rating ratingToRender = (Rating)value;
```

```
    if (isSelected) {
      setBackground(list.getSelectionBackground());
      setForeground(list.getSelectionForeground());
    } else {
      setBackground(list.getBackground());
      setForeground(list.getForeground());
    }

    setText(ratingToRender.getSource());
    setIcon(ratingIcons[ratingToRender.getValue()]);

    return this;
  }
}
```

Next, we can just change the GUI code to use the new custom renderer for the rating list:

```
private JScrollPane initRatingList() {
  //...
  ratingList.setCellRenderer(new RatingRenderer());
  //...
}
```

## ADD A RATING IN THE GUI

*In the GUI, provide a way to add a rating to the selected movie. Be sure to handle an empty source and map it to* Anonymous.

Now we need to be able to add a rating to the selected movie.

**Test 97.** Telling the logical layer to select a movie and add a rating to it, and providing specific rating value and source, causes that rating to be added to the movie that was selected.

**Test 98.** Selecting a movie, setting the rating value, and source to specific values and pressing the "Add Rating" button causes that rating to be added to the selected movie.

Here's the test in TestMovieListEditor for that function.

### Test 97: Telling the logical layer to select a movie and add a rating to it, and providing specific rating value and source, causes that rating to be added to the movie that was selected.

```
public void testAddingRating() throws DuplicateMovieException {
  Vector extendedRatings = starWars.getRatings();
  extendedRatings.add(new Rating(2, "Dave"));
```

```
        mockView.setMovies(movies);
        control.setVoidCallable(1);
        mockView.setNameField(starWars.getName());
        control.setVoidCallable(1);
        mockView.setRatingField(6);
        control.setVoidCallable(1);
        mockView.setCategoryField(Category.SCIFI);
        control.setVoidCallable(1);

        mockView.setRatings(starWars.getRatings());
        control.setVoidCallable(1);
        mockView.getRatingValueField();
        control.setReturnValue(2, 1);
        mockView.getRatingSourceField();
        control.setReturnValue("Dave", 1);
        mockView.setRatings(extendedRatings);
        control.setVoidCallable(1);
        control.activate();

        MovieListEditor editor = new MovieListEditor(movieList, mockView);
        editor.select(0);

        editor.addRating();
        control.verify();
    }
```

We need to add some methods to the MovieListEditorView interface to fetch the values for the new rating:

```
    int getRatingValueField();
    String getRatingSourceField();
```

We also need a stubbed addRating() in MovieListEditor:

```
    public void addRating() {
    }
```

OK, this compiles, but fails. The expected calls to the new methods are not being made. Also, the second call to setRatings() with the new rating is not happening. Here's the failure trace:

```
junit.framework.AssertionFailedError:
  EasyMock for interface com.saorsa.nowplaying.MovieListEditorView:
  Expectation failure on verify:
    method call setRatings([5 (Anonymous), 2 (Dave)]):
      calls expected: 1,
      received: 0
    method call getRatingSourceField(): calls expected: 1, received: 0
    method call getRatingValueField(): calls expected: 1, received: 0
```

Here's the code for addRating():

```
public void addRating() {
  if (selectedMovie != null) {
    int value = view.getRatingValueField();
    String source = view.getRatingSourceField();
    selectedMovie.addRating(value, source);
    view.setRatings(selectedMovie.getRatings());
  }
}
```

The test still fails. The failure trace is:

```
junit.framework.AssertionFailedError:
  EasyMock for interface com.saorsa.nowplaying.MovieListEditorView:
  Unexpected method call setRatings([5 (Anonymous), 2 (Dave)])
```

But this is exactly the ratings that were expected earlier. What's up? Rating doesn't have an equals() method. That's what.

We need to digress and write a test for comparing Ratings. Hold on a sec... won't that leave us with more than one test failing (the new test for Rating.equals() as well as the currently failing test? Yes and no. Yes, in that we'll have two failures reported. No, in that this test should be passing. It's the comparion that is failing; all requirements of the test are being satisfied. So let's press on and write the test for Rating.equals():

```
public class TestRating extends TestCase {
  public void testEquals() {
    final Rating aRating = new Rating(3, "Dave");
    final Rating anEqualRating = new Rating(3, "Dave");
    final Rating aDifferentRating = new Rating(2, "Jason");
    final Rating aSubRating = new Rating(3, "Dave") {
    };
    new EqualsTester(aRating, anEqualRating, aDifferentRating, aSubRating);
  }
}
```

Now we need to implement equals() and hashCode() in Rating:

```
public boolean equals(final Object anObject) {
  if (anObject == null) return false;
  if (anObject.getClass() != this.getClass()) return false;
  final Rating otherRating = (Rating) anObject;
  return (getValue() == otherRating.getValue()) &&
         (getSource().equals(otherRating.getSource()));
}
```

```
public int hashCode() {
  int result = 17;
  result = 37 * result + value;
  result = 37 * result + source.hashCode();
  return result;
}
```

This lets testEquals() pass. Now go back to our previous test. It now passes with flying colors... well, OK, just green. The next step is to add rating addition to the Swing GUI. Here's our test.

## Test 98: Selecting a movie, setting the rating value, and source to specific values and pressing the "Add Rating" button causes that rating to be added to the selected movie.

```
public void testAddingRatings() {
  JListOperator movieList =
      new JListOperator(mainWindow, new NameBasedChooser("movieList"));
  movieList.clickOnItem(0, 1);

  JComboBoxOperator ratingCombo =
      new JComboBoxOperator(mainWindow,
                            new NameBasedChooser("ratingvalue"));
  ratingCombo.setSelectedIndex(3);

  JTextFieldOperator ratingSourceField =
      new JTextFieldOperator(mainWindow,
                             new NameBasedChooser("ratingsource"));
  ratingSourceField.enterText("Dave");

  JButtonOperator addRatingButton =
      new JButtonOperator(mainWindow, new NameBasedChooser("addrating"));
  addRatingButton.doClick();

  Vector ratings = starWars.getRatings();
  assertEquals("starWars should have 2 ratings.", 2, ratings.size());

  Rating newRating = (Rating)ratings.get(1);
  assertEquals("New rating has wrong value.", 3, newRating.getValue());
  assertEquals("New rating has wrong source.", "Dave", newRating.getSource());

  JListOperator ratingsList =
      new JListOperator(mainWindow, new NameBasedChooser("ratings"));
  verifyRatings(ratingsList, starWars);
}
```

This selects *Star Wars* from the movie list, selects a rating value, enters a rating source, pushes the *Add Rating* button, verifies that *Star Wars* has the expected new rating, and verifies that it was added to the ratings list.

The initial failure of this test is due to the lack of a *ratingsource* field. We easily add one:

```java
private JPanel initDetailPane() {
  //...
  detailPane.add(initRatingList());
  detailPane.add(initRatingValueField());
  detailPane.add(initRatingSourceField());
  detailPane.add(initAddRatingButton());
  //...
}

private Component initRatingValueField() {
  List ratingIconsWithNA = Arrays.asList(CustomMovieListRenderer.icons());
  List ratingIconsWithoutNA = ratingIconsWithNA.subList(1, 7);
  ratingValueField = new JComboBox(ratingIconsWithoutNA.toArray());
  ratingValueField.setName("ratingvalue");
  return ratingValueField;
}

private Component initRatingSourceField() {
  ratingSourceField = new JTextField(16);
  ratingSourceField.setName("ratingsource");
  return ratingSourceField;
}

private Component initAddRatingButton() {
  JButton addButton = new JButton("Add Rating");
  addButton.setName("addrating");
  addButton.addActionListener(new ActionListener() {
    public void actionPerformed(ActionEvent e) {
      myEditor.addRating();
    }
  });
  return addButton;
}
```

Now the test fails due to an incorrect rating being added. We need to fill in the accessors that fetch the relevant field values:

```java
public int getRatingValueField() {
  return ratingValueField.getSelectedIndex();
}

public String getRatingSourceField() {
  return ratingSourceField.getText();
}
```

Now the test passes. Is there anything to clean up? Yes, when we added the component code, we did it quick and dirty. We need to arrange the rating addition components in a nicer way and pull their setup into a separate method. We did something very similar before, so here's the final code:

```
private JPanel initDetailPane() {
  //...
  detailPane.add(initCategoryField());
  detailPane.add(Box.createRigidArea(new Dimension(0, 5)));
  detailPane.add(initRatingsPane());
  return detailPane;
}

private Component initRatingsPane() {
  JPanel ratingsPane = new JPanel();
  ratingsPane.setLayout(new BoxLayout(ratingsPane, BoxLayout.X_AXIS));
  ratingsPane.setBorder(BorderFactory.createEtchedBorder());
  ratingsPane.add(initRatingList());

  JPanel addRatingPane = new JPanel();
  addRatingPane.setLayout(new BoxLayout(addRatingPane, BoxLayout.Y_AXIS));
  addRatingPane.setBorder(BorderFactory.createEmptyBorder(1, 10, 10, 10));
  addRatingPane.add(initRatingValueField());
  addRatingPane.add(Box.createRigidArea(new Dimension(0, 5)));
  addRatingPane.add(initRatingSourceField());
  addRatingPane.add(Box.createRigidArea(new Dimension(0, 5)));
  addRatingPane.add(initAddRatingButton());
  addRatingPane.add(Box.createRigidArea(new Dimension(0, 5)));
  addRatingPane.add(Box.createGlue());

  ratingsPane.add(Box.createRigidArea(new Dimension(5, 0)));
  ratingsPane.add(addRatingPane);
  return ratingsPane;
}
```

## REMOVE THE SINGLE-RATING FIELD

*The single-rating field no longer serves any purpose. Remove it and update the system appropriately.*

Now that everything has been updated to use multiple ratings, we can remove support for the early single-rating system.

We will start by removing setRating() in Movie. From there you compile and run the tests. When you find compile errors or failing tests, you need to investigate and either remove references to already removed code, or tweak tests to not use deleted functionality. I'll leave this as an exercise to the reader. Starting with the removal of Movie.setRating() it took about 30 minutes to clean the system of the single-rating support. Compile and run the tests (*all* the tests) continuously during this process to be sure you don't overdo it.

## RETROSPECTIVE

This has been a rather involved story. Looking back, we should have split it into two or more smaller stories. We did a lot of work in this chapter. We moved from a simple, single numeric rating per movie to a multirating system, each with a source annotation.

As part of the process, we had to revamp our persistence mechanism, moving it to its own set of classes as well as moving to a more structured format. This provides an example of letting the immediate requirements drive the addition of complexity to the system.

More and more, XML is a commonplace standard. It is the basis of many pieces of internet infrastucture. Maybe we should consider XML as *the simplest thing* when our data has any amount of structure. This story certainly would have been easier to do if we had used XML from the beginning rather than a flat text file.

# Chapter 19

# REVIEWS

*Movies can have a review attached to each rating. If there is a review there must be a source.*

## ADD A REVIEW TO RATINGS

*Add support for a single review to Rating.*

Here are the tests we want to pass when we've finished this task:

**Test 99.** A rating created without a review should answer an empty string when asked for its review.

**Test 100.** A rating created with a review should answer that string when asked for its review.

### First, some cleanup

We need to extend the concept of a *rating*. Before doing this, we should make sure that Rating is well encapsulated. When we look at how ratings are added to movies, we find these methods in Movie:

```
public void addRating(Rating ratingToAdd) {
  ratings.add(ratingToAdd);
}

public void addRating(int aRating) {
  addRating(new Rating(aRating));
}

public void addRating(int aRating, String aRatingSource) {
  addRating(new Rating(aRating, aRatingSource));
}
```

If we look further, we find that the last two methods reflect the constructors for Rating:

```
public Rating(int aRating) {
  this(aRating, "Anonymous");
}
```

```
public Rating(int aRating, String aRatingSource) {
  value = aRating;
  source = aRatingSource;
}
```

This is starting to smell like *Shotgun Surgery*, in that if we add a constructor that take a **String** review, we will likely want to add a corresponding **addRating** method. This is not a good trend. We need to clean this up before moving forward.

To do this we must replace calls to the complex **addRating** methods with a call to **addRating(Rating)** with a nested **Rating** construction. For example, the first line below needs to be replaced with the second:

```
starWars.addRating(4, "Dave");
```

```
starWars.addRating(new Rating(4, "Dave"));
```

After changing each line, we compile and rerun all the tests. This keeps us from introducing errors accidentally. If we do, we know immediately, when the code is still in mind, and in the editor.

Once we have replaced all references to a method, we can delete it. That will leave only one **addRating()** method: the one that takes a **Rating**.

## Test 99: A rating created without a review should answer an empty string when asked for its review.

Now we need to design our review handling. First, we think about what it means not to have a review. We should maintain backward compatibility if it is possible, and in this case it should be. If we use the current constructors that don't take a review, the resulting **Rating** shouldn't have a review. Now, we write this up as a test:

```
public void testNoReview() {
  Rating aRating = new Rating(3, "Dave");
  assertEquals("Rating without review should have empty review.",
               "",
               aRating.getReview());
}
```

We need to stub **Rating.getReview()**:

```
public String getReview() {
  return null;
}
```

The test fails until we fake it in **getReview()**:

```
public String getReview() {
  return "";
}
```

Now we should move aRating into the common fixture, and remove it from test-Equals():

```
private Rating aRating = null;

protected void setUp() {
  aRating = new Rating(3, "Dave");
}
```

## Test 100: A rating created with a review should answer that string when asked for its review.

Next, we need to ask, "What if a Rating like that has a review?" and "How does a Rating get a review?" The answer to the first question is that it should be able to answer it when asked. The answer to the second is that we'll start with the simplest approach, which is via a constructor. If we need to set the review after creation, we'll add the capability then. We express these answers as a test:

```
public void testWithConstructedReview() {
  Rating ratingWithReview = new Rating(4, "Jason", "Test Review");
  assertEquals("Review is incorrect.",
               "Test Review",
               ratingWithReview.getReview());
}
```

Since we're happy with how things are going and we feel confident, we'll take a bigger step and rework Rating's constructors to accommodate the review argument, as well as update getReview() to use the new field:

```
private String review = null;

public Rating(int aRating) {
  this(aRating, "Anonymous", "");
}
public Rating(int aRating, String aRatingSource) {
  this(aRating, aRatingSource, "");
}
public Rating(int aRating, String aRatingSource, String aReview) {
  value = aRating;
  source = aRatingSource;
  review = aReview;
}
public String getReview() {
  return review;
}
```

Our new test passes, and all the previous ones still do. This might be a good time to rerun AllTests. Green.

## SAVE REVIEW

*Add support to persistence for saving reviews.*

We just have one test here:

**Test 101.** If a rating has an attached review, the review is saved as the text of the <rating> element.

We already have tests in place for saving without any reviews. Nothing there will change. We also don't need to do anything relating to the saving mechanism in the interface components. All we need to worry about is that if there are reviews, they get saved properly. We can do this at the lowest level, in TestMovieListWriting. We just need a single test that verifies that saving with a review works.

## Test 101: If a rating has an attached review, the review is saved as the text of the <rating> element.

```
public void testWritingOneMovieWithReview() throws Exception {
    String starWarsOutput = "<movielist>" +
                        "<movie name = \"Star Wars\" " +
                            "category = \"Science Fiction\">" +
                        "<ratings>" +
                            "<rating value=\"4\" source=\"NY Times\" >" +
                            "Nice, fluffy, good vs evil, SciFi piece" +
                            "</rating>" +
                        "</ratings>" +
                        "</movie>" +
                    "</movielist>";

    Movie starWars = new Movie("Star Wars", Category.SCIFI);
    starWars.addRating(new Rating(4,
                        "NY Times",
                        "Nice, fluffy, good vs evil, SciFi piece"));
    movieList.add(starWars);
    writer.write(movieList);
    assertXMLEqual("Wrong output from writing a single movie list.",
                starWarsOutput,
                destination.toString());
}
```

This fails since the XML comparison fails. To get it passing, we need to work on XMLMovieListWriter:

```
private MessageFormat ratingFormatWithoutReview =
        new MessageFormat("<rating value=\"{0,number,integer}\" " +
                        "source=\"{1}\" />");
private MessageFormat ratingFormatWithReview =
        new MessageFormat("<rating value=\"{0,number,integer}\" " +
                        "source=\"{1}\">" +
            "{2}" +
            "</rating>");
```

```
//...
private void writeRating(Rating ratingToWrite) throws IOException {
  Object[] args = { new Integer(ratingToWrite.getValue()),
                    ratingToWrite.getSource(),
                    ratingToWrite.getReview() };
  MessageFormat formatToUse;

  if (ratingToWrite.hasReview()) {
    formatToUse = ratingFormatWithReview;
  } else {
    formatToUse = ratingFormatWithoutReview;
  }
  destination.write(formatToUse.format(args));
}
```

Notice how we've added a second format for ratings and renamed the previous one to better reveal its intended use. We also need to add a query (hasReview()) to Rating:

```
public boolean hasReview() {
  return review != null && review.length() > 0;
}
```

With all of this in place, the test passes. Now we need to clean up. When we added the second rating format we introduced some duplication in the format strings. Ratings should have a common core format whether there is a review or not. We need to refactor to eliminate the duplication and make the intended commonality obvious:

```
private String commonRatingFormat =
            "<rating value=\"{0,number,integer}\" " +
                "source=\"{1}\"";
private MessageFormat ratingFormatWithoutReview =
      new MessageFormat(commonRatingFormat + " />");
private MessageFormat ratingFormatWithReview =
      new MessageFormat(commonRatingFormat + ">{2}</rating>");
```

Make sure all the tests still pass, and that should do it.

## LOAD REVIEW

*Add support to persistence for loading reviews.*

Similarly to the previous task, we only need to concern ourselves with reading a MovieList that contains a review.

**Test 102.** Reading an XML stream that contains text for a rating element results in that rating having an attached review.

We need to add a test to TestMovieListReading. Just for fun, we'll take a slightly different approach this time. The existing test for reading a movie uses a fixture that uses a movie with two ratings. Let's add a review to one of them.

## Test 102: Reading an XML stream that contains text for a rating element results in that rating having an attached review.

First, a tweak to setUp():

```
oneMoviePrefix = "<movielist>" +
                "<movie name=\"Star Wars\" " +
                    "category=\"Science Fiction\">" +
                "<ratings>" +
                    "<rating value=\"3\" " +
                            "source=\"Dave\" />" +
                    "<rating value=\"5\" " +
                            "source=\"Jason\">" +
                        "Great movie!" +
                    "</rating>" +
                "</ratings>" +
            "</movie>";
```

This needs a corresponding tweak to the test:

```
public void testReadingOneMovie() throws Exception {
    //...
    Rating firstRating = (Rating)ratingIterator.next();

    //...
    assertFalse("First rating should not have a review.",
                firstRating.hasReview());

    //...
    Rating secondRating = (Rating)ratingIterator.next();

    //...
    assertTrue("Second rating should have a review.",
                secondRating.hasReview());

    assertEquals("Second rating's review is wrong.",
                "Great movie!",
                secondRating.getReview());

    //...
}
```

As expected, this test fails on the assertion that the second rating has a review. To correct that, we need to revisit processRating() in XMLMovieListReader:

```
private Rating processRating(Element ratingElement) throws IOException {
    //...
    String review = ratingElement.getTextTrim();
    return new Rating(value, source, review);
}
```

Green.

## DISPLAY REVIEW

*Add support to the GUI to display reviews.*

Now that we can handle reviews internally, it's time to make them available to the user.

**Test 103.** Telling the logical layer that a rating is selected that has no review results in the view being told to put an empty string in the review field.

**Test 104.** Telling the logical layer that a rating is selected that has a review results in the view being told to put the review string in the review field.

We start with a test in TestMovieListEditor.

## Test 103: Telling the logical layer that a rating is selected that has no review results in the view being told to put an empty string in the review field.

```
public void testRatingSelectionWithoutReview() {
  mockView.setMovies(movies);
  control.setVoidCallable(1);
  mockView.setNameField(starWars.getName());
  control.setVoidCallable(1);
  mockView.setCategoryField(Category.SCIFI);
  control.setVoidCallable(1);

  mockView.setRatings(starWars.getRatings());
  control.setVoidCallable(1);
  mockView.setRatingReviewField("");
  control.setVoidCallable(1);
  control.activate();

  MovieListEditor editor = new MovieListEditor(movieList, mockView);
  editor.select(0);
  editor.selectRating(0);
  control.verify();
}
```

Two stubs need to be added. The first is setRatingReviewField() in MovieListEditorView:

```
void setRatingReviewField(String string);
```

The other is in MovieListEditor:

```
public void selectRating(int i) {
}
```

Now we can run the new test. It fails because the expected call to setRatingReviewField() was not made. A simple change will get the test passing:

```
public void selectRating(int i) {
  view.setRatingReviewField("");
}
```

Now we've faked it. Our next test will drive us to make it work properly.

## Test 104: Telling the logical layer that a rating is selected that has a review results in the view being told to put the review string in the review field.

This test is very similar to the previous one, except that a review is present:

```
public void testRatingSelectionWithReview() {
  String davesReview = "Not bad, but kind of light.";
  starWars.addRating(new Rating(3, "Dave", davesReview));

  mockView.setMovies(movies);
  control.setVoidCallable(1);
  mockView.setNameField(starWars.getName());
  control.setVoidCallable(1);
  mockView.setCategoryField(Category.SCIFI);
  control.setVoidCallable(1);
  mockView.setRatings(starWars.getRatings());
  control.setVoidCallable(1);
  mockView.setRatingReviewField(davesReview);
  control.setVoidCallable(1);
  control.activate();

  MovieListEditor editor = new MovieListEditor(movieList, mockView);
  editor.select(0);
  editor.selectRating(1);
  control.verify();
}
```

Now we need to make selectRating() do more than return an empty string; it has to fetch the review corresponding to the selected rating and send that to the view:

```
public void selectRating(int i) {
  Rating selectedRating = selectedMovie.getRating(i);
  view.setRatingReviewField(selectedRating.getReview());
}
```

The compiler (or the editor if we are using an advanced IDE) tells us that we need to write getRating(int). When we look at Movie we see that we have getRating(), which returns the average rating. Now we add getRating(int). This is confusing—the former returns an int that is the average of all the ratings, while the latter returns the Rating at the given index. We make a note to refactor to make the intent clearer by renaming getRating() to getAverageRating(). While we're at it, getRawRating() smells funny. We'll have a closer look at it as well.

But let's get back to the problem at hand. Here's our new getRating(int):

```
public Rating getRating(int i) {
  return (Rating)ratings.get(i);
}
```

OK, green!

## Cleaning up the average rating queries

Now let's do those refactorings. The rename is easy so that we won't go into detail here. Just be sure to run AllTests after each small change if you are refactoring by hand, and afterward if you are using an automated rename.

The next item on our list is a bit more involved. The method in question, getRawRating(), is used only in MovieRatingComparator:

```
public int compare(Object o1, Object o2) {
  Movie firstMovie = (Movie)o1;
  Movie secondMovie = (Movie)o2;
  int ratingOfFirstMovie = firstMovie.getRawRating();
  int ratingOfSecondMovie = secondMovie.getRawRating();
  return ratingOfSecondMovie - ratingOfFirstMovie;
}
```

Its only use is to return -1 if the movie is unrated rather than throwing an exception. We have both a query to check if there is a rating, as well as an exception that is thrown if the rating of an unrated movie is requested. We should really only have one. I suggest that we refactor to get rid of the exception. We can do this by renaming getRawRating() to getAverageRating(), so that we now have:

```
public int getAverageRating() {
  if (hasRating()) {
    return calculateAverageRating();
  } else {
    return −1;
  }
}
```

The rename took care of the above compare() method, so it's not an issue anymore.

This rename broke the compilation of a few methods. The first is in Custom-MovieListRenderer:

```
public Component getListCellRendererComponent(...) {
  //...
  if (movieToRender.hasRating()) {
    try {
      setIcon(ratingIcons[movieToRender.getAverageRating() + 1]);
    } catch (UnratedException ex) {
    }
  } else {
    setIcon(ratingIcons[0]);
  }
  //...
}
```

In this case, we can just strip off the try–catch block:

```
public Component getListCellRendererComponent(...) {
  //...
  if (movieToRender.hasRating()) {
    setIcon(ratingIcons[movieToRender.getAverageRating() + 1]);
  } else {
    setIcon(ratingIcons[0]);
  }
  //...
}
```

We can simplify this further since now movieToRender.getAverageRating() returns -1 if the movie is unrated. The icon index calculation will now work in that case, so we have:

```
public Component getListCellRendererComponent(...) {
  //...
  setIcon(ratingIcons[movieToRender.getAverageRating() + 1]);
  //...
}
```

Running the related test verifies that this works fine.

The next problem is in TestMovieRatings():

```
public void testUnratedConstructor() {
  try {
    starTrek.getAverageRating();
    fail("Getting rating of an unrated Movie should throw UnratedMovieException");
  } catch (UnratedException ex) {
  }
}
```

Here, we can't just strip off the exception-related code... our test relies on it. But we can easily rewrite the test to use the tweaked behavior:

```
public void testUnratedConstructor() {
  assertFalse("Unrated movie should not report that it has a rating.",
             starTrek.hasRating());
  assertEquals("Average rating of an unrated movie is wrong.",
              −1,
              starTrek.getAverageRating());
}
```

The other problem is in TestMovie:

```
public void testUnratedException() {
  try {
    starWars.getAverageRating();
    fail("getRating on an unrated Movie should throw UnratedException.");
  } catch (UnratedException ex) {
    assertEquals("UnratedException should identify the movie.",
                 starWars.getName(),
                 ex.getMessage());
  }
}
```

This test is redundant. The test we just updated tested the very same behavior. We can simply delete this test.

Now we run AllTests to verify that everything passes. OK, done. We've just cleaned up our code and made it clearer. High five!

## Expose reviews in the GUI

Now we need to add review display to the Swing GUI component.

**Test 105.** Selecting a rating that doesn't have a review puts an empty string in the review field.

**Test 106.** Telling the logical layer that a rating is selected that has a review results in the view being told to put the review string in the review field.

Our first test will verify correct behavior when there is no review as well as drive the evolution of the GUI itself.

## Test 105: Selecting a rating that doesn't have a review puts an empty string in the review field.

```
public void testRatingSelectionWithoutReview() {
  JListOperator movieList =
      new JListOperator(mainWindow, new NameBasedChooser("movieList"));
  movieList.clickOnItem(0, 1);
  JListOperator ratingsList =
      new JListOperator(mainWindow, new NameBasedChooser("ratings"));
  ratingsList.clickOnItem(0, 1);
  JTextAreaOperator reviewField =
          new JTextAreaOperator(mainWindow, new NameBasedChooser("review"));
  assertEquals("There should not be a review.", "", reviewField.getText());
}
```

This fails because there isn't a TextArea named "review". Let's fix that in Swing-MovieListEditorView:

```
private JTextArea ratingReviewField = null;
//...
```

```
private Component initRatingsPane() {
  //...
  addRatingPane.add(initRatingSourceField());
  addRatingPane.add(Box.createRigidArea(new Dimension(0, 5)));
  addRatingPane.add(initRatingReviewField());
  addRatingPane.add(Box.createRigidArea(new Dimension(0, 5)));
  addRatingPane.add(initAddRatingButton());
  //...
}

private Component initRatingReviewField() {
  ratingReviewField = new JTextArea();
  ratingReviewField.setName("review");

  JScrollPane scroller =
        new JScrollPane(ratingReviewField,
                    ScrollPaneConstants.VERTICAL_SCROLLBAR_ALWAYS,
                    ScrollPaneConstants.HORIZONTAL_SCROLLBAR_NEVER);
  return scroller;
}
```

The method initRatingsPane() is getting rather large; we should make a note to clean it up (by extracting the construction of the rating detail pane) later.

This addition makes our test pass so we can do that refactoring. Here's the result:

```
private Component initRatingsPane() {
  JPanel ratingsPane = new JPanel();
  ratingsPane.setLayout(new BoxLayout(ratingsPane, BoxLayout.X_AXIS));
  ratingsPane.setBorder(BorderFactory.createEtchedBorder());
  ratingsPane.add(initRatingList());
  ratingsPane.add(Box.createRigidArea(new Dimension(5, 0)));
  ratingsPane.add(initRatingDetailPane());
  return ratingsPane;
}


private JPanel initRatingDetailPane() {
  JPanel addRatingPane = new JPanel();
  addRatingPane.setLayout(new BoxLayout(addRatingPane, BoxLayout.Y_AXIS));
  addRatingPane.setBorder(BorderFactory.createEmptyBorder(1, 10, 10, 10));
  addRatingPane.add(initRatingValueField());
  addRatingPane.add(Box.createRigidArea(new Dimension(0, 5)));
  addRatingPane.add(initRatingSourceField());
  addRatingPane.add(Box.createRigidArea(new Dimension(0, 5)));
  addRatingPane.add(initRatingReviewField());
  addRatingPane.add(Box.createRigidArea(new Dimension(0, 5)));
  addRatingPane.add(initAddRatingButton());
  addRatingPane.add(Box.createRigidArea(new Dimension(0, 5)));
  addRatingPane.add(Box.createGlue());
  return addRatingPane;
}
```

## Test 106: Telling the logical layer that a rating is selected that has a review results in the view being told to put the review string in the review field.

Now we need a test that verifies the behavior when there is a review to be displayed. First we need to tweak the fixture to add a rating with a review:

```
protected void setUp() throws Exception {
  //...
  theShining = new Movie("The Shining", Category.HORROR, 2);
  theShining.addRating(new Rating(5, "Jack", "A timeless classic"));
  //...
}
//...
```

```
public void testRatingSelectionWithReview() {
  JListOperator movieList =
      new JListOperator(mainWindow, new NameBasedChooser("movieList"));
  movieList.clickOnItem(3, 1);
  JListOperator ratingsList =
      new JListOperator(mainWindow, new NameBasedChooser("ratings"));
  ratingsList.clickOnItem(1, 1);
  JTextAreaOperator reviewField =
        new JTextAreaOperator(mainWindow, new NameBasedChooser("review"));
  assertEquals("There should be a review.",
          "A timeless Classic!",
          reviewField.getText());
}
```

This fails since setRatingReviewField() currently does nothing. It needs to fill in the new JTestArea:

```
public void setRatingReviewField(String theReview) {
  ratingReviewField.setText(theReview);
}
```

The test still fails. Let's look at the code for the rating list:

```
private JScrollPane initRatingList() {
  ratingList = new JList(new Vector());
  ratingList.setName("ratings");
  ratingList.setSelectionMode(ListSelectionModel.SINGLE_SELECTION);
  ratingList.setCellRenderer(new RatingRenderer());

  JScrollPane scroller =
        new JScrollPane(ratingList,
                        ScrollPaneConstants.VERTICAL_SCROLLBAR_ALWAYS,
                        ScrollPaneConstants.HORIZONTAL_SCROLLBAR_NEVER);
  return scroller;
}
```

We need to add a selection handler:

```
ratingList.addListSelectionListener(new ListSelectionListener() {
  public void valueChanged(ListSelectionEvent e) {
    myEditor.selectRating(ratingList.getSelectedIndex());
  }
});
```

That does it.

## Some visual cleanup

In playing with the application, we see that there are a couple of visual, aesthetic bits of weirdness:

1. Widgets resize oddly with the window size changed; combo boxes and test fields get the extra height, the review test area doesn't.

2. When a rating is selected, its review is displayed in the rating-detail area, but its value and source aren't. This looks odd.

The first issue we can fix simply by overriding the maximumSize() method of the combo boxes and text fields, like this:

```
private JComboBox initCategoryField() {
  categoryField = new JComboBox(Category.categories())  {
    public Dimension getMaximumSize() {
      Dimension size = getPreferredSize();
      size.width = Short.MAX_VALUE;
      return size;
    }};
  //...
}
```

The second issue is more involved, and is more functional. We need tests to drive it. We can do this quickly and easily by extending the tests we just wrote. First, in TestMovieListEditor:

```
public void testRatingSelectionWithoutReview() {
  //...
  mockView.setRatings(starWars.getRatings());
  control.setVoidCallable(1);
  mockView.setRatingValueField(5);
  control.setVoidCallable(1);
  mockView.setRatingSourceField("Anonymous");
  control.setVoidCallable(1);
  mockView.setRatingReviewField("");
  control.setVoidCallable(1);
  //...
}
```

That drives us to add two methods to the view interface:

```
void setRatingValueField(int i);
void setRatingSourceField(String string);
```

Now the test fails since these methods are not being called. We now need to add code to MovieListEditor.selectRating():

```
public void selectRating(int i) {
  Rating selectedRating = selectedMovie.getRating(i);
  view.setRatingValueField(selectedRating.getValue());
  view.setRatingSourceField(selectedRating.getSource());
  view.setRatingReviewField(selectedRating.getReview());
}
```

This gets testRatingSelectionWithoutReview() passing, but testRatingSelectionWith-Review fails. That's OK—as we are about to extend it to cover this situation anyway:

```
public void testRatingSelectionWithReview() {
  //...
  mockView.setRatings(starWars.getRatings());
  control.setVoidCallable(1);
  mockView.setRatingValueField(3);
  control.setVoidCallable(1);
  mockView.setRatingSourceField("Dave");
  control.setVoidCallable(1);
  mockView.setRatingReviewField(davesReview);
  control.setVoidCallable(1);
  //...
}
```

Green again. Now to revisit the corresponding tests in TestSwingMovieListEditor. Actually, we only have to extend one of them. There are two reasons for this:

1. we don't need to set method call expectations

2. if it works with a review, it will work without.

```
public void testWithReview() {
  JListOperator movieList =
      new JListOperator(mainWindow, new NameBasedChooser("movieList"));
  movieList.clickOnItem(3, 1);

  JListOperator ratingsList =
      new JListOperator(mainWindow, new NameBasedChooser("ratings"));
  ratingsList.clickOnItem(1, 1);

  JComboBoxOperator ratingCombo =
          new JComboBoxOperator(mainWindow,
                                    new NameBasedChooser("ratingvalue"));
  assertEquals("Bad rating value.", 5, ratingCombo.getSelectedIndex());
```

```
JTextFieldOperator ratingSourceField =
        new JTextFieldOperator(mainWindow,
                                new NameBasedChooser("ratingsource"));
assertEquals("Bad rating source.", "Jack", ratingSourceField.getText());

JTextAreaOperator reviewField =
        new JTextAreaOperator(mainWindow, new NameBasedChooser("review"));
assertEquals("There should be a review.",
            "A timeless classic!",
            reviewField.getText());
}
```

This drives us to implement the two methods we added to the interface earlier:

```
public void setRatingValueField(int i) {
  ratingValueField.setSelectedIndex(i);
}

public void setRatingSourceField(String theSource) {
  ratingSourceField.setText(theSource);
}
```

That gets the test to pass. Things look much better now.

## ADD A REVIEW

*Add support to the GUI to enter a review as part of adding a rating.*

There are no new tests for this task, just some enhancements of existing ones.

We start by extending testAddingRating in TestMovieListEditor since that behavior now includes a review:

```
public void testAddingRating() throws DuplicateMovieException {
  Vector extendedRatings = starWars.getRatings();
  extendedRatings.add(new Rating(2, "Dave", "Not bad."));

  //...
  mockView.getRatingValueField();
  control.setReturnValue(2, 1);
  mockView.getRatingSourceField();
  control.setReturnValue("Dave", 1);
  mockView.getRatingReviewField();
  control.setReturnValue("Not bad.", 1);
  //...
}
```

This drives the addition of getRatingReviewField() to MovieListEditorView:

```
String getRatingReviewField();
```

The test now fails because this new method is not being called. To get the test to pass we need to extend addRating() in MovieListEditor:

```
public void addRating() {
  if (selectedMovie != null) {
    int value = view.getRatingValueField();
    String source = view.getRatingSourceField();
    String review = view.getRatingReviewField();
    selectedMovie.addRating(new Rating(value, source, review));
    view.setRatings(selectedMovie.getRatings());
  }
}
```

Green. Let's move on to the GUI test in TestSwingMovieListEditorView:

```
public void testAddingRatings() {
  JListOperator movieList =
      new JListOperator(mainWindow, new NameBasedChooser("movieList"));
  movieList.clickOnItem(0, 1);

  JComboBoxOperator ratingCombo =
      new JComboBoxOperator(mainWindow,
                               new NameBasedChooser("ratingvalue"));
  ratingCombo.setSelectedIndex(3);

  JTextFieldOperator ratingSourceField =
        new JTextFieldOperator(mainWindow,
                                 new NameBasedChooser("ratingsource"));
  ratingSourceField.enterText("Dave");

  JTextAreaOperator reviewField =
        new JTextAreaOperator(mainWindow, new NameBasedChooser("review"));
  reviewField.setText("Not bad.");

  JButtonOperator addRatingButton =
        new JButtonOperator(mainWindow, new NameBasedChooser("addrating"));
  addRatingButton.doClick();

  Vector ratings = starWars.getRatings();
  assertEquals("starWars should have 2 ratings.", 2, ratings.size());
  Rating newRating = (Rating)ratings.get(1);
  assertEquals("New rating has wrong value.", 3, newRating.getValue());
  assertEquals("New rating has wrong source.", "Dave", newRating.getSource());
  assertEquals("New rating has wrong review.",
                  "Not bad.",
                  newRating.getReview());
  JListOperator ratingsList =
      new JListOperator(mainWindow, new NameBasedChooser("ratings"));
  verifyRatings(ratingsList, starWars);
}
```

This requires the following method in SwingMovieListEditorView:

```
public String getRatingReviewField() {
  return ratingReviewField.getText();
}
```

That does it. We're done. Figure 19.1 shows the final state of the application GUI.

**Figure 19.1** Final form of the application GUI.

## RETROSPECTIVE

Adding reviews to the system would seem, at first glance, to be a large task. It touches all aspects of the system from persistence to GUI. In fact, it was very simple and straightforward to add. This is one of the benefits of Test-Driven Development, refactoring, and programming by intention: it is easier to extend the code. Making a seemingly profound addition or change is no longer something to be feared.

# Chapter 20

# PROJECT RETROSPECTIVE

In this chapter we look back at the project, noting what worked well and what we might improve. This is a valuable exercise if it is your first project or your one hundred and first. Another thing we do is have a look at the design, both from an aesthetic point of view as well as from a more objective, qualitative viewpoint. We'll collect some metrics, and see what the numbers look like.

## THE DESIGN

Figure 20.1 shows the class diagram. Our design is fairly simple—we don't see any classes that are overly large or small, and none that are heavy on instance variables or operations. Classes are not overly connected. Overall, the design looks well balanced. Even though this is a small project, we should be able to maintain this level of design balance through slavishly practicing TDD and refactoring. In the next sections we will look more objectively at the design by collecting metrics that give us a more mathematical view of the design's quality. One thing to consider when looking at a design is how code is distributed:

- Are there any unusually large or small classes?

- Are there any data or function classes? These are classes that contain mostly or completely methods or instance variables, respectively.

- Are classes overly connected to, or dependent on, each other?

To determine the answers to these questions, we can collect metrics on the code. We did this using TogetherControlCenter. For each class, we collected five metrics:[1]

**LOC: Lines of Code**  The number of lines of code, excluding comments and blank lines.

This isn't a valid metric for measuring productivity or progress. Rather, it provides a high-level view of where the code is. It gives a quick way to find a class that might be too large (and are possibly doing too much and should be broken up) or too small (and are possibly not doing enough to justify their autonomy and should be merged into another class). See Figure 20.2.

**NOA: Number of Attributes**  The number of attributes (instance variables) that a class has.

---

[1] Descriptions based on the TogetherControlCenter online documentation.

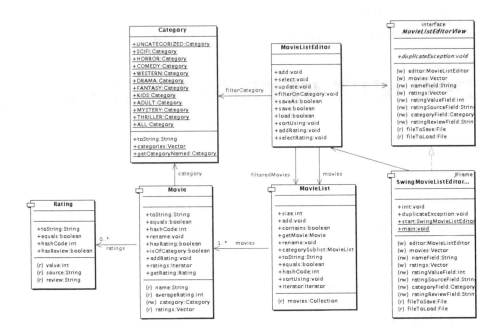

**Figure 20.1** The class diagram.

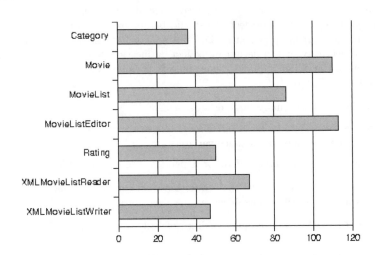

**Figure 20.2** The plot of LOC per class.

**NOO: Number of Operations**   The number of operations (methods), of all visibilities.

It is most interesting to compare the previous two metrics, as shown in Figure 20.3. An extreme imbalance between these values is indication that there may be a problem. A class that is mostly or all attributes could be a data class. Conversely, a class that

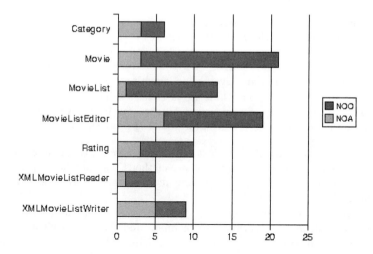

**Figure 20.3** The plot of NOA and NOO per class.

is all or mostly operations could be a function class. However, keep in mind that there should generally be more operations than attributes. Another point to remember is that accessors and mutators (aka, getters and setters) will show up as operations. This is misleading in that they are really just ways of getting to the attributes and do not often provide any functionality. As such, they should be considered part of the attribute.

**LOCOM2: The Lack of Cohesion of Methods 2**    The percentage of methods that do not access a specific attribute averaged over all attributes in the class. A high value of cohesion (a low lack of cohesion) implies that the class is well designed. See Figure 20.4.

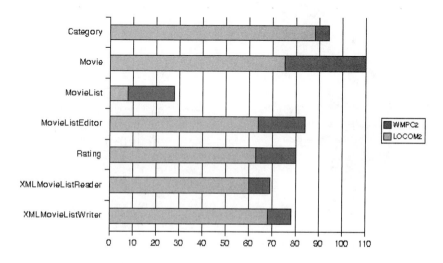

**Figure 20.4** The plot of LOCOM2 and WMPC2 per class.

All of these classes except MovieList have a fairly high LOCOM2 value, indicating a highly cohesive class. Furthermore, this indicates that MovieList may not be a good class. This isn't a great surprise since it is mostly a wrapper for the underlying collection of movies. Is this a problem? Maybe. I wouldn't worry about it now. It serves its purpose for the moment, and may evolve into something better.

The thing to remember is that these are just metrics. They don't tell you anything conclusive about the quality of your code. All they can do is give you indications of how things are going, and where to look for potential problems.

**WMPC2: Weighted Methods Per Class 2**    This is intended to measure the complexity of a class, assuming that a class with more methods than another is more complex, and that a method with more parameters than another is also likely to be more complex. See Figure 20.4.

Our classes fare quite well according to this metric. A comparatively high value for WMPC2 could indicate a class that is too complex and should be split up.

Based on these metrics, our project is in good shape. The Movie class is significantly more complex than most, but is also very cohesive. Since Movie is arguably the core class in the system, this is not unexpected.

## TEST VS. APPLICATION

An interesting thing to do is compare the amount of code we've written in the application to how much we've written in the tests.

The graph in Figure 20.5 shows a comparison between the amount of application code and test code, broken into GUI and non-GUI-related classes in each case. This is a very raw measurement, but it gives an overall impression of how much we are testing. There should be at least as much test code as application code, half as much is better.

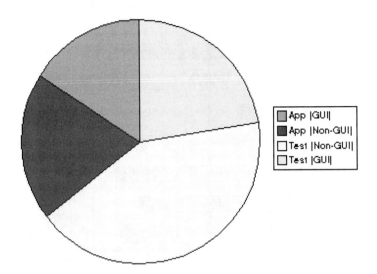

**Figure 20.5** Comparison of the amount of test and application code.

From the graph we can see that for the GUI there is a bit more test code than application code. GUIs tend to be heavy in terms of the amount of code. Properly done (i.e., highly decoupled) GUI code is primarily component creation, layout, event handling (deferring to the domain code), and presentation. Since this is straightforward code it doesn't need to be tested as heavily as complex application logic.

We can also see that there is approximately twice as much test code as application code for the non-GUI portions. This is fine, but we should start to be concerned if the test:application ratio is much more than 2:1.

# TEST QUALITY

## Jester Results

Running Jester on our application code results in a variety of changes that do not cause any test to fail. Once we trim off changes made to comments and the boilerplate (e.g., standard optimizations in equals(), toString(), hashCode(), etc), we are left with a small number of potential shortcomings, which are discussed in the following sections.

### MovieListEditor

There are two areas where Jester found potential discrepancies:

1. The case when no movie is selected. This includes deselecting a selected movie (by calling select(-1)) as well as performing operations on the selected movie when one isn't selected (specifically update() and addRating()).

2. The case when the view returns null as the file to load.

These cases are tested somewhat in the GUI tests which were not run as part of this analysis. These results do point out problems with our test coverage which need to be remedied.

### XMLMovieListWriter

This is an interesting case which can actually lead to the simplifying of the code. If you recall, before we added support for reviews, the XML element rating had no text, only attributes. When we added reviews, we placed the review in the text for the rating tag. We chose to add a second output format to handle the case where the Rating being written had a review:

```
private String commonRatingFormat =
      "<rating value=\"{0,number,integer}\" source=\"{1}\"";
private MessageFormat ratingFormatWithoutReview =
      new MessageFormat(commonRatingFormat + " />");
private MessageFormat ratingFormatWithReview =
      new MessageFormat(commonRatingFormat + ">{2}</rating>");
```

Here is the code that writes a Rating using these formats:

```
private void writeRating(Rating ratingToWrite) throws IOException {
  Object[] args = { new Integer(ratingToWrite.getValue()),
                    ratingToWrite.getSource(),
                    ratingToWrite.getReview() };
  MessageFormat formatToUse;
  if (ratingToWrite.hasReview()) {
    formatToUse = ratingFormatWithReview;
  } else {
    formatToUse = ratingFormatWithoutReview;
  }
  destination.write(formatToUse.format(args));
}
```

Jester found that it could change the condition of the if to be always true and the tests still passed. This implies that we can always simply use the first option of the if statement. Why is that? Remember that the tests compare XML structure, not text. The structure is the same in each case when there is no review—either an element with no text, or an element with an empty text. These are the same once it is parsed.

So, let's simplify writeRating() by removing the redundancy:

```
private MessageFormat ratingFormat =
      new MessageFormat("<rating value=\"{0,number,integer}\" " +
                  "source=\"{1}\">{2}</rating>");

private void writeRating(Rating ratingToWrite) throws IOException {
  Object[] args = { new Integer(ratingToWrite.getValue()),
                    ratingToWrite.getSource(),
                    ratingToWrite.getReview() };
  destination.write(ratingFormat.format(args));
}
```

Much simpler and cleaner. This is an unexpected benefit of running Jester on our code: the uncovering of some duplication.

## RatingRenderer

The issue here is due to a shortcut we took when we skipped testing the color based on selected status. If you recall, we did that because this code was identical to the code in the movie renderer which we tested more thoroughly. Maybe we shouldn't have taken that shortcut?

There are a few places where we could use an additional test or two. We didn't write any tests related to problems that can occur when opening files, for example.

## NoUnit Results

It took a while to work through several bugs in NoUnit that prevented it from running on our project code. These were all known bugs with workarounds available. After making the required changes, we had NoUnit running and providing results. These results were interesting, but not entirely surprising. The output of NoUnit's analysis is too large to reproduce here, but you can see it on our Web site with other support material for this book [URL 65].

The anonymous subclasses (e.g., event handlers) and component construction methods in the GUI are tested either not at all, or not very well. These functions are typically called from the GUI framework, and not our test code. In the GUI-based test cases they are called indirectly from the test case, again through the Swing framework.

Likewise, the custom renderers are not well tested. They are mostly boilerplate and their methods are called from the GUI framework.

Other methods that tend not to be well tested are support methods such as toString(), equals(), and hashCode(). Remember that we didn't explicitly test the latter two. We used EqualsTester to do that, so NoUnit didn't pick up the calls to them.

As we scan through the NoUnit output, we can see that the primary functional methods of the core classes are all marked green, indicating that they are tested directly.

## Clover Results

We easily ran Clover on the project, a few simple additions to the Ant build script. Results, shown in Figure 20.6, were good. Areas not tested were primarily methds such as toString() and hashcode(). One nice feature of Clover that we didn't make use of is the ability to mark sections of code that should be ignored when calculating coverage. This allows us to mark methods like toString() and not have them included in the coverage results. In some cases the untested code was error handling code that needs to be addressed. For example, there was no testing of error handling on the read and write code.

| Package | Conditionals | Statements | Methods | TOTAL | |
|---|---|---|---|---|---|
| **com.saorsa.nowplaying** | 88.7% | 87.6% | 85.7% | 87.3% | |

| Classes | Conditionals | Statements | Methods | TOTAL | |
|---|---|---|---|---|---|
| UnratedException | - | 0% | 0% | 0% | |
| DuplicateMovieException | - | 25% | 25% | 25% | |
| RatingRenderer | 100% | 58.8% | 22.2% | 50% | |
| Rating | 50% | 52.2% | 80% | 60% | |
| CustomMovieListRenderer | 100% | 70.6% | 44.4% | 64.3% | |
| MovieList | 77.8% | 70.5% | 91.7% | 75.7% | |
| XMLMovieListReader | 100% | 91.9% | 100% | 93.5% | |
| SwingMovieListEditorView | 100% | 92.7% | 98.3% | 94.1% | |
| MovieListEditor | 83.3% | 100% | 100% | 97.6% | |
| Category | - | 100% | 100% | 100% | |
| Movie | 100% | 100% | 100% | 100% | |
| MovieNameComparator | - | 100% | 100% | 100% | |
| MovieRatingComparator | - | 100% | 100% | 100% | |
| XMLMovieListWriter | 100% | 100% | 100% | 100% | |

**Figure 20.6** Results from Clover.

## Comments on the Test Quality Results

Our tests are in good shape. Jester found a couple of places where we could extend our test coverage—one where we were lazy and one where we missed testing for specific GUI behavior (the deselect case). The latter would best be dealt with by specifying what should happen when list items (both movie and rating) are deselected, and hence there is no selection. With that story in place, we would write tests and evolve the behavior to match. Jester also found an opportunity for simplification. This in itself is reason enough to use it occasionally.

NoUnit's report was reassuring: all of the important functionality was directly tested. Things found not to be tested were largely because they were called indirectly through Jemmy and the Swing framework. Thus, while NoUnit didn't detect the calls, they are being tested.

Likewise, the results from Clover weren't bad. They could be better, though. We can learn from this. The biggest problem was that we checked test coverage and quality once at the end. This is something that really should be done regularly, preferably as part of the build process. By keeping our eye on this feedback we can make corrections while they are minor. The same applies to running audits and metrics on the project. If we have an automated tool to do this (which is really a requirement), there's no excuse not to be doing it frequently. This, again, lets us take corrective action before we have a significant problem to deal with.

## OUR USE OF MOCKS

We've only used mocks for the interface view. They served us very well in that case, but could we have used them in other places to make our work easier? Likely. One possible use would be in the file loading and saving tests. There we could have used mock files, setting required return values for load tests and expectations for save tests. As the application grows and the time that the entire test suite takes to run increases, we may revisit that issue and add mocks to some of the tests, such as the file-related cases.

There are dangers in overusing mocks. The primary one is that it can make refactoring more difficult since mocks of the refactored classes need to be modified to match the new behavior. Hand-built mocks (whether using MockObjects with or without MockMaker, or not) need to be maintained like any other class in the system. On the other hand, using EasyMock can lead to overspecification in tests if you aren't careful.

Like all powerful tools, mocks are incredibly helpful and beneficial when used responsibly. Anything used to excess has the potential to create problems. Mocks are no different.

## GENERAL COMMENTS

One purpose in writing this book was to aid you, the reader, in your quest to improve your skills and your code. Another purpose was to let me think through the issues involved in TDD, mainly by having to express them clearly and understandably. I've written this section very near the end of the process, and have taken the opportunity to read through the book, looking for things that I've learned or become more convinced of.

I have, for the most part, resisted the temptation to go back and revise the code in this book. As such, it serves as a fairly accurate picture of how the development went. And as such, there are a few things I would have done differently.

One thing is that I would have used mocks more during the development of the GUI. This was a very simple application so we incurred no real penalty from using the real application code behind the GUI in our tests. Had it been a more involved application, the tests would have been noticably slow. Mocks would help avoid that.

Another thing—one more obvious and somewhat more embarrassing in hindsight— jumped out and hit me as I read through the book. Think back to the first task, specifically the test for containment in the list. I'll replicate it here for convenience, hoping that my editors don't refactor away the duplication:

```
public void testContents() {
  assertTrue("List should contain starWars.", movieList.contains(starWars));
  assertTrue("List should contain starTrek.", movieList.contains(starTrek));
  assertFalse("List should not contain stargate.", movieList.contains(stargate));
}
```

There are two things wrong with this test:

1. Checking for the containment of two movies is redundant and doesn't add much, if anything.

2. There are three assertions in this single test. I feel even more strongly now that you should always strive for a single assertion per test. In a perfect world, setUp() would build the fixture, and each test method would make a single assertion about it. Test methods this simple cease to require the message parameter for the assert.

If I were to yield to temptation, I would replace the above testContains() with:

```
public void testContains() {
  assertTrue(movieList.contains(starWars));
}

public void testDoesNotContain() {
  assertFalse(movieList.contains(stargate));
}
```

# DEBUGGING

We didn't talk about the time we spent laboriously single-stepping through our code searching for bugs. Or about painstakingly poking through data structures looking for that bad value. We didn't talk about it because we didn't do it. The write-up of the project reflects exactly what happened, down to each line of code we wrote. We did omit most of the times we ran the tests... because we did it constantly (and painlessly). We ran the tests after every change, after every compile. And many times *just to be sure*.

So... what about the debugger? Well, honestly, we never used it. I was telling someone about Eclipse and they asked what the debugger was like. After a moment of thought, I said something like, "Pretty good... I guess... I haven't used it more than a couple times...and that was mainly out of curiosity." I'd been using Eclipse almost daily for over a year at that point. He couldn't believe it.

So what's going on here? Well, once you get good at TDD you don't have much use for a debugger. This is because you are working in very small increments, adding very little code at a time.

You write a test, then write just enough code to make it pass. Once it passes, you're done with that chunk of work. When you're refactoring, you start with all the tests passing. After each small change you rerun the tests (likely, a localized subset of the entire suite). If they don't all pass, the problem is in that last little change you made. Because your tests are watching your code for bugs in such tiny increments, you never have much trouble finding a bug. It's hard to believe how well this works until you try it yourself.

Even if you were feeling brave (or foolhardy) and made a big change between tests, you simply back that change out and go through it again in smaller steps...running the tests after each step. (This is a common and humbling lesson when you are first learning TDD.)

So, yes, TDD sounds like a lot of extra work upfront (as my friend above commented), and certainly it is more work upfront than many of us are accustomed to. But it actually saves much more work on the backend (debugging) than it costs upfront. As nonintuitive as it may be, TDD saves you time. You'll find that once you acquire the feel for it, you'll work much faster than when you were using the code and debug approach. And you don't have to wait weeks to discover this higher speed: it will be obvious after just a few hours, and certainly after a couple of days. You just won't be spending all that backend time sleuthing for bugs. You'll be making rapid, steady, bug-free progress, task after task. As I keep saying, you will find it exhilarating.

## LIST OF TESTS

### Test 1: defined on Pg. 207 and implemented on Pg. 207

An empty list should have a size of zero.

### Test 2: defined on Pg. 207 and implemented on Pg. 209

Adding a movie to an empty list should result in a list with a size of one.

### Test 3: defined on Pg. 207 and implemented on Pg. 211

Adding two movies to an empty list should result in a list with a size of two.

### Test 4: defined on Pg. 207 and implemented on Pg. 214

If we add a movie to a list, we should be able to ask if it's there and receive a positive response. Conversely, we should receive a negative response when we ask about a movie that we haven't added.

### Test 5: defined on Pg. 219 and implemented on Pg. 219

The logical layer should send the appropriate list of movies to the view for display.

### Test 6: defined on Pg. 219 and implemented on Pg. 221

The GUI should have a listbox and should display a list of movies in it as requested.

**Test 7: defined on Pg. 226 and implemented on Pg. 226**

When the logical layer is asked to add a movie, it should request the required data from the view and update the movie list to include a new movie based on the data provided.

**Test 8: defined on Pg. 226 and implemented on Pg. 229**

The GUI should have a field for the movie name and an add button. It should answer the contents of the name field when asked, and request that the logical layer add a movie when the add button is pushed.

**Test 9: defined on Pg. 235 and implemented on Pg. 235**

Changing the name of a movie results in it using the new name hereafter.

**Test 10: defined on Pg. 235 and implemented on Pg. 236**

A movie can't be constructed with a null name.

**Test 11: defined on Pg. 235 and implemented on Pg. 236**

A movie can't be constructed with an empty name.

**Test 12: defined on Pg. 235 and implemented on Pg. 237**

A movie can't be renamed to a null name.

**Test 13: defined on Pg. 235 and implemented on Pg. 238**

A movie can't be renamed to an empty name.

**Test 14: defined on Pg. 239 and implemented on Pg. 239**

Indicating, to the logical layer, that a selection is made from the list causes the view to be given a value for the name field, that is, the selected movie's name.

**Test 15: defined on Pg. 239 and implemented on Pg. 241**

Selecting from the list causes the name field to be filled in with the selected movie's name.

**Test 16: defined on Pg. 239 and implemented on Pg. 242**

When an update is requested, the selected movie is renamed to whatever is answered by the view as the new name.

**Test 17: defined on Pg. 239 and implemented on Pg. 244**

When the update button is pushed, the selected movie is renamed to whatever is in the name field.

**Test 18: defined on Pg. 247 and implemented on Pg. 247**

Attempting to add a duplicate movie throws an exception and leaves the list unchanged.

**Test 19: defined on Pg. 247 and implemented on Pg. 248**

Asking the movielist to rename a movie results in its name being changed.

**Test 20: defined on Pg. 247 and implemented on Pg. 251**

Asking the logical layer to add a duplicate movie causes it to inform the presentation layer that the operation would result in a duplicate.

**Test 21: defined on Pg. 247 and implemented on Pg. 253**

Asking the logical layer to update a movie that would result in a duplicate causes it to inform the presentation layer that the operation would result in a duplicate.

**Test 22: defined on Pg. 247 and implemented on Pg. 255**

Trying to add a movie that is the same as one in the list results in the display of a "Duplicate Movie" error dialog.

**Test 23: defined on Pg. 247 and implemented on Pg. 256**

Trying to rename a movie to the name of one in the list results in the display of a "Duplicate Movie" error dialog.

**Test 24: defined on Pg. 261 and implemented on Pg. 261**

An unrated movie answers negative when asked if it is rated.

**Test 25: defined on Pg. 261 and implemented on Pg. 261**

A rated movie answers positive when asked if it is rated, and it can answer its rating when asked.

**Test 26: defined on Pg. 261 and implemented on Pg. 263**

Asking an unrated movie for its rating throws an exception.

**Test 27: defined on Pg. 264 and implemented on Pg. 264**

When asked for the renderer component, the renderer returns itself.

**Test 28: defined on Pg. 264 and implemented on Pg. 265**

When given a movie to render, the resulting test and rating image corresponds to the movie being rendered.

**Test 29: defined on Pg. 264 and implemented on Pg. 266**

When rendering an unselected item, the renderer uses its list's unselected colors.

**Test 30: defined on Pg. 264 and implemented on Pg. 267**

When rendering a selected item, the renderer uses its list's selected colors.

**Test 31: defined on Pg. 270 and implemented on Pg. 270**

Selecting a movie updates the rating in the GUI.

**Test 32: defined on Pg. 270 and implemented on Pg. 272**

Updating a movie changes its rating if a different rating was selected for it.

**Test 33: defined on Pg. 270 and implemented on Pg. 273**

Selecting a movie from the list updates the displayed rating.

**Test 34: defined on Pg. 270 and implemented on Pg. 275**

Updating a movie in the GUI changes its rating if a different rating was selected for it, and updates the display accordingly.

**Test 35: defined on Pg. 277 and implemented on Pg. 277**

A movie that hasn't explicitly been given a category should answer that it is uncategorized when asked for its category.

**Test 36: defined on Pg. 277 and implemented on Pg. 278**

If a movie is given a category when it is created, it answers that when asked for its category.

**Test 37: defined on Pg. 277 and implemented on Pg. 279**

Trying to create a movie with an invalid category (i.e., not from the predefined set) throws an exception.

**Test 38: defined on Pg. 281 and implemented on Pg. 282**

Telling the logical layer that a movie is selected causes the presentation layer to be told the category to display.

**Test 39: defined on Pg. 281 and implemented on Pg. 283**

Selecting a movie in the GUI causes the category field to be updated.

**Test 40: defined on Pg. 285 and implemented on Pg. 285**

Telling the logical layer to update and providing it with data that indicates a category change results in the GUI layer being given a new set of movies with that change reflected.

**Test 41: defined on Pg. 285 and implemented on Pg. 286**

Selecting a movie from the list, changing the value of the category, and pressing Update updates the data for that movie. When that movie is selected again, the new category is displayed.

**Test 42: defined on Pg. 289 and implemented on Pg. 290**

Requesting a sublist filtered on a specific category answers a list containing all movies of that category, and only those movies.

**Test 43: defined on Pg. 292 and implemented on Pg. 293**

Asking for a subset for the ALL category answers the original list.

**Test 44: defined on Pg. 293 and implemented on Pg. 295**

When the logical layer is told to filter on a specific category, the presentation layer is given a new list to display containing movies for the specified category.

**Test 45: defined on Pg. 293 and implemented on Pg. 296**

Telling the logical layer to select a specific movie in a filtered list rather than the complete list from actually selects the appropriate movie, in spite of being selected from a sublist.

**Test 46: defined on Pg. 293 and implemented on Pg. 297**

Telling the logical layer to update a specific movie in a filtered list rather than from the complete list actually updates the appropriate movie properly.

**Test 47: defined on Pg. 294 and implemented on Pg. 298**

A rename performed in the context of the logical layer is done in the underlying full list; that is, potential duplicates in the full list are detected.

**Test 48: defined on Pg. 294 and implemented on Pg. 299**

Selecting a category to filter on in the GUI causes the displayed list of movies to update accordingly.

**Test 49: defined on Pg. 300 and implemented on Pg. 301**

Changing the category of a movie in a filtered list causes that movie to be removed from the list. If that category is filtered on, that movie will be in the list.

**Test 50: defined on Pg. 309 and implemented on Pg. 309**

Writing an empty list to a stream writes nothing.

**Test 51: defined on Pg. 309 and implemented on Pg. 310**

Writing a list of one movie should write that movie to the stream in the format <name> | <category> | <rating>.

**Test 52: defined on Pg. 309 and implemented on Pg. 312**

Writing a list containing several movies writes each movie to the stream, one per line, in the format of the previous test.

**Test 53: defined on Pg. 313 and implemented on Pg. 313**

Telling the logical layer to "save–as" causes it to ask the presentation layer to specify a file into which it writes the movie list.

**Test 54: defined on Pg. 313 and implemented on Pg. 316**

Selecting "Save As" from the "File" menu prompts for a file using the standard file chooser. The list is written into the selected file.

**Test 55: defined on Pg. 313 and implemented on Pg. 321**

If the file selection is cancelled, nothing is written to any file.

**Test 56: defined on Pg. 322 and implemented on Pg. 322**

Telling the logical layer to "Save" causes it to save the current list to the same file as the previous "Save As" operation.

**Test 57: defined on Pg. 322 and implemented on Pg. 325**

Selecting "Save" from the "File" menu causes the list to be written into the previously selected file.

**Test 58: defined on Pg. 329 and implemented on Pg. 329**

Reading from an empty stream results in an empty list of movies.

**Test 59: defined on Pg. 329 and implemented on Pg. 330**

Reading from a stream containing the data for a single movie results in a list containing the single movie.

**Test 60: defined on Pg. 329 and implemented on Pg. 332**

Reading from a stream containing the data for several movies results in a list containing those movies.

**Test 61: defined on Pg. 333 and implemented on Pg. 333**

With the list empty, telling the logical layer to load from a file that contains data for a set of movies results in the list containing those movies.

**Test 62: defined on Pg. 333 and implemented on Pg. 335**

Choosing "Load" from the "File" menu and selecting a file containing a specific set of movie data causes the corresponding movies to be placed in the list.

**Test 63: defined on Pg. 333 and implemented on Pg. 336**

With a set of movies loaded, cancelling the load of a different set leaves the originally loaded set unchanged.

**Test 64: defined on Pg. 339 and implemented on Pg. 340**

Comparing two movies with the same name, based on name, should answer 0.

**Test 65: defined on Pg. 339 and implemented on Pg. 340**

Comparing two movies, the first having a lexically smaller name, based on name, should answer a negative integer.

**Test 66: defined on Pg. 339 and implemented on Pg. 341**

Comparing two movies, the first having a lexically greater name, based on name, should answer a positive integer.

**Test 67: defined on Pg. 339 and implemented on Pg. 342**

Comparing two movies with the same rating, based on rating, should answer 0.

**Test 68: defined on Pg. 339 and implemented on Pg. 342**

Comparing two movies, the first having a lower rating, based on rating, should answer a negative integer.

**Test 69: defined on Pg. 339 and implemented on Pg. 342**

Comparing two movies, the first having a higher rating, based on rating, should answer a positive integer.

**Test 70: defined on Pg. 339 and implemented on Pg. 342**

For the purposes of comparison, an unrated movie always has a lower rating.

**Test 71: defined on Pg. 343 and implemented on Pg. 343**

Sorting an empty list has no effect on it.

**Test 72: defined on Pg. 343 and implemented on Pg. 344**

Sorting a list, by name, that is already sorted has no effect on it.

**Test 73: defined on Pg. 343 and implemented on Pg. 345**

Sorting a list, by name, that is in reverse order puts it in order.

**Test 74: defined on Pg. 343 and implemented on Pg. 347**

Sorting a list, by rating, that is already sorted has no effect on it.

**Test 75: defined on Pg. 343 and implemented on Pg. 347**

Sorting a list, by rating, that is in reverse order puts it in order.

**Test 76: defined on Pg. 343 and implemented on Pg. 347**

Sorting a list, by rating, that has duplicates puts it in order; the duplicates being in their original order relative to one another.

**Test 77: defined on Pg. 343 and implemented on Pg. 348**

Sorting a randomly ordered list by name puts it in order, by name.

**Test 78: defined on Pg. 343 and implemented on Pg. 348**

Sorting a randomly ordered list by rating puts it in order, by name.

**Test 79: defined on Pg. 349 and implemented on Pg. 349**

Asking the logical layer to sort its list causes the associated view's list to be updated to one that is in order (order depends on what is being sorted on).

**Test 80: defined on Pg. 350 and implemented on Pg. 351**

Selecting "Sort by name" from the "View" menu causes the displayed list to be sorted by name.

**Test 81: defined on Pg. 350 and implemented on Pg. 352**

Selecting "Sort by rating" from the "View" menu causes the displayed list to be sorted by rating.

**Test 82: defined on Pg. 355 and implemented on Pg. 356**

Constructing a Movie with no arguments creates an unrated Movie.

**Test 83: defined on Pg. 355 and implemented on Pg. 356**

Add a single rating to an unrated movie. Asking for the average rating answers the rating just added.

**Test 84: defined on Pg. 355 and implemented on Pg. 357**

Add several ratings: 3, 5, and 4. Asking for the average rating answers 4.

**Test 85: defined on Pg. 355 and implemented on Pg. 358**

Add several ratings: 3, 5, 5, and 3. Asking for the average rating answers 4.

**Test 86: defined on Pg. 355 and implemented on Pg. 360**

Writing movies uses for format: <name> | <category> | <total rating> | <number of ratings>.

**Test 87: defined on Pg. 355 and implemented on Pg. 361**

Reading movies uses for format: <name> | <category> | <total rating> | <number of ratings>.

**Test 88: defined on Pg. 362 and implemented on Pg. 362**

A rating without a specified source should be anonymous.

**Test 89: defined on Pg. 362 and implemented on Pg. 366**

If we add a rating with a source to a movie, we should be able to later retrieve the source associated with the rating.

**Test 90: defined on Pg. 370 and implemented on Pg. 371**

Writing an empty list outputs an empty <movielist> pair.

**Test 91: defined on Pg. 370 and implemented on Pg. 372**

Writing a list containing one movie outputs in the adopted XML format.

**Test 92: defined on Pg. 370 and implemented on Pg. 375**

Writing a list containing one movie with multiple ratings outputs in the adopted XML format.

## SUMMARY

In this chapter we've taken a step back and had a look at the project we just did. We generated a class diagram, collected some metrics, and analyzed the quality and coverage of our tests. Our code fared well. What does this indicate? Are we especially good programmers? Maybe. It's nice to think so. However, most of the credit goes to how we worked. Test-Driven Development makes us work in small steps. This focuses us on one small problem at a time. This in turn allows us to design and code the simplest solution that we can find. This keeps our design simple. Constant refactoring keeps the combination of each *simplest* design decision as simple as possible. These techniques let us evolve a simple, clean, yet wonderfully expressive design. Furthermore, the design evolves very quickly and has an incredibly high level of quality.

# Part IV

# XUNIT FAMILY MEMBERS

Up to this point we have focused exclusively on Java. In this part of the book we take a moment to look briefly at some of the other members of the xUnit family. There are too many now to all be considered, so we will discuss only those most relevant to today's programmer.

The ordering of these chapters is arbitrary, as they are all mutually independent. The structure of each chapter is the same. We start by looking at architectural and API issues specific to the family member. The bulk of each chapter works through the same task using the language of the chapter.

Any special tricks or techniques available or applicable to each language are discussed as we go.

The task we'll use is the first task of the first story in the example project:

Make a container for movies with a way to add to it. Doesn't have to be ordered or sorted.

To implement this we'll need these tests:

**Test 1.** An empty list should have a size of zero.

**Test 2.** Adding a movie to an empty list should result in a list with a size of one.

**Test 3.** If we add a movie to a list, we should be able to ask if it's there and receive a positive response.

**Test 4.** Asking about the presence of a movie that wasn't added should result in a negative response.

In Chapter 26, the chapter on Visual Basic (it being a different sort of beast), Kay takes a slightly different approach. As in most cases, the differences are themselves instructive.

# Chapter 21

# **RUBYUNIT**

This chapter presents RubyUnit, the xUnit family member for the increasingly popular Ruby Programming language. The examples in this chapter are written using Ruby 1.6.7.

## THE FRAMEWORK

You can download RubyUnit from [URL 46]. RubyUnit includes all the expected asserts, such as:

**assert(boolean)**

**assert_equal(expected, actual)**

**assert_not_nil(object)**

As well, there are some Ruby-specific assertions, for example:

**assert_respond_to(method, object)** asserts that the **object** responds to **method**.

**assert_match(string, regex)** asserts that **string** matches against the regular expression regex.

All assertions take an optional final message parameter.

In addition to having to **require** the classes being tested, test case classes must include the following:

```
require "runit/testcase"
require "runit/cui/testrunner"
require "runit/testsuite"
```

Additionally, our test case must extend **RUNIT::TestCase**. A useful idiom is to use a template similar to the following for test cases. As when using JUnit, this allows the test case class to be run in order to run its tests. Here's the template:

```
require "runit/testcase"
require "runit/cui/testrunner"
require "runit/testsuite"

class TestSomething < RUNIT::TestCase

  RUNIT::CUI::TestRunner.run(TestSomething.suite)
end
```

## EXAMPLE

## Test 1: An empty list should have a size of zero.

```
class TestMovieList < RUNIT::TestCase
  def testEmptyListSize
    @list = MovieList.new
    assert_equal(0, @list.size)
  end
end


class MovieList
end
```

This fails with:

```
TestMovieList#test_empty_movielist F.
Time: 0.00403
FAILURES!!!
Test Results:
 Run: 1/1(1 asserts) Failures: 1 Errors: 0
Failures: 1
TestMovieList.rb:10:in 'test_empty_movielist'(TestMovieList):
  expected:<0> but was:<nil> (RUNIT::AssertionFailedError)
        from TestMovieList.rb:13
```

Now we need to fake it:

```
class MovieList
  def size
    0
  end
end
```

Green.

## Test 2: Adding a movie to an empty list should result in a list with a size of one.

The next test is:

```
def testOneMovieListSize
  @list = MovieList.new
  @starWars = Movie.new("Star Wars")
  @list.add(@starWars)
  assert_equal(1, @list.size)
end
```

This requires that we create a stub Movie class:

```
class Movie
  def initialize(aName)
  end
end
```

We also need to stub an **add** method for MovieList:

```
def add (movieToAdd)
end
```

We run the test and it fails because we've faked MovieList.size() to return 0. Now we can fake it one step better by counting the number of movies that are *added*:

```
class MovieList
  def initialize
    @numberOfMovies = 0
  end

  def size
    @numberOfMovies
  end

  def add (movieToAdd)
    @numberOfMovies += 1
  end
end
```

Our tests pass and there isn't anything in MovieList to clean up.

## Test 3: If we add a movie to a list, we should be able to ask if it's there and receive a positive response.

This test should verify that the movie that was added is really there; again we'll fake it at first:

```
def testOneMovieListContains
  @list = MovieList.new
  @starWars = Movie.new("Star Wars")
  @list.add(@starWars)
  assert(@list.containsMovieNamed?("Star Wars"))
end
```

We next need a stub containsMovieNamed? method in MovieList that fakes it for the purposes of this test:

```
def containsMovieNamed? (aName)
  true
end
```

OK, now we have some duplication in TestMovieList. The methods testOneMovieList-Size and testOneMovieListContents have a common fixture that should be extracted. But wait, what about the fixture for testEmptyListSize? It's different than the fixture used by the other tests. We not only need to extract the fixtures, but we also need to split the test case in two. Here's the result:

```ruby
class TestEmptyMovieList < RUNIT::TestCase
  def setup
    @list = MovieList.new
  end

  def testSize
    assert_equal(0, @list.size)
  end

  RUNIT::CUI::TestRunner.run(TestEmptyMovieList.suite)
end
class TestOneItemMovieList < RUNIT::TestCase
  def setup
    @list = MovieList.new
    @starWars = Movie.new("Star Wars")
    @list.add(@starWars)
  end

  def testSize
    assert_equal(1, @list.size)
  end

  def testContains
    assert(@list.containsMovieNamed?("Star Wars"))
  end

  RUNIT::CUI::TestRunner.run(TestOneItemMovieList.suite)
end
```

Notice how we've renamed the test methods when we refactored to remove the fixture-related prefix. Having a prefix like that is a good indication that we're mixing fixtures.

## Test 4: Asking about the presence of a movie that wasn't added should result in a negative response.

Now we need to test that a movie that we didn't add is, in fact, not reported as being in the list:

```ruby
def testDoesNotContain
  assert(!@list.containsMovieNamed?("Star Trek"))
end
```

This test drives us to move from fake to make in terms of keeping track of what movies have been added to the list:

```ruby
class MovieList
  def initialize
    @movies = Hash.new
    @numberOfMovies = 0
  end

  def size
    @numberOfMovies
  end

  def add (movieToAdd)
    @movies.store(movieToAdd.name, movieToAdd)
    @numberOfMovies += 1
  end

  def containsMovieNamed? (aName)
    @movies.include?(aName)
  end
end
```

We also need to extend Movie to retain its name:

```ruby
class Movie
  attr_reader :name

  def initialize(aName)
    @name = aName
  end
end
```

As you can see, we are now duplicating the information about how many movies have been added. We keep track of it explicitly (as before) and it is also available as an attribute of the Hash. To remove it, we first change size to return the information fetched from the Hash:

```ruby
def size
  @movies.size
end
```

The tests still pass, so we can remove all of the code related to explicitly counting how many movies have been added. Now MovieList is:

```ruby
class MovieList
  def initialize
    @movies = Hash.new
  end

  def size
    @movies.size
  end
```

☞

```ruby
    def add (movieToAdd)
      @movies.store(movieToAdd.name, movieToAdd)
    end

    def containsMovieNamed? (aName)
      @movies.include?(aName)
    end
  end
```

# Chapter 22

# SUNIT

This chapter presents SUnit, the xUnit family member for the Smalltalk programming language. SUnit is the granddaddy of xUnit family. It was first described by Beck in [7]. The example in this chapter uses VisualWorks Smalltalk 7 from Cincom. However, I avoided doing any GUI work, so this code should run (with possible minor tweaks) on any Smalltalk system.

## THE FRAMEWORK

The SUnit framework is included in the recent releases of VisualWorks Smalltalk [URL 43], Squeak [URL 44], and probably others that I'm not as familiar with. Versions for other varieties of Smalltalk can be found at the `xprogramming.com` Web site [URL 11].

This framework takes advantage of Smalltalk's blocks to simplify the assertion mechanism. There are several assertion calls which we will briefly list here.

## BOOLEAN ASSERTIONS

**assert: aBoolean** asserts that aBoolean is true.

**deny: aBoolean** asserts that aBoolean is false.

## BLOCK ASSERTIONS

**should: aBlock** asserts that aBlock value evaluates to true.

**shouldnt: aBlock** asserts that aBlock value evaluates to false.

## EXCEPTION ASSERTIONS

**should: aBlock raise: anExceptionalEvent** asserts that executing aBlock signals an exception identified by anExceptionalEvent. Not signaling an exception, or signaling a different exception, causes this assertion to fail.

**shouldnt: aBlock raise: anExceptionalEvent** the logical opposite of should: aBlock raise: anExceptionalEvent.

## FAILURE

**signalFailure: aString** fails immediately, providing aString as a message.

## EXAMPLE

### Test 1: An empty list should have a size of zero.

```
Smalltalk.Saorsa defineClass: #TestMovieList
  superclass: #{XProgramming.SUnit.TestCase}
  indexedType: #none
  private: false
  instanceVariableNames: 'emptyList'
  classInstanceVariableNames: ''
  imports: ''
  category: 'Saorsa'

setUp
  emptyList := MovieList new

testEmptyListSize
  self should: [emptyList size = 0]
```

When we try to accept the test method, it complains that MovieList is undefined. We define it as a stub class with nothing in it:

```
Smalltalk.Saorsa defineClass: #MovieList
  superclass: #{Core.Object}
  indexedType: #none
  private: false
  instanceVariableNames: ''
  classInstanceVariableNames: ''
  imports: ''
  category: 'Saorsa'
```

Now testEmptyListSize is accepted. When we run the test, it passes. Why? We haven't even written the size method for MovieList.

**When using methods with a common name (like size) be careful of inherited methods.**

The problem is that size is a method in Object from which we inherit. This is the Smalltalk way. Let's write a stub size method with no body and try the test again. OK. Our test now fails. Now we can write a bit of code to pass the test:

```
MovieList>>size
  ^0
```

Accept, test, green. Onward.

### Test 2: Adding a movie to an empty list should result in a list with a size of one.

This test adds one item to the list and checks that this size returns 1. This is a different fixture (i.e., not an empty list), so we start a new TestCase:

```
Smalltalk defineClass: #TestOneItemList
    superclass: #{XProgramming.SUnit.TestCase}
    indexedType: #none
    private: false
    instanceVariableNames: 'theList '
    classInstanceVariableNames: ' '
    imports: ' '
    category: 'Saorsa'


setUp
    theList := MovieList new.
    theList add: (Movie name: 'Star Wars')

testSize
    self should: [theList size = 1]
```

To get this to accept we need to define the class **Movie**:

```
Smalltalk.Saorsa defineClass: #Movie
    superclass: #{Core.Object}
    indexedType: #none
    private: false
    instanceVariableNames: ' '
    classInstanceVariableNames: ' '
    imports: ' '
    category: 'NowPlaying'


class name: aString
    ^self basicNew
       name: aString

name: aString
```

Running the tests now results in **TestOneItemList>>testSize** failing with an error because the method **MovieList>>add:** isn't understood (i.e., is undefined). We create a stub and now it fails with an assertion failure since everything runs, but we aren't really doing anything yet. This is the state we want to be in for the red bar. Now we can write some code to get the green bar back. We start by capturing the fact that a movie was added:

```
MovieList>>add: aMovie
    numberOfMovies := numberOfMovies + 1
```

To do this we need to add an instance variable to the class definition:

```
Smalltalk.Saorsa defineClass: #MovieList
  superclass: #{Core.Object}
  indexedType: #none
  private: false
  instanceVariableNames: 'numberOfMovies '
  classInstanceVariableNames: ' '
  imports: ' '
  category: 'NowPlaying'
```

Finally, we need to return that variable from size:

```
MovieList>>size
  ^numberOfMovies
```

Now TestOneItemList>>testSize passes, but TestEmptyList>>testSize fails. Why is that? Because we aren't initializing numberOfMovies to 0.

**In Smalltalk, uninitialized variables have the value nil.**

To fix this, we can add an explicit creation method (this is a class method):

```
MovieList class>>new
  ^self basicNew init
```

and an initialization method (an instance method):

```
MovieList>>init
  numberOfMovies := 0
```

With these two methods in place, we get a green bar.

## Test 3: If we add a movie to a list, we should be able to ask if it's there and receive a positive response.

The next test checks that any movies that are added are reported as being in the list:

```
TestOneItemList>>testContains
  self should: [theList containsMovieNamed: 'Star Wars']
```

For this to work, we need a containsMovieNamed: method in MovieList. We can start off by faking it:

```
containsMovieNamed: aString
  ^true
```

This makes the test pass. Now we need to test a counter-example.

## Test 4: Asking about the presence of a movie that wasn't added should result in a negative response.

```
testDoesNotContain
    self shouldnt: [theList containsMovieNamed: 'Star Trek']
```

This test drives us to add the ability to remember what movies have been added to the list. Let's take a bigger step and add a collection to hold onto them:

```
Smalltalk defineClass: #MovieList
    superclass: #{Core.Object}
    indexedType: #none
    private: false
    instanceVariableNames: 'numberOfMovies movies '
    classInstanceVariableNames: ' '
    imports: ' '
    category: 'Saorsa'

init
    numberOfMovies := 0.
    movies := Dictionary new

add: aMovie
    numberOfMovies := numberOfMovies + 1.
    movies at: aMovie name put: aMovie

size
    ^numberOfMovies

containsMovieNamed: aString
    ^movies includesKey: aString
```

If we run the tests now, they all fail (with an error) because Movie doesn't understand name. Further, Movie isn't storing its name. That's easy enough to fix:

```
Smalltalk defineClass: #Movie
    superclass: #{Core.Object}
    indexedType: #none
    private: false
    instanceVariableNames: 'name '
    classInstanceVariableNames: ' '
    imports: ' '
    category: 'Saorsa'

name
    ^name

name: aString
    name := aString
```

There, green. Now we have a little refactoring to do. We're keeping an explicit count of how many movies have been added, but this information is available from the collection of movies. The first step is to return the size of the collection:

```
MovieList>>size
  ^movies size
```

All tests still pass. Now we can go through MovieList and remove all references to numberOfMovies. The result is:

```
Smalltalk defineClass: #MovieList
  superclass: #{Core.Object}
  indexedType: #none
  private: false
  instanceVariableNames: 'movies '
  classInstanceVariableNames: ''
  imports: ''
  category: 'Saorsa'

init
  movies := Dictionary new

size
  ^movies size

add: aMovie
  movies at: aMovie name put: aMovie

containsMovieNamed: aString
  ^movies includesKey: aString
```

# Chapter 23

# CPPUNIT

This chapter presents CppUnit, the xUnit family member for the C++. The examples in this chapter are written using G++ 2.96 and CppUnit 1.8.0.

## THE FRAMEWORK

You can download CppUnit from [URL 48]. CppUnit has quite a different feel to it from the xUnit members we've looked at so far. This is largely due to the fact that C++, being compiled to native code, does not support reflection. This means that we have to do all the work ourselves. Instead of being able to have the test case class figure out what the tests are, we have to do it ourselves, like so:

```
void TestOneItemList::registerTests(TestSuite *suite)
{
  suite->addTest(new TestCaller<TestOneItemList>(
                          "testSize",
                          &TestOneItemList::testSize,
                          *this));
  suite->addTest(new TestCaller<TestOneItemList>(
                          "testContains",
                          &TestOneItemList::testContains,
                          *this));
  suite->addTest(new TestCaller<TestOneItemList>(
                          "testDoesNotContain",
                          &TestOneItemList::testDoesNotContain,
                          *this));
}
```

Assertions are also handled differently. In this case, they are implemented as macros:

```
CPPUNIT_ASSERT(condition)
CPPUNIT_ASSERT_MESSAGE(message, condition)
CPPUNIT_FAIL(message)
CPPUNIT_ASSERT_EQUAL(expected, actual)
CPPUNIT_ASSERT_EQUAL_MESSAGE(message, expected, actual)
CPPUNIT_ASSERT_DOUBLES_EQUAL(expected, actual, delta)
```

This isn't the most elegant looking solution, but it does have the beneficial effect that assertions are visually obvious.

# EXAMPLE

## Test 1: An empty list should have a size of zero.

We'll start with the test for an empty list:

```cpp
class TestEmptyMovieList : public CppUnit::TestCase {
private:
  MovieList *theList;

public:
  TestEmptyMovieList(std::string name);
  virtual void registerTests(TestSuite *suite);
  void setUp();
  void testSize();
};
TestEmptyMovieList::TestEmptyMovieList(std::string name)
  : CppUnit::TestCase(name)
{
}
void TestEmptyMovieList::registerTests(TestSuite *suite)
{
  suite->addTest(new TestCaller<TestEmptyMovieList>(
                                "testSize",
                                &TestEmptyMovieList::testSize,
                                *this));
}
void TestEmptyMovieList::setUp()
{
  theList = new MovieList();
}
void TestEmptyMovieList::testSize()
{
  CPPUNIT_ASSERT_EQUAL_MESSAGE("Empty list should be empty",
                                0,
                                emptyList->size());
}
```

Here's the stub we need to compile:

```cpp
class MovieList {
public:
  MovieList();
  int size();
};

MovieList::MovieList() {
}
```

```
int MovieList::size() {
  return 0;
}
```

This passes because our stub implementation of MovieList::size() returns 0 to keep the compiler happy.

## Test 2: Adding a movie to an empty list should result in a list with a size of one.

This test will add a movie and verify that the size is now 1. As in earlier chapters, we'll move to a new fixture for this:

```
class TestOneItemList : public CppUnit::TestCase {
 private:
  MovieList *theList;

 public:
  TestOneItemList(std::string name);
  virtual void registerTests(TestSuite *suite);
  void setUp();
  void testSize();
};

TestOneItemList::TestOneItemList(std::string name)
  : CppUnit::TestCase(name)
{
}

void TestOneItemList::registerTests(TestSuite *suite)
{
  suite->addTest(new TestCaller<TestOneItemList>("testSize",
                                              &TestOneItemList::testSize,
                                              *this));
}

void TestOneItemList::setUp()
{
  theList = new MovieList();
  Movie starWars("Star Wars");
  theList->add(starWars);
}

void TestOneItemList::testSize()
{
  CPPUNIT_ASSERT_EQUAL_MESSAGE("One item list should have one item",
                                1,
                                theList->size());
}
```

This requires that we create a stub Movie class:

```
class Movie {
 public:
  Movie(std::string aName);
};
```

```
Movie::Movie(std::string aName)
{
}
```

We also need to stub an **add** method for MovieList:

```
void MovieList::add(Movie movie)
{
}
```

This now compiles and fails with:

```
.F

!!!FAILURES!!!
Test Results:
Run: 1    Failures: 1    Errors: 0

1) test: testSize (F) line: 27 TestOneItemList.cpp
expected: 1
but was:  0
additional message:
One item list should have one item
```

Now we can fake it one step better by counting the number of movies that are *added*:

```
class MovieList {
 private:
  int numberOfMovies;

  public:
   MovieList();
   int size();
   void add(Movie aMovie);
};

MovieList::MovieList() {
  numberOfMovies = 0;
}

int MovieList::size() {
  return numberOfMovies;
}

void MovieList::add(Movie movie)
{
  numberOfMovies++;
}
```

Our tests pass and there isn't anything in MovieList to clean up.

## Test 3: If we add a movie to a list, we should be able to ask if it's there and receive a positive response.

Our next test should verify that the movie that was added is really there; again, we'll fake it at first:

```
void TestOneItemList::testContains()
{
  CPPUNIT_ASSERT_MESSAGE("Star Wars should be in the list.",
                         theList->containsMovieNamed("Star Wars"));
}
```

We next need a stub containsMovieNamed method in MovieList that fakes it for the purposes of this test:

```
bool MovieList::containsMovieNamed(std::string name)
{
  return true;
}
```

## Test 4: Asking about the presence of a movie that wasn't added should result in a negative response.

Now we need to test that a movie that we didn't add is, in fact, not reported as being in the list:

```
void TestOneItemList::testDoesNotContain()
{
  CPPUNIT_ASSERT_MESSAGE("Star Trek should not be in the list.",
                         !theList->containsMovieNamed("Star Trek"));
}
```

This, of course, fails with:

```
...F

!!!FAILURES!!!
Test Results:
Run:  3   Failures: 1   Errors: 0

1) test: testDoesNotContain (F) line: 39 TestOneItemList.cpp
  "Star Trek should not be in the list."
```

This test drives us to move from fake to make in terms of keeping track of what movies have been added to the list:

```
class MovieList {
 private:
  int numberOfMovies;
  map<std::string, Movie> movies;
```

```
  public:
   MovieList();
   int size();
   void add(Movie aMovie);
   bool containsMovieNamed(std::string name);
};
MovieList::MovieList() {
  numberOfMovies = 0;
}
int MovieList::size() {
  return numberOfMovies;
}
void MovieList::add(Movie movie)
{
  numberOfMovies++;
  movies[movie.getName()] = movie;
}
bool MovieList::containsMovieNamed(std::string name)
{
  map<std::string, Movie>::iterator result = movies.find(name);
  return result != movies.end();
}
```

We also need to extend Movie to retain its name (and add a default constructor to satisfy the requirements of map):

```
class Movie {
 private:
  std::string name;

 public:
  Movie();
  Movie(std::string aName);
  std::string getName();
};
Movie::Movie()
{
  name = "";
}
Movie::Movie(std::string aName)
{
  name = aName;
}
std::string Movie::getName()
{
  return name;
}
```

As you can see, we are now duplicating the information about how many movies have been added. We keep track of it explicitly (as before) and it is also available as an attribute of the map. To remove it, we first change size to return the information fetched from the map:

```
int MovieList::size() {
  return movies.size();
}
```

The tests still pass, so we can remove all of the code related to explicitly counting how many movies have been added. Now MovieList is:

```
class MovieList {
private:
  map<std::string, Movie> movies;

public:
  MovieList();
  int size();
  void add(Movie aMovie);
  bool containsMovieNamed(std::string name);
};
MovieList::MovieList() {
}
int MovieList::size() {
  return movies.size();
}
void MovieList::add(Movie movie)
{
  movies[movie.getName()] = movie;
}
bool MovieList::containsMovieNamed(std::string name)
{
  map<std::string, Movie>::iterator result = movies.find(name);
  return result != movies.end();
}
```

# Chapter 24

# NUNIT

WITH JAMES NEWKIRK

This chapter presents NUnit, an xUnit family member for the Microsoft .NET framework. I had the good fortune to cross paths with James as I was thinking about this chapter. I had a few questions about NUnit which I asked James, explaining my reasons. He responded and kindly offered to write and contribute the chapter. So, here's the chapter on NUnit, by one of its authors.

One thing to note: While C# and .NET are Microsoft creations, there is an open source implementation (that is progressing nicely) from Ximian, the folks behind Gnome. It's named *The Mono Project* and can be found at [URL 66].

## THE FRAMEWORK

The example is written using V1.0 of the .NET Framework and V2.0 of NUnit. See [URL 52] for the site from which NUnit can be downloaded.

### History

NUnit V1.x was written by Philip Craig in the summer of 2000. Philip released an early version in September of 2000 and was keeping the program up to date with each new version of the .NET Framework as they were being released. In February of 2002 a small group gathered to develop a new version of NUnit, one that looked less like JUnit and tried to leverage some of the capabilities of the .NET platform. The group consisted of Alexei Vorontsov, Mike Two, and James Newkirk. The one feature in .NET that we focused on was attributes. Attributes are descriptive elements that provide information about programming elements such as types, fields, methods, and properties that can be retrieved via reflection at runtime. Looking at JUnit, we saw areas where naming conventions and inheritance were used to identify test fixtures and test methods and thought that attributes provided a cleaner and more explicit approach to the same problems. This group released NUnit V2.0 in October of 2002.

### TestFixture

In order to write your first test in NUnit, you must create a class that is marked with the [TestFixture] attribute. The attribute definition is contained in an assembly called `nunit.framework.dll`. Also, you must provide a using statement that identifies the NUnit classes which are contained in the **NUnit.Framework** namespace. One thing to note is that the only requirement for the class is that it has a default constructor which means that you can place the [TestFixture] attribute on any class and it does not have to use inheritance.

```
using System;
using NUnit.Framework;

[TestFixture]
public class Something
{}
```

## Test

A test method in NUnit must be a method that is public, returns void, and has no parameters. It must also be marked with the [Test] attribute and be in a class marked with a [TestFixture] attribute.

```
[Test]
public void BlueSky()
{}
```

## SetUp

NUnit, like many xUnit implementations, has a way to allow the programmer to extract common fixture setup code and have it executed prior to each test being run.

A method can be marked with the custom attribute [SetUp] to identify it as the method that NUnit will use to build the fixture for the tests in this TestFixture. This allows for common code to be removed from the individual tests.

```
[SetUp]
public void CreateList()
{
   list = new MovieList();
}
```

## Assertion

The NUnit framework, like other xUnit frameworks, comes with the normal set of expected assertions. Since inheritance is not used to identify the test fixtures, the assertions in NUnit are static methods of a class called Assertion. This class is also defined in the NUnit.Framework namespace. The following is a sample of assert methods contained in the framework (see the class Assertion for the complete set):

```
Assertion.AssertEquals(object expected, object actual)
Assertion.Assert(boolean)
Assertion.AssertNotNull(object)
```

All of the assertion methods also take an initial parameter, which is a message that will be printed if there is a failure.

## EXAMPLE

The task is to write a class that contains a list of movies. The list should be able to determine if certain movies are in the list and it should also be able to tell you the number of movies contained in the list.

### Test 1: An empty list should have a size of zero.

We'll start by creating a test fixture to hold all of the tests called **TestMovieList**. The name of the method that will create the list and test to see if the count of movies is equal to 0 is called **EmptyList**. As you can see here they are each marked with their respective attributes.

```
using System;
using NUnit.Framework;

[TestFixture]
public class TestMovieList
{

  [Test]
  public void EmptyList()
  {
    MovieList list = new MovieList();
    Assertion.AssertEquals(0, list.Count);
  }
}
```

When I compile this test it fails since we have yet to implement the **MovieList** class. The simplest version of **MovieList** that is needed to get this to compile is as follows:

```
using System;

public class MovieList
{
  public int Count
  {
    get { return 0; }
  }
}
```

Compiling and running this yields a green bar. The first step is done. Let's go on to the next test.

### Test 2: Adding a movie to an empty list should result in a list with a size of one.

The test for this step is also in the **TestMovieList** fixture and looks like this:

```
[Test]
public void OneMovieList()
{
  MovieList list = new MovieList();
  Movie starWars = new Movie("Star Wars");
  list.Add(starWars);
  Assertion.AssertEquals(1, list.Count);
}
```

When I compile this it fails for a couple of reasons. First, I have not defined a class called **Movie** and I have not defined a method in **MovieList** called **Add**. Let's go ahead and implement them, keeping in mind the goal here is to get this test to pass, nothing else.

The simplest version of **Movie** that is needed to get this to compile is as follows:

```
using System;

public class Movie
{
  public Movie(string title)
    {}
}
```

Nothing else is needed. Remember, you need to focus on what is needed now, not in the future. Obviously, the **Movie** class is nothing more than a placeholder at this point. We also need to implement the **Add** method in **MovieList**. At first, I choose to implement **Add** like the following:

```
public void Add(Movie movieToAdd)
{}
```

Compiling and running this yields a failure. Obviously, we have to implement **Add** for the test to pass. Since we only have tests that verify that the size of the list is correct, we can still fake it somewhat by keeping track of the number of movies that were added to the list and not the contents.

```
using System;

public class MovieList
{
  private int numberOfMovies;

  public MovieList()
  {
    numberOfMovies = 0;
  }
```

```
      public int Count
      {
        get { return numberOfMovies; }
      }

      public void Add(Movie movieToAdd)
      {
        numberOfMovies += 1;
      }
    }
```

Compiling and running this yields a green bar. However, there is some code duplication in the test code. Each test method creates a MovieList class. We can extract this commonality into a SetUp method. Performing this refactoring on TestMovieList looks like this:

```
using System;
using NUnit.Framework;

[TestFixture]
public class TestMovieList
{
  private MovieList list;

  [SetUp]
  public void CreateList()
  {
    list = new MovieList();
  }

  [Test]
  public void EmptyList()
  {
    Assertion.AssertEquals(0, list.Count);
  }

  [Test]
  public void OneMovieList()
  {
    Movie starWars = new Movie("Star Wars");
    list.Add(starWars);
    Assertion.AssertEquals(1, list.Count);
  }
}
```

Compiling and running this test yields a successful result and a scan of the code indicates that there is nothing else to refactor. It's time to move on to the next test.

## Test 3: If we add a movie to a list, we should be able to ask if it's there and receive a positive response.

The test method for this test is called OneMovieListContains and is defined as follows:

```
[Test]
public void OneMovieListContains()
{
  string title = "Star Wars";
  Movie starWars = new Movie(title);
  list.Add(starWars);
  Assertion.Assert(list.ContainsMovieNamed(title));
}
```

When this is compiled it fails due to MovieList not having implemented the method
ContainsMovieNamed. Implementing a stub to get the test to pass is simple and looks
like this:

```
public bool ContainsMovieNamed(string title)
{
  return true;
}
```

Compiling and running this yields a successful result. At this point, most people
question my judgment and wonder if this is just silly. Remember, we are not done with
the task; we are moving forward step-by-step doing just enough to get the tests to pass.
We will have tests in the future that expose that this implementation is naive, but I
intend to wait until the tests expose that naiveté instead of speculating about it.

Before we move on we have some more code duplication to correct in the test
code. Looking at the test code, we see that the OneMovieListContains and OneMovieList
methods have a common setup code. However, that setup code is different from the
EmptyList setup code. The way to correct this is to split the test class into two different
classes, one called TestEmptyMovieList and the other called TestOneMovieList. Once we
move the methods into their new classes they can also be renamed. Performing this
refactoring yields the following result:

```
using System;
using NUnit.Framework;

[TestFixture]
public class TestEmptyMovieList
{
  private MovieList list;
  [SetUp]
  public void CreateList()
  {
    list = new MovieList();
  }
  [Test]
  public void Count()
  {
    Assertion.AssertEquals(0, list.Count);
  }
}
```

```
[TestFixture]
public class TestOneItemMovieList
{
    private readonly static string title = "Star Wars";
    private MovieList list;

    [SetUp]
    public void CreateList()
    {
        list = new MovieList();
        Movie starWars = new Movie(title);
        list.Add(starWars);
    }

    [Test]
    public void Count()
    {
        Assertion.AssertEquals(1, list.Count);
    }

    [Test]
    public void Contains()
    {
        Assertion.Assert(list.ContainsMovieNamed(title));
    }
}
```

Once this refactoring is complete we compile and run; everything still works so we are finished with this step.

## Test 4: Asking about the presence of a movie that wasn't added should result in a negative response.

The last test that we outlined earlier is to verify that a movie is not in the list. The test method can be implemented in either test fixture classes. In this example, it is implemented in **TestOneMovieList** test fixture and is called **DoesNotContain**:

```
[Test]
public void DoesNotContain()
{
    Assertion.Assert(!list.ContainsMovieNamed("Star Trek"));
}
```

Compiling and running the test yields the following output from NUnit:

```
NUnit version 2.0.6
....F

Tests run: 4, Failures: 1, Not run: 0, Time: 0.0300432 seconds

Failures:
1) TestOneItemMovieList.DoesNotContain :
   at TestOneItemMovieList.DoesNotContain() in testmovielist.cs:line 51
```

This test informs us that the implementation of ContainsMovieNamed is not suffi-cient given the current tests. In order to get this test to pass we need to change the implementation of MovieList to save the Movie objects that are added so that the Con-tainsMovieNamed method can determine if they are in the list. A way to implement this is with a Hashtable from the System.Collections class in the .NET Framework.

```
using System;
using System.Collections;

public class MovieList
{
  private Hashtable movies;
  private int numberOfMovies;

  public MovieList()
  {
    movies = new Hashtable();
    numberOfMovies = 0;
  }

  public int Count
  {
    get { return numberOfMovies; }
  }

  public void Add(Movie movieToAdd)
  {
    movies.Add(movieToAdd.Name, movieToAdd);
    numberOfMovies += 1;
  }

  public bool ContainsMovieNamed(string title)
  {
    return movies.ContainsKey(title);
  }
}
```

Compiling this yields a compilation failure due to the property Name not being defined in the Movie class. It's finally time to add some functionality to the Movie class.

```
using System;
public class Movie
{
  private string title;
  public Movie(string title)
  {
    this.title = title;
  }
}
```

```
    public string Name
    {
      get { return title; }
    }
  }
```

Compiling and running this yields the familiar green bar. Upon further review, however, there is a smell that exists in the MovieList class. The Hashtable class can perform the function of keeping track of the number of elements so we do not need the numberOfMovies variable. Making this change to MovieList looks like this:

```
using System;
using System.Collections;

public class MovieList
{
  private Hashtable movies;
  public MovieList()
  {
    movies = new Hashtable();
  }
  public int Count
  {
    get { return movies.Count; }
  }
  public void Add(Movie movieToAdd)
  {
    movies.Add(movieToAdd.Name, movieToAdd);
  }
  public bool ContainsMovieNamed(string title)
  {
    return movies.ContainsKey(title);
  }
}
```

Doing this refactoring has simplified the code dramatically. Reviewing the existing code along with our to-do list indicates that we are finished with the task, so let's check it back into the repository and move on to the next task.

# Chapter 25

# PYUNIT

WITH BOB PAYNE

This chapter presents PyUnit, the xUnit framework for the Python programming language. Bob Payne is the president of Electroglide Inc., a small software development firm specializing in eXtreme Programming consulting, implementation, development, and training. He is the co-founder of the Washington D.C. XP users group, an active presenter at XP conferences, and an agitator for Agile Methodologies in general.

## THE FRAMEWORK

PyUnit (`unittest.py`) is a core module in current Python distributions. This example was coded using Python 2.2.2 on Windows, but should run unchanged on virtually any Python platform. Distributions and information on Python can be found at [URL 67]. Development of the framework is ongoing under the supervision of Steve Purcell at [URL 53]. If you are doing Web development there are several test frameworks that are similar to the HTTPUnit framework in Java; these include:

**Puffin** —An XML configurable Web application/service testing framework built in Python by Keyton Weissinger. Information on the Puffin framework is available at [URL 68].

**WebUnit** —WebUnit is a unit testing framework for testing Web applications in PyUnit tests. WebUnit was developed by Steve Purcell, the author of PyUnit. Information about WebUnit can be found at [URL 69].

PyUnit has all the standard xUnit asserts and provides some name mappings to allow the use of the logically equivalent asserts. The asserts and their logical equivalents are listed below with their parameter listings (msg parameter is for an optional message):

### Testing Equivalence

Equality tests are more liberal in Python than in Java. Python generally tests for value equivalence of built-in objects and utilizes the overloadable equivalence operator for other classes.

**failUnlessEqual(first, second, msg=None)** fails if the two objects are unequal as determined by the '!=' operator.

**assertEqual(first, second, msg=None)** and

**assertEquals(first, second, msg=None)** are logically equivalent to failUnlessEqual.

**failIfEqual(first, second, msg=None)** fails if the two objects are equal as determined
by the '==' operator.

**assertNotEqual(first, second, msg=None)** and

**assertNotEquals(first, second, msg=None)** are logically equivalent to failIfEqual.

## Testing Logical comparison

Test an expression to determine if it evaluates to **true** or **false**. This evaluation is much
more liberal in Python than in most other languages because Python evaluates non zero,
non empty, or non **None** (i.e., **null**) as true. This liberal interpretation of true allows
great flexibility in assertions but can lead to false positives if care is not taken. The
comparison operators **in** and **not in** check whether a value occurs (or does not occur)
in a sequence. The operators **is** and **is not** compare whether two objects are really the
same object.

**failIf(expr, msg=None)** fails the test if the expression is **true**.

**failUnless(expr, msg=None)** fails the test unless the expression is true assert _(expr,
msg=None); logically equivalent to failUnless.

## Testing Exceptions

PyUnit provides assertions to test exception handling in applications. These assertions
test if specific exceptions are or are not raised given the evaluation of a call to an object.
If a different type of exception is thrown, it will not be caught, and the test case will
be deemed to have suffered an error, exactly as for an unexpected exception.

**failUnlessRaises(excClass, callableObj, *args, **kwargs)** fails unless an exception of
class excClass is thrown by callableObj when invoked with arguments args and
keyword arguments kwargs.

**assertRaises(excClass, callableObj, *args, **kwargs)** is logically equivalent to failUn-
lessRaises.

## Automatic Failure

PyUnit also provides a fail() method to allow programmers to create unit tests that
leverage complex conditional blocks that would not easily map to the other assertion
structures.

**fail(msg=None)** fails immediately.

## Writing tests in PyUnit

Tests in PyUnit are collected in test methods on test objects. Each test method should
have one or more assertions in the body of the method and method names should begin
with "test". Test objects must import the unittest module, extend unittest.TestCase,
and their names should begin with "Test". Optional setUp() and tearDown() methods
on test objects are used to build a fixture and clean it up after each test method is run.

The simplest form of a test is shown here:

```
Import unittest

class TestMyTestObject (unittest.TestCase):

    def testEquivalenceTests(self):
        self.assertEquals('Bob', 'Bob')

if __name__ == '__main__':
    unittest.main()
```

Tests can be collected into test suites explicitly or through introspection. While each has its advantages, I find that utilizing introspection reduces the chance that a test will be missed. The above example utilizes one form of introspection by calling the unittest.main(). When the script is run, Python will look for all objects beginning with "Test" and add them to a test suite; in turn, each method beginning with "test" will be evaluated when each TestCase in the suite is run. Order of test execution cannot be guaranteed.

## EXAMPLE

We must now write our first failing test before we can code.

### Test 1: An empty list should have a size of zero.

```
import unittest
from movie.Movie import *

class TestMovieList(unittest.TestCase):

    def testZeroLengthMovieList(self):
        movieList = MovieList()
        self.assertEquals(movieList.getSize(),0)

if __name__ == '__main__':
    unittest.main()
```

The test fails with:

```
==================================================
ERROR: testZeroLengthMovieList (__main__.TestMovieList)
--------------------------------------------------
Traceback (most recent call last):
  File "c:\python22\lib\movie\TestMovie.py", line 7, in testZeroLengthMovieList
    movieList = MovieList()
NameError: global name 'MovieList' is not defined
--------------------------------------------------
Ran 1 tests in 0.000s

FAILED (errors=1)
```

Now we will do the simplest thing that will give us a passing test. We will stub out size in the movie object to return zero.

```
class MovieList:

    def getSize(self):
        return 0
```

Green bar—the test passes with:

```
------------------------------------------------------------------------
Ran 1 tests in 0.000s

OK
```

## Test 2: Adding a movie to an empty list should result in a list with a size of one.

It is now our responsibility to expand and test for other behaviors of the MovieList object. We have also refactored the test to remove redundancy of creating an instance of MovieList and cleaning up the setUp() and tearDown() methods of the test object.

```
class TestMovieList(unittest.TestCase):

    def setUp(self):
        self.movieList = MovieList()

    def testZeroLengthMovieList(self):
        self.assertEquals(self.movieList.getSize(),0)

    def testAddMovie(self):
        self.movieList.addMovie(Movie('Star Wars'))
        self.assertEquals(self.movieList.getSize(),1)

    def tearDown(self):
        self.movieList=None
```

Red bar—the test fails with:

```
==========================================
ERROR: testAddMovie (__main__.TestMovieList)
------------------------------------------------------------------------
Traceback (most recent call last):
  File "c:\python22\lib\movie\TestMovie.py", line 11, in testAddMovie
    self.movieList.addMovie(Movie('Star Wars'))
AttributeError: MovieList instance has no attribute 'addMovie'
------------------------------------------------------------------------
Ran 2 tests in 0.000s

FAILED (errors=1)
```

Stub out the addMovie(movie) method with a pass instruction. This method returns None when it is called and does nothing.

```
class MovieList:

    def getSize(self):
        return 0

    def addMovie(self, movie):
        pass
```

Red bar—Movie object is not defined; we must stub out a Movie class. Before we do this we need to add a testMovie class to test the behavior of a Movie and stub out Movie. This class only needs to retain its name for now, so that is the only behavior we will test for.

Add test class:

```
class testMovie(unittest.TestCase):

    def testMovie(self):
        movie=Movie('Star Wars')
        self.assertEquals(movie.name, 'Star Wars')
```

Create the code for the Movie class, a simple class with only a constructor method.

```
class Movie:
    def __init__ (self, name=None):
        self.name = name
```

Red bar—MovieList is still returning 0 for all getSize() requests:

```
==============================================
FAIL: testAddMovie (__main__.TestMovieList)
----------------------------------------------------------------------
Traceback (most recent call last):
  File "c:\python22\lib\movie\TestMovie.py", line 12, in testAddMovie
    self.assertEquals(self.movieList.getSize(),1)
  File "C:\Python22\Lib\unittest.py", line 273, in failUnlessEqual
    raise self.failureException, (msg or '%s != %s' % (first, second))
AssertionError: 0 != 1
----------------------------------------------------------------------
Ran 3 tests in 0.000s

FAILED (failures=1)
```

Modify MovieList to track the size. Yes, we know this is a stupid way to do it but we also know that first we will make it work and then we will make it elegant.

```
class MovieList:

    def __init__(self):
        self.size=0

    def getSize(self):
        return self.size

    def addMovie(self, movie):
        self.size += 1
```

Green bar—All three of our tests are running at 100 percent. We could now integrate our code with the main codebase depending on our check-in strategy. Now let's add tests for the functionality to see if a movie has already been added to the MovieList.

## Test 3: If we add a movie to a list, we should be able to ask if it's there and receive a positive response.

```
class TestMovieList(unittest.TestCase):

    def setUp(self):
        self.movieList = MovieList()

    def testZeroLengthMovieList(self):
        self.assertEquals(self.movieList.getSize(),0)

    def testAddMovie(self):
        self.movieList.addMovie(Movie('Star Wars'))
        self.assertEquals(self.movieList.getSize(),1)

    def testContainsMovie(self):
        self.movieList.addMovie(Movie('Star Wars'))
        self.failUnless(self.movieList.containsMovie('Star Wars'))

    def tearDown(self):
        self.movieList=None
```

Red bar—Stub out the functionality in MovieList by simply returning True when the containsMovie(name) method is called.

```
class MovieList:

    def __init__(self):
        self.size=0

    def getSize(self):
        return self.size

    def addMovie(self, movie):
        self.size += 1

    def containsMovie(self, name):
        return True
```

Green bar—All four of our tests pass. Refactor test objects to be a bit more modular. Notice that we pulled the test for zero length list into another test object and created and then added "Star Wars" to the list of movies. The methods setUp() and teardown() are called for each of the test method invocations in that class so we do not have to worry about test crosstalk in the object.

```
class TestZeroLengthMovieList(unittest.TestCase):

    def testZeroLengthMovieList(self):
        movieList = MovieList()
        self.assertEquals(movieList.getSize(),0)

class TestMovieList(unittest.TestCase):

    def setUp(self):
        self.movieList = MovieList()
        self.movieList.addMovie(Movie('Star Wars'))

    def testOneMovieList(self):
        self.assertEquals(self.movieList.getSize(),1)

    def testContainsMovie(self):
        self.failUnless(self.movieList.containsMovie('Star Wars'))

    def tearDown(self):
        self.movieList=None
```

Green bar—Now we must extend the test to express the true intent of the contains-Movie(name) method by testing to ensure that we get a false if the movie has not been added.

## Test 4: Asking about the presence of a movie that wasn't added should result in a negative response.

```
class TestMovieList(unittest.TestCase):

    def setUp(self):
        self.movieList = MovieList()
        self.movieList.addMovie(Movie('Star Wars'))

    def testOneMovieList(self):
        self.assertEquals(self.movieList.getSize(),1)

    def testContainsMovie(self):
        self.failUnless(self.movieList.containsMovie('Star Wars'))

    def testNotContainsMovie(self):
        self.failIf(self.movieList.containsMovie('Star Trek'))

    def tearDown(self):
        self.movieList=None
```

Red bar—Extend MovieList to check if a movie has been added:

```python
class MovieList:

    def __init__(self):
        self.size=0
        self.movies=[]

    def getSize(self):
        return self.size

    def addMovie(self, movie):
        self.size += 1
        self.movies.append(movie)

    def containsMovie(self, name):
        for movie in self.movies:
            if movie.name == name:
                return True
        return False
```

Green bar—All tests pass. We are done. Or are we? We still must refactor to make the implementation of our objects as clear as possible and remove any redundancy. Our MovieList class is using a counting scheme rather than checking the length of our internal movie list.

```python
class MovieList:

    def __init__(self):
        self.movies=[]

    def getSize(self):
        return len(self.movies)

    def addMovie(self, movie):
        self.movies.append(movie)

    def containsMovie(self, name):
        for movie in self.movies:
            if movie.name == name:
                return True
        return False
```

Green bar—Done. Let's be a bit more thorough and expand our tests to check if multiple movies in the list bother us.

```python
class TestMovieList(unittest.TestCase):

    def setUp(self):
        self.movieList = MovieList()
        self.movieList.addMovie(Movie('Star Wars'))
```

```
def testOneMovieList(self):
    self.assertEquals(self.movieList.getSize(),1)

def testContainsMovie(self):
    self.failUnless(self.movieList.containsMovie('Star Wars'))

def testNotContainsMovie(self):
    self.failIf(self.movieList.containsMovie('Star Trek'))

def testMultipleMoviesInList(self):
    self.assertEquals(self.movieList.getSize(),1)
    self.movieList.addMovie(Movie('Un Chien Andalou'))
    self.assertEquals(self.movieList.getSize(),2)
    self.movieList.addMovie(Movie('Run Lola Run'))
    self.assertEquals(self.movieList.getSize(),3)
    self.failUnless(self.movieList.containsMovie('Un Chien Andalou'))
    self.failIf(self.movieList.containsMovie('Star Trek'))

def tearDown(self):
    self.movieList=None
```

Green bar—This last test is somewhat like an acceptance test since it tests multiple scenarios. Many people would argue against this level of redundancy, but for my money I believe that tests should be fragile and that some level of acceptance test should be expressed while unit-testing the application. The redundant asserts could certainly be factored out into private methods if one wishes.

# Chapter 26

# VBUNIT

WITH KAY PENTECOST

This chapter presents vbUnit, the xUnit family member for the Visual Basic platform. Kay Pentecost has agreed to write this chapter, as she has been doing TDD in VB for some time now.

## THE FRAMEWORK

This chapter presents vbUnit3 Professional, the xUnit family member for Visual Basic. There are several vbUnit implementations. The one used in this chapter is vbUnit3 Professional, version 3.06.02. vbUnit3 Professional was written by Bodo Maass, and is a commercial product. It's nicely integrated with the VB IDE, and very easy to use, so I think it's worth it. There is also a free version of vbUnit Basic on Maass' site at [URL 51]. Other versions of vbUnit are available. You can find them at [URL 11].

Installing the vbUnit3 Professional software installs it as an add-in to Visual Basic. This adds three menu items to the add-ins menu: *Show vbUnit Window* (which changes to *Hide vbUnit Window* when the window is displayed), *Run vbUnit*, and *vbUnit Options*.

To create a new project with vbUnit, select *New Project* from the File menu. On the *New Project* window, select *vbUnitTestDLL* as the project type. This opens a vbUnit project (the default name is **vbUnitTestDLL**) with two classes: the first test fixture (**vbuTestFixture**) and the test suite (**vbuTestSuite**). You can and should rename these classes and files to be meaningful in your project.

The fixture implements the **IFixture** interface and instantiates a variable for the **IAssert** class. This gives us a selection of assertion methods, including:

```
Assert.Verify(Boolean)
Assert.StringsEqual(expected, actual)
Assert.LongsEqual(expected, actual)
```

As expected, the **Assert** methods each have the optional message parameter.

The **IFixture** interface provides two methods: **IFixture_Setup** and **IFixture_TearDown**. As you'll see, you can use these methods to put common set up and tear down code for the tests when we refactor in the project. **IFixture_Setup** runs before every test, and **IFixture_TearDown** runs after every test.

The default Fixture already has a failing test:

```
Public Sub TestFail()
    mAssert.Verify False, "hello"
End Sub
```

To get your first green bar, you need to change the preceding **False** to **True**.

## EXAMPLE

### Getting Started with vbUnit

We start by opening a new project in VB6. We select *vbUnitTestDLL* as the type of project. This creates a project (that I renamed to **vbuMovie**), a test fixture (renamed to **vbuMovieFixture**), and a test suite (renamed to **vbuMovieSuite**). Figure 26.1 shows the environment. The vbUnit window is docked above the *immediate* window.

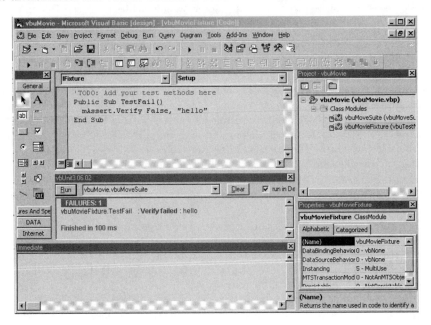

**Figure 26.1** The Visual Basic environment.

We expect that clicking the *Run* button will give us a red bar, but instead it gives us a message saying that a user-defined type is not found. That's because we changed the name from **vbuTestFixture** to **vbuMovieFixture**. The test suite **vbuMovieSuite** is looking for the old name. We can fix that by changing the code in the **vbuMovieSuite** to look for **vbuMovieFixture**.

```
suite.AddFixture New vbuMovieFixture
```

Now, clicking the *Run* button on the vbUnit window gives us a red bar. It failed. But we haven't really done anything yet...so what's wrong?

Nothing's wrong. I like to start with the failing test provided by vbUnit...just to confirm that it's set up and working correctly (see Figure 26.2).

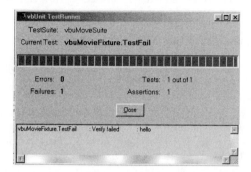

**Figure 26.2** The vbUnit window with a failed test.

To find the method that failed, we double-click on the test result line:

`vbuMovieFixture.TestFail : Verify failed : hello`

which brings us to the highlighted line of code:

    mAssert.Verify False, "hello"

Aha! If **Verify** is **False**, which it is here, the test will fail. Now we've confirmed that vbUnit is working correctly...so we can change the **False** to **True**, and get a green bar—the passing test.

Now the vbUnit window has the text:

`OK (1 Test, 1 Assertion) Finished in 3.821 seconds`

So now, having warmed up with a small test that vbUnit is correctly installed and the project is running, we're ready to start the real work.

## Creating the MovieList Functionality

Our first test will be the test for an empty MovieList. And it looks pretty much like the first Java test:

    mAssert.LongsEqual 0, EmptyList.Size, "Size of empty list should be 0."

Next, we need to dimension **EmptyList** as a MovieList.

    Dim EmptyList As New MovieList
    mAssert.LongsEqual 0, EmptyList.Size, "Size of empty list should be 0."

This won't compile, of course. We have no class MovieList yet. The error message is:

```
user-defined type not found
```

So, we add a class to the test and name it MovieList. Now the test fails again because we have no method called Size:

```
Method or data member not found
```

At this point, the test requires a MovieList class, which we gave it, and a method in MovieList called Size. We know that the method should return zero for this case. And that's *all* we really know.

Oh, we figure the MovieList object will eventually hold a list of movies. And the size of the MovieList will be the number of movies it holds. If we were doing some other style of programming, we might create some movies, put them in the MovieList, and count them, wouldn't we? Well, then we'd have to decide what a movie looked like, and how to put movies into the list, and so on and so on and so on.

But all the test is asking for is a Size method that returns zero. So that's all we have to do. We *do the simplest thing that could possibly work*, and create a Size method that returns zero.

```
Public Function Size() As Long
    Size = 0
End Function
```

And run the test. And if we typed everything correctly, we get a green bar!

Once the test runs, we can look at the code for opportunities to refactor, but there's not much here to do. We're ready to do the next test, which we'll call TestSizeAfter-AddingOne, just as we saw in Chapter 10. This test will confirm that when we add a movie to the list, the list knows there's one movie in there. Our assertion will be:

```
mAssert.LongsEqual 1, oneItemList.Size, "List should have 1"
```

To set up for the assertion we need to:

```
Dim oneItemList As New MovieList
Dim StarWars As Movie
Set StarWars = New Movie
oneItemList.Add StarWars
```

The compiler will complain until we have a Movie class and an Add method, so we add a Movie class and put an empty Add method in MovieList. Now, running the tests, we get a red bar.

It failed because the Size method is only returning zero, and the Add method doesn't do anything.

So we're going to let the Add method increment a counter that tracks how many movies we've added. Notice that at this point we don't care anything else about the movie or the movie list—just that when we add a movie the movie list knows it has one more movie.

So we'll create a private variable, NumberOfMovies.

```
Private NumberOfMovies As Long
```

Now we can increment NumberOfMovies in the Add method, and have the Size method return the number of movies.

Our MovieList class looks like this now:

```
Private NumberOfMovies As Long

Public Function Size() As Long
  Size = NumberOfMovies
End  Function

Public Function Add(aMovie As Movie)
  NumberOfMovies = NumberOfMovies + 1
End Function
```

Do we think the next test will run correctly the first time? Let's try it:

```
Public Sub TestSizeAfterAddingTwo()
  Dim twoItemList As New MovieList
  Dim StarWars As Movie
  Dim StarTrek As Movie
  Set StarWars = New Movie
  Set StarTrek = New Movie
  twoItemList.Add StarWars
  twoItemList.Add StarTrek
  mAssert.LongsEqual 2, twoItemList.Size, "List should have 2"
End Sub
```

As we expected, this gives us a green bar. Now, looking at the code for opportunities to refactor, we see a lot of duplication. What's duplication? Duplication appears whenever we do something more than once...even when we use different names in different methods. We're dimensioning a new MovieList, for example, in almost every method:

```
Dim EmptyList As New MovieList
Dim oneItemList As New MovieList
Dim twoItemList As New MovieList
```

In each case, it's just a MovieList, although we named methods to tell us what kind of a MovieList they are.

So, we can move this to the Setup method in vbuMovieFixture. We also dimension and instantiate two Movie objects, so we can put that code in the Setup, too. We'll put the Dim statements in the General section of the class so they have class-wide scope.

```
Private StarWars As Movie
Private StarTrek As Movie
Private movieList As MovieList
```

```
Private Sub IFixture_Setup(assert As IAssert)
  Set mAssert = assert
  Set MovieList = New MovieList
  Set StarWars = New Movie
  Set StarTrek = New Movie
End Sub
```

And, of course, we want to release memory in TearDown:

```
Private Sub IFixture_TearDown()
  Set movieList = Nothing
  Set StarWars = Nothing
  Set StarTrek = Nothing
  Set mAssert = Nothing
End Sub
```

When we press the run button, if it still gives us a green bar, we can delete the duplicated code so the dimension statements and the instantiations go away. All that is left in each test is the MovieList.Add method, and the assert that we are testing.

Now we know how many movies are in the MovieList...but we don't know anything about the MovieList other than that.

So our next test will be to see if, once we put a movie in the MovieList, if MovieList knows it's in there.

```
Public Sub TestContents
  movieList.Add StarWars
  mAssert.Verify movieList.ContainsMovieName("Star Wars")
End Sub
```

The compiler will remind us that we haven't written a contains method, yet. So we create a method in MovieList called ContainsMovieName.

```
Public Function ContainsMovieName(NameOfMovieToCheckFor As String) As Boolean
```

And, of course, the simplest thing we can do is to have Contains return True.

```
ContainsMovieName = True
```

As I do this, I really like the feeling I get when the green bar appears. The more functionality I add, the more confidence the green bar gives me.

We don't actually have to refactor, yet. We can add another test to check that a movie that has not been added returns False when we call ContainsMovieName. This time, we don't call the Add method.

```
Public Sub TestNotContains
  mAssert.Verify Not (MovieList.ContainsMovieName("Star Wars"))
End Sub
```

When this fails, we can write the functionality that actually checks the contents of the MovieList.

```
Public Function ContainsMovieName(NameOfMovieToCheckFor As String) As Boolean
    Dim movie As Movie
    Contains = False
    For Each movie In Movies
      If movie.title = NameOfMovieToCheckFor Then
        ContainsMovieName= True
        Exit For
      End If
    Next movie
```

We haven't dimensioned Movies yet. Movies will be a collection that will hold the movies for MovieList.

So we dimension Movies in the general section of the MovieList class, so it's available to the entire class.

```
Private Movies As New Collection
```

Now that we've got a collection, we can refactor the add method to actually add a movie to movieList, instead of just incrementing NumberOfMovies. Then, we can use the Collection method, Count, to find out the Size of the MovieList.

First, we add a line to the MovieList.Add method:

```
Movies.Add
```

We see that we're incrementing **NumberOfMovies** to get the **MovieList.Size**. Now, however, we have the collection **Movies**, so we can use the **Collection Count** method to get the number of movies. We add the line:

```
Size = Movies.Count
```

to the MovieList.Size method and delete the

```
Size = NumberOfMovies
```

The first thing we need here is a movie title. So we'll add **Title** properties to **Movie**:

```
Private mTitle   As String
Public Property Get Title() As String
  Title = mTitle
End Property

Public Property Let Title(aTitle As String)
  mTitle = aTitle
End Property
```

And we'll add the title to the movie in the IFixture_SetUp:

```
StarWars.Title = "Star Wars"
StarTrek.Title = "Star Trek"
```

Green bar!!

This runs and gives us a green bar, so we can delete the NumberOfMovies dimension statement, and the assignment of NumberOfMovies to Size.

And here we have to do some thinking. Is a Movie ever going to exist without a title? No. We don't want any titleless movies hanging around...the only time we'd have a titleless movie would be some sort of movie object we use as an iterator, and it would never be directly instantiated. So a Movie *must* have a title. We can't do that with a constructor like we could in other object-oriented languages.

To make sure that every movie has a title, we need some sort of factory object to create movies. Let's call it Studio, and give it a method of MakeNewMovie.

Now, of course, we hear our pair yelling "Test first, test first!"

OK. Point taken. Create a new test fixture called vbuTestStudioFixture. Here's the test:

First, the assert, since we do that before anything else.

```
mAssert.StringsEqual "Star Wars", StarWars.Title, "Title should be 'Star Wars'"
```

Then we add the assignment, before the assert:

```
Set StarWars = Studio.makeNewMovie("Star Wars")
```

To get this to run, we need the Studio class, the makeNewMovie method. We already have the Title property in Movie.

So we dimension a Studio object, and we create the Studio Class.

We put this in the vbuTestStudioFixture:

```
Dim Studio As New Studio
```

And we create this in the Studio Class:

```
Public Function makeNewMovie(MovieTitle As String) As Movie
   Dim movie As New Movie
   movie.Title = MovieTitle
   Set makeNewMovie = movie
End Function
```

Now we change the assignments in the IFixture_SetUp of the vbuMovieFixture for the new functionality.

```
Private Studio As New Studio

Set StarWars = Studio.makeNewMovie("Star Wars")
Set StarTrek = Studio.makeNewMovie("Star Trek")
```

Green bar!

Now we can modify the IFixture_SetUp in vbuTestMovie to use the new functionality:

```
Private Sub IFixture_Setup(assert As IAssert)
   Set mAssert = assert
   Set MovieList = New MovieList
   Set StarWars = Studio.makeNewMovie("Star Wars")
   Set StarTrek = Studio.makeNewMovie("Star Trek")
End Sub
```

OK, now we have three classes: Studio, Movie, and MovieList. These classes allow us to add movies to a list and check that the list contains them...and the code is pretty straightforward and clean.

Here are the classes in their most recent form:

First, Movie:

```
Option Explicit

Private mTitle As String

Public Property Get Title() As String
   Title = mTitle
End Property

Public Property Let Title(aTitle As String)
   mTitle = aTitle
End Property
```

Next, MovieList:

```
Option Explicit

Private Movies As New Collection

Public Function Size() As Long
   Size = Movies.Count
End Function

Public Sub Add(aMovie As movie)
   Movies.Add aMovie
End Sub

Public Function ContainsMovieName(NameOfMovieToCheckFor As String) As Boolean
   Dim movie As movie
   ContainsMovieName = False
   For Each movie In Movies
     If movie.Title = NameOfMovieToCheckFor Then
       ContainsMovieName = True
       Exit For
     End If
   Next movie
End Function
```

```
Public Function makeNewMovie(MovieTitle As String) As movie
   Dim movie As New movie
   movie.Title = MovieTitle
   Set makeNewMovie = movie
End Function
```

Finally, Studio:

```
Option Explicit

Public Function makeNewMovie(MovieTitle As String) As movie
   Dim movie As New movie
   movie.Title = MovieTitle
   Set makeNewMovie = movie
End Function
```

There are more things we can do: we can change MovieList into a real collection; we can set the Movie class to be Public Not Createable so that programs outside of the DLL can only create Movies by going through Studio; we can add functionality to Movie, MovieList, and Studio as it's needed.

But we don't need it yet, so this is a good place to stop!

# Appendix A

# EXTREME PROGRAMMING

> *'Tis noble Kent, your friend.*
> *- King Lear, Act 5 Scene 3*
> *William Shakespeare*

This appendix does not try to be an exhaustive overview of eXtreme Programming (XP). Its purpose is to provide a very brief introduction to XP as background to the discussion of Test-Driven Development.

## THE AGILE REVOLUTION

Since the late 1990s the field of software development has been undergoing something of a revolution. It had been fairly common knowledge for some time among more open-minded practitioners that the field was in trouble. Projects were delivered late, cost much more than was expected, and/or did not deliver the originally requested features. Additionally, programming was often a stressful job with programmers feeling overworked and underappreciated.

In 1994 The Standish Group published a report that brought these problems into the light. The now-famous *Chaos Report* [21] documented that only 16 percent of projects were completed successfully. A follow-up report[22] included the significant finding that the likelihood of a project succeeding diminished the more people worked on it, the more it cost, or the longer it took. What did successful projects look like? They were low cost, short, and done by small teams.

Around this time, several thought leaders in the field began to develop software development processes that increased the chances of success. Two of the most notable were Ward Cunningham and Kent Beck, who called their idea "eXtreme Programming."

In 2001 several of the people involved in this development approach met to discuss this trend and their ideas. This meeting led to the *Agile Manifesto*[URL 6], which is included as part of this chapter, in a sidebar. The group that wrote the manifesto forms the core of what is now *The Agile Alliance*[URL 5].

For more information on Agile Software Development, see [13], [24], [33].

How are agile methods different from traditional ones? At first glance it seems that there is nothing new here. Most seasoned developers will see practices that they have been using some time. So what's the big deal?

Traditional (i.e., non-agile) methodologies advocate and usually try to enforce a defined and repeatable process. This is based on the belief that software can be manufactured. In essence, these are industrial-era approaches.

Agile methodologies are, in contrast, post-industrial. They use introspection, retrospection, and adaptation to allow people to self-organize based on the application of

---

### Manifesto for Agile Software Development

We are uncovering better ways of developing software by doing it and helping others do it. Through this work we have come to value:

**Individuals and interactions** over processes and tools
**Working software** over comprehensive documentation
**Customer collaboration** over contract negotiation
**Responding to change** over following a plan

That is, while there is value in the items on the right, we value the items on the left more.

| | | |
|---|---|---|
| Kent Beck | James Grenning | Robert C. Martin |
| Mike Beedle | Jim Highsmith | Steve Mellor |
| Arie van Bennekum | Andrew Hunt | Ken Schwaber |
| Alistair Cockburn | Ron Jeffries | Jeff Sutherland |
| Ward Cunningham | Jon Kern | Dave Thomas |
| Martin Fowler | Brian Marick | |

©2001, the above authors. This declaration may be freely copied in any form, but only in its entirety through this notice.

---

a set of practices that lead to an emerging process. This idea is expressed in one of the Agile Alliance's principles: "The best architectures, requirements, and designs emerge from self-organizing teams"[URL 6]. See the sidebar for all of the principles behind the Agile Manifesto.

## EXTREME PROGRAMMING

eXtreme Programming, commonly referred to simply as XP, is one of the most agile of the agile processes.

XP is defined by four values and a set of practices. However, XP is more than this, more than just doing the practices. It is a way of creating software that embodies the values. The practices are activities that we do in order to learn XP. Beck sees the practices as being much the same as etudes that help one learn and internalize techniques in playing a musical instrument.

## THE FOUR VARIABLES

No discussion of XP can begin without talking about the four variables: cost, time, quality, and scope. We look at each, how they are interrelated, and how they relate to a project and its risk.

**Cost** Every project has a cost. This includes equipment, facilities, and man-hours. Especially man-hours.

## Principles Behind the Agile Manifesto

- Our highest priority is to satisfy the customer through early and continuous delivery of valuable software.

- Welcome changing requirements, even late in development. Agile processes harness change for the customer's competitive advantage.

- Deliver working software frequently, from a couple of weeks to a couple of months, with a preference to the shorter timescale.

- Business people and developers must work together daily throughout the project.

- Build projects around motivated individuals. Give them the environment and support they need, and trust them to get the job done.

- The most efficient and effective method of conveying information to and within a development team is face-to-face conversation.

- Working software is the primary measure of progress.

- Agile processes promote sustainable development. The sponsors, developers, and users should be able to maintain a constant pace indefinitely.

- Continuous attention to technical excellence and good design enhances agility.

- Simplicity—the art of maximizing the amount of work not done—is essential.

- The best architectures, requirements, and designs emerge from self-organizing teams.

- At regular intervals, the team reflects on how to become more effective, then tunes and adjusts its behavior accordingly.

**Time** Every project takes time.

**Quality** Every project results in a system with a certain level of quality.

**Scope** Every project consists of a certain set of functionality.

The really interesting thing is how these variables interact. If you increase cost by adding people to the project, velocity will often decrease (due to the costs of integrating the additional people) and, hence, time will increase. On the other hand, increasing the cost by buying faster or better equipment or facilities can boost your velocity and thus decrease time. You cannot decrease time simply by dumping more money into a project, especially early in the project. In fact, you are limited in what you can achieve by controlling cost.

Time is often dictated by external constraints such as trade shows, investor requirements, and business commitments. Because of this, time is often relatively fixed.

Quality can be variable, but lowering the quality of the system has serious negative impact. No worker is happy for long if they are coerced into producing goods of poor quality. This can lead to a serious morale issue. Also, low quality code is harder to extend and maintain. If you try to shorten the time required by limiting quality, it will surely backfire.

Scope is the thing that is most easily controlled. This entails adding or removing functionality from the requirements of the project. By using a few simple techniques, XP makes this work very well. One important technique is to always be working on the most important outstanding feature, according to the customer. That ensures that if unimplemented features are later removed (thereby reducing scope), the most important things have already been done.

One mistake that people make is thinking that they can control all four variables. This is impossible. Cost, time, quality, and scope are interrelated such that the value of any one depends on the values of the others. What this means in practical terms is that you can control at most three of the four, but never all four. If you attempt to control all four, your project will most likely fail and will certainly be a miserable one to work on.

## THE VALUES

The reason XP is so successful lies in the four values it is built upon:

1. Communication
2. Simplicity
3. Feedback
4. Courage

We'll examine each of these values in turn.

## Communication

Communication is of paramount importance in XP. This is evidenced in several of its practices:

- Programming is done in pairs.
- There is a stand-up meeting every morning.
- The team works in an open space.
- There is a customer in the room with the team.
- Heavy use is made of shared white-boards.
- Information of general interest is displayed in a prominent location.

These practices promote open, honest communication between programmers, between programmers and customers, and with management.

## Simplicity

The value of simplicity cannot be overstated. Keeping the code and the design as simple as possible increases the clarity, understandability, extendability, and maintainability of the system.

Exactly what is *simplicity*? In the context of XP, Beck[8] defines the simplest system by using four criteria (in order of decreasing importance). The code is simple if it:

- runs all the tests
- reveals all the intention
- has no duplication, and
- uses the fewest possible classes and methods.

## Feedback

Without honest, continuous feedback everything else falls apart. Feedback is what keeps everyone in sync. It is what enables the programmers to deliver the system that the customer really wants.

Feedback takes many forms and occurs at many levels on many timescales. This can range from the feedback you get from running your tests on a minute-by-minute basis, the ongoing feedback from your pair-programming partner, the feedback from the team in the daily meeting, through to feedback from the customer during iteration planning when they tell you how you're doing in terms of overall direction.

## Courage

Courage is required to do XP. It takes courage to make sweeping changes to working code to make it clearer or just *better*. Having a broad test suite gives you confidence, but courage still has to come from inside. It takes courage to tell your customer that they can't have another feature added without deferring to something else. It takes courage to throw away code.

## THE PRACTICES

In this section we'll have a brief look at each of the XP practices. For more detail see [6], [8], [26], and [URL 12].

## Whole Team

Software development is a cooperative game[13]. There are several players, including programmers, coach, customers, management, and users. All these players are on the same team, and the goal is for everyone to win. Everyone works together to do that. On a practical note, the core players (programmers, coach, and ideally customer) sit in the same room so there is minimal barriers to communication.

## Planning Game

There are two aspects to the planning game: release planning and iteration planning. The former deals with what can be accomplished by a certain date, while the latter deals with what to do next on a day-to-day basis.

**Release Planning**   In an XP project, requirements exist in the form of stories that are written by the customer. Each story briefly describes a single aspect of functionality (sometimes called a feature) that is testable. The programmers estimate the cost of each story. Based on that information and their knowledge of the priority[1] of each story, the customer sketches out the order in which stories should be done. We accept that this plan is inaccurate and we will adjust it as we go, as the velocity of the team changes, and as the customer changes their mind about scheduled stories or comes up with new ones. This set of stories is then divided into iterations (each of which last between one and three weeks) based on how much work the team can get done per iteration.

**Iteration Planning**   Each release is made up of a series of iterations. At the beginning of each iteration the development team sits down and brainstorms each story that is scheduled for that iteration. The result is a set of tasks for each story. These tasks are then estimated.[2] Then each programmer signs up for a selection of tasks that they can accomplish in this iteration. They know how much work they got done during the previous iteration and assume that they will get the same amount done this time. This same rule of thumb is used to estimate how much the team as a whole can accomplish in an iteration. This is then used in release planning to divide stories into iterations. They sign up for that much work. This is the concept known as *yesterday's weather*...odds are that you'll get the same amount done today as you did yesterday. If a programmer finds that they have time left toward the end of the iteration, they will look for more work. If a programmer is running out of time (i.e., has too much work), they will defer some or pass it to another programmer who has time left.

The key thing to remember about the planning game is that the *planning* is more important than the plan.

## Small Releases

By keeping releases small and frequent we get more rapid feedback from users. Releases should be no larger than several months' worth of work. As mentioned before, releases are split into iterations. While the size of releases can vary depending on external constraints, iterations are a fixed size: between one and three weeks. Historically, two weeks has been the most popular iteration size, but recent experiences are favoring one-week iterations.

## Customer Tests

As stated in previous sections, the customer writes the requirements as a set of stories. They also write a test (or tests) for each story so that everyone knows when that story has been successfully implemented in full. These are the customer tests and are also known as *acceptance tests* since they indicate when a story's implementation is acceptable. Ideally, the customer has their tests ready for the programmers to use (i.e., run) before the associated stories are scheduled.

## Simple Design

Design for today, not for some potential future. By working test-first we constrain our design to what is required to pass the test. By refactoring as required, we keep the

---

[1]The priority of a story is based on its business value to the customer.

[2]Task estimates are at a finer level of granularity than story estimates, and are more accurate since there is now more information to work with.

design clean and simple. That's one reason why I claim this is a book about design, not about testing.

## Pair Programming

Every line of code (test and production) is written by two programmers sitting at a single computer. The most common, uninformed objection to pair programming is that you have two people doing one person's work. But it's more than two people writing code together. There is an ongoing, real-time code review in progress. The partner (the person not typing) can be thinking strategically, while the driver (the person typing) thinks tactically. Because of this, the partner can suggest what the next test should be, what names should be used, where refactoring is warranted, etc. Also, because there is always someone available to talk to, problems can be talked through and brainstormed as needed.

There have been studies on the effectiveness of pair programming. One was presented at the XP2000 conference[37, Chapter 14] which found that using pair programming took only 15 percent more time and that the extra development cost would be repaid in quicker and cheaper testing, QA, and support. Another study was presented at XP2002[38] which found that pair programming increases job satisfaction among programmers.

The social aspect of pair programming should not be undervalued either. Programmers are people, and people are social animals.

## Test-Driven Development

Write tests first and let that drive your design and coding. That's what this book is all about. One of the beneficial side effects of TDD is that you end up with a comprehensive test suite. This gives you confidence to refactor. If the tests run before refactoring (and they *must*) and they run after, you can be confident that you haven't changed the behavior of the code.

## Design Improvement

As you program, you write a small test (just enough to fail), then write a small bit of code (just enough to pass the failing test). This can lead to poorly designed or poorly structured code. So the next step is to refactor to make the code clean again.

By refactoring as required, we continuously make the design better, a little at a time. This makes the code as simple, clear, and intent-revealing as possible.

## Collective Code Ownership

Everybody owns everything. Anybody can change any code as required. This, especially combined with pair programming, allows and encourages everyone to get familiar with all (or at least most) of the codebase. It also enables refactoring in that if anyone sees a problem, they can fix it. It lets the team work as fast as possible since you never have to wait for the owner of the code to make the change you need.

## Continuous Integration

In XP you never go for very long without integrating your work with the codebase. There are several beneficial results:

- Integration is never a headache because there are minimal differences between the codebase and your work.

- The codebase is always very close to the most current state of the system, typically within hours.

- Your working copy is never very far from the baseline codebase in the repository so you never have the chance to diverge much.

It is very important to stay this close to the codebase because of collective ownership. Anyone is able to work on any part of the code. The longer you go without integrating, the more likely it is that someone has made changes that conflict with yours.

At the very least, you should integrate after you finish each task. It is even better to integrate after each test-code-refactor cycle. That way you are integrating every 15–30 minutes. When you're doing this, it's especially important to have your tests run quickly, because before integrating you have to verify that *all* the tests run.

Never, *never*, *NEVER* leave anything unintegrated at the end of the day. If you can't integrate before you leave for the day, throw it out and start fresh in the morning. If a task takes longer than a day to do, either the task is too complex (and has to be broken up) or your solution is too complex (and you need to find a simpler one). In either case, start over.

## Coding Standard

In order to support collective ownership, everyone on the team needs to conform to the same coding standard. This allows everyone to be comfortable working on any of the code since it all looks the same. What this standard is doesn't matter. The main thing is that everyone adheres to it. For obvious reasons, it makes sense to use a standard close to something that is common in the industry.

## Common Vocabulary

Everyone involved in the project must use a common vocabulary for talking about the project. This has often been accomplished through the use of a metaphor.

The metaphor is a shared, simple description of the system. It must be shared by everyone involved and so should be cast in terms that everyone understands. For example, the C3 project at Chrysler (the original XP project) used a metaphor of an assembly line to describe the payroll system they were building. Everyone at Chrysler understood assembly lines.

Not only does the metaphor provide a common understanding of the system's operation, it also provides a source for names in the system. This tightly couples the code itself with the shared understanding that has developed.

## Sustainable Pace

If you can't stay awake, you can't program. If you can't think, you can't program. Our industry has made a hero of the programmer that works until the wee hours of the morning, kept awake (and possibly alive) on a diet of pizza, chips, and cola. Nobody can last long that way. On an XP project, you stop work when you are ready to. When you've put in a good day you go home, get some rest, and have some fun. That way you can come back the next morning rested, refreshed, and ready to work at your top effectiveness. By doing this, you can keep up the pace indefinitely, and not worry about burning out before the project is completed.

## SUMMARY

eXtreme Programming is one of the most revolutionary movements in the history of programming. It rejects the pomp and ceremony of the heavy methodologies that are standard in our industry. It turns the focus away from processes that spell out what everyone on the project has to do, and when. It eschews the use of complex tools and technological solutions in favor of people doing the simplest thing that could work. Instead of trying to nail down and predict all requirements and timelines at the beginning of the project, it encourages the customers to think up new requirements and change direction throughout the project. Instead of trying to fully design the system before the first line of code is written, it evolves the system in small steps, *just enough* at any one time.

In short, it lets programmers program, have a life, and have fun doing it.

# Appendix B

# AGILE MODELING

WITH SCOTT AMBLER

> *We fortify in paper and in figures,*
> *Using the names of men instead of men:*
> *Like one that draws the model of a house*
> *Beyond his power to build it; who, half through,*
> *Gives o'er and leaves his part-created cost*
> *A naked subject to the weeping clouds*
> *And waste for churlish winter's tyranny.*
>
> *- Henry IV, part 2, Act 1 Scene 3*
> *William Shakespeare*

Some people will tell us that "if you're taking a test-driven development (TDD) approach to development that you don't need to model." Those people are completely and utterly wrong. These are probably the exact same people who also told us that "you don't model on an eXtreme Programming (XP) project," and they were completely and utterly wrong about that, too. The best thing that can be said about them, I guess, is that at least they're consistent.

In this chapter we explore the following issues:

- The myths surrounding modeling

- An introduction to Agile Modeling (AM)

- What are agile models?

- Agile Modeling and TDD

## THE MYTHS SURROUNDING MODELING

Before we explore the relationship between modeling and TDD, I first want to dispel some myths that you may have about modeling. My experience is that the people who tell you that TDD and modeling don't go together typically don't have a very good understanding of modern approaches to modeling, and in particular have little or no experience with Agile Modeling (AM). In the August 2001 issue of *Software Development* [URL 63] Scott explored the following misunderstandings that people have about modeling:

**Model = Documentation.** The reality is that the concepts of *model* and *document* are orthogonal—we can have models that aren't documents and documents that aren't models. A sketch on the back of a paper napkin is a model, as is a drawing on a whiteboard, as is a collection of Class Responsibility Collaboration (CRC) cards, as is a low-fidelity user interface prototype built from flip chart paper and sticky notes. These are all valuable models, yet questionable documents.

**You Can Think Everything Through From the Start.** Project teams suffering from this myth often produce significant amounts of documentation instead of what their users actually want—working software that meets their needs. We need to recognize that we can't think all the minutiae through, that the programmers likely won't follow the detailed guidance provided by the models anyway, and that our models need to evolve over time in an iterative and incremental manner. The fundamental reality is that only our code is ever truly in sync with our code.

**Modeling Implies a Prescriptive Software Process.** The reality is that we can model in an agile manner, as we'll see later in this chapter.

**You Must "Freeze" Requirements.** The good news is that by freezing our requirements early in the life cycle, the customer is likely to get exactly what they asked for; the bad news is that they likely won't get what they actually need. The reality is that change happens, so we need to embrace this fact and act accordingly.

**Your Design is Carved in Stone.** This is similar to the desire to freeze requirements, the main difference being that management wants to ensure that every developer is marching to the same tune by following *the design*. The result is that developers either build the wrong things, or build the right things the wrong way, to conform to *the design*. The reality is that nobody is perfect; even the best designers aren't going to get it right the first time. Furthermore, if we don't freeze the requirements, then by implication we cannot freeze the design—changes to the requirements will force changes to the design. The best way to look at it is that the design isn't finished for a given release until we've shipped the code.

**You Must Use a CASE Tool.** I often create a model to think through an issue, such as how we might architect one aspect of the system, allowing myself and/or my coworkers to move forward and implement what we just modeled. As a result, I often don't need a significant CASE tool to support my modeling efforts—a white board or stack of index cards often suffices. My experience is that CASE tools are fine as long as they provide the best value for our investment in them, but that most of the time I simply don't need one to model successfully. Yes, I'll often use tools such as Together/CC [URL 34] because it generates significant amounts of Java scaffolding code and ERWin [URL 45] because it generates database schemas. Both of these tools help me to fulfill the true purpose of software development: the creation of software that meets the needs of my users. Having said that, the vast majority of my modeling efforts are still done by using simple tools, not sophisticated modeling tools.

**Modeling is a Waste of Time.** The reality is that we are very often more productive sketching a diagram, developing a low-fidelity prototype, or creating a few index cards, in order to think something through before we code it. Productive developers model before they code. Furthermore, modeling is a great way to promote communication between team members and project stakeholders because you're talking through issues, coming to a better understanding of what needs to be built and building bonds between everyone involved with the project in the process.

**The World Revolves Around Data Modeling.** Many organizations hobble their new development efforts by starting with a data model. Often this is the way the organization has always done things; the data community has a political death grip on the IT department and therefore does everything in their power to ensure that they control the software development projects, or the legacy database(s) are such a mess that we have no other choice. The reality is that we have a wide variety of models at our disposal—use cases, business rules, activity diagrams, class diagrams, component diagrams, user interface flow diagrams, and CRC models to name a few—and data models are merely one such option. We need to use the right model(s) for the job.

**All Developers Know How to Model.** Modeling skills are gained over years of experience and only when a developer chooses to gain them. As the agile community will tell us, people need to work together and to balance off one another's strengths. Everyone should have the humility to understand that they don't know everything and therefore they can always learn something important from everyone else: modelers can learn details of a certain technology from a programmer and programmers can learn valuable design and architecture techniques from modelers. My personal philosophy is that everyone is a novice, including myself.

By understanding the myths surrounding modeling and dealing with them effectively, we put yourself, our project team, and our organization in a position where we can develop software effectively. Agile Modeling (AM) describes an effective approach to modeling and documentation that works well within a TDD environment.

## AN INTRODUCTION TO AGILE MODELING (AM)

The Agile Modeling (AM) methodology [2] [URL 8] is a chaordic collection of practices—guided by principles and values—that should be applied by software professionals on a day-to-day basis. AM is not a prescriptive process, in other words, it does not define detailed procedures for how to create a given type of model. Instead, it provides advice for how to be effective as a modeler. AM is *touchy-feely* in that it is not hard and fast—think of AM as an art, not a science.

An agile modeler is anyone who models follows the AM methodology applying AM's practices in accordance with its principles and values. An agile developer is someone who follows an agile approach to software development. An agile modeler is an agile developer. Not all agile developers are agile modelers.

AM has three goals:

1. To define and show how to put into practice a collection of values, principles, and practices pertaining to effective, lightweight modeling. What makes AM a catalyst for improvement isn't the modeling techniques themselves—such as use case models, class models, data models, or user interface models—but how to apply them productively.

2. To address the issue of how to apply modeling techniques on software projects taking an agile approach, such as eXtreme Programming (XP) [8] or Feature Driven Development (FDD) [36]. Sometimes it is significantly more productive for a developer to draw some bubbles and lines to think through an idea, or to compare several different approaches to solving a problem, than it is to simply start writing code. There is a danger in being too code-centric—sometimes a quick sketch can avoid significant churn when we are coding.

3. To address how we can improve our modeling activities following a *near-agile* approach to software development, and in particular project teams that have adopted an instantiation of the Unified Process such as the Rational Unified Process (RUP) [30] or the Enterprise Unified Process (EUP) [3]. Although we must be following an agile software process to truly be agile modeling, we may still adopt and benefit from many of AM's practices on non-agile projects.

## AM Values

The values of AM include those of XP—*communication, simplicity, feedback,* and *courage*—and extend it with *humility.* It is critical to have effective communication within our development team as well as with and between all project stakeholders. We should strive to develop the simplest solution possible that meets all of our needs and to obtain feedback regarding our efforts often and early. Furthermore, we should have the courage to make and stick to our decisions, and have the humility to admit that we may not know everything, that others have value to add to our project efforts.

## AM Principles

The principles of AM include the importance of *assuming simplicity* when we are modeling and *embracing change* as we are working because requirements do in fact change over time. We should recognize that *incremental change* of our system over time enables agility and that we should strive to obtain *rapid feedback* on our work to ensure that it accurately reflects the needs of our project stakeholders. Agile modelers realize that *software is the primary goal*, although they balance this with the recognition that *enabling the next effort is the secondary goal*. We should *model with a purpose*, if we don't know why we are working on something, then we shouldn't be doing so, and that we need *multiple models* in our development toolkit in order to be effective. A critical concept is that models are not necessarily documents, a realization that enables us to *travel light* by discarding most of our models once they have fulfilled their purpose. Agile modelers believe that *content is more important than representation*, that there are many ways we can model the same concept yet still get it right. To be effective modelers we need to *know our models*. To be effective teammates we should realize that *everyone can learn from everyone else*, we should *work with people's instincts*, and that *open and honest communication* is often the best policy to follow to ensure effective teamwork. Finally, a focus on *quality work* is important because nobody likes to produce sloppy work, and that *local adaptation* of AM to meet the exact needs of our environment is important. The following summarizes the principles of AM.

**Assume Simplicity**    As we develop we should assume that the simplest solution is the best solution.

**Content Is More Important Than Representation**    Any given model could have several ways to represent it. For example, a UI specification could be created using sticky notes on a large sheet of paper (an essential or low-fidelity prototype), as a sketch on paper or a whiteboard, as a "traditional" prototype built using a prototyping tool or programming language, or as a formal document including both a visual representation as well as a textual description of the UI.

**Embrace Change**    Accept the fact that change happens. Revel in it; change is one of the things that make software development exciting.

**Enabling the Next Effort is Your Secondary Goal**   Our project can still be considered a failure even when we deliver a working system to our users—part of fulfilling the needs of our project stakeholders is to ensure that our system is robust enough so that it can be extended over time. As Alistair Cockburn [13] likes to say, when we are playing the software development game our secondary goal is to set up to play the next game.

**Everyone Can Learn From Everyone Else**   Agile modelers have the humility to recognize that they can never truly master something, there is always opportunity to learn more and to extend your knowledge. They take the opportunity to work with and learn from others, to try new ways of doing things, to reflect on what seems to work and what doesn't.

**Incremental Change**   To embrace change we need to take an incremental approach to our own development efforts, to change our system a small portion at a time instead of trying to get everything accomplished in one big release. We can make a big change as a series of small, incremental changes.

**Know Your Models**   Because we have multiple models that we can apply as agile modelers we need to know their strengths and weaknesses to be effective in their use.

**Local Adaptation**   It is doubtful that AM can be applied *out of the box*; instead, we will need to modify it to reflect the environment, including the nature of the organization, the team, the project stakeholders, and the project itself.

**Maximize Stakeholder Investment**   Our project stakeholders are investing resources—time, money, facilities, and so on—to have software developed that meets their needs. Stakeholders deserve to invest their resources the best way possible and not to have them frittered away by our team. Furthermore, stakeholders deserve to have the final say in how those resources are invested or not invested. If it was our money, would we want it any other way?

**Model With a Purpose**   If we cannot identify why and for whom we are creating a model, then why are we bothering to work on it all?

**Multiple Models**   We have a wide range of modeling artifacts available to us. These artifacts include, but are not limited to, the diagrams of the Unified Modeling Language (UML), structured development artifacts such as data models, and low-tech artifacts such as essential user interface models [1].

**Open and Honest Communication**   People need to be free, and to perceive that they are free, to offer suggestions. Open and honest communication enables people to make better decisions because the quality of the information that they are basing them on is more accurate.

**Quality Work**   Agile developers understand that they should invest the effort to make permanent artifacts, such as source code, user documentation, and technical system documentation of sufficient quality.

**Rapid Feedback**   Feedback is one of the five values of AM, and because the time between an action and the feedback on that action is critical, agile modelers prefer rapid feedback over delayed feedback whenever possible.

**Software is Your Primary Goal**   The primary goal of software development is to produce high-quality software that meets the needs of our project stakeholders in an effective manner.

**Travel Light**   Traveling light means that we create just enough models and documentation to get by.

**Work With People's Instincts**   As we gain experience at developing software, our instincts become sharper, and what our instincts are telling us subconsciously can often be an important input into our modeling efforts.

## AM Practices

To model in an agile manner we must apply AM's practices appropriately. Fundamental practices include *creating several models in parallel, applying the right artifact(s)* for the situation, and *iterating to another artifact* to continue moving forward at a steady pace. *Modeling in small increments*, and not attempting to create the magical *all encompassing model* from our ivory tower, is also fundamental to our success as an agile modeler. Because models are only abstract representations of software, abstractions that may not be accurate, we should strive to *prove it with code* to show that our ideas actually work in practice and not just in theory. *Active stakeholder participation* is critical to the success of our modeling efforts because our project stakeholders know what they want and can provide us with the feedback that we require. There are two fundamental reasons why we create models: either we *model to understand* an issue (such as how to design part of the system) or we *model to communicate* what our team is doing (or has done). The principle of *assume simplicity* is supported by the practices of *creating simple content* by focusing only on the aspects that we need to model and not attempting to create a highly detailed modeling, *depicting models simply* via use of simple notations, and *using the simplest tools* to create our models. We travel light by *discarding temporary models* and *updating models only when it hurts*. Communication is enabled by *displaying models publicly*, either on a wall or internal Web site, through *collective ownership* of our project artifacts, through *applying modeling standards*, and by *modeling with others*. Our development efforts are greatly enhanced when we *consider testability, apply patterns gently*, and *reuse existing artifacts*. Because we often need to integrate with other systems, including legacy databases as well as Web-based services, we will find that we need to *formalize contract models* with the owners of those systems. The following summarizes the practices of AM.

**Active Stakeholder Participation**   Project success often requires a significant level of involvement by project stakeholders—senior management needs to publicly and privately support our project, operations and support staff must actively work with our project team towards making the production environment ready to accept our system, other system teams must work with ours to support integration efforts, and maintenance developers must work to become adept at the technologies and techniques used by our system.

**Apply Modeling Standards**   Developers should agree to and follow a common set of modeling standards on a software project. A good source of modeling standards and guidelines is the book *The Elements of UML Style* [4] and [URL 64].

**Apply Patterns Gently**   Effective modelers learn and then appropriately apply common architectural, design, and analysis patterns in their models. However, both Martin Fowler [17] and Joshua Kerievsky [28] believe that developers should consider easing into the application of a pattern and apply it gently.

**Apply the Right Artifact(s)**   This practice is AM's equivalent of the adage *use the right tool for the job*; in this case we want to create the right model(s) to get the job done. Each artifact—such as a UML state chart, an essential use case, source code, or data flow diagram (DFD)—has its own specific strengths and weaknesses, and therefore is appropriate for some situations but not others.

**Collective Ownership**   Everyone can work on any model, and ideally any artifact on the project, if they need to.

**Consider Testability**   When we are modeling we should be constantly asking ourselves "How are we going to test this?" because if we can't test the software that we are building, we shouldn't be building it.

**Create Several Models in Parallel**   Because each type of model has its strengths and weaknesses, no single model is sufficient for our modeling needs. By working on several at once we can easily iterate back and forth between them and use each model for what it is best suited.

**Create Simple Content**   We should keep the actual content of our models—requirements, analysis, architecture, or design—as simple as we possibly can while still fulfilling the needs of our project stakeholders. The implication is that we should not add additional aspects to our models unless they are justifiable.

**Depict Models Simply**   We should use a subset of the modeling notation available to us—a simple model that shows the key features that we are trying to understand, perhaps a class model depicting the primary responsibilities of classes and the relationships between them, often proves to be sufficient.

**Discard Temporary Models**   The vast majority of the models that we create are temporary working models—design sketches, low fidelity prototypes, index cards, potential architecture/design alternatives, and so on—models that have fulfilled their purpose but no longer add value now that they have done so.

**Display Models Publicly**   This supports the principle of *open and honest communication* on our team because all of the current models are quickly accessible to them, as well as with our project stakeholders because we aren't hiding anything from them.

**Formalize Contract Models**   Contract models are often required when an external group controls an information resource that our system requires, such as a database, legacy application, or information service. A contract model is formalized with both parties mutually agreeing to it and ready to mutually change it over time if required.

**Iterate To Another Artifact**   Whenever we find that we are having difficulties working on one artifact (perhaps we are working on a use case and find that we are struggling to describe the business logic), that's a sign that we should iterate to another artifact. By iterating to another artifact we immediately become *unstuck* because we are making progress working on that other artifact.

**Model in Small Increments**   With incremental development we model a little, code a little, test a little, then deliver a little. No more *big design upfront* (BDUF) where we invest weeks or even months creating models and documents.

**Model to Communicate**   One reason why we model is to communicate with people external to our team or to create a contract model.

**Model To Understand**   The most important application of modeling is to explore the problem space, to identify and analyze the requirements for the system, or to compare and contrast potential design alternatives to identify the potentially most simple solution that meets the requirements.

**Model With Others**   Software development is a lot like swimming—it's very dangerous to do alone.

**Prove it With Code**   A model is an abstraction, one that should accurately reflect an aspect of whatever you are building. To determine if it will actually work, we should validate that our model works by writing the corresponding code.

**Reuse Existing Resources**   There is a wealth of information that agile modelers can take advantage of by reusing them.

**Update Only When It Hurts**   We should update an artifact such as a model or document only when we absolutely need to (when not having the model updated is more painful than the effort of updating it).

**Use the Simplest Tools**   The vast majority of models can be drawn on a whiteboard, on paper, or even on the back of a napkin. Note that AM has nothing against CASE tools—if investing in a CASE tool is the most effective use of our resources, then we should do so and then it to the best of its ability.

At its core, AM is simply a collection of techniques that reflect the principles and values shared by many experienced software developers. If there is such a thing as agile modeling, then are there also agile models? Yes.

## WHAT ARE AGILE MODELS?

A model is an abstraction that describes one or more aspects of a problem or a potential solution addressing a problem. Traditionally, models are thought of as zero or more diagrams plus any corresponding documentation. However, non-visual artifacts such as collections of CRC cards, a textual description of one or more business rules, or the structured English description of a business process are also models. An agile model is a model that is just barely good enough. But how do we know when a model is good enough?

Agile models are just barely good enough when they exhibit the following traits:

**Agile models fulfill their purpose.**   Sometimes we model to communicate, perhaps we need to communicate the scope of our effort to senior management, and sometimes we model to understand, perhaps we need to determine a design strategy to implement a collection of Java classes. If we don't know why we need to create something, then don't create it; that wouldn't be agile.

**Agile models are understandable.**   Agile models are understandable by their intended audience. A requirements model will be written in the language of the business that our users comprehend, whereas a technical architecture model will likely use technical terms that developers are familiar with. For example, the whiteboard sketch in Figure B.1 is straightforward and easy to understand—it isn't perfect but it gets the message across. The modeling notation that we use affects understandability—UML use case diagrams are of no value to our users if they don't understand what the notation represents. In this case we would either need to use another approach or educate them in the modeling technique. Style issues, such as avoiding crossing lines, will also affect understandability—messy diagrams are harder to read than clean ones [4]. The level of detail in our models and simplicity also affect understandability.

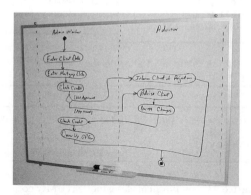

**Figure B.1** A whiteboard sketch of a business process.

**Agile models are sufficiently accurate.**    Models often do not need to be 100 percent accurate, they just need to be accurate enough. For example, if a street map is missing a street, or it shows that a street is open but we discover it's closed for repairs, do we throw away the map and start driving mayhem through the city? Not likely. We might decide to update our map; we could pull out a pen and do it ourselves or go to the local store and purchase the latest version (which still might be out of date), or we could simply accept that the map isn't perfect but still use it because it is good enough for our purposes. We don't discard our street map the minute we find an inaccuracy because we don't expect the map to be perfect nor do we need it to be. Some project teams can tolerate inaccuracies whereas others can't: the nature of the project, the nature of the individual team members, and the nature of the organization will decide this.

**Agile models are sufficiently consistent.**    An agile model does not need to be perfectly consistent with itself or with other artifacts to be useful. If a use case clearly invokes another in one of its steps, then the corresponding use case diagram should indicate that with an association between the two use cases that is tagged with the UML stereotype of <<Include>>. The diagram is clearly inconsistent with the use case specification, yet the world hasn't come to an end. In an ideal world, all of our artifacts would be perfectly consistent but the world isn't ideal nor does it need to be. There is clearly an entropy issue to consider regarding accuracy and consistency. If we have an artifact that we wish to keep as official documentation, then we will need to invest the resources to update it as time goes on, otherwise it will quickly become out of date and useless. The data model of Figure B.2 is missing a few recently added columns, yet it still provides very good insight into your database schema. There is a fine line between spending too much time updating documents and not enough. As an aside, Figure B.2 follows the proposed UML notation for data modeling described at [URL 7].

**Agile models are sufficiently detailed.**    A road map doesn't indicate each individual house on each street. That would be too much detail and thus would make the map difficult to work with. However, when a street is being built, I would imagine the builder has a detailed map of the street that shows each building, the sewers, electrical boxes,

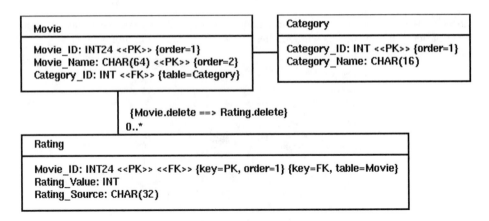

**Figure B.2** A physical data model (UML notation).

and so on in enough detail that makes the map useful to him. This map doesn't depict the individual patio stones that make up the walkway to each, once again that would be too much detail. Sufficient detail depends on the audience and the purpose for which they are using a model—drivers need maps that show streets, builders need maps that show civil engineering details. Similarly, Figure B.1 clearly doesn't provide a detailed description of the XYZ business process, nor is it perfect, but it does get depicted at a sufficiently detailed level. I've worked on many projects where a couple of diagrams drawn on a whiteboard that are updated as the project goes along were sufficient to describe the architecture.

**Agile models provide positive value.** A fundamental aspect of any project artifact is it should add positive value. Does the benefit that an architecture model brings to our project outweigh the costs of developing and (optionally) maintaining it? An architecture model helps to solidify the vision to which our project team is working towards, which clearly has value. But, if the costs of that model outweigh the benefits, then it no longer provides positive value. Perhaps it was unwise to invest $100,000 developing a detailed and heavily documented architecture model when a $5,000 investment resulting in whiteboard diagrams recorded via digital snapshots would have done the job.

**Agile models are as simple as possible.** We should strive to keep our models as simple as possible while still getting the job done. Simplicity is clearly affected by the level of detail in our models, but it also can be affected by the extent of the notation that we apply. For example, Unified Modeling Language (UML) class diagrams can include a myriad of symbols, yet most diagrams can get by with just a portion of the notation. We often don't need to apply all the symbols available to us, so we limit ourselves to a subset of the notation that still allows us to get the job done. Often a CRC model is sufficient to explore the business domain or the detailed design of our software, an example of which is depicted in Figure B.3, so we don't even need to create a UML class diagram.

Therefore, the definition for an agile model is that it is a model that fulfills its purpose and no more; is understandable to its intended audience; is simple; sufficiently accurate, consistent, and detailed; and investment in its creation and maintenance pro-

**Figure B.3** Several CRC cards.

vides positive value to the project. In other words, an agile model is just barely good enough.

# Appendix C

# ONLINE RESOURCES

This appendix presents a categorized and annotated list of URLs that are referenced in the book.

## FORUMS

Here you will find a selection of online places to talk with others about TDD and/or XP. This includes mailing lists, newsgroups, forums, etc.

[URL 1] **Yahoo JUnit Group**
⇒ groups.yahoo.com/group/junint

Discussion of JUnit and its use.

[URL 2] **Yahoo XP Group**
⇒ groups.yahoo.com/group/extremeprogramming

Discussion of eXtreme Programming practices and principles.

[URL 3] **Yahoo TDD Group**
⇒ groups.yahoo.com/group/testdrivendevelopment

Discussion of the theory and practice of test-driven development.

[URL 4] **Yahoo Refactoring Group**
⇒ groups.yahoo.com/group/refactoring

This is a forum for discussions about refactoring, including tools associated with refactoring. It is a place to share and discuss new and old refactorings in a variety of software languages.

## INFORMATION ON AGILE PROCESSES

[URL 5] **The Agile Alliance**
⇒ www.agilealliance.org

The Agile Alliance is a non-profit organization dedicated to promoting the concepts of agile software development, and helping organizations adopt those concepts.

[URL 6] **The Agile Manifesto**
⇒ www.agilemanifesto.org

This site contains the text of the manifesto, information about the manifesto and its authors, and a list of signatories (and a way to become one).

[URL 7] **The Agile Data Homepage**
⇒ www.agiledata.org

A good source of information about how data can be treated with agility. Hosted by Scott Ambler.

[URL 8] **The Agile Modeling Homepage**
⇒ www.agilemodeling.com

The home of the Agile Modeling "movement." See Appendix B for an introduction. Hosted by Scott Ambler.

# INFORMATION ON EXTREME PROGRAMMING

[URL 9] **XP123**
⇒ www.xp123.com

William Wake's site, full of articles and information about XP.

[URL 10] **The Refactoring Homepage**
⇒ www.refactoring.com

Martin Fowler's site dedicated to refactoring.

[URL 11] **XProgramming.com: An eXtreme Programming Resource**
⇒ www.xprogramming.com

The canonical XP site, maintained by Ron Jeffries.

[URL 12] **eXtreme Programming: A Gentle Introduction**
⇒ www.extremeprogramming.org

Don Wells' site, a very nicely done introduction to XP.

[URL 13] **eXtreme Programming Roadmap**
⇒ `www.c2.com/cgi/wiki`

The granddaddy of XP sites. This is where it all began. This is a wiki (the original) so it's a forum for discussion as well as an information source.

# JUNIT-RELATED SOFTWARE

[URL 14] **JUnit Resources**
⇒ `www.junit.org`

This is the place to get the latest versions of the programmer test frameworks in the xUnit family. There are also extensions and articles about programmer testing.

[URL 15] **JUnitPerf**
⇒ `www.clarkware.com/software/JUnitPerf.html`

JUnitPerf is a collection of JUnit test decorators that help you measure the performance and scalability of functionality contained within existing JUnit tests.

[URL 16] **JUnitPP**
⇒ `junitpp.sourceforge.net`

JUnitPP is an extension of the JUnit framework. It provides some additional functionality that makes JUnit more flexible and simple to use. It provides a test data repository, command line arguments, and an improved TestRunner supporting a built-in repetition counter and multithreading on the command line.

[URL 17] **Daedalos JUnit Extensions**
⇒ `www.daedalos.com/EN/djux`

The Daedalos JUnit Extensions (djux) extend the JUnit testing framework in various ways. They allow specifying TestResources that are available during the whole test cycle. Using test resources speeds up unit tests, because time-consuming initializations are only done once and remain active over a complete series of test runs. Furthermore, they allow you to integrate external testing tools as well as to perform specific database tests inside JUnit tests.

At the site you can download the current version of the Daedalos JUnit Extensions and find additional information about unit testing, future releases, and examples.

[URL 18] **xmlUnit**
⇒ `xmlunit.sourceforge.net`

XML can be used for just about anything, so deciding if two documents are equal to each other isn't as easy as a character for character match. XMLUnit allows you to compare XML documents and strings.

### [URL 19]  Gargoyle Software's JUnit Extensions
⇒ `gsbase.sourceforge.net`

A collection of classes that are helpful when writing JUnit test cases.

### [URL 20]  NoUnit
⇒ `nounit.sourceforge.net`

NoUnit allows you to see how good your JUnit tests are. It generates a report from your code to graphically show you how many of your project's methods are being tested, and how well.

This is invaluable if you have code that doesn't have a suite of programmer tests.

If you are practicing TDD, then this shouldn't be required since all the code is there as a direct result of a test requiring it. But not a bad idea, anyway...bad stuff happens.

### [URL 21]  Jester - the JUnit test tester
⇒ `jester.sourceforge.net`

Jester finds code that is not covered by tests. It does this by making systematic (and independent) changes to your code, compiling, and running your test suite. If changing the code results in the tests still passing 100 percent, then a potential problem is flagged.

### [URL 22]  The Clover code coverage analyser
⇒ `www.thecortex.net/clover`

Clover instruments your source code, gathers execution counts on a line-by-line basis when you run your test suite (or run the code in whatever way you want), and generates reports from the resulting data. This is very handy if you want to find out how comprehensive your tests are. And you should want to find that out.

### [URL 23]  The Mock Objects framework
⇒ `www.mockobjects.com`

The Mock Objects project is a generic programmer testing framework whose goal is to facilitate developing programmer tests in the mock object style.

[URL 24] **MockMaker**
⇒ `mockmaker.sourceforge.net`

MockMaker is a program for creating source code for mock object classes that work with the MockObjects framework (required parts of the framework are included in the MockMaker download).

[URL 25] **EasyMock**
⇒ `www.easymock.org`

EasyMock is a framework for dynamically creating mock object at runtime. A big advantage of this is that specifications for the mocks are included as part of the test and not in yet another class.

[URL 26] **Mockry**
⇒ `mockry.sourceforge.net`

Mockry is another tool to create mockobjects.

## JUNIT-RELATED INFORMATION

[URL 27] **JUnit: A Starter Guide**
⇒ `www.diasparsoftware.com/articles/JUnit/jUnitStarterGuide.html`

by J. B. Rainsberger
After reading how critical the JUnit community is of JUnit's documentation, we decided to create some.

[URL 28] **Simple Smalltalk testing: With patterns.**
⇒ `www.xprogramming.com/testfram.htm`

The original xUnit article, by Kent Beck.

[URL 29] **Test infected: Programmers love writing tests.**
⇒ `junit.sourceforge.net/doc/testinfected/testing.htm`

The classic treatise on TDD, by Kent Beck and Erich Gamma.

[URL 30] **JUnit primer.**
⇒ `www.clarkware.com/articles/JUnitPrimer.html`

Another great introduction to using JUnit, by Mike Clark.

[URL 31] **Refactoring test code.**
  ⇒ www.cwi.nl/~leon/papers/xp2001/xp2001.pdf

An excellent article on smells in test code and what to do about them. Presented at XP2001, by Arie van Deursen, Leon Moonen, Alex van den Bergh, and Gerard Kok.

## TOOLS

[URL 32] **The Eclipse Project**
  ⇒ www.eclipse.org

You can find the latest versions of the open source Eclipse IDE here, as well as articles, forums, etc. relating to Eclipse. Eclipse now includes the JUnit plugin as part of the build.

[URL 33] **Idea**
  ⇒ www.intellij.com/idea/

Full Java IDE with extensive refactoring support.

[URL 34] **Together Control Center**
  ⇒ www.togethersoft.com

TogetherSoft's IDE and UML modeling tool.

[URL 35] **jBuilder**
  ⇒ www.borland.com/jbuilder

Borland's Java IDE has some refactoring support.

[URL 36] **Jakarta ANT**
  ⇒ jakarta.apache.org/ant

The standard way to write build scripts for Java.

[URL 37] **CruiseControl**
  ⇒ cruisecontrol.sourceforge.net

A continuous integration tool from Martin Fowler and the folks at ThoughtWorks.

[URL 38] **The Smalltalk Refactoring Browser**
  ⇒ chip.cs.uiuc.edu/users/brant/Refactory

The original refactoring power tool.

[URL 39] **jFactor**
⇒ www.instantiations.com/jfactor

A Java refactoring tool from Instantiations (who have been making tools for the OO world for a long time). It is a refactoring plugin.

[URL 40] **RefactorIT**
⇒ www.refactorit.com

A Java refactoring tool from Aqris that works with jBuilder, Sun ONE Studio, NetBeans, and jDeveloper.

[URL 41] **CodeMorpher**
⇒ www.xptools.com

A Java refactoring tool from XP Tools AB that helps find smells, suggests appropriate refactorings, and performs refactorings. Available as a stand-alone application that interoperates with most Java IDEs and as a plugin for Borland's JBuilder.

[URL 42] **Retool**
⇒ www.chive.com/products/retool

Retool is a refactoring tool from Chive Software. It is an add-in for Oracle 9i, JDeveloper, and Borland JBuilder 4/5.

[URL 43] **VisualWorks Smalltalk by Cincom**
⇒ www.cincom.com/smalltalk

VisualWorks is the direct descendant of the original Smalltalk systems from XEROX PARC. XEROX spun off ParcPlace to commercialize Smalltalk-80. This evolved into VisualWorks and was subsequently bought by Cincom, who has continued to develop and evolve it.

[URL 44] **Squeak**
⇒ www.squeak.org

Squeak is an open, highly-portable Smalltalk-80 implementation whose virtual machine is written entirely in Smalltalk, making it easy to debug, analyze, and change. To achieve practical performance, a translator produces an equivalent C program whose performance is comparable to commercial Smalltalks.

Squeak is available for free via the Internet at this and other sites. Each release includes platform-independent support for color, sound, and network access, with complete source code. Originally developed on the Macintosh, members of its user community have since ported it to numerous other platforms.

[URL 45] **ERWin by Computer Associates**
   ⇒ www3.ca.com/Solutions/Product.asp?ID=260

AllFusion ERwin Data Modeler is an industry-leading data modeling solution that
can help you create and maintain databases, data warehouses, and enterprise data
models.

## OTHER XUNIT FAMILY MEMBERS

[URL 46] **Testing Framework for Ruby**
   ⇒ homepage1.nifty.com/markey/ruby/rubyunit/index_e.html

On this page you can download the latest version of RubyUnit and find documentation and related tools (e.g., a Ruby implementation of a mock objects
framework).

[URL 47] **Testing Framework for Smalltalk**
   ⇒ www.xprogramming.com/testfram.htm

On this page you can download the latest version of SUnit. SUnit is now included
in the standard distribution of Cincom VisualWorks Smalltalk.

[URL 48] **Testing Framework for C++**
   ⇒ cppunit.sourceforge.net

On this page you can download the latest version of CppUnit, find documentation, and get involved. CppUnit was originally a port of JUnit done by Michael
Feathers of Object Mentor.

[URL 49] **Testing Framework for C++**
   ⇒ unitpp.sourceforge.net

On this page you can download the latest version of Unit++. This is an alternative xUnit implementation for C++ which takes a different approach. It isn't
a port of JUnit, rather it is a redesign and rewrite in C++. As such, it takes
advantage of C++'s capabilities and idioms.

[URL 50] **Testing Framework for Perl**
   ⇒ perlunit.sourceforge.net

On this page you can download the latest version of PerlUnit.

[URL 51] **Testing Framework for Visual Basic**
   ⇒ www.vbunit.com

On this page you can download the latest version of vbUnit.

[URL 52] **Testing Framework for C# and .NET**
⇒ nunit.org

On this page you can download the latest version of NUnit.

[URL 53] **Testing Framework for Python**
⇒ pyunit.sourceforge.net

The home on PyUnit and its ongoing development.

# COMPANIES

[URL 54] **Adaption Software, Inc.**
⇒ www.adaptionsoft.com

Adaption is the company founded and run by the author of this book.

Adaption Software uses its expertise in Extreme Programming (XP) and Test-Driven Development, as well as its high level of software craftsmanship to provide:

1. Consulting services for companies adopting TDD or XP;

2. Training courses for individuals and organizations who wish to learn TDD or XP;

3. Software development consulting services using XP.

[URL 55] **The Pragmatic Programmers**
⇒ www.pragmaticprogrammer.com

The online home of The Pragmatic Programmers, the company built by Dave Thomas and Andy Hunt.

[URL 56] **Clarkware Consulting, Inc.**
⇒ www.clarkware.com

Clarkware Consulting, Inc. provides pragmatic software architecture, design, development, and performance consulting and mentoring services. Mike Clark offers his personal experience and leadership in tailoring these services for your project to quickly deliver maximum business value. He has a reputation for delivering high-quality software rapidly and predictably, and a passion for helping clients build better software faster. He also offers customized training and mentoring to help you quickly become productive using agile design and testing tools that any budget can afford.

[URL 57]  **Daedalos Consulting GmbH**
⇒ www.daedalos.com

The company that employs Jens Uwe Pibka. Kent Beck worked with this company
for a couple of years as well.

[URL 58]  **ThoughtWorks, Inc**
⇒ www.thoughtworks.com

The consulting/contracting company for which Martin Fowler works.

[URL 59]  **Gargoyle Software, Inc.**
⇒ www.gargoylesoftware.com

Mike Bowler's company.

[URL 60]  **TogetherSoft**
⇒ www.togethersoft.com

Maker of the Together line of products.

# MISCELLANEOUS

[URL 61]  **The Coad Letter**
⇒ bdn.borland.com/coadletter

The Coad Letter focuses on these key areas: competitive strategy, adaptive process, modeling, design, and test-driven development. This site is a specialized
e-newsletter source and online community dedicated to developing, discussing,
and advancing these topics.
The Coad Letter is a service provided by Peter Coad and colleagues.
I (Dave Astels) am editor of the TDD edition.

[URL 62]  **Brad Appleton's AVL Tree tutorial**
⇒ www.enteract.com/~bradapp/ftp/src/libs/C++/AvlTrees.html

A freely available public domain AVL tree library written in C++.

[URL 63]  **Software Development**
⇒ www.sdmagazine.com

Software Development magazine.

[URL 64] **The Modeling Style Homepage**
 ⇒ www.modelingstyle.info

A good source of modeling standards and guidelines. Hosted by Scott Ambler.

[URL 65] **The support page for this book.**
 ⇒ www.adaptionsoft.com/tddapg.html

A page with supplemental information, additional chapters, discussion forum, links to online resources, corrections, downloadable code, etc.

[URL 66] **The Mono project**
 ⇒ www.go-mono.com

An effort to create an open source implementation of the .NET Development Framework.

Mono includes: a compiler for the C# language, a runtime for the Common Language Infrastructure (also referred to as the CLR), and a set of class libraries.

[URL 67] **The Python Language**
 ⇒ www.python.org

The online home of Python.

[URL 68] **The Puffin Homepage**
 ⇒ www.puffinhome.org

The online home of Puffin: an XML configurable Web application/service testing framework built in Python by Keyton Weissinger.

[URL 69] **The WebUnit Homepage**
 ⇒ webunit.sourceforge.net

The online home of WebUnit: a unit testing framework for testing Web applications in PyUnit tests. WebUnit was developed by Steve Purcell, the author of PyUnit.

# Appendix D

# ANSWERS TO EXERCISES

This appendix contains answers to the exercises in the book, with pointers back to where the exercise appeared.

**Exercise 1:**  *from Categories on page 279*
Refactor TestMovie to use a single Constructor Method that we just added to Movie.

**Answer 1:**

```
public class TestMovie extends TestCase {
  private Movie starWars = null;

  protected void setUp() {
    starWars = new Movie("Star Wars", null, −1);
  }

  public void testMovieName() {
    assertEquals("starWars should have name \"Star Wars\".",
                 "Star Wars",
                 starWars.getName());
  }

  public void testNullName() {
    String nullString = null;
    try {
      new Movie(nullString, null, −1);
      fail("null name should have thrown IllegalArgumentException.");
    } catch (IllegalArgumentException ex) {
    }
  }

  public void testEmptyName() {
    try {
      new Movie("", null, −1);
      fail("empty name should have thrown IllegalArgumentException.");
    } catch (IllegalArgumentException ex) {
    }
  }
```

```java
public void testToString() {
  assertEquals("starWars should have toString of \"Star Wars\".",
               "Star Wars",
               starWars.toString());
}

public void testEquals() {
  final Movie a = new Movie("Star Wars", null, -1);
  final Movie b = new Movie("Star Wars", null, -1);
  final Movie c = new Movie("Star Trek", null, -1);
  final Movie d = new Movie("Star Wars", null, -1) {
  };
  new EqualsTester(a, b, c, d);
}

public void testRenaming() {
  String newName = "Star Trek";
  Movie aMovie = new Movie("Star Wars", null, -1);
  aMovie.rename(newName);
  assertEquals("Renaming should change the name.",
               newName,
               aMovie.getName());
}

public void testNullRename() {
  Movie aMovie = new Movie("Star Wars", null, -1);
  try {
    aMovie.rename(null);
    fail("null rename should have thrown IllegalArgumentException.");
  } catch (IllegalArgumentException ex) {
  }
}

public void testEmptyRename() {
  Movie aMovie = new Movie("Star Wars", null, -1);
  try {
    aMovie.rename("");
    fail("empty rename should have thrown IllegalArgumentException.");
  } catch (IllegalArgumentException ex) {
  }
}

public void testCopyConstructor() {
  Movie copyOfStarWars = new Movie(starWars);
  assertNotSame("A copy should not be the same as the original.",
                starWars,
                copyOfStarWars);
  assertEquals("A copy should be equal to the original.",
               starWars,
               copyOfStarWars);
}
```

```
    public void testUnRated() {
      assertFalse("starWars should be unrated.", starWars.hasRating());
    }

    public void testRatedMovie() throws UnratedException {
      Movie fotr = new Movie("Fellowship of the Ring", null, 5);
      assertTrue("fotr should be rated", fotr.hasRating());
      assertEquals("fotr should be rated at 5.", 5, fotr.getRating());
    }

    public void testUnratedException() {
      try {
        starWars.getRating();
        fail("getRating on an unrated Movie should throw UnratedException.");
      } catch (UnratedException ex) {
        assertEquals("UnratedException should identify the movie.",
                     starWars.getName(),
                     ex.getMessage());
      }
    }

    public void testUncategorized() {
      assertEquals("starWars should be uncategorized.",
                   "Uncategorized",
                   starWars.getCategory());
    }

    public void testScienceFiction() {
      Movie alien = new Movie("Alien", "Science Fiction", -1);
      assertEquals("alien should be Science Fiction.",
                   "Science Fiction",
                   alien.getCategory());
    }

    public static void main(String[] args) {
      junit.textui.TestRunner.run(TestMovie.class);
    }
  }
```

**Exercise 2:**   *from Categories on page 279*
Refactor the tests again, this time removing the unneeded Movie creation.

**Answer 2:**

```
    public class TestMovie extends TestCase {
      private Movie starWars = null;

      protected void setUp() {
        starWars = new Movie("Star Wars", null, -1);
      }
```

```java
public void testMovieName() {
  assertEquals("starWars should have name \"Star Wars\".",
               "Star Wars",
               starWars.getName());
}
public void testNullName() {
  String nullString = null;
  try {
    new Movie(nullString, null, -1);
    fail("null name should have thrown IllegalArgumentException.");
  } catch (IllegalArgumentException ex) {
  }
}
public void testEmptyName() {
  try {
    new Movie("", null, -1);
    fail("empty name should have thrown IllegalArgumentException.");
  } catch (IllegalArgumentException ex) {
  }
}
public void testToString() {
  assertEquals("starWars should have toString of \"Star Wars\".",
               "Star Wars",
               starWars.toString());
}
public void testEquals() {
  final Movie a = new Movie("Star Wars", null, -1);
  final Movie b = new Movie("Star Wars", null, -1);
  final Movie c = new Movie("Star Trek", null, -1);
  final Movie d = new Movie("Star Wars", null, -1) {
  };
  new EqualsTester(a, b, c, d);
}
public void testRenaming() {
  String newName = "Star Trek";
  starWars.rename(newName);
  assertEquals("Renaming should change the name.",
               newName,
               starWars.getName());
}
public void testNullRename() {
  try {
    starWars.rename(null);
    fail("null rename should have thrown IllegalArgumentException.");
  } catch (IllegalArgumentException ex) {
  }
}
```

```java
public void testEmptyRename() {
  try {
    starWars.rename("");
    fail("empty rename should have thrown IllegalArgumentException.");
  } catch (IllegalArgumentException ex) {
  }
}

public void testCopyConstructor() {
  Movie copyOfStarWars = new Movie(starWars);
  assertNotSame("A copy should not be the same as the original.",
                starWars,
                copyOfStarWars);
  assertEquals("A copy should be equal to the original.",
               starWars,
               copyOfStarWars);
}

public void testUnRated() {
  assertFalse("starWars should be unrated.", starWars.hasRating());
}

public void testRatedMovie() throws UnratedException {
  Movie fotr = new Movie("Fellowship of the Ring", null, 5);
  assertTrue("fotr should be rated", fotr.hasRating());
  assertEquals("fotr should be rated at 5.", 5, fotr.getRating());
}

public void testUnratedException() {
  try {
    starWars.getRating();
    fail("getRating on an unrated Movie should throw UnratedException.");
  } catch (UnratedException ex) {
    assertEquals("UnratedException should identify the movie.",
                 starWars.getName(),
                 ex.getMessage());
  }
}

public void testUncategorized() {
  assertEquals("starWars should be uncategorized.",
               "Uncategorized",
               starWars.getCategory());
}

public void testScienceFiction() {
  Movie alien = new Movie("Alien", "Science Fiction", -1);
  assertEquals("alien should be Science Fiction.",
               "Science Fiction",
               alien.getCategory());
}
```

```
    public static void main(String[] args) {
      junit.textui.TestRunner.run(TestMovie.class);
    }
}
```

**Exercise 3:**   *from Categories on page 281*
The customer identified these categories: *Science Fiction, Horror, Comedy, Western,
Drama, Fantasy, Kids, Adult, Mystery, Thriller.* Add these to **Category**.

**Answer 3:**

```
    public class Category {
      private String name = null;

      private Category(String categoryName) {
        name = categoryName;
      }

      public static final Category UNCATEGORIZED = new Category("Uncategorized");
      public static final Category SCIFI = new Category("Science Fiction");
      public static final Category HORROR = new Category("Horror");
      public static final Category COMEDY = new Category("Comedy");
      public static final Category WESTERN = new Category("Western");
      public static final Category DRAMA = new Category("Drama");
      public static final Category FANTASY = new Category("Fantasy");
      public static final Category KIDS = new Category("Kids");
      public static final Category ADULT = new Category("Adult");
      public static final Category MYSTERY = new Category("Mystery");
      public static final Category THRILLER = new Category("Thriller");
    }
```

**Exercise 4:**   *from Categories on page 283*
Extend **setCategoryField()** to make **testSelecting()** pass.

**Answer 4:**

```
    public void select(int i) {
      if (i == -1) {
        selectedMovie = null;
      } else {
        selectedMovie = movies.getMovie(i);
        view.setNameField(selectedMovie.getName());
        view.setCategoryField(selectedMovie.getCategory());

        try {
          view.setRatingField(selectedMovie.getRating() + 1);
        } catch (UnratedException e) {
          view.setRatingField(0);
        }
      }
    }
```

**Exercise 5:**   *from Categories on page 283*
What problem does this cause? Why? Fix it.

**Answer 5:**   It breaks testUpdating(), testUpdatingWithSameName(), and testDupli-
cateCausingUpdate because they don't expect the calls to setCategoryField().

Here are the updated methods. We just need to add expectations for the calls to
setCategoryField():

```
public void testUpdating() {
    Vector newMovies = new Vector();
    newMovies.add(starWars);
    newMovies.add(new Movie("Star Trek I", Category.SCIFI, 5));
    newMovies.add(stargate);
    newMovies.add(theShining);

    mockView.setMovies(movies);
    control.setVoidCallable(1);

    mockView.setNameField("Star Trek");
    control.setVoidCallable(1);
    mockView.setRatingField(4);
    control.setVoidCallable();
    mockView.setCategoryField(Category.SCIFI);
    control.setVoidCallable(1);

    mockView.getNameField();
    control.setReturnValue("Star Trek I", 1);
    mockView.getRatingField();
    control.setReturnValue(6, 1);

    mockView.setMovies(newMovies);
    control.setVoidCallable(1);

    control.activate();

    MovieListEditor editor = new MovieListEditor(movieList, mockView);
    editor.select(1);
    editor.update();

    control.verify();
}
public void testUpdatingWithSameName() {
    Vector newMovies = new Vector();
    newMovies.add(starWars);
    newMovies.add(new Movie("Star Trek", Category.SCIFI, 5));
    newMovies.add(stargate);
    newMovies.add(theShining);

    mockView.setMovies(movies);
    control.setVoidCallable(1);
```

```
      mockView.setNameField("Star Trek");
      control.setVoidCallable(1);
      mockView.setRatingField(4);
      control.setVoidCallable();
      mockView.setCategoryField(Category.SCIFI);
      control.setVoidCallable(1);

      mockView.getNameField();
      control.setReturnValue("Star Trek", 1);
      mockView.getRatingField();
      control.setReturnValue(6, 1);

      mockView.setMovies(newMovies);
      control.setVoidCallable(1);

      control.activate();

      MovieListEditor editor = new MovieListEditor(movieList, mockView);
      editor.select(1);
      editor.update();

      control.verify();
    }

  public void testDuplicateCausingUpdate() {
    mockView.setMovies(movies);
    control.setVoidCallable(1);

    mockView.setNameField("Star Trek");
    control.setVoidCallable(1);
    mockView.setRatingField(0);
    control.setDefaultVoidCallable();
    mockView.setCategoryField(Category.SCIFI);
    control.setVoidCallable(1);

    mockView.getNameField();
    control.setReturnValue("Star Wars", 1);

    mockView.duplicateException("Star Wars");
    control.setVoidCallable(1);

    control.activate();

    MovieListEditor editor = new MovieListEditor(movieList, mockView);
    editor.select(1);
    editor.update();

    control.verify();
  }
```

**Exercise 6:**   *from Categories on page 284*
We used the toString() method to get the value for the category field, as well as the value from the expected Category to compare against the field contents. What's the problem that we have with the system in its current state? (Hint: look at Category.) Fix it.

**Answer 6:**   We haven't defined Category.toString() so it just uses the default from Object. This gives a consistent result, and so our test passes. However, it's not human readable. To fix it we need to add toString() to Category:

```
public String toString() {
  return name;
}
```

**Exercise 7:**   *from Categories on page 286*
Make the required changes to Movie and TestMovieListEditor.

**Answer 7:**   Add a mutator for category tp Movie:

```
public void setCategory(Category aCategory) {
  category = aCategory;
}
```

In TestMovieListEditor, add an expectation for the call to getCategoryField() in testUpdatingWithSameName():

```
public void testUpdatingWithSameName() {
  Vector newMovies = new Vector();
  newMovies.add(starWars);
  newMovies.add(new Movie("Star Trek", Category.SCIFI, 5));
  newMovies.add(stargate);
  newMovies.add(theShining);

  mockView.setMovies(movies);
  control.setVoidCallable(1);

  mockView.setNameField("Star Trek");
  control.setVoidCallable(1);
  mockView.setRatingField(4);
  control.setVoidCallable();
  mockView.setCategoryField(Category.SCIFI);
  control.setVoidCallable(1);

  mockView.getNameField();
  control.setReturnValue("Star Trek", 1);
  mockView.getRatingField();
  control.setReturnValue(6, 1);
  mockView.getCategoryField();                 // this line added
  control.setReturnValue(Category.SCIFI, 1); // this line added
```

```
    mockView.setMovies(newMovies);
    control.setVoidCallable(1);

    control.activate();

    MovieListEditor editor = new MovieListEditor(movieList, mockView);
    editor.select(1);
    editor.update();

    control.verify();
  }
```

**Exercise 8:**   *from Filter on Category on page 290*
Write a toString() method for MovieList.

**Answer 8:**

```
    public String toString() {
      StringBuffer buf = new StringBuffer("[");
      Iterator movieIterator = movies.iterator();
      boolean first = true;

      while (movieIterator.hasNext()) {
        Movie aMovie = (Movie) movieIterator.next();
        if (!first) {
          buf.append(' ');
        }

        first = false;
        buf.append('"');
        buf.append(aMovie.getName());
        buf.append('"');
      }
      buf.append(']');
      return buf.toString();
    }
```

**Exercise 9:**   *from Filter on Category on page 292*
Write an equals() method for MovieList. Start by adding a test to TestMovieListWith-
PopulatedList.

**Answer 9:**    First, the test:

```
    public void testEquals() throws DuplicateMovieException {
      MovieList equalList = new MovieList();
      equalList.add(starWars);
      equalList.add(starTrek);
      equalList.add(stargate);

      MovieList unequalList = new MovieList();
      unequalList.add(starWars);
      unequalList.add(stargate);
```

```
    new EqualsTester(movieList, equalList, unequalList, null);
  }
```

Then the **equals()** method (be sure you didn't forget hashCode()):

```
  public boolean equals(Object o) {
    if (o == this) return true;
    if (o == null) return false;
    if (o.getClass() != this.getClass()) return false;

    MovieList aMovieList = (MovieList)o;
    return movies.equals(aMovieList.movies);

  }

  public int hashCode() {
    return movies.hashCode();
  }
```

**Exercise 10:**  *from Filter on Category on page 292*
Extend the fixture to support this test.

**Answer 10:**

```
    //...
    private MovieList scifiList = null;
    private MovieList thrillerList = null;
    private MovieList horrorList = null;

    protected void setUp() throws Exception {
      //...
      scifiList = new MovieList();
      scifiList.add(starWars);
      scifiList.add(starTrek);
      scifiList.add(stargate);

      thrillerList = new MovieList();
      thrillerList.add(redOctober);
      thrillerList.add(congo);

      horrorList = new MovieList();
      horrorList.add(theShining);
      horrorList.add(carrie);
    }
```

**Exercise 11:**  *from Filter on Category on page 296*
Make the required updates to add filteredMovies.

**Answer 11:**

```
public class MovieListEditor {
  private MovieList filteredMovies;

  public MovieListEditor(MovieList movieList, MovieListEditorView aView) {
    movies = movieList;
    filteredMovies = movieList;
    view = aView;
    view.setEditor(this);
    updateMovieList();
  }

  private void updateMovieList() {
    view.setMovies(new Vector(filteredMovies.getMovies()));
  }
}
```

**Exercise 12:**   *from Persistence on page 311*
Extract the fixture code from the two tests into setUp().

**Answer 12:**

```
public class TestMovieListWriter extends TestCase {
  StringWriter destination = null;
  MovieList movieList = null;

  protected void setUp() {
    destination = new StringWriter();
    movieList = new MovieList();
  }

  public void testWritingEmptyList() throws Exception {
    movieList.writeTo(destination);
    assertEquals("Writing an empty list should produce nothing.",
            "",
            destination.toString());
  }

  public void testWritingOneMovie() throws Exception {
    String starWarsOutput = "Star Wars|Science Fiction|4\n";
    Movie starWars = new Movie("Star Wars", Category.SCIFI, 4);
    movieList.add(starWars);
    movieList.writeTo(destination);
    assertEquals("Wrong output from writing a single movie list.",
            starWarsOutput,
            destination.toString());
  }

  public static void main(String[] args) {
    junit.textui.TestRunner.run(TestMovieListWriter.class);
  }
}
```

**Exercise 13:**   *from Persistence on page 314*
Add the method stubs and declarations we need in order to get the test compiling.

**Answer 13:**    In MovieListEditor:

```
public void saveAs() {
}
```

In MovieListEditorView:

```
File getFile(String string);
```

And in SwingMovieListEditorView:

```
public File getFile(String pattern) {
  return null;
}
```

**Exercise 14:**   *from Persistence on page 321*
Make the required change to TestMovieListEditorFileOperations.testSaving().

**Answer 14:**

```
public void testSaving() throws Exception {
  mockView.setMovies(movies);
  control.setVoidCallable(1);
  mockView.getFile();
  control.setReturnValue(outputFile, 1);
  control.activate();

  MovieListEditor editor = new MovieListEditor(movieList, mockView);
  assertTrue("Editor should have saved", editor.saveAs());
  FileAssert.assertSize("Save As-ed file has wrong size.",
                        expected.length(),
                        outputFile);
  FileAssert.assertEquals("Save As-ed file has wrong contents ",
                          expected,
                          outputFile);
  control.verify();
}
```

**Exercise 15:**   *from Persistence on page 325*
Fix the add() related tests in TestMovieListEditor.

**Answer 15:**

```
public void testAdding() throws DuplicateMovieException {
  String LOST_IN_SPACE = "Lost In Space";
  Movie lostInSpace = new Movie(LOST_IN_SPACE, Category.SCIFI, 3);
  Vector moviesWithAddition = new Vector(movies);
  moviesWithAddition.add(lostInSpace);

  mockView.setMovies(movies);
  control.setVoidCallable(1);
  mockView.getNameField();
  control.setReturnValue(LOST_IN_SPACE, 1);
  mockView.getCategoryField();
  control.setReturnValue(Category.SCIFI, 1);
  mockView.getRatingField();
  control.setReturnValue(3, 1);
  mockView.setMovies(moviesWithAddition);
  control.setVoidCallable(1);
  control.activate();

  MovieListEditor editor = new MovieListEditor(movieList, mockView);
  editor.add();

  control.verify();
}

public void testDuplicateCausingAdd() {
  mockView.setMovies(movies);
  control.setVoidCallable(1);

  mockView.getNameField();
  control.setReturnValue("Star Wars", 1);
  mockView.getCategoryField();
  control.setReturnValue(Category.SCIFI, 1);
  mockView.getRatingField();
  control.setReturnValue(5, 1);

  mockView.duplicateException("Star Wars");
  control.setVoidCallable(1);
  control.activate();

  MovieListEditor editor = new MovieListEditor(movieList, mockView);
  editor.add();

  control.verify();
}
```

**Exercise 16:**   *from Persistence on page 325*
Fix up the add related tests in TestSwingMovieListEditorView.

**Answer 16:**

```
public void testAdding() {
  String LOST_IN_SPACE = "Lost In Space";
  Movie lostInSpace = new Movie(LOST_IN_SPACE, Category.SCIFI, 3);
  movies.add(lostInSpace);

  JTextFieldOperator newMovieField =
          new JTextFieldOperator(mainWindow,
                      new NameBasedChooser("name"));
  newMovieField.enterText(LOST_IN_SPACE);

  JComboBoxOperator ratingCombo =
          new JComboBoxOperator(mainWindow,
                      new NameBasedChooser("rating"));
  ratingCombo.setSelectedIndex(4);

  JComboBoxOperator categoryCombo =
          new JComboBoxOperator(mainWindow,
                      new NameBasedChooser("category"));
  categoryCombo.setSelectedIndex(1);

  JButtonOperator addButton =
          new JButtonOperator(mainWindow,
                        new NameBasedChooser("add"));
  addButton.doClick();

  JListOperator movieList =
          new JListOperator(mainWindow,
                        new NameBasedChooser("movieList"));
  ListModel listModel = movieList.getModel();
  assertEquals("Movie list is the wrong size", movies.size(),
                listModel.getSize());

  for (int i = 0; i < movies.size(); i++) {
    assertEquals("Movie list contains bad movie at index " + i, movies.get(i),
                listModel.getElementAt(i));
  }
}

public void testDuplicateCausingAdd() {
  JTextFieldOperator newMovieField =
          new JTextFieldOperator(mainWindow,
                        new NameBasedChooser("name"));
  newMovieField.enterText(starWars.getName());
  JComboBoxOperator ratingCombo =
          new JComboBoxOperator(mainWindow,
                        new NameBasedChooser("rating"));
  ratingCombo.setSelectedIndex(4);

  JComboBoxOperator categoryCombo =
          new JComboBoxOperator(mainWindow,
                        new NameBasedChooser("category"));
  categoryCombo.setSelectedIndex(1);

  JButtonOperator addButton =
          new JButtonOperator(mainWindow,
                        new NameBasedChooser("add"));
  addButton.pushNoBlock();
```

```
        checkDuplicateExceptionDialog();
        JListOperator movieList =
            new JListOperator(mainWindow,
                              new NameBasedChooser("movieList"));
        checkListIsUnchanged(movieList);
    }
```

**Exercise 17:**  *from Persistence on page 334*
Do the split: TestMovieListEditorFileOperations into TestMovieListEditorSaving and Test-MovieListEditorLoading.

**Answer 17:**

1. Rename TestMovieListEditorFileOperations to TestMovieListEditorSaving.

2. Create TestMovieListEditorLoading, copying loading related parts of TestMovie-ListEditorSaving:

```
        public class TestMovieListEditorLoading
                extends CommonTestMovieListEditor {
          private Vector emptyMovies;
          private File inputFile;

          protected void setUp() throws Exception {
            super.setUp();
            inputFile = File.createTempFile("testSaving", "dat");
            inputFile.deleteOnExit();
            emptyMovies = new Vector();
          }
          public void testLoading() throws Exception {
            mockView.setMovies(emptyMovies);
            control.setVoidCallable(1);
            mockView.getFileToLoad();
            control.setReturnValue(inputFile, 1);

            mockView.setMovies(movies);
            control.setVoidCallable(1);
            control.activate();

            MovieListEditor editor = new MovieListEditor(new MovieList(),
                                                mockView);
            assertTrue("Editor should have loaded.", editor.load());
            control.verify();
          }
          public static void main(String[] args) {
            junit.textui.TestRunner.run(TestMovieListEditorLoading.class);
          }
        }
```

**Exercise 18:** *from Persistence on page 335*
In looking at adding another test to TestSwingMovieListEditorFileOperations, we notice
that we have some code debt. The *Rule of Three* has kicked in. This is the third test,
and as we think about it we see that there are a few lines of code duplicated in each
test. Time to refactor. What do we need to do?

**Answer 18:** Each test begins with these three lines that need to be moved to the
end of setUp() and removed from the two existing tests:

```
menubar = new JMenuBarOperator(mainWindow);
fileMenu = new JMenuOperator(menubar, "File");
fileMenu.push();
```

**Exercise 19:** *from Sorting on page 345*
What does the fixture look like?

**Answer 19:**

```
public class TestMovieListSortingByName extends TestCase {
  private MovieList sortedList = null;
  private MovieNameComparator nameComparator = null;
  private Vector sortedMovies = null;
  private MovieList emptyList = null;

  protected void setUp() throws Exception {
    emptyList = new MovieList();
    sortedMovies = new Vector();

    sortedMovies.add(new Movie("A", Category.SCIFI, 5));
    sortedMovies.add(new Movie("B", Category.SCIFI, 4));
    sortedMovies.add(new Movie("C", Category.SCIFI, 3));
    sortedMovies.add(new Movie("D", Category.SCIFI, 2));
    sortedMovies.add(new Movie("E", Category.SCIFI, 1));
    sortedMovies.add(new Movie("F", Category.SCIFI, 0));
    sortedMovies.add(new Movie("G", Category.SCIFI, -1));

    sortedList = new MovieList();
    Iterator i = sortedMovies.iterator();
    while (i.hasNext()) {
      sortedList.add((Movie) i.next());
    }
    nameComparator = new MovieNameComparator();
  }

  //...
}
```

**Exercise 20:**   *from Multiple Ratings on page 357*
Do the extraction of the fixture.

**Answer 20:**

```java
public class TestMovieRatings extends TestCase {
  private Movie starTrek = null;

  protected void setUp() throws Exception {
    starTrek = new Movie("Star Trek", Category.SCIFI);
  }
  public void testUnratedConstructor() {
    try {
      starTrek.getRating();
      fail("Getting rating of an unrated Movie should throw UnratedMovieException");
    } catch (UnratedException ex) {
    }
  }
  public void testAddingOneRating() throws Exception {
    starTrek.addRating(3);
    assertEquals("Bad average rating of 1.", 3, starTrek.getRating());
  }
  public static void main(String[] args) {
    junit.textui.TestRunner.run(TestMovieRatings.class);
  }
}
```

**Exercise 21:**   *from Multiple Ratings on page 362*
What is the problem, and how do we fix it?

**Answer 21:**   The expected saved data strings don't include a rating count value. They need to be updated to:

```java
public class TestMovieListEditorSaving extends CommonTestMovieListEditor {
  protected void setUp() throws Exception {
    super.setUp();
    expected = "Star Wars|Science Fiction|5|1\n" +
               "Star Trek|Science Fiction|3|1\n" +
               "Stargate|Science Fiction|0|0\n" +
               "The Shining|Horror|2|1\n";
    extendedExpected = expected + "The Fellowship of The Ring|Fantasy|5|1\n";
  }
  //...
}

public class TestSwingMovieListEditorFileOperations extends TestCase {
  protected void setUp() throws Exception {
    //...
    savedText = "Star Wars|Science Fiction|5|1\n" +
                "Star Trek|Science Fiction|3|1\n" +
                "Stargate|Science Fiction|0|0\n";
    extendedSavedText = savedText + "The Shining|Horror|2|1\n";
  }
}
```

**Exercise 22:** *from Multiple Ratings on page 377*
Convert TestMovieListEditorSaving as required.

**Answer 22:**

```java
public class TestMovieListEditorSaving extends XMLTestCase {
  protected MockControl control = null;
  protected MovieListEditorView mockView = null;
  protected Vector movies = null;
  protected Movie starWars = null;
  protected Movie starTrek = null;
  protected Movie stargate = null;
  protected Movie theShining = null;
  protected MovieList movieList = null;
  private String expectedPrefix;
  private String expected;
  private File outputFile;
  private Movie fotr;
  private String extendedExpected;
  private Vector extendedMovies;

  public TestMovieListEditorSaving(String name) {
    super(name);
  }

  protected void setUp() throws Exception {
    String parser = "org.apache.xerces.jaxp.DocumentBuilderFactoryImpl";
    XMLUnit.setControlParser(parser);
    XMLUnit.setTestParser(parser);

    starWars = new Movie("Star Wars", Category.SCIFI, 5);
    starTrek = new Movie("Star Trek", Category.SCIFI, 3);
    stargate = new Movie("Stargate", Category.SCIFI, -1);
    theShining = new Movie("The Shining", Category.HORROR, 2);

    movies = new Vector();
    movies.add(starWars);
    movies.add(starTrek);
    movies.add(stargate);
    movies.add(theShining);

    movieList = new MovieList();
    movieList.add(starWars);
    movieList.add(starTrek);
    movieList.add(stargate);
    movieList.add(theShining);

    expectedPrefix = "<movielist>" +
                     "<movie name=\"Star Wars\" " +
                         "category=\"Science Fiction\">" +
                       "<ratings>" +
                         "<rating value=\"5\" " +
                                 "source=\"Anonymous\" />" +
                       "</ratings>" +
                     "</movie>" +
```

```
                              "<movie name=\"Star Trek\" " +
                                    "category=\"Science Fiction\">" +
                          "<ratings>" +
                            "<rating value=\"3\" " +
                                      "source=\"Anonymous\" />" +
                          "</ratings>" +
                        "</movie>" +
                        "<movie name=\"Stargate\" " +
                              "category=\"Science Fiction\">" +
                          "<ratings></ratings>" +
                        "</movie>" +
                        "<movie name=\"The Shining\" " +
                              "category=\"Horror\">" +
                          "<ratings>" +
                            "<rating value=\"2\" " +
                                        "source=\"Anonymous\" />" +
                          "</ratings>" +
                        "</movie>";
      expected = expectedPrefix + "</movielist>";

      fotr = new Movie("The Fellowship of The Ring", Category.FANTASY, 5);
      extendedExpected = expectedPrefix +
                      "<movie name=\"The Fellowship of The Ring\" " +
                              "category=\"Fantasy\">" +
                          "<ratings>" =
                            "<rating value=\"5\" " +
                                        "source=\"Anonymous\" />" +
                          "</ratings>" +
                        "</movie></movielist>";

      extendedMovies = new Vector(movies);
      extendedMovies.add(fotr);

      outputFile = File.createTempFile("testSaving", ".dat");
      outputFile.deleteOnExit();

      control = EasyMock.controlFor(MovieListEditorView.class);
      mockView = (MovieListEditorView)control.getMock();
      mockView.setEditor(null);
      control.setDefaultVoidCallable();
    }
    public void testSaving() throws Exception {
      mockView.setMovies(movies);
      control.setVoidCallable(1);
      mockView.getFileToSave();
      control.setReturnValue(outputFile, 1);

      mockView.getNameField();
      control.setReturnValue(fotr.getName(), 1);
      mockView.getCategoryField();
      control.setReturnValue(Category.FANTASY, 1);
```

```
            mockView.getRatingField();
            control.setReturnValue(fotr.getRating() + 1, 1);
            mockView.setMovies(extendedMovies);
            control.setVoidCallable(1);
            control.activate();

            MovieListEditor editor = new MovieListEditor(movieList, mockView);
            assertTrue("Editor should have saved", editor.saveAs());
            assertXMLEqual("Save As-ed file has wrong contents ",
                           expected,
                           contentsOf(outputFile));

            editor.add();
            assertTrue("Editor should have resaved", editor.save());
            assertXMLEqual("Saved file has bad contents.",
                           extendedExpected,
                           contentsOf(outputFile));
            control.verify();
        }

    private String contentsOf(File aFile) throws IOException {
        FileInputStream fstream = new FileInputStream(aFile);
        int size = fstream.available();
        byte[] buffer = new byte[size];
        fstream.read(buffer);
       return new String(buffer);
        }

    public void testCancelledSaving() throws Exception {
        mockView.setMovies(movies);
        control.setVoidCallable(1);
        mockView.getFileToSave();
        control.setReturnValue(null, 1);
        control.activate();

        MovieListEditor editor = new MovieListEditor(movieList, mockView);
        assertFalse("Editor should not have saved.", editor.saveAs());
        control.verify();
        }

    public static void main(String[] args) {
        junit.textui.TestRunner.run(TestMovieListEditorSaving.class);
        }
    }
```

**Exercise 23:**   *from Multiple Ratings on page 377*
Update MovieListEditor.save() to make it work.

**Answer 23:**

```
public boolean save() throws IOException {
  if (outputFile == null) {
    return false;
  }
  FileWriter writer = new FileWriter(outputFile);
  new XMLMovieListWriter(writer).write(movies);
  writer.close();
  return true;
}
```

# BIBLIOGRAPHY

[1] Scott W. Ambler. *The Object Primer: The Application Developer's Guide to Object Orientation.* Cambridge University Press, New York, 2nd edition, 2001. www.ambysoft.com/theObjectPrimer.html.

[2] Scott W. Ambler. *Agile Modeling: Effective Practices for Extreme Programming and the Unified Process.* John Wiley & Sons Publishing, New York, 2002.

[3] Scott W. Ambler. Enterprise unified process white paper. Technical report, Ronin International, 2002. www.ronin-intl.com/publications/unifiedProcess.htm.

[4] Scott W. Ambler. *The Elements of UML Style.* Cambridge University Press, New York, 2003. www.ambysoft.com/elementsUMLStyle.html.

[5] Dave Astels. Refactoring with UML. In *Proceedings of XP2002: 3rd International Conference on eXtreme Programming and Flexible Processes in Software Engineering*, pages 67–70, 2002. Available at `ciclamino.dibe.unige.it/xp2002/atti`.

[6] David Astels, Granville Miller, and Miroslav Novak. *A Practical Guide to eXtreme Programming.* The Coad Series. Prentice Hall, 2002. ISBN 0-13-067482-6.

[7] Kent Beck. Simple smalltalk testing: With patterns. Available at `www.xprogramming.com/testfram.htm`.

[8] Kent Beck. *Extreme Programming Explained: Embrace Change.* The XP Series. Addison Wesley Longman, 2000. ISBN 0-201-61641-6.

[9] Kent Beck. *Test-Driven Development: By Example.* Addison Wesley Longman, 2002. ISBN 0-321-14653-0.

[10] Joshua Bloch. *Effective Java Programming Language Guide.* Addison Wesley Longman, 2001. ISBN 0-201-31005-8.

[11] Marko Boger, Thorsten Strum, and Per Fragemann. Refactoring browser for UML. In *Proceedings of XP2002: 3rd International Conference on eXtreme Programming and Flexible Processes in Software Engineering*, pages 77–81, 2002. Available at `ciclamino.dibe.unige.it/xp2002/atti`.

[12] Peter Coad, Mark Mayfield, and Jonathan Kern. *Java Design: Building Better Apps and Applets.* Yourdon Press Computing Series. Prentice Hall, 2nd edition, 1999. ISBN 0-139-11181-6.

[13] Alistair Cockburn. *Agile Software Development.* Addison Wesley Longman, October 2001.

[14] Michael Feathers. The humble dialog box. *Published online*, 2002. Available at `www.objectmentor.com/resources/articles`.

[15] Martin Fowler. The refactoring home page. `www.refactoring.com`.

[16] Martin Fowler. *Refactoring: Improving the Design of Existing Code*. Addison Wesley Longman, 1999. ISBN 0-201-48567-2.

[17] Martin Fowler. Is design dead? In *Extreme Programming Examined*, chapter 1, pages 3–17. Addison Wesley Longman, 2001. Also available at `www.martinfowler/articles/designDead.htm`.

[18] Tammo Freese. Easymock: Dynamic Objects for jUnit. In *Proceedings of XP2002: 3rd International Conference on eXtreme Programming and Flexible Processes in Software Engineering*, pages 2–5, 2002. Available at `ciclamino.dibe.unige.it/xp2002/atti`.

[19] E. Gamma, R. Helm, R. Johnson, and J. Vlissides. Design Patterns: Abstraction and Reuse in Object-Oriented Designs. In O. Nierstrasz, editor, *Proceedings of ECOOP'93*, Berlin, 1993. Springer-Verlag.

[20] Erich Gamma and Kent Beck. jUnit: A cook's tour. *Jave Report*, May 1999. Available at `junit.sourceforge.net/doc/cookstour/cookstour.htm`.

[21] The Standish Group. The CHAOS report, 1994.

[22] The Standish Group. CHAOS: A recipe for success, 1999.

[23] Peter Haggar. *Practical Java Programming Language Guide*. Addison Wesley Longman, February 2000.

[24] Jim Highsmith. *Agile Software Development Ecosystems*. Addison Wesley Longman, March 2002. ISBN: 0-201-76043-6.

[25] Andrew Hunt and David Thomas. *The Pragmatic Programmer*. Addison Wesley Longman, 2000. ISBN 0-201-61622-X.

[26] Ron Jeffries. XProgramming.com: An extreme programming resource. `www.xprogramming.com`.

[27] Ron Jeffries, Ann Anderson, and Chet Hendrickson. *Extreme Programming Installed*. The XP Series. Addison Wesley Longman, 2001. ISBN 0-201-70842-6.

[28] Joshua Kerievsky. Patterns and XP. In *Extreme Programming Examined*, chapter 13, pages 207–220. Addison Wesley Longman, 2001.

[29] Joshua Kerievsky. *Refactoring to Patterns*. Not yet published, 2002. Drafts available online at `www.industriallogic.com/xp/refactoring`.

[30] P. Kruchten. *The Rational Unified Process: An Introduction*. Addison Wesley Longman, 2nd edition, 2000.

[31] Tim Mackinnon. xUnit testing—a plea for assertEquals. In *Proceedings of XP2002: 3rd International Conference on eXtreme Programming and Flexible Processes in Software Engineering*, pages 170–171, 2002. Available at `ciclamino.dibe.unige.it/xp2002/atti`.

[32] Tim Mackinnon, Steve Freeman, and Philip Craig. Endo-testing: Unit testing with mock objects. In *Extreme Programming Examined*, chapter 17, pages 287–301. Addison Wesley Longman, 2001. Available at `www.mockobjects.com/endotesting.html`.

[33] Robert C. Martin. *Agile Software Development: Principles, Patterns, and Practices.* Prentice Hall, 2003. ISBN 0-13-597444-5.

[34] Pete McBreen. *Software Craftsmanship.* Addison Wesley Longman, 2002. ISBN 0-201-73386-2.

[35] Ivan Moore. Jester—A junit test tester. In *Proceedings of XP2001: 2nd International Conference on eXtreme Programming and Flexible Processes in Software Engineering*, pages 84–87, 2001.

[36] Stephen R. Palmer and John M. Felsing. *A Practical Guide to Feature-Driven Development.* Prentice Hall, 2002.

[37] Giancarlo Succi and Michele Marchesi, editors. *Extreme Programming Examined.* The XP Series. Addison Wesley Longman, 2001. This is a collection of papers from the XP2000 proceedings. ISBN 0-201-71040-4.

[38] Giancarlo Succi, Michele Marchesi, Witold Pedrycz, and Laurie Williams. Preliminary analysis of the effects of pair programming on job satisfaction. In *Proceedings of XP2002: 3rd International Conference on eXtreme Programming and Flexible Processes in Software Engineering*, pages 212–215, 2002. Available at `ciclamino.dibe.unige.it/xp2002/atti`.

[39] Arie van Deursen and Leon Moonen. The video store revisited—thoughts on refactoring and testing. In *Proceedings of XP2002: 3rd International Conference on eXtreme Programming and Flexible Processes in Software Engineering*, pages 71–76, 2002. Available at `ciclamino.dibe.unige.it/xp2002/atti`.

[40] Arie van Deursen, Leon Moonen, Alex van den Bergh, and Gerard Kok. Refactoring test code. In *Proceedings of XP2001: 2nd International Conference on eXtreme Programming and Flexible Processes in Software Engineering*, pages 92–95, 2001. Available at `www.cwi.nl/~leon/papers/xp2001/xp2001.pdf`.

[41] William C. Wake. *Refactoring Workbook.* Addison Wesley Longman, 2003. ISBN 0-321-10929-5.

# INDEX